THE ASSOCIATION FOR SCOTTISH LITERARY STUDIES
NUMBER THIRTY-FIVE

THE DEVIL TO STAGE

FIVE PLAYS BY JAMES BRIDIE

*

EDITORIAL ADVISER: HAMISH WHYTE

THE ASSOCIATION FOR SCOTTISH LITERARY STUDIES

The Association for Scottish Literary Studies aims to promote the study, teaching and writing of Scottish literature, and to further the study of the languages of Scotland.

To these ends, the ASLS publishes works of Scottish literature (of which this volume is an example); literary criticism and in-depth reviews of Scottish books in *Scottish Studies Review*; short articles, features and news in *ScotLit*; and scholarly studies of language in *Scottish Language*. It also publishes *New Writing Scotland*, an annual anthology of new poetry, drama and short fiction, in Scots, English and Gaelic. ASLS has also prepared a range of teaching materials covering Scottish language and literature for use in schools.

All the above publications are available as a single 'package', in return for an annual subscription. Enquiries should be sent to:

> ASLS, Department of Scottish Literature, 7 University Gardens, University of Glasgow, Glasgow G12 8QH. Telephone/fax +44 (0)141 330 5309 or visit our website at **www.asls.org.uk**

A list of Annual Volumes published by ASLS can be found at the end of this book.

THE ASSOCIATION FOR SCOTTISH LITERARY STUDIES

THE DEVIL TO STAGE

FIVE PLAYS BY JAMES BRIDIE

Edited by

GERARD CARRUTHERS

GLASGOW

2007

*

First published in Great Britain, 2007
by The Association for Scottish Literary Studies
Department of Scottish Literature
University of Glasgow
7 University Gardens
Glasgow G12 8QH

www.asls.org.uk

Hardback
ISBN: 978 0 948877 70 4

Paperback
ISBN: 978 0 948877 71 1

Frontispiece (p.vii): James Bridie's 1944 Christmas card to Alastair Sim
Reproduced by kind permissions of the Trustees of the National Library of Scotland
and Professor Ronald Mavor

A catalogue record for this book
is available from the British Library.

The Association for Scottish Literary Studies acknowledges
support from the Scottish Arts Council towards
the publication of this book.

Typeset by AFS Image Setters Ltd, Glasgow
Printed and bound by Bell & Bain Ltd, Glasgow

CONTENTS

ACKNOWLEDGEMENTS

For advice, for information, for practical support, and for saving me from error, I am grateful to Valentina Bold, Amanda Brend, Martin Carruthers, John Corbett, Sarah Dunnigan, Douglas Gifford, David Goldie, David Hamilton, David Hutchison, Colin Kidd, Alison Lumsden, Kirsteen McCue, Margery Palmer McCulloch, Jan McDonald, George Philp, Julie Renfrew, Ronnie Renton, Alan Riach, Adrienne Scullion and Kenneth Simpson. Dr Matthew Dunnigan was particularly helpful in advising me on aspects of medicine and medical history in Bridie's plays. The calm efficiency of Duncan Jones, General Manager of the Association for Scottish Literary Studies, has been very much appreciated in seeing this project to a conclusion, as has the assistance of Hamish Whyte, who has acted all along as a most wise and patient General Editor. It is a particular pleasure to acknowledge the intellectual and moral support and advice of James Bridie's son, Professor Ronald Mavor. I am grateful too to Bridie's modern literary representative, Nick Quinn of The Agency, London. Also, I could not have undertaken this work without the helpfulness and professionalism of the staffs of special collections at the British Library, Glasgow University Library, the Mitchell Library, Glasgow, and the National Library of Scotland. I am especially grateful to the University of Glasgow, and to the Department of Scottish Literature which thereafter bore extra burden, for granting me a sabbatical period from 2004 to 2005, during which time the crucial spade-work on this edition was dug.

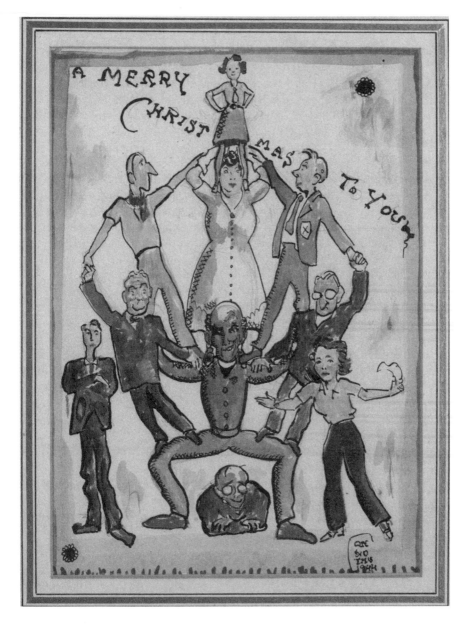

James Bridie's 1944 Christmas card to Alastair Sim, with Bridie himself appearing under Sim, the latter seen in costume as Mr. Bolfry.

INTRODUCTION

James Bridie, pen-name of Osborne Henry Mavor (1888–1951), merits not a single mention in *The Cambridge History of Twentieth-Century English Literature* (2004), a book that despite its title offers coverage also of Scottish literature of the period. In a skilfully succinct chapter on theatre between the wars, Maggie B. Gale essays the major dramatic trends of the day including the intellectualism of George Bernard Shaw, the expressionism of Somerset Maugham and J. B. Priestley, and the national (Irish) drama of Sean O'Casey.[1] Bridie, *the* Scottish dramatist of ideas, an extensive user of poetic symbolism and anti-naturalism in his work, and the individual who, arguably, did more than anyone else to establish a theatrical infrastructure in Scotland in the first part of the twentieth century, has fallen out of the story. In the context of the wider English-speaking world, perhaps, Bridie is viewed (if at all) merely as a sub-Shavian writer, staging long moral arguments but with a flippancy and inconsequentiality that seem to defeat any firm, purposeful conclusions such as are often to be found in the much more politically driven Shaw. Bridie is absent also from a chapter by Trevor R. Griffiths in *The Cambridge History* that covers the 1940s.[2] However, in the registering of Scottish drama of social realism and class conflict in their periods, Joe Corrie, Ena Lamont Stewart and Robert McLeish are all picked up on the radar of Gale and Griffiths. Griffiths' treatment nods towards the increasing dominance of a Brecht-influenced theatre of political commitment in 1950s Britain and the consequent "kitchen sink" drama of the 1960s, contexts in which Bridie's kind of drama was very rapidly superseded. The attendant later trajectory of Scottish theatre itself into the gritty realism and class polemic of the Royal Lyceum Theatre in Edinburgh and of the 7:84 Scotland Company has likewise confirmed the marginalisation of Bridie's work. Bridie's explicit hostility to "the Glasgow Unity Theatre Company's entire aesthetic", this company which from 1941 put huge effort into contemporary issues-led work and attracting working-class audiences, and his low opinion of the work of Ena Lamont Stewart, has seen him become engrained in the minds of much of the modern Scottish theatrical establishment as a bygone grandee of middle-class Scottish culture.[3] His plays now little performed (though far from the large urban centres of Scotland, Pitlochry Festival Theatre has maintained a creditable continuous record in staging his work), Bridie is victim, in Alasdair Cameron's words, "in a great tradition of national amnesia".[4]

Paradoxically, part of the reason for Bridie's erasure in Scottish consciousness has to do with his consummate success as a cultural activist in helping to create some of the most solid institutional fabric for the arts in Scotland. His legacy here has been wide, lasting and transcends whatever limitations of outlook have been imputed to him personally. Bridie is an important figure in ushering in a new age of professionalism, away from its previous amateurism, in Scottish theatre. He was a board member of the Scottish National Players whose driving motivation was, as their name suggests, the establishment of a Scottish national theatre. If this aim was not actually achieved, institutionally, until the twenty-first century, the group's seasons in Glasgow, its far-reaching tours of Scotland and even some performances in London helped create an audience and an appetite for Scottish subject-matter from the 1920s onward that has endured. Bridie himself wrote his first performed play and a subsequent three for the SNP between 1928 and 1934. Amateur or semi-professional as its actors were, nonetheless the SNP proved a large platform from which a stable professional acting class was gradually to establish itself in Scotland (the SNP energy is apparent in David Hutchison's statistic that they presented "131 full-length and one act plays" between 1921 and 1947).[5] In 1942 Bridie became the first chair of the Scottish Committee of the Council for the Encouragement of Music and the Arts (later the Scottish Arts Council) which involved long, frequent and arduous meetings in London as well as in Edinburgh. The Citizens' Theatre which opened (with underwritten funding from CEMA) at the Atheneaum, Glasgow, in October 1943, later moving to the Gorbals area, was largely founded as a result of Bridie's artistic vision of a resident, professional theatre company in Glasgow.[6] As well as adopting a workaday attitude as a board member for "the Citz", where he was regularly consulted on every aspect of its operations, Bridie wrote for it three plays, *The Forrigan Reel*, *Lancelot* and *John Knox*, between 1944 and 1947 (to say nothing of a pantomime in 1945). To this profile ought to be added his activities in encouraging the establishment of the Edinburgh International Festival for which, in 1948, Bridie worked, amidst a breathtaking assembly of talent, to bring about a stunning landmark production of Sir David Lyndsay's *Ane Pleasant Satire of the Thrie Estaitis* (*c.*1556) with fellow playwright Robert Kemp (adapter), Tyrone Guthrie (director) and Cedric Thorpe Davie (musical director), to say nothing of a superb cast of actors. With this production a circle had been completed by Bridie, whose *The Sunlight Sonata* twenty years earlier had provided a modern morality play for Scotland diagnosing widespread spiritual atrophy in somewhat similar mode, including generic experimentation, to that found in Lyndsay's sixteenth-century masterpiece.

Manifestly, Bridie ploughed a great amount back into Scottish culture and yet his relation to the Scottish literary "revival" of the twentieth century is complex. On excellent terms with the likes of Neil Gunn (who had also been involved initially in writing for the Scottish National Players) and, especially, Eric Linklater (who shared with Bridie a similarly riotous acerbity as a writer), his co-existence with the high-priest of the Scottish "literary renaissance", Hugh MacDiarmid, was far from easy. MacDiarmid's *Contemporary Scottish Studies* (1926) had called for a drama distinct from that of England, which would take particular heed of "the distinctive factors of Scottish psychology".[7] Bridie's dramatic Scottish character studies most certainly occupy the terrain for which MacDiarmid had called. Also, Bridie's use of Scots in many plays (including perhaps poking some gentle fun at MacDiarmid, the great reviver of Scots poetry, in the hexameter-verse-speaking Beelzebub in *The Sunlight Sonata*, shortly after the poet had made his plea for a distinctive Scottish drama) represents a sustained literary use (and provided much material for the Scots National Dictionary) in a manner that was all that MacDiarmid might have wished. MacDiarmid, the nationalist and communist firebrand, attempted on several occasions to provoke argument with Bridie, the latter, secure as a much more commercially successful writer as well as public figure, largely ignoring such attempts (though in 1945 he felt compelled to respond when MacDiarmid had "regurgitated a quantity of bile" against his beloved "Citz").[8] In a lecture on "The Scottish Character as it was viewed by Scottish Authors from Galt to Barrie" for the Greenock Philosophical Society in 1937 Bridie had been humorously sceptical in the face of MacDiarmid's gloomy pronouncement that Scottish expression was cowed and neutered through contamination by English culture:

> Mr. MacDiarmid – another Scotsman in disguise, by the way, for his right name is C. M. Grieve – is the most considerable Poet this country has produced since Burns. He has therefore some right to be heard. He is also in some sense, a Scottish Character himself. He might be listed as a totey, pernickety, sometimes rigwoodie stug.[9]

The mixture here of inseparable compliment and rebuttal is pure Bridie at his oxymoronic best. MacDiarmid is a "stug" or a sharp stabber, a chisel even, while MacDiarmid's own Scots vehemence, mimicked by Bridie, defeats the MacDiarmidist premise that abject cultural surrender is already accomplished. Pricking with a forked tongue is a technique that Bridie used frequently in his drama.

Bridie, perhaps, is not entirely trusted by the most culturally nationalist versions of Scottish literary history for having been such a success in London's West End.[10] Over sixty per cent of Bridie's work was premiered in England, a state of affairs that speaks not so much of the "Jock on the make", as it does of Scotland's fledgling institutional fabric in theatre, which, in time, Bridie did so much to help bring to maturity. Long and fruitful relationships with such prodigious directors as H. K. Ayliff and Bridie's fellow Scot, the actor–director Alastair Sim (to say nothing of performances in Bridie's work by the cream of British acting talent in the 1930s and '40s), show him to be a playwright operating at the centre of both the network of British theatrical high craftsmanship and box-office success. Overtures from film producers such as Sir Alexander Korda and Alfred Hitchcock (who wanted Bridie to work in Hollywood, though the playwright was finally reluctant to invest his energies here) confirm Bridie's reach in his own time. In turn, Bridie's production values were expansive. This is true in his giving wide expressive canvas to the Scottish "character" in, for instance, the riotously funny *Gog and Magog* (1948) based on the doggerel poet William McGonagall, which premiered at the Arts Theatre, London. Conversely, he used the Scottish stage, most especially the Citizens' Theatre Company, for such lavish productions as his classical extravaganza, *The Queen's Comedy* (1950). Among other works of the international dramatic canon, Bridie's particularly successful adaptations of Ibsen for the Citizens', both *Hedda Gabler* and *The Wild Duck*, show him as a man determined to do as much as he could to associate with Scotland that literary form which historically his country had been most iconoclastic towards.

As with the "message" of so many of his plays, Bridie's own views, and perhaps even his personality, are not easy exactly to define (what is urgently wanted is an applied biography of Mavor/Bridie to bring into focus not only his own life and work but also to provide a reassessment of an era of formative Scottish cultural development from the 1920s to the 1940s, that is perhaps taken too much for granted in modern commentary). Winifred Bannister comments, "Bridie's political views were rather like his religion: so liberal minded, so humanitarian that they were unfixed."[11] Assuredly agnostic, seemingly a comfortable professional man, for much of his life as a medico (most notably becoming consulting physician to the Victoria Infirmary in Glasgow and Professor of Medicine at Anderson's College, Glasgow), he worried over the historical and spiritual condition of humanity as much as any other writer. Gerald Wheales produced a hugely engaged treatment of Bridie's drama in 1961 that clearly saw the playwright as a highly significant figure (not coincidentally did Wheales' *Religion in Modern English Drama* appear before the watershed 1960s downgraded the significance of "metaphysical" writers like Bridie in the light of others of more sociologically materialist and politically activist concerns). Wheales suggests that across Bridie's oeuvre we find that "some kind of belief is necessary", even though belief in the religious, the political, or even "simply" in humanity, remains open to contradiction amidst the selfish, rapacious behaviour which humans constantly exhibit.[12] This is the moral universe which Bridie essays, one where good and evil, right and wrong, form a constant dialectic, but in which no absolute versions of these opposing values present themselves. It is a chilling aspect of Bridie's work that humanity's exertions in evil (in a Robert Knox or an Adolf Hitler figure even) as much as in its pious rectitude might show the grandiose and ultimately empty conceit of the species. Bridie's plays mirror the in turn noisy frivolity and noisy seriousness of humanity, and, with cheerful scepticism, extracting the positive of performativity, the playwright contents himself that he has been at least entertaining. Bridie's own self-description as an artist and as a man was frequently glib, throwaway or even self-deprecating, and yet twentieth-century Scottish culture has no-one of greater dynamism.[13] Frequently, it is mere hyperbole to suggest that an individual has packed several careers into one life, but in the case of Dr. Mavor and Mr. Bridie this was true.

The present selection of plays publishes the historically significant *The Sunlight Sonata*. It would be difficult to imagine this work (so deeply imbued with the mores of the late-1920s Glasgow upper middle classes) being performed today, but it remains entertaining to read and, instructively, contains the seeds of Bridie's later methods. In fantastic scenario, metaphysical message and Scots dialogue it is an index of Bridie's ambition to reinhabit the stage with Scottish, as well as more universal, attitudes and concerns. The other four plays chosen (as with at least five others not included: *Tobias and the Angel, John Knox* (1947), *Gog and Magog, Mr. Gillie* (1950) and *The Baikie Charivari or the Seven Prophets*) might all fruitfully be performed in the present day. All of these narrate dramatic, even (with breezy irony) melodramatic, stories that might keep any audience gripped. Bridie's dialogue and characterisation are, in turn, grim, witty, philosophical and poignant; human tragedy and comedy are both credibly accounted for in his oeuvre. Actually no more ponderous than the work of a Samuel Beckett or a Harold Pinter, nonetheless Bridie's scripts might be somewhat edited for performance in line with the more readily active tastes of the modern audience.[14] If Bridie's plays might be seen, generally, as deficient in "sexual politics and [especially their] treatment of women", in the present publication, *The Anatomist, A Sleeping Clergyman* and *Daphne Laureola* all feature strong female characters which would present fulsome roles for such fine actors as Kate Dickie, say, Cate Blanchett or Tara Fitzgerald.[15] A revival of seriously mounted Bridie performance is very much overdue, and it is astonishing that such continues to be resisted in Scottish theatre, especially, which owes this dramatist so much.

James Bridie's first performed play, *The Sunlight Sonata* (1928), provided a typically elusive start to the dramatist's career as it was billed under the authorship of "Mary Henderson". Premiered at the Lyric Theatre in Glasgow, it has been given scant attention by critics who tend to see it, with some justification, as little more than a mere frolic or an extended joke. Bridie himself referred to the play's "amateur crudities"; however, it is an important historical document attesting to the inspiration of John Brandane, fellow playwright and lifelong friend who helped galvanise the fervour with which Bridie sought to supply material for the Scottish National Players, and it marked the start of the playwright's very fruitful relationship with Tyrone Guthrie, whose first professional production this was. It is worth noting, also, that the appearance of Beelzebub, speaking here a rich Scots, sets up a recurrent device in Bridie's drama: diabolic intervention in the world as a means of casting a razor-sharp light on the mores of human behaviour. Bridie's finely bleak last play, *The Baikie Charivari or the Seven Prophets* (1952), features the devil as incisive commentator on society, politics and culture (and as with *The Sunlight Sonata* resonant in voice in sonorous verse). Bridie, then, right until the end of his oeuvre scrutinised human behaviour in the light of this dark perspective in a way that raised the question, was it the devil or human beings who chilled the blood more? Comically, in *The Sunlight Sonata*, a group of middle-class Glaswegians on a picnic near Loch Lomond are anaemically, or pettily, sinful (they have no real sense of the dark and gambol merely in the sunlight) while around them the three graces and the forces of hell play out an ever more riotous attempt to impinge meaningfully on their lives. Bridie has in his sights the spiritually denuded life of modern humanity and his own seemingly throwaway comment on the play, "I wrote it on a Sunday and had to ring up a clergyman of my acquaintance to find out exactly who the Seven Deadly Sins were. He did not know", is not so much to be taken at face value but as confirming his deep and enduring diagnosis, as first set out in *The Sunlight Sonata*, that the "progress" of history is one where the human moral skin becomes, if anything, thicker.[16]

The Anatomist, originally performed in Edinburgh in 1930 by the Masque Theatre Company, was Bridie's first London production. It was played at the new Westminster Theatre in 1931 under the direction of Tyrone Guthrie, and it was a palpable hit better received, in fact, in the British capital than it had been previously in Scotland.[17] The enduring popularity of *The Anatomist* (it has probably been performed only less frequently among the Bridie oeuvre than another 1930 offering, *Tobias and the Angel*) is rooted in its fascinatingly macabre historical matter which surrounds the Burke and Hare "Body Snatching" scandal in Edinburgh during 1828. The "shock value" of the drama is heightened by the fact that Bridie despatches his material with an apparently throwaway humour, not least in his genre-tagging of the text. The published edition describes the play as "a lamentable comedy" and, synonymously, there are elements of *grand guignol* and farce in the handling of both the body of the main murdered character, the prostitute Mary Paterson, and of the eponymous anatomist, Robert Knox, the man of path-breaking experimental science who receives the dubiously acquired cadavers of Burke and Hare. Added to this, the playfulness of Bridie in *The Anatomist* is disconcertingly mirrored by the habitual frivolity of Knox's utterances. One might turn to Bridie's identification of farce as being particularly marked in his artistic palette, and to his 1939 lecture, "The Theatre", where he offers this definition: "Farce comes from the Italian *farcio*, I stuff. It means a haggis. It means an hour or two filled with anything that comes into the heads of the author or the actors."[18] Bridie's ludic lens in this lecture, however, is alternated with a long-sighted, grim lyricism as he considers the entertainment needs of the theatrical audience: "If [. . .] the spectators are conscious of the passage of time, the dreadful progress of the Universe towards destruction and nothingness, the play has failed."[19]

Robert Knox is, like Bridie in his lecture, a person who switches between bluff evasiveness and portentous declamation. He is an oxymoronic creation, a "Justified Sinner" or "a monstrous fine fellow" (p.93) as he describes himself, the man who wishes to further the understanding of human anatomy, but whose labours might as much be about tearing at the human body because he is a sociopath as about medical advancement.[20] He is the man who facetiously mocks the drawing-room lovers' tiff of his assistant, Walter Anderson, and fiancée, Mary Belle Dishart, for being histrionic and yet who wishes to hear the mob cry in his own wake, "Crucify him!" (p.53). On one hand, his protean capacity (describing himself in turn as a "jig-maker" for, as theatrical audience to, as judge of, and surgeon to, the quarrel between Walter and Mary Belle) provides for him a traditional shape-changing, devilish quality. He is Satan-like too as he talks in riddles. We see this in his exchange with Walter, who, much to his fiancée's disapproval, has deferred a potentially comfortable married living as a General Practitioner so as to carry on a while longer his pure research as assistant to Knox, and who appeals to the latter for understanding:

WALTER Am I in the right? Have I been a fool?
KNOX You are in the right to be a fool, and a fool to be in the right.
(p.53)

Is Knox pathetically deficient in empathy and feeling, or evil in not caring that his anatomy-room subjects have been murdered to order? Is he a man lacking in vision or too full of missionary zeal, seeing himself as "the apostolic successor of Cuvier" (p.93)? In one of a number of ironies and in a peculiar piece of poetic justice, Knox, hating the mob, is rescued by a mob – of "Knoxites" led by his most contemptible student, Raby. Similarly, despising drawing-room propriety, emblem of the bourgeois society which for long turns a blind eye to his dealings with Burke and Hare, Knox is forced at the end of the play to lecture in the Dishart drawing-room when the way to his university demonstrating-room is barred by hostile hoi polloi. Knox throughout might be deliberately constructing his own melodramatic "stage-devilment", but Bridie in the ironic texture of his play is enjoying the last laugh. Knox, ultimately, is bashed about and confined by his author in a way analogous to the victims of Burke and Hare. No human can ever really be master amidst "the dreadful progress of the Universe towards destruction and nothingness".

A Sleeping Clergyman (1933) also features a universe where God or good moral purpose is essentially absent (a lack signalled by the clergyman who slumbers through the narration of much of the play's action) and where human agency is embodied in a surfeit of sinister medicos. Continuing another of Bridie's fruitful theatrical relationships, the play was first directed by H. K. Ayliff at the Malvern Festival Theatre, thereafter running for nine months at the Piccadilly Theatre, London. The play electrified audiences, also perhaps marking the highpoint of Bridie's critical estimation in his own lifetime as "not a few observed that the mantle of Shaw had fallen on Bridie's shoulders".[21] Bridie himself was to write in *One Way of Living* that it "was the nearest thing to a masterpiece I shall probably write".[22] Albeit not without lashings of typical ironical reserve, Bridie's play has some general resonance with the likes of Shaw's *Man and Superman* (1902) which posits the evolutionary creativity of humanity as replacement for outworn moral prerogatives. The energy force that runs through the Cameron family during the best part of fifty years which the play chronicles is amoral and coldly ruthless, to the extent even of murder, but ultimately is responsible for finding a vaccination against a pandemic illness sweeping through the world and decimating the population (based, clearly, upon the catastrophic influenza outbreak of 1918). One way of reading the trajectory of the Cameron family saga is that good comes from bad as benefit to mankind is ultimately affected through individual genius; however, the genetically transmitted talent that finds the cure remains as essentially selfish and disconnected at the end of the play in the person of Charles Cameron the second, as in the case of his grandfather, Charles Cameron the first, at its start. The latter is deeply odious, enjoying the fact that his pregnant girlfriend will be cheated out of the respectability of marriage with his imminent death, which occurs from tuberculosis while his great intellectual potential remains unfulfilled. Cameron the second has military decorations that he cares not a jot about, consorts coldly with prostitutes and, in general, has the same lack of empathy for social and human connection as his grandfather, even though outwardly more seemingly conformist in these spheres and recognised as a great scientist. Rightly, John Thomas Low has made much of the inspiration for part of Bridie's play in the infamous 1857 case of Madeleine Smith in Glasgow, tried for the murder by poison of her lover, Emile L'Angelier.[23] Most likely guilty of the crime, Smith presented a scrupulously respectable façade in court to disguise a nature, clearly, that was hugely self-centred and passionately wild. Her guilt or lack of it was found by the jury to be "not proven", in that uniquely Scottish verdict, and it should be no surprise, therefore, that her case exercised the interest of Bridie with his taste for resonating dubiety. His plays are full of characters such as Robert Knox, or the similarly expedient but also criminally complicit Dr. William Marshall in *A Sleeping Clergyman*, whom society finds it convenient, even practical, morally to wink at so that their energies might remain at large. So far as Bridie himself is concerned, one feels, the moral or immoral condition of humanity is ultimately "not proven" when weighed against the more vital sphere of inspirational, as often as not, amoral, action which blindly propels the advancement of human culture and progress for good or ill. We see something of this cool, non-moral, empirical eye of Bridie's when, provocatively, he writes in 1941 while World War II rages around him:

> [. . .] if everybody had been [living ordinary lives] there wouldn't have been any Hitler or Jesus or Genghis Khan or Pasteur or George Stevenson or Copernicus or James Watt or Shakespeare or Napoleon or Robespierre or Lenin & nothing would have happened except the steady pressure of dull blackguards on top until the human race died – at about 6000BC – from inanition.[24]

Of course, as in the letter just quoted from, so too in his dramas, Bridie looks on the human activity, the "progress" of the world with a humour, if not exactly redemptive, at least bracingly honest.

In *Mr. Bolfry*, first performed in 1943 at the Westminster Theatre under Alastair Sim's direction, we have the depiction of the drab and petty reality of World War II on the ground as opposed to the notion of an epic struggle between good and evil. On the face of it, the play's sardonic view of the importance of great historic events does nothing for contemporary homeland propaganda (and shows the relatively relaxed view of the censor at this time). Bolfry, a high-ranking diabolic official conjured from hell by some bored young people in the Highlands, claims to be ignorant of the present conflagration and is unexcited about its possibilities for lasting mayhem:

> I should think some lunatic has been able to persuade his country that it is possible to regiment mankind. I should think the people he has persuaded are my old friends the Germans. They are sufficiently orderly and sufficiently stupid so to be persuaded. I should conjecture that mankind has risen in an intense state of indignation at the bare possibility of being regimented. I should think that the regimenters will succeed in hammering their enemies into some sort of cohesion. Mankind will then roll them in the mud for a bit and then pull them out and forget all about them. They will have much more interesting things to attend to – such as making money and making love. (p.211)

Anne Greene's reading of the play sees Bolfry as "a Blakean–Shavian Devil whose function it is to set the individual free", and, in the light of the passage just quoted, we can see why she reaches this conclusion.[25] Bolfry, indeed, rails against the puritanical, Calvinist minister, Mr. McCrimmon, at whose manse his niece, Jean, is staying along with the billeted soldiers Cohen and Cully. And these young people, symbols of an almost entirely secular and (by today's standards) mildly hedonistic life, have sought out Bolfry as counterbalance to the grim overlordship of McCrimmon. What they find in the devil, however, is a useless, negative mirror image of McCrimmon (Bolfry dresses in similar clerical garb), and a generally similar aloof detachment from the world that seemingly confirms McCrimmon's view of the importance of attending to that abstraction, "the soul".

Summoned in the night by the sounds of the illicit séance, McCrimmon encounters Bolfry and reckons him to be a nightmare-vision of his own sinful nature (one triggered by a possibly alcoholic past). The dualism of McCrimmon–Bolfry, however, merely confirms Jean's witticism about the highland "Wee Free" community: "It's got the best record for church attendance and the highest illegitimacy rate in the Kingdom" (p.181). Nothing more, in fact, is to be learned about the ideal life from Bolfry than from McCrimmon; they *are* two parts of a whole, but define rather than merely oppose one another. The idea of goodness and sinfulness conform a structure of morality which leads to extremes in categorisation and, as a result also, in human behaviour. The "struggle" between good and evil is, in fact, comically undercut as McCrimmon, knife in hand, eventually chases Bolfry out into the night and drives him over a cliff and into the sea. Evil is, in orthodox terms, "defeated" in this scenario, but in obviously crude fashion, so that both McCrimmon and Bolfry, ultimately, are belittled in the farcical ending to their encounter. The notorious finale to Bridie's play, when, the next morning reality restored, Bolfry's left-behind umbrella walks out in front of the protagonists, confirms the bathos. In response to this sight the minister's wife's summation is deliberately purblind: "Och, well, dear me, a walking umbrella's nothing to the things that happen in the Bible. Whirling fiery wheels and all these big beasts with the three heads and horns. It's very lucky we are that it was no worse. Drink up your tea" (p.226). We are back to a world that comfortably, smugly, accommodates both the sacred and the mundane. It might be suggested that, implicitly, both the overdetermined matter of the former and the unimaginative essence of the latter are equally critiqued in *Mr. Bolfry*. Human beings both, on the one hand, create rather ridiculous metaphysical systems and, on the other, content themselves with a threadbare sense of reality. Hyperactivity and laziness: these, in Bridie's perception, are all too often the defining and coexisting markers of human behaviour.

Daphne Laureola (1949) was Bridie's biggest theatrical hit, performed first at Wyndham's Theatre in the West End of London in a year-long run starring Edith Evans and produced by Laurence Olivier. Highly symbolic text and poignant psychological study (involving Bridie's most extended female character creation), the play, like *Mr. Bolfry*, elides nitty-gritty human contingency (here a post-war Britain of rationing) and a strongly emphasised mythical under-felt (the tale of Apollo's desire for Daphne). The Apollo-character is Ernest Piaste, resident at the Young Christian Men's Association and student of astronomy and economics, rather than prophetic Greek god. Amidst the threadbare conditions of a formerly fashionable Soho eatery, he falls in love with the Daphne-figure, Lady Pitts. Daphne, turned into a laurel tree to protect her from Apollo's attentions, is here in Lady Pitts already transformed into a pretty specimen by her ancient millionaire husband, Sir Joseph, whom she attends, suitably enough, in his conservatory (the Daphne genus being a particularly prized collector's item in the laurel family). Ernest's longing for Lady Pitts represents a kind of love among the ruins. He is émigré from communist-overrun Poland and first encounters her at a French restaurant in London, *Le Toit Aux Porcs*, now peddling the most basic menu, accommodating minor black marketeers and featuring a dangerous hole in the floor as a result of structural damage during the Blitz.

The deliberately heavy symbolism of *Daphne Laureola* is added to by Lady Pitts' name representing, on the face of it, infernal possibility for Ernest. Truly, he burns with unrequited love and seems denied in the most flagrant fashion when, on the demise of Sir Joseph, his beloved marries Vincent, her chauffeur. Ironically, however (as the Apollo–Daphne myth tells us), it is Lady Pitts who is cruelly assailed by Ernest. His ardent desire, with which the audience is likely, initially, to have an amount of sympathy, is simply another of the male-centred contexts which habitually surround Lady Pitts. She is the elegant product of the rectory, a first-class honours scholar from Cambridge University, and obtains the drudgery of an office job in a Birmingham factory (the extent of the independence won for her by her qualifications) from which she is "rescued" by the admiration of her ancient baronet. Now finding herself widowed and the object of desire of an overserious and humourless young man (humorously, Ernest is of Scottish Presbyterian stock on his mother's side) whose amorousness is of the instant and prefabricated calf-love kind, she chooses the man whose attentions are, at least, of some practical use to her. Vincent has routinely extracted her, as he does at *Le Toit Aux Porcs* in the first act of the play, from her solitary drunken peregrinations; and he is a man, perhaps, whose rough possessiveness is more honest than either that of Sir Joseph or Ernest. In giving herself to Vincent, she is, to some extent, removing herself from the pedestal of goddess and attempting to become merely a woman (whose relationship with her chauffeur prior to her husband's death, it is hinted, has been more than merely professional). The cast of mildly loathsome supporting characters form a chorus *manqué*, as they comment on the main events of the play with a mixture of the morally platitudinous and class fawning at the restaurant and at Lady Pitts' home to which, in her drunken bonhomie at *Le Toit Aux Porcs*, she has invited them. Their utterances form a striking counterpoint to the overexuberant declamations of love from Ernest and the altogether more poignant plaintiveness of Lady Pitts' speeches, which demonstrate her intelligent self-identification of her hopeless situation. On watching the play performed, Tyrone Guthrie wrote to Bridie in a rapture over Lady Pitts' soliloquies, saying "[w]hat a poet you could be if you weren't such a goddamned *amateur*", with the implication that Bridie wastes the more sublime aspects of his expression in intermingling these with characters and material that is altogether more mundane, flippant and throwaway.[26] In fact, as *Daphne Laureola* and other plays show, Bridie is a dramatist acutely attuned to the poetry that the human condition recurrently creates and the pathetic and even ludicrous reality in which it is often played out. Bridie's oeuvre is full of alternate taunting of, and tenderness for, humanity. Of which of these is it finally deserving is a question Bridie recurrently asks of his audience, a question which it is difficult satisfactorily to answer even today. Bridie strives, as Hope says at the end of *A Sleeping Clergyman*, "Whether the world is worth it or not".

Endnotes

[1] Maggie B. Gale, 'Theatre and Drama Between the Wars' in Laura Marcus and Peter Nicholls (eds), *The Cambridge History of Twentieth-Century English Literature* (Cambridge University Press: Cambridge, 2004), pp.318–334.
[2] Trevor R. Griffiths, 'Drama and the New Theatre Companies' in *The Cambridge History of Twentieth-Century English Literature*, pp.494–509.
[3] Neil Cooper, Obituary for Ena Lamont Stewart, *The (Glasgow) Herald* (16th February 2006), p.20.
[4] Alasdair Cameron, 'Bridie: The Scottish Playwright' in *Chapman* No. 55–56 (Spring 1989) [124–132], p.124. The same issue of *Chapman* contains Maurice Fleming's useful review of Ronald Mavor's *Dr. Mavor and Mr. Bridie*, pp.121–123; Allen Wright's 'Kelvinside, Kirriemuir and the Kailyard', pp.134–137; Tony Paterson, 'James Bridie: Playwright as Impressario?', pp.139–145; and Ronald Mavor, 'Bridie Revisited', pp.146–151. As ever, Edwin Morgan is hugely insightful in a short but wide-ranging piece in his 'James Bridie', a talk given to the English Association in 1967, first published in *Scottish International* (November 1971), and reprinted in *Essays by Edwin Morgan* (Carcanet: Cheadle, 1974), pp.232–241. For an excellent summary of Bridie's dramatic career and cultural involvements, see Alasdair Cameron and Adrienne Scullion, 'James Bridie and Scottish Theatre' in Douglas Gifford, Sarah Dunnigan and Alan MacGillivray, *Scottish Literature in English and Scots* (Edinburgh University Press: Edinburgh, 2002), pp.619–627.
[5] David Hutchison, '1900–1950' in Bill Findlay (ed.), *A History of Scottish Theatre* (Edinburgh University Press: Edinburgh, 1998), p.224; for more on the Scottish National Players and Bridie's involvement see also Hutchison's *The Modern Scottish Theatre* (Molendinar Press: Glasgow, 1977), pp.43–57 & pp.72–78; and, for an incisive and highly lucid summary of twentieth-century Scottish theatre, generally, and Bridie's place in it, his 'Theatres, Writers and Society: Structures and Infrastructures of Theatre Provision in Twentieth-Century Scotland' in Ian Brown (ed.), *The Edinburgh History of Scottish Literature Volume 3* (Edinburgh University Press: Edinburgh, 2007), pp.142–150.
[6] See the entry on Bridie, written by Eric Linklater (revised by David Hutchison) in *The New Dictionary of National Biography* (Oxford University Press: Oxford, 2004); for the scale and intensity of Bridie's cultural activism, the two sources that shed indispensable light are Winifred Bannister, *James Bridie and His Theatre* (Rockliff: London, 1955) and Ronald Mavor, *Dr. Mavor and Mr. Bridie* (Canongate and The National Library of Scotland: Edinburgh, 1988). For Bridie and the Citizens' Theatre, as well as Bannister and

Mavor, see Cordelia Oliver, *Magic in the Gorbals* (Northern Book: Famedram, 1999); and *A Conspectus to Mark the Citizens' 21st Anniversary as a Living Theatre in Gorbals Street Glasgow* (Glasgow, 1964), including 'James Bridie, a Tribute' (first written in 1956), pp.9–10, in which J. B. Priestley already complains that Bridie 'seems the most undervalued dramatist of his stature known to me' (p.9). Jan McDonald's unpublished lecture, ' "We simply could not wait" – James Bridie and the Citizens' Theatre', delivered for the 50th anniversary of the School of Drama in 2001 (and soon to be deposited in the Scottish Theatre Archive, University of Glasgow Library Special Collections), was most helpful; I am grateful to Professor McDonald for providing me with a copy of her lecture. See also Donald Campbell's excellently written *Playing for Scotland: A History of the Scottish Stage 1715–1965* (Mercat Press: Edinburgh, 1996) for the long context.

[7] In 'Towards a Scottish National Drama: John Brandane' (first published 8th January 1926) see Hugh MacDiarmid, *Contemporary Scottish Studies* edited by Alan Riach (Carcanet: Manchester, 1995), (pp.235–243) p.241.

[8] Letter from James Bridie 11th January 1945 to the editor of the *Scots Independent* where the playwright responds to MacDiarmid's charge (in which the poet probably hoped to hint at Bridie's jealousy of Robert McLellan) that the Citizens' Theatre had announced the performance of McLellan's *Jamie the Saxt*, without any actual intention to perform it. Bridie responded in his letter to MacDiarmid's charge, seeing the poet as a hater of the Citizens' and in the following terms, 'if I did not realise that this represents Mr. MacDiarmid's habitual reflex to everything practical conceived for the benefit of Scotland, I should take the liberty of calling him a damned liar' (see typescript of letter in Glasgow University Library Special Collections [GB 247 STA Bridie 96]).

[9] James Bridie, 'The Scottish Character as it was viewed by Scottish Authors from Galt to Barrie' ('The John Galt Lecture for 1937': Greenock, 1937), p.19.

[10] It should be acknowledged too, however, that Bridie at times enjoyed something of a prickly relationship to Scottish theatre audiences. William Power encapsulates something of this when, in 1932, he writes: 'James Bridie, not long ago, wrote an icily scathing letter to a London paper about the ape-like behaviour of a Glasgow audience which, through some collective misapprehension, found itself at a really good play' in Power, 'Community Drama and the Renaissance: A New Theatre Public', reprinted in Margery Palmer McCulloch (ed.), *Modernism and Nationalism: Literature and Society in Scotland 1918–1939* (Association for Scottish Literary Studies: Glasgow, 2004), p.138.

[11] Bannister, *James Bridie and His Theatre*, p.36.

[12] Gerald Weales, *Religion in Modern English Drama* (University of Pennsylvania Press: Philadelphia, 1961), [pp.79–90] p.81.

[13] For a full-length study of Bridie's drama that makes much of the difficulty of reading Bridie's outlook, see Helen L. Luyben, *James Bridie: Clown and Philosopher* (University of Pennsylvania Press: Philadelphia, 1965). A further useful study, especially in reading the awkward moral and spiritual status of Bridie's main protagonists, is Ernest G. Mardon, *The Conflict Between the Individual and Society in the Plays of James Bridie* (William MacLellan: Glasgow, 1972).

[14] See the very interesting prompt script for *The Anatomist* among the papers of Alastair Sim held at the National Library of Scotland, where Sim, as he did for other Bridie offerings, made his own directorial alterations and excisions in dialogue (MS.31069). Clearly, Bridie was happy to leave such final decisions to those such as Sim whose theatrical sensibility he trusted, and there is no reason why some of Bridie's texts might not be practically edited in the light of modern performance requirements.

[15] Alasdair Cameron and Adrienne Scullion, 'James Bridie and Scottish Theatre', p.626.

[16] Quoted in Mavor, *Dr. Mavor and Mr. Bridie*, p.63.

[17] See Bannister, *James Bridie and His Theatre*, pp.62–63.

[18] 'The Theatre. A Paper Read to the Thirteen on the Evening of 24th November 1939' (Glasgow, 1939), p.2.

[19] 'The Theatre', p.3.

[20] For a fuller discussion of *The Anatomist* along the lines argued here, see Gerard Carruthers, 'Two Bridie Plays: *The Anatomist* and *Mr. Bolfry*' in Douglas Gifford, Sarah Dunnigan and Alan MacGillivray (eds), *Scottish Literature* (Edinburgh University Press: Edinburgh, 2002), pp.627–635.

[21] Mavor, *Dr. Mavor and Mr. Bridie*, p.77.

[22] James Bridie, *One Way of Living* (Constable: London, 1939), p.278.

[23] John Thomas Low, *Doctors, Devils, Saints and Sinners: A Critical Study of the Major Plays of James Bridie* (Ramsay Head Press: Edinburgh, 1980), pp.23–24.

[24] Quoted in Mavor, *Dr. Mavor and Mr. Bridie*, pp.107–108.

[25] Anne Greene, 'Bridie's Concept of the Master Experimenter' in *Studies in Scottish Literature* No.2 (1964), [pp.96–110], p.100.

[26] Mavor, *Dr. Mavor and Mr. Bridie*, p.127.

THE SUNLIGHT SONATA

OR

TO MEET THE SEVEN DEADLY SINS

A FARCE-MORALITY

IN

A PROLOGUE, AN INTERLUDE, A DEMONSTRATION, AN APOTHEOSIS AND AN EPILOGUE

To Tyrone Guthrie

Persons in the Play

MARCUS GROUNDWATER, C.B.E., D.L., J.P.. . . . . A builder
MAGGIE GROUNDWATER . . . . His wife
2nd-LT. HAMISH HECTOR MATHIESON GROUNDWATER . Their son
MATTHEW PETTIGREW. . . . . An artist
THE REV. SOMERLED CARMICHAEL, B.D., B.LITT.. . . . A clergyman
MRS. CARMICHAEL . . . . His wife
ELSIE CARMICHAEL . . . . Their daughter

BEELZEBUB	FAITH
SUPERBIA	HOPE
INVIDIA	CHARITY
IRA	
ACCIDIA	
AVARICIA	
GULA	
LUXURIA	

PHŒBUS APOLLO (who does not appear in person)

1

DESCRIPTION OF CHARACTERS

GROUNDWATER: Æt. 54. Well-dressed, round, chubby, and hard, but not incapable of sentiment. An elder in Carmichael's church, *(a)* because it is good for trade, *(b)* because he is afraid of God. He has an educated Glasgow accent, and speaks broadly when he is angry or trying to be funny.

MRS. GROUNDWATER: Æt. 30? 40? 50? A gross, over-dressed, over-eating blonde. A great patron of beauty parlours and restaurants.

HAMISH: A perfect little gentleman. Æt. 21. Beautifully dressed. Easily polite. Fettes, Sandhurst, and the Highland Light Infantry. His parents are proud and a little afraid of him.

PETTIGREW: Æt. 35. A sulky oaf of a painter. Long dark hair. Blue chin. Pink collar. Peacock blue tie. Light old Harris tweeds. Chain smoker. Groundwater is his Mæcenas and is getting a little impatient at the slowness with which Pettigrew fulfils his contracts.

CARMICHAEL: Æt. 40. Light grey suit and clerical collar. A big, handsome man with a powerful voice. His manner is reserved and suggests that he is well aware that he looks and sounds rather magnificent.

MRS. CARMICHAEL: Æt. 38. Ill-dressed, bleach-haired. Nervously quick in her talk and movements. Has the air of a drudge, but there is more than a suspicion that this is principally histrionic.

ELSIE: Æt. 19. A pretty girl. Plays tennis very well, golf fairly well, and dances superlatively well when she gets the chance. Dressed by a good tailor. An atheist in religion. Her parents obviously get on what nerves she has.

THE THREE GRACES: The Graces are three handsome but uneventful Pantomime Fairy Queens. On the top of Charity's wand is a tiny telephone. On the top of Faith's a miniature barometer. On the top of Hope's – a Star.

BEELZEBUB: Six feet high. Bald. He wears little horns like Emil Jannings' in the Faust film. His face is painted bright blue, but apart from this his face is that of a lovable old gentleman inclining to embonpoint. He speaks the Doric. He wears a long black cloak with a green lining, green sleeves with pointed white cuffs turned back over his knuckles, black kid gloves, and a dark blue doublet and hose. He carries his tail over his arm.

SUPERBIA: All the Sins are as small as possible, but Superbia is the tallest of them. She is thin and ivory pale. She wears a black velvet hunting-dress springing into an arum lily collar, hawking gloves, spurred scarlet boots, a purple passion flower over one pointed ear, and a long Pompadour cane.

IRA: Is dressed in rags of every shade of red from magenta to vermilion. Her hair is red and she has a pale face and black devil eyebrows. A dagger is in her belt. Her legs are bare and scratched, and she has hairy brogues on her feet.

ACCIDIA: A slut in dusky blue rags, tangled neutral-coloured hair and jade earrings. Her expression is woebegone, and she must indicate sullenness as well as sloth.

AVARICIA: Is a male. He is the conventional miser, but young, elfish and sprightly. Yellow tunic and brown stockings. Pale hair, little horns, a tiny peaked chin beard and a peaked face. His nose is bright scarlet. He jingles as he walks.

GULA: Also a male. Falstaff as a boy. He wears a mask representing a sensual expressionless face. His Elizabethan garments have burst in places.

INVIDIA: Is the smallest of the Sins. Neatly dressed in green with an iron chain necklace. Pale face and eyes and hair.

LUXURIA: The youngest of the Sins. A baggage. She is dressed in a leopard skin and exiguous underwear, a smilax wreath, a quantity of cheap jewellery and high-heeled shoes. She is a restless, unpleasant little thing, always scratching herself or teasing Ira.

PROLOGUE

Part of Glen Falloch at the head of Loch Lomond. The stage represents a flat of green turf surrounded by heather, one or two birches, and a mountain ash. A third of the stage at back L. is occupied by a sloping heath-clad platform, on top of which is a huge boulder. The back cloth is painted to represent a rugged and conventionalised Highland landscape, showing very little sky. The stage, on the rise of the curtain, is in inky darkness except for one star, high up R. When he is revealed by the lightning, BEELZEBUB is seen to be standing on the boulder. In the darkness he is heard intoning the following hexameters in a deep baritone with an accent in which broad Ayrshire and schoolroom pedantry are nicely blended.

BEELZEBUB Now is the butt o' the nicht. The muckle black Bens are about me.
Dour and cauld and deid. What are the Bens to me?
Give me the bonny wee glens with the quick brown whispering water,
And Life in the burn, in the linn, by the river shadowed with cities.
Life in the muir and the wood and the clachan – flittering, fighting,
The rat and the bat and the cleg; the otter, the owl and the adder;
The lean sculduddery cat and the slaters under the ruckies;
Maggots in dead men's eye-sockets; eels in the deep cold loch;
The sweating caird and his wife and weans in bed in the bothy
Wi' the plaid well over the lugs for fear of my wise horngollochs
That peek and peer and turn and hirple and crawl in their armour
Into the ears and the nose and the eyes and into the brain-pan,
Into the very soul. . . . The thoughts. The thoughts. The thoughts.
O for the living heart of a man. What are the Bens to me?
Man. Man. Man.
You're feart o' me, you're feart o' me,
Droll wee slug wi' the shifty e'e!
Raise your praise to the Ancient of Days.
I prevent you in all your ways.
Your heavy hosannas sink to me.
To me you pray in horrible psalm
For the single eye and the grasping palm –
"Play the game, Lord, play the game.
Commit us not to the worm and the flame.
Save us from boils and leprosy,
Prosper our cheating and let us be!
Benedicamus, Domine! Amen."

(A silence)

4

It's lonely for Princes of Darkness up here in the hills.
Ye blasted sarcophagous bings! Aye, sit there silent and glower!
Where's your civility? Tell me. I'll set you to rights!
Take ye that. Take ye that. Take ye that.

(Thunder and lightning)

. . . Aye, weel ye may wag your pows!

(A storm. There is a lull. A silvery burst of community giggling breaks out. The stage is lit with a baleful red glow. The SEVEN DEADLY SINS are revealed crouching in the foreground.)

BEELZEBUB Eh? What's that, what's that? I heard laughing. . . . Is a'body there? It isna' the day nor the hour for a Sabbath of Witches.

(SUPERBIA advances. The evil light intensifies gradually.)

SUPERBIA Is that you, Master?
BEELZEBUB I'm Master o' deils and hobgoblins, o' poltergeists, witches and fays. Which of the boiling are you in your duddie bit braws? Come your ways oot o' the mirklins. Walk widdershins by me. . . . Deil hain us! A vaudie bit smatchet. What name do they ca' ye?
SUPERBIA I am the Lady Superbia. The first of the Seven Deadly Sins. Those are the others. I forget their names.
BEELZEBUB It was you got my excellent crony, the Son of the Morning, the sack. Ye Inferiority Complex! . . . Get ower. Get oot o' my sicht.

(IRA advances)

Man! Here's a bit maggie-rab partan! And what's like the matter wi' you?
IRA I'm Anger. My Christian name is Ira.
BEELZEBUB Losh save us and a'! Whatna dirdum! Awa' and coo in the corner.

(INVIDIA advances)

INVIDIA Master, I am Envy. My proper name is Invidia, but nobody thinks it worth while calling me by my proper name. I should have come before Ira. But I don't suppose you care.
BEELZEBUB Not a rap, not a scrap, not a maik. I've a routh of your sort at hame. Awa' to your Mother's Meeting. Next. . . . Who's next yin? That's richt. Take your time!

(ACCIDIA advances)

ACCIDIA I'm Accidia, you know. Sheer damned laziness and the black dog on the back and all that sort of thing. One of the Neuroses, you know. Psychasthenia to my friends. I'm rather Slavonic, they say.

BEELZEBUB (*irrelevantly*) Of the oak-headed natives of Britain, it is said "They shall never be Slavs." But they're doing their damndest, the craturs. Move on, lassie. Don't go to sleep.

(*AVARICIA advances*)

AVARICIA Good-morning, Master.

BEELZEBUB Your name, then, you nippit wee spirlie. Or is that giving something away?

AVARICIA Not at all, Master. It's Thrift, really, as a matter of fact – Avaricia in Latin.

BEELZEBUB And how are they all in the North? Nay, you can keep your counsel and anything else you can get. And wha is this creeshy pockpud?

GULA Gula, Master, Gula. Gutsy Gilbert. Salivating Sam. You don't happen to have a pork-pie about you, Master?

BEELZEBUB A what?

GULA A pig tart, Master.

(*The SINS murmur a protest at his cheek*)

BEELZEBUB (*looking severely at him*) Keep you your gab for engorging. And carry your belly ow're there. Yin, Twa, Three, Fower, Five, Six. It runs in my heid there were Seven.

(*LUXURIA advances*)

LUXURIA Hello!

BEELZEBUB What's that?

LUXURIA Hello, Daddy!

BEELZEBUB Daddy! In the name o' – What do they call you?

LUXURIA Luxuria, dearie. Isn't it a pretty name? Of course they call me other names too, but I never forget that I'm a lady, whatever people say. A nasty, low, common lot they are. No education.

BEELZEBUB Get owre wi' the lave, you randy. You're wantin' a skelping. (*Thunder*)
From the antres dark of Pandemonium
I come.
To throw my shadow on the roofs of men
Again.
For years are dreary in yon sulphur ditch
Of which
The LANDLORD girns in perpetuity
To me
Of all his woes. He has seen better days,
He says.
Eternal tedium; eternal doom,

6

And gloom.
I tell you it was getting past a joke.
I spoke
To Lucifer about it.
He said, "Oh!
Then go
And take a jaunt into the cooler air
Up there,
Report in full on everything you see
To me.
See if the Seven Deadly Ones are quite
All right,
And make the rascals demonstrate to you
A few
Small tricks. And tell me if they shirk
Their work."
And so from Hateful Pandemonium
Agog, agog to quit that dismal place,
To put you through your paces I have come.
How are my little friends the Human Race?
SUPERBIA You'd hardly believe how proud they are.
They're proud of their accents or having a car,
Or of knowing a knight or the name of a winner,
Or of putting on hard-boiled shirts to dinner;
Or of taking a bath or of not taking beer.
There's nothing too silly or mean or queer
For the People to peacock and boast and shout
And be unbearably vain about.
IRA *and* **INVIDIA** Oh, the fights and the fun and the fret and the fuss
Since they handed their politics over to us.
AVARICIA All the noble and the wise
Swear by Private Enterprise.
Zaharoff and Bernard Shaw
Preach the Economic Law.
Ire and Envy run the Left;
I uphold the banner of Theft,
And my stock was never higher.
GULA *and* **ACCIDIA** We are the end of every man's desire.
Even if they do get fat,
What of that?
LUXURIA Oh, I'm not going to play this silly round game. I'm the best of
the lot. I'm Self Expression. I'm Personality. That's what I am. I'm the only
one who really interests them.
BEELZEBUB Sins. Why have you come here, far on a ghostly moorland?

7

Cannot you move them in dreams to murder and envy and lust? Am I to bear to the LANDLORD ill words of his profitless vessels?

SUPERBIA We are waiting.

INVIDIA You see, they are having a picnic up here to-morrow.

AVARICIA Seven of them. We've marked them down. It's a sort of a competition. Seven of us. Seven of them. One each.

INVIDIA Huh! Mathematics!

IRA Yes, Master, and I hope you intend to see fair play. Last time—

INVIDIA Now, Ira, don't annoy the Master.

IRA Don't annoy him? You cringing, sneaking, evil-minded little hag, it wouldn't take much to make me lose my temper with you.   *(Thunder)*

BEELZEBUB Now. Now. Now. Now. Stay at peace, ye besoms. *(He clears his throat)*

> The world is asleep like a peerie, bumming round on its peg.
> The veil'd moon trails her mantle along the shores of the ocean.
> The unsleeping, uncaring stars look coldly down and behold us.
> Sleep little Sins and rest for a while, poor babies of sorrow.

INVIDIA On the spur of the moment. Yes. An impromptu. . . . Rest till the morrow.

CURTAIN

End of Prologue

INTERLUDE

Played before the Curtain

Enter CHARITY. To her FAITH and HOPE.

FAITH Why, bless my buttons, what is this I see?
Surely it can't be little Charity!
Good-morning, dearie, how are you to-day?
HOPE I hope the nathty headache'th quite away.
CHARITY Quite better, thanks. I took a Fairy Powder.
But what a night! The thunder growing louder,
The lightning growing nearer every minute.
It's my belief, my dears, the Devil's in it.
HOPE That'th funny now. Thince the thtorm thtarted brewing
I've felt convinced there mutht be thomething doing.
CHARITY Whenever an important Devil comes
I feel the rheumatism in my thumbs.
Last night I felt it – felt it something cruel.
HOPE Do say it'th better now, my prethiouth jewel.
CHARITY Yes, thank you. Faith, dear, what have you to say?
FAITH I know we're going to have a lovely day.
And I remarked to Hope when you came in
That we might take the Morris for a spin
Right up to Crianlarich, just us three
And drop in to Ardlui for our tea.
CHARITY But what about that Devil? What do you think?
I heard the waste pipe in the kitchen sink
Go horribly last night. A gurgling sound,
As if some big upheaval underground
Were going on. Do you remember, dear,
It happened last time Ashtaroth was here?
Hope, dearie, I'm alarmed. What do you say?
Is there a great big Devil on his way?
HOPE I hope not, preciouth.
FAITH Anyway, we'll see.
We'll all go up Lochlomondside for tea,
Since the barometer *(she consults one at the top of her magic wand)* . . . is
    now set fair.
I must go now. So long. I'll see you there. *(Exit)*
CHARITY Faith! Hi! Oh, well, perhaps we'd better go,
Although she does take things for granted so.
She is a love! But listen, Hope, I doubt

9

To-day there'll be bad influences about.
I don't half like the portents.
HOPE Never mind.
The wortht may come, but good remainth behind.
Thomewhere, at anyrate, the thun is shining
And every thtorm cloud has a thilver lining.
So let us hope – er – that the betht man winth.
Lithten. How are thothe darling Deadly Thinth?
CHARITY Busy as bees, the dears. Quite happy too.
How can they realise the harm they do?
I love Luxuria. She is such a child.
Gula's good-natured. Ira's a little wild
But so straightforward. Sloth's so quiet and nice.
Superbia's a girl you look at twice.
And poor Invidia, things are hard for her.
And Avaricia's such a gatherer
And picker up of things. Oh, what a joy
To parents when they have a careful boy.
HOPE They are a little trying now and then,
But naughty children make the finetht men.
You wait a million years or tho and thee
How abtholutely lovely they will be.
CHARITY Of course they will. But I must go, my dear.
I'm hoping to inspire a profiteer
(Such a nice man) to give a pound or two
To help a most deserving kangaroo
Who sprained his ankle yesterday, in the Zoo.
HOPE Tho long, love.
CHARITY Cheery-bye bye.
HOPE Tootleoo.   *(Exeunt)*

End of Interlude

THE DEMONSTRATION

The scene is the same as that in the Prologue, but it is bathed in sunshine. A picnic party has practically finished the eating part, and the fragments are being returned to baskets and hampers. MRS. CARMICHAEL and ELSIE are packing; MRS. GROUNDWATER is fanning herself with a newspaper and having a sort of Indian summer of a picnic all to herself with two sandwiches and what is left of a pint of Ayala. The MEN have gone down to the river to wash dishes, except PETTIGREW, who is lying on his back in the scanty shade of the big rock.

MRS. C. Aren't they lovely. All the hills. Do look at them!

ELSIE Thanks. I've seen them.

MRS. C. You needn't snap my nose off, Elsie. *(Shouting to the men)* Do hurry up with the dishes. What a time you take!

ELSIE It's ridiculous to start packing just as soon as we have finished.

MRS. G. Especially when we haven't finished.

MRS. C. Oh, I'm so sorry, Mrs. Groundwater. You were so quiet I didn't notice. But really, I mean, it's so nice to say to yourself: "There now, that's over. We can have the rest of the afternoon to ourselves."

ELSIE We have, anyhow.

MRS. G. Now, do you know, I don't quite agree with you, Mrs. Carmichael. I think it's so nice to sort of prolong the picnic. I mean it's so nice to see the things still lying about as if we were going on and on and on, like as if it was some beautiful dream of eternity.

MRS. C. It is easy for you to talk that way, Mrs. Groundwater. You have a rich husband, and you can afford to take things easy. But it's very, very different for a poor parson's wife. She has to keep at it, at it all the time, and never faint by the wayside. And you've no idea what a delight it is for her to say, once in a while: "There now. The work's done."

ELSIE Oh, I think that's all bilge, personally. What work? You go about making work for yourself; fuss, fuss, fuss all the time. You make heavy weather out of nothing.

MRS. C. Elsie darling, don't say "bilge". Mrs. Groundwater, may I have that bottle now? They come in so handy for this sort of thing and that sort of thing and little odds and ends. Are you quite finished?

MRS. G. Quite, quite, quite.

> For pleasures are like poppies spread.
> You pluck the fowl, its bloom is shed.
> Or like the Borealis lights a tumptytum amid the storm.
> Or like the snowball in the river
> A moment white then melts into the liquid mass.

MRS. C. Dear me, yes. How true that is!

(BEELZEBUB and his SINS appear like a row of Jacks in the Box over the summit of the rock. GLUTTONY, ANGER, and SLOTH and ENVY are more prominent than the other three. The conversation interests them. The party is unaware of BEELZEBUB and his SINS.)

MRS. C. There now! That's that. Oh, those men! It will be time to go home before we have the dishes packed. Hello, Mr. Pettigrew, I thought you had gone with them.

PETTIGREW No, I thought . . . I say, I can't help in any way, can I?

(ACCIDIA pops round the corner of the rock and twitches anxiously at his sleeve. IRA makes violent signals to ELSIE.)

ELSIE Oh, no, Mr. Pettigrew. We have almost quite finished. But we have been tremendously bucked all through by your moral support.

(BEELZEBUB looks bored. He is keeping a score in a little book. A certain liveliness is seen among the SINS as the conversation illuminates each individual characteristic.)

PETTIGREW *(sulking)* Oh, very well then. *(He lies back and stares at the sky)*

MRS. G. Elsie dear, would you very much mind looking in my husband's attache case for the liqueur chocolates? Yes. Over there. I think they round off a little snack like this so nicely. Don't you?

(ELSIE passes the chocolates with a sneer)

MRS. G. *(helping herself)* Do have one, dear. Mrs. Carmichael. Please. Mr. Pettigrew. Now put them back beside me. I love liqueur chocolates . . .

> The same that oft times hath
> Charmed magic casements opening on a prospect of pearly seas in
>   fairyland.

I do so love that. It's from the poem about the vintage that hath been chilled for an hour or so in the garden earth. Something about a blushful Hippopotamus. After all, there's nobody like Shelley. Are you fond of Shelley, Mrs. Carmichael?

MRS. C. I have so little time for reading, nowadays.

(CARMICHAEL, GROUNDWATER and HAMISH come in carrying cups, glasses, saucers and plates)

MARCUS I'm awfully sorry, Mrs. Carmichael, but Hamish broke one of your plates. It was a cracked one anyway, but that's no excuse for carelessness.

MRS. C. Oh, it doesn't matter really. They are cheap old things. We can't afford to pay much for crockery.

MRS. G. How very naughty of you, Hamish. Hamish, I've been looking everywhere for the opera creams we bought at Balloch. You had them last.

HAMISH We didn't buy them. The Padre bought them. He's got them, I expect.

MR. C. Ah, yes. So I have. Won't you have one, Mrs. Groundwater?

MRS. G. You spoil me, Mr. Carmichael. We've just been having such an interesting talk about poetry.

MR. C. How very highbrow of you, Mrs. Groundwater. I imagined that ladies talked of much more worldly matters when they laughed alone.

MRS. G. Dear me, Mrs. Carmichael, how badly you have brought him up!

MR. C. I am afraid my upbringing was complete before my wife and I ever met.

MRS. G. Isn't that awful, now. How dull for her. I made a man of Marcus, here, and enjoyed doing it. He knows we talk of other things than servants and scandal, don't we, duckums?

MARCUS Yes. You talk about food.

MRS. G. Ho! I suppose you live on air like a seraph or something. Do tell the Minister what you said when those kidneys were underdone last Friday. Hmph! Perhaps you'd better not, and you a ruling elder! . . . But seriously, Mr. Carmichael, I think it's just dreadful how unintellectual people have become since the War. They think of nothing but dancing and amusing themselves. Don't you think the world is going to the— getting worse instead of better?

MR. C. I should be sorry to think so, Mrs. Groundwater, but there is little doubt that a gross spirit of materialism is abroad.

(At this point BEELZEBUB hides a leer behind his hand, and SUPERBIA, who has found the scene rather tedious, sits up and takes notice)

I should be sorry to think myself lacking in sympathy for my fellow-creatures – I am glad to say that spiritual pride has never been one of my failings. . . .

(BEELZEBUB and SUPERBIA think this is great fun and applaud him silently)

. . . You know, Mrs. Groundwater, comprendre tout, c'est tout pardonner – to understand everything is to forgive everything. . . .

MRS. G. Thanks, I know French very well.

MR. C. I know that, but I was correcting myself. I hate lapsing into a foreign language when the homely, natural tongue will serve quite as well. It is a beastly affectation, and I have to be for ever on my guard against it. Where was I?

HAMISH You were starting in to give the young generation a sharp telling off, Padre.

MR. C. Was I, indeed?

HAMISH Yes, you were. Personally I don't think they're so bad.

MARCUS What way not?

HAMISH They're a bit full of oats and so on, but there's far more palliness nowadays and less poodlefaking and square pushing and so forth, if you know what I mean.

MARCUS What in all the earth have poodles to do with it?

HAMISH Oh, poodlefaking. *You* know.

MARCUS I don't.

HAMISH Well, I mean you can take a girl out and jazz about a bit and go home, and never any suggestion of mucking about and what not. My feeling is, it's a lot healthier.

MARCUS Mr. Carmichael just about hit the nail on the head when he mentioned materialism. I don't mind a little fun myself so long as it's understood that there are more important things. But people nowadays have lost all sense of proportion. There's no spiritual-mindedness about these days. Everybody's out to enjoy himself without a thought either to his business or to his immortal soul. It's fair sickening. Well. Well. What are we going to do now, eh? What are we going to do now? Let's do something. The time's getting on.

MRS. C. Now, let me think. What was that nice round game we had at the Mothers' Tea Party, Elsie?

ELSIE Oh, round game! I wish I'd brought my knitting.

MRS. C. I wish you had, Elsie.

MRS. G. I don't see why we need do anything. I'm quite happy as I am. Peace, perfect peace, with loved ones far away. Oh, I believe I'm going to have a little hiccup. Mr. Carmichael, would you mind passing my vanity bag? It has some of those nice strong little peppermints in it. Thank you so much.

MRS. C. Somerled dear, I think perhaps it would be as well if you three men took the hampers to the car. Then we'd have everything shipshape and settle down to enjoy ourselves.

MARCUS (*sitting down*) Mrs. Carmichael, I've done quite enough work for one day. There's Pettigrew. He hasn't done a hand's turn. I don't see why even an artist shouldn't do a job of work now and again. If a man does not work neither shall he eat. The pastor and I will have a smoke. Pettigrew and Hamish can take the hampers. Hamish, Pettigrew, you take the hampers. You and Mrs. Carmichael thinking of taking a daunder up the glen, Maggie? (*He takes out a cigar case*)

MRS. C. Well, what do you think, Mrs. Groundwater?

(MRS. GROUNDWATER *does not hear her*)

MARCUS Oh, I remember, Carmichael. You always smoke a pipe. I like a good cigar myself now and again. I put these in my pocket at the Infant

Health Luncheon. The Corporation do you pretty well in that way at any rate.

MRS. C. It looks as if these two men wanted to be left alone, Mrs. Groundwater.

(HAMISH pulls the unwilling PETTIGREW to his feet and the two carry off the luncheon baskets, R.)

MRS. G. Have you such a thing as a cigarette, Mr. Carmichael? Oh! Oh! Oh!

MRS. C. What is the matter, dear?

MRS. G. I feel so funny and faintish.

MR. C. What is it? Can we do anything?

MARCUS It's nothing. She has those turns often. It will pass off in a minute. Mrs. Carmichael and Elsie will oxter you down to the burn, Maggie. Rub her behind the ears with a wet handkerchief, Mrs. Carmichael. That always brings her round.

(The two women help MRS. GROUNDWATER to her feet, and slowly the three go out L.)

MR. C. I do hope it's nothing serious.

MARCUS Serious? Not a bit. It used to be serious enough when we had to call in a doctor at two guineas a time to put her in bed and give her baking soda.

MR. C. Oh, come now. You are rather hard on the doctors.

MARCUS Not at all. I've a sort of sneaking admiration for doctors all the same. The second oldest profession in the world and still going strong. But that's by the way. See here, listen, Mr. Carmichael. I wanted a word with you by yourself. I wanted to tell you that I am very hurt and displeased at the attitude of the Business Committee of the Kirk Session.

MR. C. Now just in what way have they displeased you, Mr. Groundwater?

MARCUS It's about this building contract. You know perfectly well that as a ruling elder I had no wish or inclination to quote for it. But ever since the rebuilding scheme came on the tapis last spring certain individuals have been nag nag nagging and pestering me to take over the contract. Thought they would get the work done on the cheap because I happened to be a prominent figure in the Church. Now, after I had quoted a cut-throat price I won't make a penny piece out of, here they go behind my back and ask Wyllie & Symington for a quotation.

MR. C. I know nothing about business, Mr. Groundwater, but my information is that Wyllie & Symington are prepared to do the job for a considerably smaller sum.

MARCUS They've quoted at one thousand and fifty-five pounds below my offer. They're making you a present of it.

MR. C. You know I never cant, Mr. Groundwater. I abominate cant. But it runs in my mind that gifts to the Lord never go unrepaid.

MARCUS Gifts to the Lord! You know perfectly well that I'm as generous as my neighbour. I practically put in the new organ myself. But there's a limit. There's the Economic Law, and that's God's Law – you can say what you like. Supply and Demand, and fair, untrammelled competition. This offer of Wyllie & Symington's is sheer damned foolishness. Of course they'll put the loss down to advertising expenses, but that isn't business. . . . See here, Mr. Carmichael, you've said yourself I'm a very valued member. We've been more like friends than a Minister and Elder, the pair of us. And there's Hamish taken a notion to Elsie. It's like we'll be closer connected still, before very long. And now I've been put on the University Court it'll be bad luck or bad guidance if I can't get my spiritual adviser made a Doctor of Divinity before the year's out. I'll tell you what, I'll make you a fair offer. I'll cut down my price £500 and count that as a wedding present to the young folks, and you'll put your foot down on this Wyllie & Symington business. After all, you're the shepherd of the flock. You should have some say in the way they spend their money.

MR. C. I've already told you I don't understand business.

MARCUS But this isnae business. It's on a higher plane altogether. Pure, undiluted friendship. £500 doesnae grow on every bush.

MR. C. As I say, I don't understand business. I never indulge in highfaluting, but my mind is occupied by what I conceive to be more important matters. I am quite willing to leave money matters to Mr. Lang, Bailie Dallas, Sir John Small, Mr. Shillitto and yourself.

MARCUS But, God bless my soul, there's not a business man among the bunch of them except myself.

MR. C. Then perhaps you will be able to convert the others to your views. I wash . . .

MARCUS But listen, Mr. Carmichael . . .

MR. C. I wash my hands . . .

MARCUS But you cannae do that, Mr. Carmichael. Though I say it that shouldn't, I've a big following in the congregation, and if I was reluctantly compelled to give up my sittings there would be a stampede to the doors that would bring the whole jing bang about your ears.

MR. C. Please allow me to finish what I was going to say. I wash my hands of the whole matter.

MARCUS Well, I'm not responsible for your ablutions, but, my God, you'll be sorry for it.

MR. C. I have yet to be sorry for anything I have done in all my life.

MARCUS Do you tell me? Imphm. Well, it aye takes a beginning, and you'll start being sorry next month if that Wyllie & Symington tender goes through.

MR. C. Look here. Are you THREATENING me?

(BEELZEBUB *shows interest, and* IRA, AVARICIA *and* SUPERBIA *are dancing with excitement*)

ELSIE (*singing without*) "One fine day a ship . . ." (*and so on from* "Madame Butterfly")

MARCUS Threatening you? I know my place better. You're awful thin in the skin to-day. It's not for me to say, but I repeat it, you'll regret it all your life if you let these incompetent rascals put a finger on your new Kirk. They've made a bonny mess of the houses of Corporation tenants, never mind the House of God! The rest was only daffing. You should cultivate a sense of humour.

MR. C. No one has ever accused me of lacking a sense of humour before. As a matter of fact I have a very fine sense of humour.

MARCUS Fine I know it. Fine I know it. You had the Rotary Club in fits last month. I could hardly keep from smiling myself. Well, Elsie, how's the invalid?

ELSIE (*entering, sitting down on the slope and taking out a cigarette*) Oh, she's all right. She's getting a recipe for something sweet and beastly from Mumsie. . . . What an excruciatingly jam day!

MR. C. The modern young woman has no more respect for her mother tongue than she has for her parents, Mr. Groundwater.

MARCUS Oh, they're great wee rascals. I like them fine.

(*He looks admiringly at* ELSIE, *whose attitude shows rather unstudied grace than virgin modesty. The* SINS, *except* LUXURIA, *look depressed and irritable.*)

And what conventions are you turning tapsalteerie this winter, Miss Elsie? You'll have to come round some evening and teach me this new Cincinnati Dip. We see no young folks about the house now Hamish is away to his depôt.

(HAMISH *and* PETTIGREW *come back*)

Oh, here's the sodger boy himself. Hamish, what about a party?

HAMISH A what?

MARCUS A party. Some night. For Miss Elsie.

HAMISH Oh, a *party*. How topping. It's a dear old word "party". Crackers and conundrums and things. And a cake, with eighteen candles for Elsie's birthday.

ELSIE Nineteen, you fool.

(HAMISH *laughs and sits down in front;* PETTIGREW *in front of him*)

MARCUS Well, Pettigrew. There's a picture for you. Less expense in paint

17

and more fun than when you took Maggie's portrait. I doubt you'd no' be any quicker in getting done with it either.

PETTIGREW I'd like very much to paint Miss Carmichael, if she'd let me.

(Enter the two married women)

MRS. G. Oh, don't let him, Elsie. When he did my portrait it was the most fatiguing thing I ever endured. Tiresome! I must have eaten pounds of olives and salted almonds. He might have been painting Buckingham Palace, the time he took. From cellar to attic.

MRS. C. Are you quite recovered, Mrs. Groundwater?

MRS. G. Quite, thanks. So silly of me. But I think if there's a tiny half bottle of that nice Ayala left, and perhaps a chicken sandwich. . . .

PETTIGREW I'll get it for you, Mrs. Groundwater.

(ACCIDIA goes out R.)

MRS. G. Thank you so much. A cushion, Hamish.

(She sits down and automatically gets to work on the liqueur chocolates)

I can't think why I was so silly. So undignified too. Oh, what wouldn't I do to be strong and well like you, Elsie. What a nice young man Mr. Pettigrew is, and such a clever, clever artist.

MARCUS Oh, he's clever enough. He got £30 in advance out of me last September for a six-foot-by-four landscape he said was nearly ready. With cows in the foreground. It's not everybody could do that, I can tell you. I don't mean do cows – do me, I mean. The Haunting Melody, he called it. Haunting! All I know is there's been no manifestation over my sitting-room mantelpiece, and I'm beginning not to believe in ghosts.

MRS. C. He certainly doesn't seem to kill himself with overwork. I expect he has money of his own.

MARCUS Not a stiver. Not a maik. He lives by his wits, if you ask me.

MRS. G. Oh, but that's the artistic temperament.

MR. C. He has marvellous technique. It is a pity he has to wait so long and so patiently for inspiration.

HAMISH Feel like manging up the funny old burn for a brief space, old Elsie?

ELSIE No, thanks.

MRS. C. Do go, Elsie. There's plenty of time, but don't be late.

ELSIE No. I'm quite happy as I am. I'm in a state of poisoned rapture. The sun and the hills and what not. I have no time for vulgar intrigues with pococurantic young modern mutts. I'm a kelpie or something.

MR. C. Pococurantic?

HAMISH Oh, dammit. These are harsh words.

MRS. C. I wish you wouldn't say "mutts", Elsie.

(PETTIGREW arrives with viands for MRS. GROUNDWATER; ACCIDIA following)

MARCUS Wait a bit. I've got a pack of cards. Let's play Nap or something. We can play for matches.
HAMISH Oh, what fun.
ELSIE How murderously attractive.
MRS. G. No. Let's just sit still and enjoy ourselves. Let's bask in the sun like wild-eyed bucolic Ludo eaters. No, Lotos eaters. I wonder whether they were nice. Lotoses, I mean.
ELSIE Like anaemic artichokes, I should think.
MR. C. Well, I don't know what you people propose to do, but I, personally, am going to sleep.

(He settles himself comfortably. He suits the action to the word. MRS. CARMICHAEL arranges a cushion below his handsome head. PETTIGREW begins a drawing. HAMISH looks alternately at it and at ELSIE, who is thinking long, long thoughts.)

ELSIE What are you doing, Mr. Pettigrew?
PETTIGREW Oh, drawing.
ELSIE Me?
PETTIGREW Yes.
ELSIE Am I lovely?
PETTIGREW Yes.
HAMISH Let me see.
MARCUS *(who has taken out a pocket-book)* 5, 7, 9, 8, 2, 3 and carry 3 is 37. Three to carry. Ach, to blazes.

(He tilts his hat over his eyes and lies back)

HAMISH I wish I could draw like that. Not a bit like, but damn clever.
PETTIGREW *(chewing a pencil and rubbing with his thumb)* God bless you, Mr. Copperfield.
HAMISH Heigh, sirs! It's a damn fine day.

(He settles and stares at ELSIE. MRS. GROUNDWATER is nodding. So is her husband. MRS. CARMICHAEL takes out a novel and pretends to read, stealing sharp, angry glances at MRS. GROUNDWATER the while. The tinkle of a distant river is heard.

BEELZEBUB looks at the SINS and they look at BEELZEBUB. ACCIDIA is the only Sin who is not entirely shamefaced. But in fine she knows that all this is none of her doing. BEELZEBUB begins to speak in a harsh penetrating whisper.)

BEELZEBUB "Melodious birds sing madrigals" . . .
By Eblis' guts,

A bonny like covey of Sins for to louse on the World!
Could you pervert a monkey? Could you, by Hell's black reek?
SUPERBIA By Rhadamanthus, sir, you do us wrong,
How can men sin when they are warmed and fed?
Hold up your gash black hand athwart the sun;
Then, Master, you shall see what will befall.
BEELZEBUB Tyach! . . . Ye pernickety craturs. Look. Are ye satisfied now?

(He holds forth his hand and spreads his fingers. Immediately the stage grows gloomy as BEELZEBUB's hand blocks the rays of the sun. The SINS creep forward from the rock and form a semicircle round the picnic party. BEELZEBUB watches intently like a great broken-winged bat. MRS. GROUNDWATER sneezes and shivers. She wakes. The SINS are ranged behind their appropriate victims.)

MRS. G. I had such a lovely dream. I was lunching in a big hotel. And now it's cold.

(She seizes an unfinished sandwich)

Hello, Mr. Carmichael. Are you awake too? What were you dreaming about?
MR. C. I dreamed . . . dreamed that I went up to Heaven to the sound of golden trumpets and there – above the cherubim – there was a Fourth Seat. You pitiful fat woman. How dare you speak to ME?
MARCUS Eh? What's that? What are you saying to my wife? Fat, is she? Fat, eh? Whose car did you drive out in? Who paid for it and the tax and the petrol and the insurance and the damned lazy devil of a showfoor? You maybe, you blithering, cocksure sky-pilot?
MR. C. Ha! So that's the way of it?
MARCUS See here. You'll return that twenty quid I lent you when you got your call. Plus interest. And pretty quick too. I'll teach you to put a spoke in my wheel and diddle me out of my rightful profits, you preachifying pauper. Doll about in my car, and look down your nose at me.
PETTIGREW *(tearing up his drawing)* Oh, stow your gab the lot of you. You make my soul sick.

(He rolls over on his back and ACCIDIA tickles his chin. LUXURIA turns up her little nose in contempt.)

MR. C. I have no words to express . . .
MRS. C. What's that? Who drove out in your car? *Your* car! The car you stole from your workmen and customers. You cheat, you. You war profiteer. Who ate all my sandwiches and my veal and ham pie? All you brought was half a dozen of cheap fizzy wine and that fat sow over there drank every drop of it herself. You dirty, stingy old miser.
MARCUS Stingy. Listen to that! You're mad. You're mad!

MR. C. You shut up.

MRS. C. You're better than I am, I suppose, and that's why I have to slave, slave, slave my life out keeping up appearances for that vain, sulky, conceited, bellowing bull over there.

MR. C. Woman! What is this I hear?

MRS. C. You hear just what you are, Somerled Carmichael! And your wife's a nobody. All the pious, prayerful women in their fox furs come slavering over you and pity you for not having a harem of buxom voluptuous beauties like them instead of a wee, shilpit, beaten thing like me.

MR. C. Well, well, well, well, well! What viper is this I have nourished in my bosom?

ELSIE *(screaming with anger)* Be quiet, will you? Be quiet both of you or I'll kill you. I've had to put up with your dull pomposity, Dad, and your fussy cattishness, Mother, for all these years, and now you break out in your true colours and disgrace me before my friends. You rotten, rotten, rotten, dirty pair. Damn you, damn you, damn you!

MRS. C. Ha, you'd like *her* for a mother would you? *(Nods over to MRS. GROUNDWATER and leers at her)*

MARCUS Listen you here, Carmichael.

MR. C. I'm listening, you mangy dog. *(They glare)*

HAMISH *(who is crawling upstage to ELSIE on all fours like a tomcat)* What lots of pretty legs you have, grandma!

ELSIE Get away, you!

HAMISH *(jumping up and springing at her)* You darling devil, I'll bite your heart out.

(They fall together on the slope fighting furiously. Enter CHARITY in haste.)

CHARITY Oh, Faith! Oh, Hope! Oh hurry up. Do. Please. I know you're breathless, but you must be quick.

ELSIE Let go, you swine. I'll murder you.

TABLEAU

CARMICHAEL is standing over GROUNDWATER in a threatening attitude. MRS. GROUNDWATER is stuffing herself with sandwiches and liqueur chocolates and washing them down with champagne. She is now in the contented stage of alcoholism. MRS. CARMICHAEL on hands and knees is looking at her with evil glee and encouraging her to drink. PETTIGREW is lying supine with his eyes shut and a sneer on his face. CHARITY rings a little bell on the top of her magic wand and unhooks a little microphone.

CHARITY Hello. Yes. Number One, The Firmament.

Hello. Hello. Hello. Yes. Are you there?
Phœbus Apollo, for the love of Mike,
What are you doing with the sunshine, please?
PHŒBUS (*distant but silver clear*) A Devil has put his hand across the sun.
CHARITY Oh, bite it then. Bite it. Be quick. Be quick.
PHŒBUS I'll throw a sun spot at it. Will that do?
CHARITY Oh, don't ask questions. Do it. Do be quick.

(*BEELZEBUB suddenly withdraws his hand, uttering a devilish exclamation. The sun shines out.*)

BEELZEBUB Something has burned my hand.
CHARITY And serve you jolly well right!
BEELZEBUB Was it for this I burst the crust of Mount Etna with flames?
Whatna jaunt for a Deil! O ye skinny wee Sins,
What have I got for my jaunt but an awfu' sair finger?
Atchye. . . . O Moloch grant patience . . . ye charity weans!
I'll awa to my sulphurous baths and my cunning masseurs.
You can dae what ye like wi' the folk, for I'll never come back.

(*He descends, and sooty smoke rises. The SINS creep desolate to the shelter of the rock. The PICNIC PARTY look at one another in amaze. CHARITY withdraws to the wings and stands looking on, dabbing her nose with a little lace handkerchief.*)

MR. C. I don't know what to say.
MARCUS Well, better not say it. The time's getting on. We'd better be getting back to the Rolls-Royce. Hamish, take your mother's other arm. Upsy daisy. Easy does it.
MRS. G. (*weeping*) And I was so happy. So very, very happy.
MR. C. (*to his wife*) Come along then, dear. I . . . in fact . . . I . . . This is the first time in my life I have been at a loss for an appropriate remark. I say, Pettigrew. Do get up. We're going home.

(*Alarums and excursions. At last ELSIE, the THREE GRACES and the SEVEN DEADLY SINS are left in possession of the stage.*)

FAITH You are the Limit. Yes, indeed you are.
I must say this time you have gone too far.
HOPE What Faith has said is absolutely true.
An INSTITUTION is the place for you!
LUXURIA Oh, please don't send us to an Institution.
SUPERBIA Shut up, Luxuria.
CHARITY Yes. I'm afraid it is the only way.
I will arrange to have it done to-day.

ELSIE Excuse me, are you Charity? I was at one of your dances last winter.

CHARITY Yes, Miss Carmichael, I am Charity.

ELSIE Joking apart, are you really going to send them to an Institution? Where they'll have prayers morning and evening and cocoa at eleven?

CHARITY *(relapsing into prose)* Well, I mean what else can I do?

HOPE They can't behave themthelveth.

FAITH It will do them all the good in the world.

ELSIE Well, if you do it will be the most CALAMITOUSLY cruel thing I ever heard of. Poor little things, how can they help being Sins? They don't know any better and they have to express their personalities somehow. Besides, what on earth am I to do without them? . . . Charity, Faith, Hope! Leave me my little deadly sins. I'll tell you what, I'll look after them. Maternal instinct and so forth. You won't know them in a year or two. Is it a bet? Can I?

CHARITY O very well. I simply can't say No.
Have your own way about it. . . . Oh, hello!
Some sandwiches and things! I say, Hooray!
We haven't had a bite to eat to-day.

(The GRACES, with merry giggles, begin a small picnic on what MRS. GROUNDWATER has left)

ELSIE How just too devastatingly dear of you! Good-bye then. . . . Now Superbia and Ira, don't look so sullen. Wipe that beastly rouge off your face and pull down your leopard skin, Luxuria. Avaricia, take your hands out of your pockets. Gula, you can't have any of these sandwiches. The Aunties need them all. Invidia, stop pinching Luxuria. Pull up your stockings, Accidia. Now come along. You'll be late for supper, and I've got a date with Hamish for the Diner Dansant.

(ELSIE goes out leading SUPERBIA and IRA by the hand. The others follow sheepishly.)

CHARITY *(laughing at some joke or other)* Hello. One, Firmament.
Phœbus, is that you?
Here, could you let us have an hour or two
More daylight for a special treat. To-night.
Charity speaking. Yes, thanks. Quite all right.
How splendid of you. Thank you. Yes. Quite well.

(Hangs up receiver)

I wonder if old B. got safe to Hell.

FAITH The very same thought that occurred to me.
Hope, dearie, won't you ring him up and see?

HOPE All right. *(She takes receiver from CHARITY)* Thix, thix, thix, Pandemonium.
CHARITY She lisps in numbers for the numbers come.
HOPE Hello. Yeth. No. Hello. Hello. No. No.
Number engaged? All right. Yeth. Yeth. Hello!
Exthcuthe me. There'th a buthing. Can you hear?
Beelthebub? Hope thpeaking. . . .

(A flash. Black out leaving the AUNTIES under a single broad spotlight.)

Dear, dear, dear!
FAITH Always the same bad loser. Never mind.
Evil is but as piffle in the wind.
Come wind, come rain, come tempest, hail or rack
Virtue is still the same good horse to back.

(Bell rings)

CHARITY Yes. Yes. Is that you, Pandemonium? Yes. Listen, Faith, he says "A Time will Come!"
FAITH He says so, does he? Very well. We'll see. *(Lights go up)* Ho! Ho!
CHARITY Ha! Ha!
HOPE Hehehehehehe!

CURTAIN

THE APOTHEOSIS

The Scene is a sort of lounge-drawing-room with big French windows. Curtains can be pulled over them and a suburban garden can be seen through them. The room is in SIR MARCUS GROUNDWATER's house in Kelvinshields, near Glasgow. The time is late summer. Five years have passed since the dreadful events before the Interval. LADY GROUNDWATER, on her face the Peace (ruffled occasionally by an attack of waterbrash) that Passeth All Understanding, is reclining on a semi-invalid couch and darning socks. She is plainly dressed, but a piece of thermogene unskilfully tucked into her bosom adds a subdued note of colour. In the garden an aged man in a sleeved waistcoat is raking a gravel path. Man? When he takes off his nasty old hat to wipe his steaming brow we are startled to observe little horns sprouting from his forehead. He is BEELZEBUB. CHARITY enters, wearing enough of the costume of a serving-maid to indicate that she is that for the present. She carries a tray with letters and medicine on it.

CHARITY I've took the letters from the letter-box.
Now then, my lady, lay aside them socks. . . .
My! What a lovely day! How blue the Heavens is!
I almost misremembered your elevenses.
LADY G. Oh, thank you so much, Jane. I didn't know it was so late. Time does fly, doesn't it? The hands of the clock go round so, it makes a person giddy to look at them. Do you remember – of course, you must – where it says:

> Ah! catch the flitting moments where they flit,
> Gather the something rosebuds while you can,
> Nor all your tears wipe out a jot of it . . .?

(A bland but urgent hiccough interrupts her)

Pardon me . . . I always say . . . Beg pardon . . . I always say. Dear me I'll be forgetting my home address next. What is it I always say, now?
CHARITY Now, mum, I mean, my lady, I should say,
Don't bother trying to recall to-day
The nice remark you say you always say,
For if you always are a saying it,
We're sure some time to get the benefit.
If I may make so bold as ask a question,
How do you find the nasty indigestion?
LADY G. Oh, much better, thank you. Much, much, much, much, much

25

better. And by the way, *would* you very much mind asking Faith to keep the kitchen door shut? I don't know why it is, but I do dislike the smell of cooking. I hate to feel that way, even about a smell, but we're poor bodies and we can't help ourselves. You'll tell her, won't you?

CHARITY Of course I will now, bless your tender heart;
And Faith, I'm sure, will take it in good part.

(She sees the GARDENER and starts)

This afternoon I fancied I could see
Glittering scales below the apple-tree,
And now who's that? . . . Oh, only old Macpherson!
I took him for a very different person
Just for an instant! . . . Deary me to-day!
Drink up your bismuth and I'll clear away.

(LADY GROUNDWATER drinks and CHARITY, all of a flutter at what she thought she saw, clears away and goes out. LADY G. gets up and totters to the gramophone. She starts it playing, I am sorry to say, the Barcarole from the "Tales of Hoffman". She sits down to her socks again with a contented sigh. She hums the air a semitone higher than it is played on the gramophone. SIR MARCUS wanders in. He is as restless as ever, but he has lost purpose. He looks always a little puzzled, these days.)

LADY G. Oh, hello, Marky! You gave me quite a little fright. I thought you had gone to the office.

MARCUS Oh, no, no, no, no. I thought. . . . No. I've got twa-three things to do. Hello! Letters?

LADY G. Dear me, yes! I forgot all about them. *(They open letters)*

MARCUS Aye, aye. What's the tune?

LADY G. It's a bit of Schumann's "Unfinished Symphony". Do you mind it?

MARCUS No. I like a bit of religious music now and again. It gives me a kind of a delightful sort of dwawm.

LADY G. Such an awful pity he didn't finish it. It begins with Fate knocking at the door, or else it's a man buried alive knocking on his coffin-lid. I forget which. I must ask Mrs. Carmichael. I think it's so nice. . . . Yes, knocking on the lid, I think it is.

MARCUS I thought yon was a scratch on the record.

LADY G. No, no. It's at the beginning. Before you came in. . . . Dear me!

MARCUS What's the matter, hen?

LADY G. The Carmichaels. Stop the record, please, lovey. . . . The Carmichaels are coming to lunch. Tuts, tuts.

MARCUS What way, "Tuts"?

LADY G. I've just remembered that girl Elsie's up from London – I mean down from London for the weekend. It's in all the papers. It's awfle awkward.

MARCUS How awkward?

LADY G. Hamish, of course. You know. The poor boy. He's never got over it.

MARCUS Ugh, I don't believe he gives her a thought.

LADY G. Marky, a mother knows. Besides, nobody seems to think of anybody but Elsie these days. You can't get away from her. See. There she is in the "Tatler" again.

MARCUS Aye! And very nice too.

LADY G. I suppose you have to, if you're a great author. But I wouldn't get photographed in MY bath, even if I'd written the Bible and the "Pilgrim's Progress". However, I suppose it's a lady photographer took it.

MARCUS And you think Hamish . . .? Oh, he'll get over it. He'll get over it all right.

LADY G. I wonder. I don't know. Marky, if I had treated you cruelly long, long ago. If I had married wee Slimmen the way Ma wanted me to. Would you . . . would you be the man you are to-day?

MARCUS It's a question. Maybe no'. Maybe no'. Aye, aye, Imphm. . . . What's for lunch?

LADY G. I never ask, these days. It's funny. I used to be quite interested in my meals. I leave it all to Faith, now. She's a splendid plain cook. So economical.

MARCUS Tyach! Economy! Rice pudding three days running. I'll tell you this, she'd be better of a wee bit less economy and more imagination.

LADY G. Well, I always say, better a loaf of bread and quietness therewith than an army with banners. And rice pudding's so wholesome. And she made last Sunday's *gigot* do till Friday – yesterday.

MARCUS But why? We're not so hard up as all that comes to.

LADY G. Well, you see, I always think it's such a good example to them that are not so – so fortunate as we are.

MARCUS Aye, aye. And there's a lot of them like that. Hard times. We should be very thankful. A lot. Here's a note from Mistress Steviston. . . . What did I give last year to her Do-you-believe-in-Fairies Guild?

LADY G. I forget. It's such a good, good cause. "Do you believe in fairies?" It's such a pretty idea, I think. I often think we're further off from Heaven than when we were a girl. At least I was a girl. You weren't of course.

MARCUS Oh, what a damned shame!

LADY G. Yes, it is, isn't it? . . . What is?

MARCUS This letter. It's from the Bank. About that bill I backed for Wyllie & Symington.

LADY G. Wyllie and . . .? Oh, you mean the builder people who were so nasty about that contract for the church extension? Years ago.

MARCUS They might well be nasty. After all it was kind of thoughtless of me to put up the new church hall for nothing. They were having a hard struggle just then, and the contract would maybe have brought them bye the bit. . . . But I'm afraid there'll be trouble over the head of this bill. . . . I've bitten off more nor I can chew. I'll have to see . . . what . . . Puir auld Symington! They tell me he has varicose veins in his leg. And him near seventy.

LADY G. It is a hard life for the old.

(GROUNDWATER goes to the window to hide his emotion. He notices BEELZEBUB.)

MARCUS Oh, good-morning, Macpherson.

BEELZEBUB Good-morning to you, Sir Marcus. I trust that I see you in health?

MARCUS Pretty fair. Pretty fair. The midges bad this morning?

BEELZEBUB I love the wee busy bit things as if I had been their faither. Maybe I am, in a way. . . . How is her leddyship keeping?

MARCUS Fine, thanks, fine. Macpherson's asking for you, Maggie.

LADY G. Oh, good-morning, Macpherson. I had a wee walk round the garden this morning with Miss Hope. Your new parabola is going to be a great success. What was it you were going to train over it, now?

BEELZEBUB I thocht, if your leddyship pleases, to bigg it wi' ramblers and hops.

LADY G. Doesn't that sound a little unrestful. But I suppose life is like that, isn't it?

MARCUS No rest for the wicked. No rest for the wicked.

BEELZEBUB And ye're no sae far wrang, I may tell ye. . . . By the Blistering Grids of Gehannum!

(He goes, muttering angrily)

LADY G. What did he say?

MARCUS He's a wee bittie free with his language. A character though. Fine old Scotch type. I think I'll raise his wages.

(HAMISH comes in. He has left the Army. He is in Holy Orders. He salutes his Mamma and nods respectfully to his Father.)

MARCUS 'Morning, Hamish.

LADY G. Well, Lambikin?

HAMISH Good-morning, Mother. Good-morning, Dad.

MARCUS And where have you been all morning?

HAMISH I was breakfasting with the Bish.

LADY G. Is it quite respectful to call your Bishop, Bish?

HAMISH Oh, we don't call him that to his face, of course. Not that he'd mind, really. He's a very good sort, the old Bish.

LADY G. Such a nice man. I do think the Scottish Episcopal Church is so distinguy.

HAMISH What exactly do you mean, Mother?

LADY G. Oh, I don't know. It's the atmosphere that's so nice. Having breakfast with Bishops, and so on.

MARCUS The United Free Church is good enough for me. They're a persecuting lot, Bishops.

LADY G. Oh no, Marky! Don't you remember the Trial of the Thirty-nine Bishops, when they lit such a bonfire – and candles and things in Smithfield Market, Bloody Mary of Argyle, you know. That's HISTORY! And their gaiters and little black kilts. What did he say to you, Hamish?

MARCUS Well, I don't know. I draw the line at Popery, and there's a . . .

LADY G. But it wasn't the Pope, darling. It was the Bishop. The Pope lives in the Vacuum in Venice. What did the Bishop say to you, Hamish?

HAMISH Well, there were several of us, and he just sloshed around a kind word here and a chatty remark there, and so forth. Very matey and all that. About evangelicals and that sort of merchant.

LADY G. I know. I used to love Wordsworth's "Evangelic" when I was a little girl. . . . Hamish, I'm so glad you left the Army.

HAMISH Oh, absolutely.

LADY G. And you never regretted it, son?

HAMISH Not a scrap. I'd no option, really. You remember the chappie in the Bible who got it as it were where he lived and decided to cut it all out henceforward? I mean, CONVICTION and all that sort of rot. After that – that day on Loch Lomond some sort of something or other said to me, "You're for it, old tough; you're blowing up merrily, for a mucker . . ."

LADY G. It was a Higher Power speaking to you, Hamish.

HAMISH Yes, I know. . . . And then . . . Well, I mean, I ask you? I as near as touch joined the Salvation Army. . . . I don't know why I am talking all this rot. . . . Hello! There are the Carmichaels.

MARCUS They're coming to lunch.

LADY G. Are they . . . is it just Mister and Missis?

HAMISH Yes. Why?

LADY G. Oh, nothing. It's just that . . . No, it's nothing. That'll be all right. Shout to them to come in by the window, Marcus.

MARCUS Hey! Mr. Carmichael! *(He goes out)*

LADY G. Darling, it's as well to prepare you. Elsie may be coming. They expected her to be with them.

HAMISH Elsie? Oh, yes. What about it?

LADY G. I'm so glad you take it so calmly. So very, very glad.

HAMISH Mater, I've been trying to tell you. I'm different now. I mean, girls are a wash-out so far as I'm concerned. I'm joining a celibate order.

LADY G. What is it celebrated for?

HAMISH Celibate, celibate! I mean they take a vow not to – to marry and all that sort of thing. Renounce the Flesh in a way.

LADY G. Ah! Vegetarians!

HAMISH No, no. Not necessarily. . . . Good-afternoon, Mrs. Carmichael. Good-afternoon, sir.

(The CARMICHAELS come in, followed by SIR MARCUS. CARMICHAEL has grown a beard and an inferiority complex. His clothes are only semi-clerical, but he wears a white necktie. MRS. CARMICHAEL's haggard expression is intensified by an almost continuous smile – a watery beam.)

MRS. C. How do you do, Mr. Hamish. How are you, Lady Groundwater?

LADY G. Quite, quite well. Now, do sit down. You must be tired. How do you do, Mr.Carmichael?

CARMICHAEL Quite well, thank you, Lady Groundwater. May my wife and I congratulate you in person – offer our very respectful congratulations on the well-deserved honour His Majesty has been pleased to bestow upon your household?

MRS. C. Oh, it's so nice and we're so pleased. Somerled and I feel quite grand now, knowing titled people. I find myself bringing your name into conversation oftener than ever.

LADY G. Oh dear me, we're getting quite used to it already. We are just the same plain, simple folk we always were.

> "Proud rank is but a penny stamp,
> For a' that and so forth."

MARCUS Plain, douce folk.

LADY G. Come and take off your things, Mrs. Carmichael. Dear me, it's ages since you crossed our doorstep. You must give me all the news. You're *such* a stranger. *(They go out)*

HAMISH I'll take your hat and stick.

CARMICHAEL Oh, please don't trouble. I . . .

HAMISH Oh, rot. I'm going anyhow. *(He goes)*

MARCUS Have a cigar.

CARMICHAEL Dare I, do you think? Well. . . . Thanks. It will be a great treat. But perhaps if you don't mind, I'll keep it till after luncheon. And, Sir Marcus, just before the ladies come down, may I have a word with you?

MARCUS Surely, surely. What is it?

CARMICHAEL I hate to bother you with my affairs on – on a day like this, but you've been so kind, and as I may not have another opportunity while Mrs.— I beg your pardon, Lady Groundwater is upstairs. . . .

MARCUS Go on, sir, go on. We're auld freens, the twa o' us.

CARMICHAEL Well, to come to the point, as you can't fail to have noticed, since my – ah – nervous breakdown I have – the congregation has – well, in point of fact, I've lost whatever grip I had on the congregation. They've been most awfully kind and forbearing. But my sermons, for instance – you don't mind my talking about myself? – my sermons seem to have lost – well, inspiration – if they ever had any. I'm beginning to doubt it.

MARCUS I wouldn't say that. Very thoughtful and scholarly I've always thought them.

CARMICHAEL No. It's kind of you to say so, and you've been very loyal. But others are drifting away. Quite excusably, of course. Please don't imagine that I blame them. As you know I've repeatedly asked to be relieved of my charge.

MARCUS Well, we won't hear of it. And that's all that's about it.

CARMICHAEL It's beautiful of you, and it warms my heart to hear you say it. But I've taken the liberty of raising the question individually with Mr. Lang, Bailie Dallas, Mr. Shillitto and others, and practically the whole Session are in favour of my retirement.

MARCUS Well, it's not fair! It's most unfair. I'll settle that lot of . . . Oh, dear me! Mr. Carmichael, I doubt I'm getting old. I haven't the fight in me that I once had. But if doubling my freewill offering will do any good. . . .

CARMICHAEL No, no, no. I'll never be able to repay you for all you have done. But it's not only the sermons. I've lost hold. I tell you the truth is that I'm not worthy to be a minister of the Gospel. Look here! Is there any job I could do in your firm? A timekeeper, or something. No, I'm not accurate enough for that. A – a hod-carrier?

MARCUS Are you serious?

CARMICHAEL Dead serious. I daren't go on. I daren't.

MARCUS But you're an educated man.

CARMICHAEL No, no. Not even that. I was at a Scottish Public School. . . . I know a little Greek and Latin and a little Hebrew.

MARCUS The Hebrew might help you in a commercial career. . . . But you've just got me all muddled up. I don't know where I am these days. I've lost purpose. I . . .

(*Enter HOPE with a sheaf of papers. She wears horn-rimmed spectacles to show that she is a Secretary.*)

HOPE Thir Marcuth, I have brought the . . . Oh, dear me!
Thethe thpecth have made me I can hardly thee;
I didn't know you were engaged jutht now
Thethe paperth hardly matter anyhow.

MARCUS This is Miss Hope, Mr. Carmichael. She's my Secretary now, you know. We've solved the Servant Problem. Miss Hope and her two sisters have come to us as domestic helps. Lady helps.

HOPE I'm thure I hope tho. For it ith quite true
A girl can be a help and a lady too.

(Re-enter LADY GROUNDWATER and MRS. CARMICHAEL)

LADY G. Fancy! Mrs. Carmichael has never seen Mr. Pettigrew's new picture of me. There it is, Mrs. Carmichael.

MRS. C. Oh, how lovely!

LADY G. It's not really like, of course. It's modern, you see. But Mr. Pettigrew paints the Soul. That's really my soul, not me.

MRS. C. And a kind, sweet soul it is.

LADY G. Not at all. Not at all. Now, now, now, now, Mrs. Carmichael. . . . Every now and again I think it's good – I mean the picture – and then I sort of don't.

HOPE I think it's lovely, Mum, I really do.

How ith that clever Mr. Pettigrew?

LADY G. He's in London now. Doing awfully well. Didn't you know? You knew of course, Mrs. Carmichael?

MRS. C. Well. . . . Elsie wrote. . . . She hasn't time to write often, poor girl, but she said . . . well, something about . . . about Mr. Pettigrew and her . . . Of course she was only in fun. I mean to say, Lady Groundwater, even if their idea of fun nowadays is a little BROAD, it doesn't matter if the heart's in the right place, does it? . . . At any rate, she seems to have adopted Mr. Pettigrew, in a way.

LADY G. The kind-hearted girl! And he's a great credit to her. Done so well. Did you see his photograph in this week's "Tatler", talking to a Duchess in pyjamas? And they say his pictures are worth thousands of pounds, now.

HOPE Thouthandth of poundth a picture! Oh, I thay!

They mutht be happy up Parnathuth way!

LADY G. Art is a marvellous gift. Thousands of pounds!

MARCUS Sit down, everybody. Sit down, sit down. You were speaking of Elsie. Any news of her? We half thought we'd have the pleasure of seeing her to-day. She's a big swell now, I hear.

THE CARMS *(together)* Well, you see, Elsie . . .

MRS. C. I'm so sorry, dear.

CARMICHAEL No, no. You go on, dear.

LADY G. I think Elsie's done so marvellously. Girls nowadays are very lucky. In my day a poor girl with no private means would have thought herself a very lucky girl to be making – how much is it?

MARCUS Nine hundred pounds a week, they say.

LADY G. Nine hundred pounds a week before she was twenty-five. Very lucky. . . .

MRS. C. Yes. It is a great comfort, in a way, that she has done so well. She was always an enthusiastic, hardworking girl. I don't grudge her a penny of it.

CARMICHAEL One could have wished, perhaps, that she had chosen some other occupation – or occupations, for she appears to have several.

MARCUS I don't know many occupations where a working girl can earn £900 a week. She must have cornered the only possible ones. Of course, money isn't everything. But it shows you are appreciated.

(BEELZEBUB appears in the garden, gazing at some approaching mystery)

CHARITY (at the door) The famous artist, Mr. Pettigrew.

(A resplendent PETTIGREW enters, and advances to his hostess with firm, rapid steps. CHARITY again glimpses BEELZEBUB through his disguise. Her shriek cuts through the welcoming noises.)

CHARITY IN NOMINE ANGELORUM! – Is it YOU?
LADY G. Jane! My dear!
HOPE Charity, love, whatever is the matter?
CHARITY Skittles! I've gone as batty as a hatter!
Pardon, m'lady, I was quite unnerved.
Faith ast me to announce that lunch is served.

(Exeunt HOPE and CHARITY whispering excitedly. BEELZEBUB has vanished.)

MARCUS What's ado with the lassie?
LADY G. I never knew her go like that before. I hope she doesn't take fits or anything. . . . I'm so sorry, Mr. Pettigrew. Such a delightful surprise. You'll stay for lunch, I hope?
PETTIGREW Yes. I shall.
LADY G. And Miss Carmichael. She's your – your guardian or partner or something, isn't she? Is she coming too?
PETTIGREW She is not my guardian, she is my mistress.
MARCUS Oh, I say! I mean to say. Look here.
PETTIGREW She arrived this morning with her suite in the Royal Scot. In a specially built saloon. Full of orchids. She says you are not to wait for luncheon. She will be here presently.
LADY G. Oh, but we must wait. It's no trouble at all.
PETTIGREW I think you had better do what Elsie says.
MARCUS But it's an awful-like thing to start without her when she may be here any minute.
PETTIGREW I THINK YOU HAD BETTER DO WHAT ELSIE SAYS!

(They stare at him. He takes LADY GROUNDWATER's arm and they march, in amaze, from the room. The stage is empty for a full minute. The long melodious note of a very expensive motor horn is heard approaching. It stops. There is a trill of laughter like that heard at the "butt of the night" in the Prologue. It stops also. In a full orchestral silence, ELSIE enters by the French window. She is dressed with the most

33

expressive wickedness – probably in black velvet. The SINS have stayed in the garden, but their sign manual is on her face. She smokes an enormous black cigarette in a huge holder and stands surveying the audience with a basilisk stare. SHE SHOULD PLAY BLATANTLY FOR A LAUGH, even to the extent of saying to an invisible chauffeur-footman: "Georges, will you tell Animaxander to see that the baby leopard gets his Alenbury?" . . . To her HAMISH, on his way to lunch. He starts twice – once on seeing her, and a second time on recognising her.)

HAMISH Oh, hello! Miss Carmichael. And all that sort of thing.

ELSIE Hello! And what is *your* name?

HAMISH Who, me? I'm Hamish. . . . Groundwater, you know. Didn't you recognise me?

ELSIE You have changed. Are you going to a fancy dress ball?

HAMISH No. Oh, no! I'm not.

ELSIE Then why are you so gaily dressed? Why are you dressed like the Private Secretary?

HAMISH Oh, that! I'm in Orders now, you know.

ELSIE Is that a Department or a Place?

HAMISH No. Neither. Holy Orders, you know. The Clergy, you see. I'm a clergyman, and all that sort of thing.

ELSIE Sit down and talk to me.

HAMISH Well, it's just lunch-time, you see. In fact they've begun. They're having it just now. Perhaps we'd better . . .

ELSIE Sit down, I tell you! Don't stand there prattling when I tell you to do something. Don't you know who I am?

(They sit on the couch)

HAMISH Well, I've heard you've become a bit of a celebrity.

ELSIE O Fame! Fame! Fame! Or do you mean a notoriety?

HAMISH Well, fellows say things, don't they? You write movie scenarios and novels and you act a bit, don't you?

ELSIE Hamish, I should love to hear you describing a thunderstorm. You'd say it was a bit noisy, wouldn't you, darling?

HAMISH Well, so it is, isn't it?

ELSIE And the Atlantic Ocean's a bit wet, and you are a little ignorant. . . . By Blood! You stammering little provincial lout. I was once in love with you!

HAMISH Oh, I don't think so, really. Sort of matey only. Mild boy and girl stuff. Nothing in it, really.

ELSIE There was. There was. I adored you. Passionately. My skin crinkled when you looked at me. A lovely feeling. I adore you still.

HAMISH Oh, look here. Listen. Shut up. I mean. That's all bilge.

ELSIE Kiss me. Blast your eyes, kiss me. Kiss me if it kills you.

HAMISH Easy on. I've cut all that out now, Elsie. Be a man. Pull yourself together. I'm a priest. Chuck it!

ELSIE Take that and that. A priest should feel hellfire fanning his cheek – just once – if it blisters him. Ah, my lover!

HAMISH (getting up) You ought to be ashamed of yourself. I'm surprised at you. You used to be a decent sort of girl.

ELSIE You don't like my cantharides kisses, darling?

HAMISH No, I don't. Nor any kind. Nor you either. You've degenerated most frightfully.

ELSIE I know I have. God help me. I know I have. Save me, Hamish.

HAMISH Save you from what?

ELSIE From worse than death. Sit down here and save me from worse than death.

HAMISH Don't try to be funny.

ELSIE Try to be funny? *Try* to be funny? Do you know that the readers of the "Sabbath Pictorial" decided by a HUGE majority that I'm the wittiest woman in the world? Eh? Do you know that I've made Dukes and Duchesses and Royalties and Ambassadors splutter the soup all over the table?

HAMISH Dirty pigs!

ELSIE And Archbishops and Poets and Cardinals and Dictators. . . . Oh, come and have some lunch!

HAMISH I think we'd better.

ELSIE No, but honestly. You can't possibly understand how my personality has developed. You read what is supposed to be all about me in the "Queen", and "Homes and Gardens" and the "Spectator" and "News of the World". But it's not me a bit. It's only people like Wells and Barrie and Beverley Nichols who really understand me, and even they are nowhere near the real ME. But I'm growing quite egocentric. Tell me all about yourself, Hamish. Have you read my new book?

HAMISH No, I haven't. I hear it's a bit near the knuckle even for these days. No decent fellow would read it. Besides, it's impossible to get a copy.

ELSIE Of course, I forgot. The dear Home Secretary! But you don't know him. You don't know anything. Go in to lunch, you reinforced-concrete-headed nincompoop!

HAMISH Very well. May I have the pleasure?

ELSIE No, you mayn't. Go in and say I'm coming. And leave the door open.

(HAMISH goes out)

Let me see. Which Sin shall I take with me? Oh, yes. Gluttony hasn't had a square meal for hours. Gula, you little pig!

(GULA, fat, oily, in an Eton suit, his hair neatly parted, enters by the chimney)

GULA Here I am, lady.

ELSIE You are to lunch with me to-day. It is the old Groundwater woman's luncheon. You remember her. You should enjoy it.

GULA By gum, I should, lady.

(A buzz of chatter comes from the inner room)

ELSIE Ha! He has told them I'm coming. Remember not to speak with your mouth full.

GULA I shall not speak at all, lady.

(GULA and ELSIE enter the luncheon-room. BEELZEBUB appears at the window, the SIX SINS ranged behind him. There is a rumble of thunder and the stage darkens perceptibly.)

THE SINS Can't we go in now, Master?

INVIDIA That fat little brat got in all right.

LUXURIA The Aunties are nowhere to be seen.

THE SINS Do let's go in, Master!

SUPERBIA What do we care for the Aunties, anyway?

IRA If they do pack us off to an Institution it's better than working overtime for that cat of a girl.

ACCIDIA It's better than working at all.

AVARICIA They'll be RUINED, I tell you, if we don't get in. It's only Christian to go in, Master.

THE SINS Please let us, Master?

BEELZEBUB Bide a wee then, ye cockiemajinkies, till I spy out the land.

(He enters the rooms. A loud buzzing of flies is heard as he crosses into the room. It darkens still more.)

Wheesht, wheesht! Ye flies of the Air. They'll hear ye. Fly silently.

(After a swift cautious look through the keyhole, BEELZEBUB takes a Hand of Glory from his pocket and lights the fingertips at a petrol lighter)

Hist! Hist!
The Deid Man's Fist.
Nippit from off a gallows medlar, close by the wrist.
Bale licht
Burn bricht.
Shine ill beams on ill hap.
OLEOC NI ES IUQ RETSON R-R-R-RETAP!
Sleep ye that sleep;

Wake ye that wake;
Be as the deid for SATHANAS' sake!

(GULA comes rushing out as if shot from a gun)

GULA Oh, Master! Oh, Master! Rissoles and rice-pudding, Master. Rissoles and rice-pudding!
BEELZEBUB Haud you your wheesht or I'll melt you. Awa' and eat worms in the garden!

(GULA finds a worm to eat and joins the group of SINS)

BEELZEBUB House! Vacuum cleaned and garnished!
House! Lacquered and polished and varnished!
Open your yetts to the Seven De'ils, waur nor they were before!

(The SINS burst in. BEELZEBUB sits down to the piano.)

BALLET OF THE SEVEN DEADLY SINS

(SUPERBIA lies on a couch and feigns to sleep. The SINS creep out except ACCIDIA who fans SUPERBIA and smooths her pillow. Enter LUXURIA, who tickles the sleeper with a peacock's feather. SUPERBIA awakes and rings a little bell. Enter INVIDIA with a gown and slippers. Pas de Quatre. SUPERBIA, INVIDIA, LUXURIA and ACCIDIA. INVIDIA and LUXURIA tend SUPERBIA before a mirror. ACCIDIA sits gloomily at the foot of the couch. Enter GULA who pays court to SUPERBIA. Minuet. INVIDIA goes to the door and beckons AVARICIA. IRA bursts from the chimney. AVARICIA and GULA fight. GULA catches sight of LUXURIA and breaks off the battle to make love to her. Dance. GULA sets to LUXURIA, AVARICIA to SUPERBIA, ACCIDIA and INVIDIA posing at opposite corners and IRA threading in and out of the set.)

(Enter FAITH, HOPE and CHARITY)

THE SINS Pests and Pandemics! The Aunties!

TABLEAU

CHARITY I knew I wasn't wrong, O Safety Pins,
Hope, if it ain't those naughty little Sins!
FAITH I never saw a sight so − so obscene.
Beelzebub, whatever do you mean?

(She snatches the Hand of Glory from the piano, blows it out and throws it into the garden. BEELZEBUB sits heavily down on the keys. The lights

go up. *The SINS scuttle for cover. IRA is unsuccessful in hiding and remains in full view. Enter GROUNDWATER.)*

MARCUS What's this, eh? What's this? MacPherson, you're drunk!

BEELZEBUB I am a life-long teetotaller. By Eblis, you do me a wrong.

MARCUS I do, do I? Well, you'll take a fortnight's pay. Where's my cheque-book. Here it is. "The League of Pussy's Protectors"? Well, they'll have to do without *that* fiver, anyhow.

(He pulls out a cheque, tears it up, and writes another, crossing it)

Here. Take that. And get to Hell out of here.

THE SINS He's crossed it. He's crossed the cheque!

(BEELZEBUB takes the cheque, but drops it at once, casts an evil glance on GROUNDWATER and backs quickly through the window, registering impotent rage)

FAITH That was the very way to make him go.

Sir Marcus, you've done better than you know.

MARCUS Oh, you're there, Faith, are you? Lady Groundwater will have a word or two to say to you about that lunch. Plain cook you call yourself? More plain than cook. It wasn't fit for a pig.

FAITH It was, it was!

HOPE Now, now, Thir Marcuth, that ith not the cathe.

Bethideth, that ith no way to thpeak to Faith.

MARCUS Yes it is. And to you too. . . . I'm beginning to think you know as much about bookkeeping as she knows about boiling an egg. And that's nothing, nothing.

CHARITY Sir Marcus, do be careful what you say.

Much more and we might have to go away.

MARCUS And would I break my heart if you did? No, I wouldn't. Much more of you three and I'd have high-faluted my way to the Silly House. Aye, and had a chat with the Official Receiver on the way. I feel as if you'd sucked the soul out of me. It's my belief you are nothing but a pack of vampires.

FAITH Vampires! He called us vampires! Oh, my hat!

Hope, did you ever hear the like of that?

HOPE I hope you won't regret it all your life;

And Mr. Hamish and your lady wife.

(Enter LADY GROUNDWATER and ELSIE, MRS. CARMICHAEL following)

LADY G. Oh, and you didn't tell me where you got that lovely necklace, Elsie.

ELSIE Oh, that's the wages of sin – paid in advance.

LADY G. I thought the wages of sin was death or something.

ELSIE Did you?

LADY G. Oh, you're there, Faith. Faith, the rissoles were burnt to bricks and the rice-pudding was singed. It made me so ill I think I fainted. I came all over queer. Now please understand I won't have it. Hope, go and order the car. We are going to the Malmaison for a proper lunch. Charity, come upstairs and help me and Mrs. Carmichael on with our things. Come along, Mrs. Carmichael. Come, Elsie.

(Exeunt CHARITY and LADY GROUNDWATER)

MRS. C. *(to ELSIE)* Elsie, I must say this, if that was a specimen you showed us at lunch of the manners you've learnt from your fine friends, you needn't have been ashamed to introduce your poor, commonplace parents to them.

LADY G. *(without)* Do hurry, Mrs. Carmichael. I'm dying of starvation.

MRS. C. *(sotto voce)* Greedy fat beast.

(She goes out. GROUNDWATER is staring with a half-burnt crossed cheque in his hand. FAITH, by the window, is forgotten but defiant. HOPE is soothing her. ELSIE sits on the couch and covers her face with her hands.)

ELSIE There's something wrong. There's something wrong.

(CARMICHAEL comes in)

CARMICHAEL Groundwater!

MARCUS Well?

CARMICHAEL Look here. What I said before lunch. Forget it, will you? I've not been myself since – since my nervous breakdown. I've been . . . I was lost in a mist on Goat Fell. It was palpable almost, that mist. Cloying, hindering my every step. Well, just now . . . at luncheon . . . it suddenly cleared away. My doubts . . . everything like that . . . all gone. I am SURE again. Sure of my message. Sure of myself. A most extraordinary experience. Saul on the road to Damascus.

MARCUS Aye. It wasn't bad Burgundy. The last of the bin. I'm glad you liked it.

CARMICHAEL I see. You think I'm drunk. You and the like of you can't be expected to recognise inspiration when you see it. I don't care what you think, but I want you to forget what I said about resigning.

MARCUS Aye. Well, I was just swithering about it. We'll see. We'll see after your sermon to-morrow.

CARMICHAEL Yes. You'll see. By God, you'll hear a sermon to-morrow.

(He dashes out by the French window in an ecstasy)

MARCUS Hey! Mr. Carmichael! The man's daft!

(He follows. Enter HAMISH. He carries a glass of port in his hand. He is slightly flown with wine.)

HAMISH Hello, old Elsie! Where are the others?
ELSIE What? . . . I don't know.

(The SINS become bolder. HOPE goes out after GROUNDWATER. FAITH remains.)

HAMISH Elsie, was that all right, what you said at lunch that you're a millionaire?
ELSIE Yes. . . . I suppose so.
HAMISH Honest?
ELSIE More or less.
HAMISH Listen, you're looking dashed lovely. Sort of drooping. See here, what about it?
ELSIE What about what?
HAMISH What about what you said about me converting you, and so forth? I'll start whenever you like. Now, if you like.
ELSIE What are you talking about?
HAMISH You know what I'm talking about. The Dad has blued all his siller on Cat and Dog homes and things, and we haven't a bean, and you're rolling in it; but I don't care. I'll make you care for me if you'll let me.
ELSIE *You* will?
HAMISH Yes, me. If you think I've no guts because I'm a parson, why that's easily settled.

(He tears off his collar, puts down his glass and puts his arms round her)

Elsie. . . . Sweetheart! Elsie, look at me. What's up? It's not that frightful tick Pettigrew – in there swilling port – is it? He's a frightful tick, really. Look at me.
ELSIE *(laughing)* You do look a mutt. Do you know, a Prince of the Blood Royal shot himself on my doorstep last week?
HAMISH Well, they've probably cleared him away by now. And I don't mind that sort of thing really. I'm very broad-minded. I'm not perfect myself, even, if it comes to that.
ELSIE No, I don't suppose you are.
HAMISH What about it, then?
ELSIE I don't know. I'm in such a funk, somehow. I feel as if virtue had gone out of me, though I don't think I'd any to go. I feel sure of only one thing.
HAMISH What is that, said he, anxiously?
ELSIE That no more Princes will shoot themselves on my doorstep – except by accident. . . . Oh, I'd better marry you, I think.
HAMISH Good business. Extraordinarily good business.

(They embrace. Enter PETTIGREW. He is no longer gorgeous, no longer dynamic. His hands are in his trousers pockets.)

PETTIGREW Aye, aye! Well, good-afternoon.
ELSIE *and* **HAMISH** Good-afternoon.
PETTIGREW Good-afternoon, Cook.
FAITH Good-afternoon.

(PETTIGREW slouches out)

HAMISH Lord, I didn't see you, Cook. I beg your pardon.
FAITH I'm sure it's granted, sir.
Oh, sir, you must be very good to her.
HAMISH Oh, absolutely, what?

(The SINS gather in a respectful semicircle round the Happy Pair. FAITH takes the Stage.)

EPITHALAMION RECITED BY FAITH

Phœbus is throned and Hymen's torch is lit
And we had better make the best of it.
So to this happy blend of rib and dust
If evil spirits come (as come they must),
As reverent servitors let them attend,
Utterly purposed never to offend.
Let Avarice keep the wolf-pack from the door
And Envy polish up the parquet floor.
Let soft Luxuria deck the wanton bride
And Gula keep the inner man supplied.
Let capable Superbia nurse the kids
And Ira whack them, as the Bible bids.
Let Sloth transport the family jars away.

On these conditions only let them stay –
To stimulate, to comfort, to sustain,
Or, at the least, perhaps to entertain.
And do remember, dears, in the event
Of fire, flood, families or accident,
That you can count eternally on me
And my sweet sisters, Hope and Charity.

CURTAIN

EPILOGUE

If at this Point some fool calleth "Author, Author," and if the Audience take it up in accents free of menace, or even if the Fireman in the pit hath to be bribed to raise the cry and it be but taken up by the Programme Sellers, ACCIDIA will advance before the Curtain and will say:

I suppose, strictly speaking, I am the Author of this piece. But I feel very strongly that I must acknowledge my indebtedness to my little friends, Pride, Envy and Avarice, without whose continual encouragement this Play would never have been written. I cannot but refer, moreover, to that great Patron and Master of all young Dramatists, dear Beelzebub, without whose direct inspiration this Play might never have been written.

This Play is really a sort of Propaganda Play. In these days when all sorts of fancy and synthetic vices are being hourly imported from Europe and America, it is up to us to show by our enthusiastic support that Great Britain is still the best breeding-ground for the good old-fashioned Sins that made our fathers what they were.

Good-night, children. Good-night, all the little Imbeciles. Good-night, everybody. Good-night. Good-night.

THE END

THE ANATOMIST

A LAMENTABLE COMEDY OF KNOX, BURKE AND HARE AND THE WEST PORT MURDERS

To Rona Mavor

Persons in the Play

MISS AMELIA DISHART
MISS MARY BELLE DISHART
WALTER ANDERSON L.R.C.S., Edinburgh. A Demonstrator in Anatomy
JESSIE ANN . . . . A Maid-servant
ROBERT KNOX, M.D. . . . . A Lecturer in Anatomy
AUGUSTUS RABY . . . . A Student of Anatomy
THE LANDLORD OF THE THREE TUNS
MARY PATERSON . . . . A Woman of the Town
JANET . . . . A Servant-girl
DAVIE PATERSON . . . . Porter at Surgeons' Hall
WILLIAM BURKE
WILLIAM HARE
Sundry STUDENTS of Anatomy

Author's Note

The Play. – This play is a reversion from the modern type of chronicle play to a type less concerned with historical facts than with entertainment. The action is limited to four short scenes, a simple fictitious narrative is unfolded, and no more characters are introduced than are necessary to the development of the fable.

The principal figure is Robert Knox, the anatomist, who was so theatrical in his life and habit that it is possible to transfer him almost bodily to the stage. A few heightened effects have been added, and his rhetorical style has been adapted slightly to fit modern standards, but I believe the character as it stands in the play is a fair deduction from what we know of the man.

The Character of Knox. – Lonsdale, his biographer, describes him as follows:

> Dr. Knox was slightly above the middle stature, and his person realised the definition of a muscular, 'tight-made' man. . . . His wide chest and powerful shoulders and rather long arms presented something of the *physique* of the wrestler; but no such characters for a moment vied with the gentlemanly air and pronounced intellectuality of the man himself.

Mr. Lonsdale is a frank Knoxophile.

> His carriage was upright, his walk firm and soldierly. . . . The apparent restlessness of both his features and framework bespoke the versatile Frenchman more than the 'canny Scot'. The atrophied condition of his left eye, the large nose and full mouth were heightened in force by strong lines and a coarseness of features incident to the worst form of confluent small-pox. He had a strikingly fine head, that shone in all its baldness. . . . The muscles of Knox's face were seldom at rest when his brain was occupied. These involuntary twitchings were far from agreeable, especially those which affected his underlip, the crossing of which from side to side produced a kind of smacking noise. Co-ordinate or alternating with transfacial movements, the neck was extended, the shoulders raised, and the arm drawn to the side. . . .

'He was bland in manner and full of pleasantry,' Mr. Lonsdale says, but his extracts from Knox's *obiter dicta* suggest little blandness and rather a brutal form of pleasantry.

He was a dandy. He wore a dark puce or black coat and a fancy waistcoat; a high cravat passed through a diamond ring; a prominent shirt-collar; rings, watch-seals, chains and pendants; dark trousers and shining boots. He wore gold spectacles and no braces. He did not usually wear a patch on his blind eye, but he definitely should in this play. He gestured when he lectured.

He had a bitter heart: he had served at Waterloo and in South Africa; he was eloquent and full of bulldog pluck. He defied the Church, the University and Public Opinion for years after his scandal. He had a well-stocked mind and kept the largest possible proportion of his stock in the shop window. He really did contribute to Science. He was the most popular lecturer in Britain. He had a grim and fantastic humour. He had a nasty tongue at medical meetings and elsewhere. He was fascinating to women. His biographer says, 'He married a person of inferior rank.' This person bore him several children, and died. It would interest Mr. Shaw to know that he was an anti-vivisectionist. He turned his blind eye to the methods by which he was supplied with corpses for dissection, and this, for a time, clouded his reputation and threatened his safety. He continued researching, working and lecturing in Edinburgh for thirteen years, but during those years he was laying up for himself a more serious source of trouble than the resetting of murdered bodies. He essayed Higher Criticism in a very mild and tentative way. This finished him. Edinburgh could forgive him his earlier offence but it could not forgive him his last. He fled to Glasgow and thence to London, a broken and discredited man of fifty-one years of age. He was thirty-six or thirty-seven at the time of the play.

No solution to the mystery of Knox's attitude in 1828 is suggested. Perhaps Mary's (in Act Three) is nearest the truth, though she only says it to hurt him.

The West Port Murders. – In 1828 the demand for anatomy subjects far exceeded the supply. Corpses came to Leith from London and the Continent. The bootleggers of the time supplemented these by digging up corpses from graves. They were sturdy, adventurous rascals and were reinforced by a few enthusiastic amateurs, of whom Liston, the surgeon whose long splint still survives in first-aid sets, was one. Burke and Hare were people of a different stamp. They came from Ireland and lived on whisky in a slum. They paid for the whisky by keeping lodgers. One of these, an old pensioner, died, and his body was sold to Knox. The second was an unconscionable time in dying, and Hare put a pillow over his face. From that time on it was easy money, and probably sixteen persons were trapped and murdered by the pair in a year. Some of these were well-known Edinburgh characters. The incaution of their race led to their discovery. Hare turned King's Evidence and Burke was hanged.

Characters and Incidents in the Play. – The incident of Mary Paterson is taken from life. She was recognised on 'the table' by William Fergusson, who later became President of the Royal College of Surgeons of England. Fergusson is represented in the play by Walter Anderson, a fictitious character. The Disharts are also fictitious, but Knox *was* fond of music and of ladies. Raby is fictitious and is intended to symbolise the dog-like loyalty of Knox's students when the clouds were thick around him. Davie Paterson, the go-between, is an actual character. For some reason or other he became rather a hero.

The play does not pretend to be anything but a story with an historical background. If it illustrates anything, it is the shifts to which men of science are driven when they are ahead of their times. The 'mob' should be very careful in its choice of objects for persecution; for stoning the prophets is not so good for their morale as many adepts of martyrdom would have us believe.

If some facetiæ seem in bad taste in the presentation of so grim a subject, I plead de Quincey as a precedent.

J. B.
Glasgow, September 1929.

ACT ONE

The withdrawing-room at the DISHARTS'. MARY BELLE DISHART is at her piano. MISS AMELIA DISHART, her elder, is embroidering by the dying light from the window. WALTER ANDERSON is watching MARY and turning over her music. The time is autumn in 1828.

MARY I attempt from love's sickness to fly in vain,
        Since I am myself my own fever and pain.
        No more now, fond heart, with pride shall we swell:
        Thou canst not raise forces enough to rebel.

        For love has more power and less mercy than fate
        To make me seek ruin and love those that hate.
        I attempt from love's sickness to fly in vain,
        Since I am myself my own fever and pain.

WALTER Thank you very much.
AMELIA I have heard you sing better, Mary Belle.
MARY I know. I am in poor voice to-night. I don't know why.
WALTER I thought you sang it with great feeling and expression.
MARY Oh, feeling! Yes.

(She looks at her sister, who rises)

AMELIA The light is almost gone. How lovely and sad these autumn evenings are! We shall miss them when we go abroad next month.
WALTER Don't go abroad, Miss Amelia. . . . I think the evenings are more beautiful in Scotland than anywhere else in the whole world.
AMELIA In the whole world, Walter? You must be the great traveller to pass your judgments on so wide an area.
WALTER Well, I have been to Calais and to Madeira.
MARY You are quite the Christopher Columbus.
WALTER And you are suddenly very waggish. I rejoice to see you have become sprightly again.
MARY I rejoice, sir, in your rejoicings.
WALTER Mary, I . . . Will you sing again?
MARY No, indeed I will not.
AMELIA Walter, I think you are a sufficiently old friend of the family to excuse my leaving you and my sister together for a few moments. We expect another guest to-night – a gentleman – and I have some instructions to give to Jessie Ann. We may overlook the proprieties for once in a way, may not we?
WALTER Of course, Miss Amelia. Permit me . . .
MARY We have pulled each other's hair and torn each other's clothes often enough in the past. Is it wise to leave us together?

AMELIA I cannot think why Walter comes here at all. You are making him blush with your coarseness. Don't mind her naughtiness, Walter. Her heart is in the right place.

WALTER I hope so, indeed, Miss Dishart. As a student of anatomy I hope so. It is tidier so.

AMELIA You are being indelicate now. I doubt I should not leave you after all.

MARY Do go away, Amelia. You are filling the room with a dreadful draught and poor Walter will be frozen to the door-handle, and what will your dear Mr. Knox think?

WALTER Dr. Knox? Is he coming to-night?

AMELIA Oh, yes. Poor soul, he is lonely! And he is so fond of female society. And he does love Mary Belle and me to accompany him with his flute. He plays shockingly, poor soul. And he has married, we are told, so unhappily. Mrs. Knox cannot or will not go out with him. They say she is hardly presentable. He is so kind to her too.

MARY You are sorry for an Irish tinker in the street, but you do not ask him in to your with-drawing-room.

AMELIA Mary Belle, please do not talk in that way. Mr. Knox is a most interesting man. Such a fund of information! And he is Walter's hero. You must not speak ill of Walter's hero.

MARY I cannot congratulate either Walter on his hero or you on your – on your protégé.

AMELIA Mary Belle dear, what has come over you to-night? You are quite unlike yourself.

MARY I am fey, I think. Amelia, your great bear of a surgeon will be upon us at any moment. And I will not be left alone with sulky Walter and ogreish Dr. Knox. Do hurry, dearest.

AMELIA I shall be back presently. Be good.

(She goes)

MARY Well, Walter?

WALTER Well?

MARY Amelia was right. I sing Purcell abominably.

WALTER Oh, no! I thought . . .

MARY Ah, 'with feeling and expression', yes. With too much feeling. 'To make us seek ruin and love those that hate.'

WALTER If you are referring to me you are treating me most cruelly. You know and you know that I love you tenderly, devotedly.

MARY Perhaps.

WALTER What do you mean?

MARY You know very well what I mean.

WALTER On my honour I do not. Tell me.

MARY Your honour! It is a pretty honour that forces a lady to say what she never should say.

WALTER Oh, don't tell me it is the same old quarrel again. I hoped and believed that it was all done with.

MARY Why may we not marry?

WALTER But we shall marry, my heart's love! Only we must wait. Others can wait. Why should not we?

MARY Wait, wait, wait! I am sick of waiting. Three of my friends were married this summer. I shall have no bridesmaids left.

WALTER But you agreed. . . . You said you would wait twenty years if need be.

MARY I know I did. Don't be so ungentlemanly as to cast that up to me. *(MARY picks up a skein of wool and twists it in her hands)* How you humiliate me!

WALTER Mary . . .

MARY Uncle Matthew talked about it all this afternoon. He asked again whether you would accept the money he will lend you to commence practice in Fife. He says he can't understand why you won't take his offer. We could marry in spring, he says.

WALTER Mary, I explained to you why I could not commence practice in Fife. I thought you understood.

MARY Of course I understand. I understand only too well. You love your loathsome dissecting-rooms and your horrible Dr. Knox better than you love me.

WALTER You know that's not true. And please don't speak in that way of Dr. Knox.

MARY "Don't speak in that way of Dr. Knox"? It is how everyone speaks of Dr. Knox. He *is* horrible. He is conceited. He is overdressed. He is ugly. He is pompous. He's rude. And they say worse things of him than that.

WALTER Who says so? What do they say?

MARY Never mind.

WALTER But I *do* mind. I insist upon knowing.

MARY You *insist*, Dr. Anderson?

WALTER I do insist. Mary, you of all people must not have your judgment corrupted by malicious lies. It is intolerable that . . .

MARY Walter, please don't gesticulate. You will knock down the what-nots. Besides, I am in no mood to admire it. Pray sit down. Here. *(She gives him her wool to hold and begins to wind)* Now you are bound. I wish I could gag you too.

WALTER Mary. Tell me. What lies have you heard against Dr. Knox?

MARY They are not lies. . . . Well, he is a married man and he is for ever dancing attendance on unmarried females.

WALTER Dr. Knox's domestic life has been a tragedy.

MARY There is no compulsion upon him to transform it into a French farce. . . . Besides . . .

WALTER Besides what?

MARY Well, besides, everybody knows that he is hand in glove with the sack-'em-up men.

WALTER With the *what*?

MARY With the sack-'em-up men. The body-snatchers. The resurrectionists. It is utterly dreadful to think . . .

WALTER It *is* dreadful. It is dreadful to hear you talking thieves' slang – worthy of the lips that invented the lie but unspeakably unworthy of yours.

MARY You can't deny it. *Do* hold my wool properly. Everyone says it. . . . Walter, dear, I'm horribly unhappy.

WALTER Who has been filling your head with this? I can't bear to hear you talking of such things. Oh, put down that damned wool!

MARY Oh, Walter, you've fankled it all up. It will take hours to unravel.

WALTER Mary, if I went to Fife I should be profaning something – something greater than my love for you.

MARY Your own selfish personal inclinations.

WALTER No, no, no, no! I have to fight them. God knows how I have to fight them. They tell me to go to Fife. To marry you at once. I adore you. My whole soul aches for you.

MARY I see. Only it aches a little bit more for the great, one-eyed, bald-headed, nasty Dr. Knox; and just a little bit more for your horrid dead people. You are like a cannibal. Oogh! I dreamed last night that you were a black, moulting carrion crow, pecking, pecking— You come here reeking of mortality. It's disgusting.

WALTER It isn't disgusting. It's beautiful. Lovely, intricate human bodies. It teaches me to see God.

MARY That's blasphemous.

WALTER No, no, no. Mary, if only you . . . It's God's work. Anatomy is God's work. He made us and we ought to know how. It is as if they had taken the noblest of an artist's works and locked them in a dark gallery and barricaded the door. We are breaking down the barricade. We'll go on. . . . We'll make manifest God's work to man! We will! . . . Oh, I can't express myself. Ask Knox. He'll tell you. He knows.

MARY God's work! God and Dr. Knox! A singular association! Indeed I cannot think why my sister does not forbid him the house.

WALTER Forbid Dr. Knox the house! Oh, very pleasant. Miss Dishart at least has some dim conception that his visits are an honour, ma'am, an honour!

MARY You dare to speak to me like that!

WALTER Listen to me. Knox will be remembered when Buonaparte and Wellington are forgotten. His work in the comparative anatomy of the eye . . .

MARY Dr. Anderson, you are beside yourself. Please go away.

WALTER Forgive me, Mary.

MARY You are unpardonable.

WALTER You are right. I am not myself to-night.

MARY I think you are yourself to-night. I think I have never known your true self till to-night. I count myself fortunate to have discovered you – in time. Here is your ring.

WALTER I won't take it. This is a foolish quarrel.

MARY I am foolish, am I? I talk thieves' slang, do I? I am unladylike, am I?

WALTER I said no such thing. I said it was a foolish quarrel, and so it is.

MARY It is NOT. You must choose between me and Dr. Knox.

WALTER I choose both. I will have both. I will make you see my point of view.

MARY You will never drag me so low as that. This is your last chance. I will share the affections of a gentleman with nobody. Which do you choose?

WALTER Oh, my God, what shall I do?

(MAID knocks, and enters)

(Enter DR. KNOX. He carries a flute in its case. The room has darkened, and his presence appears to make it darker.)

MAID Dr. Knox!

KNOX You rehearse some theatricals? I intrude, as usual.

MARY No, no, Dr. Knox. We are very much obliged by your visit. We were expecting you. My sister will be here presently. Walter, do you light the candles, please. Be seated, sir.

KNOX I thank you, ma'am. Well, Mr. Anderson, you tear yourself from your studies to sport with Amaryllis in the shade. I am interested to observe this in you, sir. Madam, do I interrupt your idyll?

MARY I don't know what you mean, sir. Jessie Ann, tell Miss Dishart that the Doctor is here.

(The MAID goes out)

KNOX I'll explain my meaning, if you are really an anxious inquirer. I take any amount of trouble with a truly anxious inquirer. I do, do I not, Mr. Daphnis Anderson?

MARY You are facetious, Mr. Knox.

KNOX Your only jig-maker.

MARY If you will excuse me, I shall go fetch my sister.

WALTER No.

MARY No? Let me pass, please, Mr. Anderson.

WALTER Mary. We cannot leave things as they are. Listen. Dr. Knox will speak for me. He'll tell you, Mary. Mary, do listen.

MARY I can't conceive what Mr. Knox will think of you. Open the door, please.

(She goes out)

KNOX *Une affaire des tendresses*, I perceive. You are a sad rogue, Anderson, I fear.

WALTER Sir, I—

KNOX Not a word, not a word. Keep your amours to yourself. I am not a good natural confidant. Besides, I wanted to talk to you about something. What was it, now? Eureka! I have it. Was it you who gave that dolt Raby a head to dissect?

WALTER Yes, sir. This morning.

KNOX And why, pray? Do you think that dissecting-room subjects are so easily come by that I can afford to have them mangled by that imbecile?

WALTER Well, sir, he hadn't yet dissected the head. He's a dull fellow, sir, but conscientious and anxious to learn.

KNOX *Ach, Gott!* Then he is a *rara avis*. But he may fly to the Himalayas and learn from the vultures who mutilate the liver of poor Prometheus by the most up-to-date Edinburgh methods. Or, better still, send him to my worthy and honoured colleague, the Professor of Anatomy. I won't have him in my rooms.

WALTER I think you do him an injustice, sir. There are many worse students than old Raby.

KNOX *C'est vrai. C'est juste.* There are. Mr. Anderson, when I survey the brutish faces of the youths ranged round my lecture-room, I thank my Maker that I once studied the habits of the hyena. I presented a communication on them, sir, to the Royal Society. I have no doubt you are too occupied with petticoats to have read it, sir, but it is in the library.

WALTER I have read the paper, sir.

KNOX This is fame, sir. This is glory. It is worth all the labour of stuffing these Bartholomew pigs for the slaughter to have awakened a glimmer of interest in one of them. If you would follow my instructions without question, I should be better pleased. But that is too much to hope for.

WALTER Very well, sir. I shall make an arrangement with Raby.

KNOX Send him out to rob graveyards. It is all the ass is fit for.

WALTER If you are serious, sir, I must tell you that that is no part of my duty.

KNOX What, pray, is no part of your duty?

WALTER Arranging churchyard raids. I disapprove of them very strongly.

KNOX You do, do you? We will have you in the Militia, with a cocked hat and a blunderbuss. You are a prig, Mr. Anderson.

WALTER You are not very kind to me, Dr. Knox.

KNOX Would you like to weep on my bosom? You looked on the verge of tears when I arrived. You appear to be enjoying a merry evening.

WALTER Damnation! To-night I meet the two people I most reverence in the world, and they make me a butt. I had better go home.

(Enter AMELIA and MARY BELLE)

KNOX Mademoiselle, your humble servant. I have been annoying Mr. Walter Anderson.

AMELIA Ah, you must not do that, Dr. Knox. Mr. Walter is under my especial protection.

KNOX He is indeed happy. How are you?

AMELIA I am very well indeed, thank you. Pray sit down and tell us the news. Walter has been very silent all evening. He is a poor gossip.

KNOX In Mr. Walter's trade and mine that is a high qualification.

AMELIA Oh, do you think so? I used to rely on old Dr. Bell for all the crack of the country-side. Mamma used to say he was better than a clergyman.

KNOX His scandal was more piquant, ma'am.

AMELIA Ah, I would not say that. What a pity Mr. Sidney Smith went away. What a chatterbox! And a minister of the gospel, too. Mamma adored him.

KNOX He is a Canon now, I am told.

AMELIA And a very explosive one, too. Did you know him, Doctor?

KNOX No, ma'am.

AMELIA I did so admire his writing in the *Review*. So polished. So unlike those boors in *Maga*. Little Mr. Macaulay is writing now in the *Review*.

KNOX Ah?

AMELIA Mary Belle, have you the latest number? Yes. On Machiavelli. He was here last night. Not Machiavelli – Mr. Macaulay; and he told us. He was very proud. He is a chatterbox, if you like. Have you read his essay?

KNOX On Machiavelli?

AMELIA Yes.

KNOX I have no time for the follies of young scribblers. What does he say of Machiavelli?

AMELIA He makes some sort of a hero of him. I cannot think why. I myself think Machiavelli was a great rascal.

KNOX You are wrong, ma'am, you are wrong. He had the hall-mark of greatness upon him.

AMELIA And what is the hall-mark of greatness?

KNOX To be assailed by the mob.

MARY Mercy! When everyone is telling us that the voice of the people is the voice of God!

KNOX Ladies, I have, as you know, fought against the French at some personal danger. If there is such a thing as physical courage, I do not possess it; but I would give all I have for the proud and happy privilege of standing with my back to the wall and my pistols in my hand, with a thousand of the *canaille* before me, ravening for my blood.

AMELIA It is a strange wish. But your cause would, of course, be a good one?

KNOX What do I care for the cause? I have no opinions I would die for. But if I heard but once the noble patriotic cry, 'Crucify him!' I would know my cause was good.

AMELIA You are making yourself quite hot, Mr. Knox.

WALTER But you have heard the cry already, Mr. Knox. The University—

KNOX Want my blood. I was referring to the full-throated bellow of the mob. Not the squeak of vampire flittermice.

AMELIA You should go into Parliament, Mr. Knox. How well you speak.

KNOX Miss Amelia, how beautifully and tenderly you make us ranting actors look absurd. Shall we practise on the flute? Miss Mary Belle, your harp has shed its garments and fallen from the willow. Shall we have a trio? What have you been playing?

"I attempt from love's sickness to fly. . . ."

WALTER But, Mr. Knox – do pardon me a moment – you say you have no opinions you would die for. But surely you must feel, must know you are right?

KNOX Right about what, my disciple?

WALTER Oh, everything. You stand up so boldly against the schools, and the clergy, and – and the talk of all the drawing-rooms. You preach a gospel. You *must* have confidence in it?

KNOX Only a fool is sure of himself until the mob denies him. The learned Regius Professor, Alexander Monro the Third, would think he was right, if he could think at all. But I am not such a dolt.

MARY You hear that?

KNOX Hoho!

AMELIA Let us have some music.

WALTER No, no. You don't know how important this is to me. If you are being witty, please tell me. I have no sense of humour.

MARY Walter, you must not.

WALTER Please, Mary. I am at my wits' end.

KNOX No very long journey. What is the matter with you?

WALTER To-night I have been offered the choice between my dearest happiness and another year's work at anatomy. I risked my happiness – I may have lost it – to work with you. Am I in the right? Have I been a fool?

KNOX You are in the right. You have been a fool. You are in the right to be a fool, and a fool to be in the right.

MARY Mr. Knox . . .

AMELIA Now, now, now, now, now, now. Dr. Knox has come to practise on the flute and not to be deeved with dull family matters.

KNOX Family matters are never dull, ma'am. That is a mistake you ladies make. Come. I shall be the Judge in Chambers. What is the cause?

WALTER Sir, Miss Mary Belle Dishart says . . .

KNOX I don't want to hear what she says, sir. She will say it herself. What have you to say?

(Enter the MAID)

MAID Please, Miss Amelia—

AMELIA What is it, Jessie Ann?

MAID Please, ma'am, are you at home to a Mr. Baby?

AMELIA Mister who, girl?

MAID Mr. Baby. An English-spoken gentleman.

WALTER Oh, pardon me, Miss Dishart. She means Mr. Raby. I took the liberty of asking him to come. He is a medical student. He comes from Warwickshire, I think. He has very few friends in Edinburgh, and I thought to ask permission to present him. He is very well connected. . . .

KNOX Ha! He is also most conscientious and anxious to learn. He ceased this evening, at my urgent request, to pursue his studies at Surgeons' Square, but I have no doubt his exclusiveness and genteel connections will appeal to other poor devils of Lecturers in Anatomy in this city.

AMELIA And he's kicking his heels downstairs all this time! Show the gentleman up, Jessie Ann.

(Exit MAID)

AMELIA Why don't you simply say he is a friend of yours, Walter? He is welcome if he is, and I'll soon get his biography out of him for myself.

KNOX And this cause these two people were about to bring before me?

AMELIA The cause can wait. It is a pack of nonsense, anyway.

(Enter the MAID and RABY)

MAID Mr. Baby.

(She goes)

AMELIA How do you do, Mr. Raby? Will you present Mr. Raby, Walter?

WALTER May I present Mr. Augustus Raby, Miss Dishart. Miss Mary Belle Dishart, Mr. Raby. Dr. Knox, I think you already know Mr. Raby. He is a student of yours.

KNOX He was.

AMELIA Dr. Knox has been speaking so kindly of you, Mr. Raby. Do you sit down by me.

RABY Most happy.

AMELIA Have you been long in Edinburgh, Mr. Raby?

RABY Not very. No. Not very.

AMELIA We are enchanted that Walter should have asked you to come to see us. He is a very old friend of ours, and his friends are very welcome. You are a native of England, Mr. Raby?

RABY Yes. Yes, ma'am.

AMELIA Where is your home?

RABY Oh, I lodge in the Canongate.

AMELIA No. I mean your real home. In England.

RABY Sutton Bottom.

AMELIA And where is that? In which county?

RABY Bucks.

AMELIA I have never been there, but I am told it is a very beautiful county.

RABY Oh, in parts. Parts are so-so.

AMELIA And parts are not so so-so. But that is like all other counties. Even our own Midlothian. Do you like Edinburgh, Mr. Raby?

RABY Yes.

AMELIA It is an interesting old city. Every stone speaks of history. Doesn't it?

RABY Yes. It does.

AMELIA Do you like negus?

RABY Oh, yes, ma'am.

AMELIA Mary Belle, will you prepare the negus and ask Jessie Ann to bring it up?

MARY Very well, Amelia.

(She goes out)

AMELIA The nights are drawing in now. Walter, draw the curtains. You will find the autumn nights shorter here than in England, Mr. Raby?

RABY Yes, ma'am.

AMELIA What is your honest opinion of Scotland, Mr. Raby? We Scots are always anxious to know how "ithers see us".

RABY Pardon?

AMELIA You know our poet Burns has a couplet:

> "O wad some poo'er the giftie gie us
> To see oorsel's as ithers see us."

But no doubt that sounds barbarous to you.

RABY Yes, ma'am. I mean, no, ma'am.

AMELIA Do you find the Scots tongue easy to understand?

RABY No, ma'am.

WALTER How is the reading getting on, Raby? Have you finished that text-book I lent you?

RABY A bit slowly, sir. I am rather slow, sir, as you know. But I'm sticking to it. I'm determined to get through, this time, sir. Oh, and I wanted to ask you, sir – you know where it says that about the development of the spinal cord in the chick embryo . . .

WALTER Will you talk to me about it to-morrow? Oh – yes – I forgot. . . . In any case, will you see me at Surgeons' Hall to-morrow morning, early?

RABY Yes, sir. I will.

WALTER I have something to talk to you about.

RABY Yes.

AMELIA I am told you work very hard, Mr. Raby.

RABY Oh, I don't know. So-so.

AMELIA Oh, you are too modest. Is he not, Doctor?

KNOX I have no means of judging. I have never had occasion to shock his modesty.

AMELIA But surely that is not the only way of appraising modesty, to shock it!

KNOX It is the only way I know, ma'am.

AMELIA Doctor, you are terrible. Are his lectures full of terrible things like that, Mr. Raby?

RABY Oh, no, ma'am. Nothing of the sort. They're wonderful. About bones and joints and so forth . . . and bowels.

AMELIA And *what?*

RABY Oh, it doesn't matter really. What I mean is . . . Yes.

(Re-enter MARY and JESSIE ANN, with a tray full of materials for negus. JESSIE ANN goes out, and during the ensuing conversation MARY prepares and hands round the negus, accepting WALTER's help with a bad grace.)

KNOX He says that what I teach him doesn't matter. You hear that, Miss Amelia?

AMELIA No, I don't. I will not have Mr. Raby teased. Walter, will you be so good as to hand me the Album of Neapolitan Views? I want to show them to Mr. Raby. Are you fond of Naples, Mr. Raby?

RABY Yes, ma'am. I like them very much.

(KNOX snorts)

AMELIA My sister and I visited Naples last year. This is Mount Vesuvius. At night, particularly, it is a very awe-inspiring sight.

RABY It must be, ma'am.

AMELIA Have you been to Naples?

RABY No, ma'am.

AMELIA Tons of molten lava are thrown into the air.

RABY Yes, ma'am.

AMELIA This is the Bay. But no pictorial representation can give the remotest idea of the depth of azure presented by the still waters in the sunlight.

RABY No, ma'am. Very deep, I'm sure.

AMELIA Do have some negus.

RABY Thank you, ma'am.

AMELIA Do you like negus? No. I asked you that before.

KNOX With the deepest respect, Miss Amelia, may I draw your attention to this? However fascinating the lunge and riposte of your conversation with Mr. Raby, it was not to listen to intellectual dialogue that I came here. I came here to play on the flute. It became clear that a domestic imbroglio made the atmosphere impossible for the flute until the tangle was resolved. I was about to resolve it when Mr. Raby entered like a high wind from Mount Olympus. May we not proceed where we left off?

AMELIA Really, Mr. Knox, I am very indulgent with you, but this is intolerable.

KNOX I find it so, ma'am. I shall go.

AMELIA You will do nothing of the sort. Sit down and behave yourself. I am very, very angry with you. Mr. Raby, please don't mind him.

RABY I don't, ma'am. At least . . .

KNOX At least? Well? At least . . .?

AMELIA Mister Knox! Well, perhaps Mr. Raby will excuse us. I know it seems inhospitable, but—

RABY *(sitting tight)* Nothing to excuse, ma'am, really.

AMELIA We shall be charmed to see you any other evening you care to call, Mr. Raby.

RABY *(sitting tight)* Very good of you, ma'am, I'm sure.

AMELIA *(going towards him)* So if you . . .

(RABY gets up)

KNOX Oh, let him stay. He might as well be a pig in an Irishman's cabin for all the notice he will take. I know. I have lectured to him. Let him be the jury. Sit down, you fool. Fifteen good asses and true concentrated and sublimated into one sublime and concentrated ass. Hold your tongue and listen. Miss Amelia, forgive me. I may not appear so, but I am a very sensitive man. I am conscious of a suppressed atmosphere of strife. If there is a battle, I insist on taking part. Now, Miss Mary Belle Dishart, let us have your story.

AMELIA I simply will not allow this sort of thing.

KNOX Why not, ma'am? Why not? We have a hidden abscess here, an impostume. Let us have incision. Let us imbrue.

AMELIA Mr. Knox, you may mix metaphors till you are black in the face. I will not have it in my house.

KNOX You mean that you will not talk about it. You have it already, and in your house. Be a sensible woman.

AMELIA I never in all my life heard the like of this.

KNOX Then do not forgo a new experience. It is always a mistake to forgo a new experience. Miss Mary Belle, I am waiting.

MARY Waiting for what, sir?

KNOX For what you have to say.

MARY I doubt you will hardly be pleased with what I have to say.

KNOX Signorina, I do not solicit your compliments. I am unaccustomed to compliments. I ask you to add honesty to your natural beauty and wit, and to add dispatch to all three.

MARY Amelia!

AMELIA It is not the least use appealing to me.

MARY You asked this gentleman to our house.

AMELIA When I asked him, he gave no evidence of being lunatic.

WALTER Miss Amelia, pray listen. You misunderstand Mr. Knox's eccentricity of manners. He . . .

KNOX *Dieu vous remercie, mon Prince.*

WALTER This cannot go on. Mary and I are near breaking-point.

MARY We reached breaking-point half-an-hour ago.

WALTER This must be settled. Mr. Knox can help us. Pray, pray don't anger him. Let him go his own way. Mary! My sweetheart! If ever you had any regard for me, tell Dr. Knox our difficulty. If you will not, I don't know what I shall do.

AMELIA I think you had better, Mary Belle. More of this and we shall all be raving – except Mr. Raby.

MARY Very well. What does it matter? . . . Mr. Knox, Mr. Anderson and I were affianced. We were to be married this year. Since you appointed him your assistant, he has altered his plans.

WALTER My darling, no. No, no, no!

KNOX You must not say "My darling, no, no, no, no," while the witness is giving evidence. Pray proceed, Signorina.

MARY My uncle, Sir Matthew Goudie, has offered him an advance of £1,000 that he may commence medical practice in Fife. Now. At once. He has refused it.

KNOX Quite rightly. He is unfit to start practice. He is better than most, but he is not yet fit to be responsible for human lives.

MARY He is. He is. Or he never will be. Besides that was not his excuse for breaking his word to me.

KNOX And what was his excuse?

MARY He said he was doing God's work. He said he was engaged on an heroic task. He said if he went to Fife he would be – he would be profaning something holier than his – than his love for me.

KNOX He said all that, did he?

WALTER Yes; and I meant it.

KNOX No doubt you did. And you, my dear young lady, took all this play-acting *aux grands sérieux?*

WALTER Mr. Knox!

MARY It was. I knew it was. Play-acting! That's what it was.

KNOX Be calm. Be calm. Be calm. Ninety per cent of all the amatory game is play-acting. And by far the most delightful part. Compose yourself. I have no doubt he meant what he said. But he had a far better reason for breaking his engagement with you.

WALTER I did not break my engagement.

KNOX Hold your tongue, you. Miss Mary Belle, I can quite understand that the pursuit of science may appear mean and trivial to a young female brought up on Shakespeare, crewel-work and the use of the musical glasses. But life, my dear young lady, is not all assemblies and quadrilles, or even dressing, bathing and smacking babies.

MARY Don't you dare speak like that to me. I am not a child. If you had the least sensibility you would feel – as Walter *knows* – that if he had been a poet or a musician or – or inspired in any way, I would have followed him barefoot through the world, or waited for him to the end of time.

KNOX That would have been very foolish of you.

MARY What do I care for foolishness or wisdom? I know what is right. I know Walter.

KNOX He is better employed than in making foolish jingles or spoiling canvas in the attempt to copy what cannot be copied.

MARY Better employed! He is employed on work I abhor. He cuts up dead bodies. He does it because he likes it. He is mad. He is *infected*, as people are infected with typhoid fever. That is my opinion of your dissecting, if you would like to know.

KNOX What do I care for your opinions? I am a man of science. I want your reasons.

MARY You want me to argue. I can't argue. I won't argue.

KNOX You prefer to jump to conclusions.

MARY Of course I do. Every sensible person does. All women jump to conclusions, just as all men crawl on their hands and knees, looking for them, counting every cobble-stone and never arriving, or arriving at the wrong place.

(AMELIA has taken up her sewing. WALTER is listening intently. RABY is looking foolish.)

KNOX But look at the trouble your leaping causes! *Nam fuit ante Helenam, femina teterrima causa belli.*

MARY I don't know Latin.

KNOX You should study the classics. I have just quoted Horace to the effect that Helen was not the first female to raise a rumpus.

AMELIA Doctor, you are being very naughty. I do think you might help, instead of parading your classics. The poor young people are in sad trouble.

KNOX Trouble! They know nothing of trouble. Let them go, as I did, to the deserts of South Africa, and hunt carnivora across the wastes, accompanied only by ape-like Caffres . . .

AMELIA Yes, yes. You have told us. You must have had a terrible time. But black men can't be any worse than black thoughts. And, besides, you said you could settle things.

KNOX I did. Come, my dear. We are straying from the point. Let us have your absurdities. I am all ears. Mr. Raby, will you stop looking at me in that manner? I *have* only one eye. This patch covers an eyeless socket.

AMELIA Doctor!

KNOX Your pardon. Proceed, Miss Mary Belle.

MARY Dr. Knox, you appear to find this situation humorous. I find it humiliating. Walter tells me that this occupation which keeps us apart is God's work. You tell me he is play-acting when he says so. You have answered my question with jeers. I don't understand. I *must* understand. Won't you tell me what you mean?

KNOX My dear, we all seek to explain ourselves in big words and windy notions. The wise disregard these things. Our friend Walter has a sacred thirst of which he is only half-conscious. The vulgarian, the quack and the theologian are confronted with the Universe. They at once begin to talk and talk and talk. They have no curiosity. They know all about it. They build a mean structure of foolish words and phrases, and say to us, "This is the World." The comparative anatomist *has* curiosity. He institutes a divine search for facts. He is unconcerned with explanations and theories. In time, when you and I are dead, his facts will be collected and their sum will be the Truth. Truth that will show the noblest thing in creation, how to live. Truth that will shatter the idol Mumbo Jumbo, before which man daily debases his magnificence. Truth . . .

MARY No doubt that is very fine. But it is all words, too.

KNOX It is a religion. It is a passion.

MARY It is a very horrid sort of religion.

KNOX My dear young lady, it is less horrid than the religions of most of mankind. It has its martyrs, it has its heresy-hunts, but its hands are clean of the blood of the innocent.

MARY Are they?

KNOX Of course they are.

MARY Do you call the hands of a resurrectionist clean?

KNOX Of the blood of the innocent.

MARY Grave-robbing is worse than murder.

KNOX Madam, with all respect, you are a pagan atheist to say so. If you believed in an immortal soul, why should you venerate the empty shell it has spurned in its upward flight? And with a false veneration, too. The anatomist alone has a true reverence for the human body. He loves it. He knows it.

MARY He pays ruffians to tear it from the grave where loving hands have laid it. Your friend Mr. Liston, the surgeon, goes himself and beats the guardians, like the pot-house bully he is.

KNOX Bob Liston is no friend of mine. I abhor his methods.

MARY Where do *you* get your bodies from?

(A pause)

KNOX How should I know? My duty is to teach.

MARY Ah!

KNOX My child . . . *(He tries to take her hands)* You love my friend. To love is to understand. Try to understand that he is doing great things, of which not the least is to sacrifice a part of his happiness.

WALTER Mary . . .

MARY Mr. Anderson, your presence here is inexpressibly painful to me. I am greatly obliged to Dr. Knox for his attempt to put me in the wrong. But he has only convinced me how right I am. I cannot look at one of the three of you without a shudder. I feel as if you had lifted a lid and showed me a glimpse of unspeakable things. Will you excuse me? I'll retire.

AMELIA Oh, darling, darling!

WALTER Then that's the end. You can go to hell. If you want me you'll find me in the gutter!

(He dashes rudely out)

KNOX Mr. Raby, perhaps it would be well if you followed him to his gutter and exercised a restraining supervision on his wallowing.

RABY Eh? I don't quite follow, sir.

KNOX Go after him and see he comes to no harm. I cannot afford to lose a good assistant.

RABY Very well, sir. Good-night, ma'am, and thank you very much for a pleasant evening. Good-night, ma'am. Good-night, sir.

(He bows himself out)

KNOX And God's benison on you, sir. . . .

> "To arms! to arms!" the fierce virago cries,
> And swift as lightning to the combat flies.
> All side in parties, and begin the attack;
> Fans clap, silks rustle, and tough whalebones crack.
> Heroes' and Heroines' shouts confusedly rise,
> And bass and treble voices strike the skies.
> No common weapons in their hands . . .

MARY Mr. Knox!

KNOX No common weapons . . .

MARY Mr. Knox, it is the common talk of this town that you are generally admired by persons of our sex. And this in spite of your hideous face and cynical, filthy, scandalous tongue. There is one lady who does not share their admiration. She loathes and detests and abhors you and all your ways. And she wishes you a very good-night.

(Exit MARY)

KNOX Poor things. Poor hearts.

AMELIA Your sentiment rings abominably false, Dr. Knox.

KNOX False, Miss Amelia! I have never in my life been accused . . . Well, perhaps it does. What does it matter?

AMELIA My sister's happiness matters to me a very great deal. And Walter's too.

KNOX I did my best, Miss Amelia. But we who are groping among the roots of life cannot be expected to take too seriously the whimsies of the creatures of the air. You are crying! You mustn't cry. It congests the conjunctival sac. Let us consult Schubert. Let us hear what Rossini has to say on the quarrels of lovers. Come.

AMELIA Ah, no. I couldn't play for you to-night, Doctor.

KNOX I insist. Look –

"I attempt from love's sickness to fly in vain."

Strike up!

(He begins to play, extremely badly, on his flute. MISS AMELIA struggles helplessly with laughter, tears and his accompaniment.)

CURTAIN

ACT TWO

Scene One

A low dive in the Canongate of Edinburgh – "the Three Tuns".

The only occupants are the LANDLORD, dozing behind his bar, and WALTER ANDERSON, drinking solus at a little table in the corner. He is drunk.

(An hour or so has passed since Act One.)

WALTER Nebby.

LANDLORD Aye, Doctor?

WALTER Nebby, bring m'nother shot of gin.

LANDLORD Right you was, Professor. *(He brings it)* Ye're out for a bit o' fun the nicht, Doctor?

WALTER Fun? Fine fun. Nebby, my girl has thrown me over. D'ye call that funny? Eh?

LANDLORD No. I wouldna just. Providential, maybe, but no' just funny.

WALTER If you had called that funny, I would have figged you. I would have tapped your claret.

LANDLORD Nae doubt. Nae doubt.

WALTER I would. You thinkawouldn't?

LANDLORD Oh, you're a braw lad wi' the maulies, Mr. Walter.

WALTER I see. You think I'm drunk. Well, I don't care for your opinion. Nor for anybody's opinion. I do what I like. Y'understand?

LANDLORD Aye, aye.

WALTER I'm the only judge of what I do. I don't ask anybody's opinion.

LANDLORD Aye. You're fine upstanding lads, you o' the Surgeons' Hall.

WALTER You hold your mouth about the Surgeons' Hall.

LANDLORD Aye. We're well to hold our mouth aboot the Surgeons' Hall. There's owre mony Bow Street runners cam' to the toon the day. . . . Was ye waiting for onybody?

WALTER May I ask whether that is any of your business?

LANDLORD There's nae harm in speirin'. But Merryandrew, the Sack-'em-up man, was here and awa' hauf an hour bye; wi' a' his gang, Spune and Moudie-warp and Praying Howard. I'm feared ye're owre late. There was word o' a job out by Mid-Calder. But Dr. Liston, he was in and awa' wi' them. Ye're owre late.

WALTER Blast your eyes, you ought to ken very well I've no truck with the resurrectionists. Nor me nor Dr. Knox.

LANDLORD Aye, weel. No offence.

WALTER You'll take that back. No, not the gin. Bring another one. . . . Damned ruffians! Moudie-warp, indeed!

LANDLORD *(bringing gin)* Oh, I kenned fine you werena' in the way of business wi' the Sack-'em-up boys. But I thocht maybe you was game for a ploy.

WALTER And so I am. But not with Bob Liston and his friend Spune. Not by a long, long, long, long way, Nebby. Discretion. That's what I believe in. Discretion. You think no anatomist has a conscience. Well, some have.

LANDLORD I can weel believe that.

WALTER Well, Miss Ma— I mean a certain young person does *not* believe it. You believe that?

LANDLORD Aye, aye. I believe that.

WALTER Well, if sh'can't believe that, I'm finished with her. Un'stand? Finished with her. I go my own way aft' this. Don't care whatappens. Aft'll got my own life to live. No woman can bully me. I'm going to have—

(LANDLORD has returned to his bar)

jolly good evening. Tha's what I'm going to have. Bring 'nother drink.

(Enter MARY PATERSON and JANET. MARY is a glorious-looking creature. It is not apparent till she speaks that she has been drinking. She has a loud, harsh voice and her dialect is sometimes mincing and affected and sometimes pure Calton gutter-talk. The contrast between her speech and her appearance is indescribable. JANET is a colourless, frightened wisp who has much earlier in the evening decided that a joke can be carried too far.)

MARY P. Nebby.

LANDLORD Good-e'en to you, Mary.

MARY P. My bonnie wee Nebby! Jennie, Nebby's my only joe. Nebby, this is Janet.

LANDLORD Good-e'en to you, mistress.

MARY P. Jennie, is he no' bonnie? His neb is like a red, red rose that's newly sprung in June. If ye tak' him frae me, I'll kill ye.

LANDLORD Wheesht, wheesht, Mary.

MARY P. I'll misguggle your thrapple. I'll mashackerel ye to rights. And I'll no wheesht, Mr. Nebby. Wheesht to a leddy, indeed! I'll wheesht ye.

JANET Wheesht, Mary. Come on awa' hame.

WALTER Nebby, introduce me to your lady friends.

LANDLORD This is Mistress Mary Paterson and a freen' o' hers.

WALTER Your servant, ma'am; 'n yours, ma'am.

MARY P. And what may your name be, sir?

LANDLORD He's Mr. Wotherspoon, frae Dalkeith.

WALTER He is nothing of sort. Nothing of sort. I am Dr. Walter Anderson – at your service. . . . Don't you tell lies about me! D'you hear?

LANDLORD Aye. I hear.

WALTER May I beg f'you to join me in a glass of cordial?

MARY P. With great pleesure. We are mich obleeged.

WALTER Pleasure's mine. What may I order for you?

LANDLORD I ken what Mistress Paterson takes. Awa' you, and sit doon. Ye'll mak' a better impression that way.

(The party sit at WALTER's table. The LANDLORD brings drinks. An air of tipsy gentility pervades the scene. MARY takes off her bonnet.)

MARY P. The evenings is beginning to draw in.

WALTER Yesh. I think autumn evenings are more beautiful in Scotland than anywhere else in the whole . . . Oh, dear me! Dear me! *(He begins to weep)*

MARY P. Puir wee thing wi' your mouth a' treacle and your tail a' parritch and your heid a' wumps! What are ye greetin' for?

WALTER I – I said that before, to-night.

MARY P. Tuts! I didnae hear ye. It's a' richt, my wee hen.

WALTER It's not that. I don't object to repeating myself. Now and again. But it reminded me— *(He weeps again)*

MARY P. Nownie! Nownie! Was it a lassie that was bad to ye?

WALTER How did you know?

MARY P. Oh, I ken mair nor I let dab, as the man said. Nownie, nownie! Wha' ca'd ye partan-face, my bonnie wee pet lamb?

WALTER You're very kind to me. You're as kind and good as you are bonnie. And you *are* bonnie! What m'nificent hair! Like polished copper.

MARY P. Now, now, young man, none of that. That's not genteel. Dry your eyes on your mooshwar and sit up like a wee gentleman.

WALTER But honestly I mean it. I'll never forget your kindness to me. You'll never know what you've done for me. How can I repay you – ever?

MARY P. Weel, if ye dinna let poor Jennie die of thirst . . .

JANET Nae mair, Mary. We've had plenty. Come on awa' hame.

WALTER A thousand pardons. Landlord, same again. Mary, your hair is like fallen beech leaves. 'N as shoft as shilk. It's beautiful hair.

(As the LANDLORD is bringing the drinks, enter DAVID PATERSON)

MARY P. See! – stop it.

WALTER Davie! Dear old Davie! Davie, my long-lost brother! Come away in, Davie. We're having a party, Davie. Bring Davie's tipple, Nebby. Now comes in the sweet o' the night!

PATERSON Most kind of you, Dr. Anderson, I'm sure. But I couldnae think o' presuming . . .

WALTER Not a word. Miss Mary, may've the honour t' present to you my friend 'n colleague, Davie Paterson. Lord High Seneschal to the Great Dr. Knox. Same name, b' Jove – Paterson! Your Uncle Davie.

MARY P. I'm sure he is no uncle of mine, Dr. What's-your-name.

WALTER Oh, can't be sure. Can't be sure. These are naughty times, Miss Mary.

MARY P. *(laughing uproariously)* Come on, then, Uncle. Your wee niece'll sit on your knee.

PATERSON I'm sure it's real kind of you, miss. If the Doctor has no objection, begging his pardon.

WALTER Not least in world. Here's y' jolly good health. Interestin' reunion. Happy family gathering. Proudest moment in my life.

(He falls on a seat, and would fall on the floor if JANET didn't catch him)

MARY P. Aw, the puir wee soul. They shouldnae tak' that amount of drink, Mr. Paterson. See; we'll hap him up.

(WALTER is stretched on a bench, and MARY puts her shawl over him)

WALTER Chaos is come again.

PATERSON Are ye all richt, Doctor?

WALTER I'm all right, but the world's all wrong. It's spinning backwards through the constellations and the ether is full of thunder and lightning.

MARY P. Is that not awful, now? Just you go to sleep for a wee, and it'll be all richt in a wee while.

WALTER Do you think I had better? Very well; I will.

(He goes to sleep)

PATERSON Well, ma'am, what's the clash o' the toon?

MARY P. Sh! Sh!

PATERSON Faith, you'll no' wake him this side of to-morrow morning. The deil couldnae wauken him.

MARY P. Weel, dinna you try.

PATERSON Och, ye're awfu' backsettin' the nicht.

MARY P. Will you keep your hands off me, ye blasted crult? Sit down and be at peace, and tak' your dram, or tak' your mangy carcase out o' here.

PATERSON Och, I'm no' wantin' your conversation.

(A silence. MARY smooths WALTER's hair.)

MARY P. Can ye sew cushions and can ye sew sheets,
      And can ye sing Balaloo
      When the bairnie greets?
      Then ho and baw birdie
      Then ho and baw lamb,

Then ho and baw birdie, my boonie wee lamb.
Hey Oh, hyooch Oh, what'll 'a *dae* wi' ye?
Black's the life I lead wi' the hale o' ye –
Mony o' ye and little to gie ye.
Hey Oh, hyooch Oh, what'll I dae *wi'* ye?

(She sings the refrain twice. After the first time she repeats the third last line wearily and bitterly to herself.)

(Enter BURKE and HARE. They take a high-backed settle by the fireside.)

BURKE It's a fine night, Mister Nebby, glory be to God, an' I'm that dry that me throat feels the like of the insides of a lime-kiln. Will you give us a couple gills of malt? An' be quick about it.
LANDLORD Hae you the siller to pay for it?
BURKE Silver is it? Holy St. Joseph, will you listen to him, Bill! Silver is it? There's what's better than silver, a note. And you can take an' nail it to the counter, if you've a mind to, so long as we have drink for the worth of it.
LANDLORD There's the stink of the mort-cloth on it, Mr. Burke.
HARE Will you hould your prate. That's no way to speak to your betters. Stink, indeed! It 'ud make a cat laugh to hear you talkin' of stinks an' you livin' in a mouldy old shebeen the like of this.
BURKE Yes, an' you hold yours along with him, or I'll give you a puck in the gob that'll make ye. And as for you, Mister Nebby, it 'ud be far better for you to keep reddnin' that ugly nose of yours with your rotten rum than to be smellin' out stinks where there is none. Let you bring us our drinks and stop your blatherin'.

(LANDLORD retires. PATERSON comes over to BURKE and HARE.)

PATERSON Fine night.
HARE It is that.
PATERSON How's trade with ye?
HARE Oh, not so bad. I've seen it worse.
PATERSON Well?
BURKE Well what?
PATERSON Have ye the like of a shot for us the morn?
HARE Musha, they're not so easy come by as all that. Why, man alive, we brought you one last week.
PATERSON I know that. But Mr. Knox is aye at me to get more. Ssht.

(LANDLORD brings drinks)

HARE Give us a glass for Mr. Paterson, will you, Mister Nebby. You'll have a drop with us, won't you?
PATERSON Nay, b' Heavens. I don't drink with you.

HARE Oh, glory be, you won't, won't ye. Well, that laves the more for us that will. *Slainthe.*

BURKE *(to HARE)* Here's lookin' towards ye. *(Drinks)* And it's what I'm tellin' you, Mr. Paterson, it's no shot we have for you in the mornin'.

PATERSON Come along, Burke. You've aye served us well before at a pinch. The session's just started and they havenae the subjects tae gang round.

HARE Dear me, is that so? Now supposin', I say supposin', we did obleege the Doctor, what would he be willin' to give for it these bad times?

PATERSON Ye ken weel the price. Seven pounds. An' it's more than ye'd ever get from Lizars or even the Professor.

HARE Your sowl to glory. What's that? Seven pounds. An' we've got to get it in a hurry. It's crazy you are with your seven pounds. Think of the risk, man! Why, the last one we brought you paid us seven ten.

PATERSON A mouldy auld body that dropped to bits when I took it out the tea-kist.

BURKE It's jokin' you are, Mr. Paterson. Mouldy indeed!! A fine fresh body it was. I never handled better. An' the divil's own trouble we had gettin' it anyway. I know where there is a grand one we could get for ye quick, but it would cost you ten pounds. The Professor himself has offered us more. But I'm thinkin' we'd sooner a fine gentleman like Dr. Knox 'ud have it. Not forgetting that honest man his janitor.

PATERSON I'll gi'e eight. I'll get me heid in me hands for it, but I'll gi'e ye eight.

BURKE *(to HARE)* Has Nellie been down to see your missus to-night?

HARE Musha! How would I know?

BURKE It's what I was thinkin', that if the four of us took a little jaunt as far as Portobello the salt say air would do us a power of good. I haven't been that way for a long time. What do ye say, Bill?

HARE There's nothin' I'd like better this blessed minit and no mistake, than to be stravagin' down to the say an' to be fillin' me lungs with the fine fresh air instead of sittin' here talkin' blather in a rotten stinkin' old den the like of this.

BURKE We'll, if we're goin', we better start early in the mornin'.

PATERSON But, Mr. Burke . . .

BURKE Good-night to you, Mr. Paterson. Bill, you better slip down and borrow a loan of Grogan's ass-cart. He's got new tackling for the donkey. And I'll get Nellie. An' you can drive it round to my place shortly after five.

HARE *(rising)* I'll start this minit or he'll be off on his round with it. An' it's the fine time we'll have with the little birds fair burstin' themselves with song an' the sunlight fit to dazzle your eyes an' it shinin' on the say. And it's there you'll find cockles and periwinkles enough to feed an army.

BURKE And meself an' Nellie will be wadin' in the say. Hurry up now, will ye?

PATERSON Can't you wait a minute, Mr. Burke? I'll make you a better offer. I'll give you two pounds now this minute, and seven more when you bring the shot. I canna say fairer than that, can I?

HARE An' what'll it come to altogether?

BURKE Nine pounds.

HARE Nine pounds is it? Well, I'd not say but that might be worth doin' somethin' for. You can lave it to us.

PATERSON Mind, if ye bring another auld rickle of bones you can just take it back where you found it, and never darken ma doors again. Now, mind. A guid fresh young juicy corp.

HARE You're the fine juicy one yourself and that's no lie. Well, lave it to us; we'll find you one. Though the blessed St. Patrick himself knows it's the divil's job to get them. What with sentries at the cemetries and militia rampagin' the town, it's hard set a man is to earn an honest livin' be the sweat of his brow.

BURKE Come on with the money, for we have a night's work before us yet, if you want your shot in the morning.

PATERSON Mind, the same time as usual. And none of last month's capers, Hare coming up the High Street drunk in the full light of day with a box on his back with a shot in it. Half-past four, mind you, and no later.

HARE We'll be there on time all right. So don't get flustered. And it's little light there be at that time to see whether I'm drunk or sober I am. Won't you have a small one with us now, Mr. Paterson, just to clinch the bargain?

PATERSON No. I've the young doctor owre by to see safe. And forbye, I've no notion to take a dram wi' you and wake up the morn on a marble table, wi' Dr. Knox fumbling among my tripes. Eh? Ha, ha!

HARE Ha, ha, ha!

BURKE Ha!

(RABY appears at the door, questing)

RABY Oh, hello, Paterson. And so on.

PATERSON Good-evening to you, Mr. Raby.

RABY I say, have you seen Dr. Anderson, eh? The Chief told me to take charge of him, and I'm damned if I haven't lost him.

PATERSON There he is, over there, Mr. Raby, sir. I must say he's in bonny-like hands. A wheen o' Jezebels. I'll leave him to you, sir. If ye bring him up to the Square later, we'll play the pump on him. It's the best thing to do.

RABY Oh, right. Very good. Aye, aye, and all that sort of thing.

PATERSON Good-night to you, sir. And, see here, sir. Dinna lose sight of him again.

RABY Oh, *au revoir*.

(Exit PATERSON)

(RABY goes over to ANDERSON, whose head is in the lap of the sleeping MARY. He shakes ANDERSON's shoulder. ANDERSON sits up abruptly without waking MARY.)

RABY Now, sir. Now, Doctor. You must come home. Indeed you must.

WALTER Whassa? That you, Raby? You're a good fellow, Raby. Goodnight.

MARY P. *(waking up)* Eh! Deevil sain us! What's this, now, the wind's blown in?

RABY It's all right, my good girl. I'm taking him home.

MARY P. Who are you?

RABY It doesn't matter really.

MARY P. I'll come wi' ye.

RABY Oh, dear, no! You'll do nothing of the sort. Come along, Doctor, get up. Now you go to bye-byes again, like a good young lady, or I'll call a constable.

(He gets his hand under WALTER's armpit, and hoists him to his feet)

MARY P. You will, you tinker's messan! You will, you deil's brat! Awa' wi' you, you gentry pup! I ken the likes o' you. You call yoursel' a man? You wouldnae mak' a pair o' breeks for a man!

JANET Mary, Mary, come on awa' hame.

WALTER Where's Mary?

MARY P. *(attempting to get up, but restrained by JANET)* I'm here, my lamb.

WALTER Wan' speak to Mary. Oh, goo' Lor', I'm sleepy. Did you notice her hair, Raby? Beautiful!

RABY Come along, sir. Steady does it.

(They go out)

JANET Now, Mary Paterson, you'll just sit still. You'll just sit still, Mary Paterson. This is an awful-like place to bring a decent girl to. An awful-like place. You should think shame, Mary.

MARY P. Och, sneck up!

(HARE gets up and comes over, bowing politely as he approaches)

HARE Good-evenin' to you, Miss.

MARY P. And what is your business to interfere and put your ugly phiz between me and me lady friend?

HARE Business is it? None at all. It's only I was wonderin' could it be yourself was singin' like an angel from heaven and I comin' in through the passage beyond.

MARY P. Aye, maybe.

HARE I thought it might be, an' yet I wasn't sure. Then when I cem in an' seen you all dressed up so grand, says I to myself, a pretty girl that's all dolled up as fine as a peacock is hardly likely to have a voice like a weeshy little nightingale. But I was wrong, I see. So it was yourself I heard singin' so soft and low that it would melt the heart in a man to be listening to the like of it. Well now, wonders will never cease. Would you be vexed with me now if I asked you to let me oil that lovely throat of yours with a drop of Nebby's best?

MARY P. It looks to me you've a hantle ower muckle to say, Mr. Man. But I'll drink wi' ye, for I've a gullet like a hearthstane in hell, this very nicht.

JANET Ach, Mary, come awa' hame. I dinna like his looks, Mary. He's got a face like a warlock. I'm frichtit. Come awa' hame.

MARY P. Tyach. Haud your wheesht. He's a wee shilpit cratur. I could crack him like macaroni if I minded. And he's a nice weel-spoken chiel. It's the last time ever you come out wi' me, Mistress.

HARE You don't like me looks, don't you? Well, if you don't you can go and look at a picture. And who cares what you like anyway, so long as me little sweetheart here'll have a drink with me?

MARY P. Here's to your good health, Mister Irishman.

HARE *(to JANET)* Come along and let's be friends. Have a drop yourself.

(JANET declines)

MARY P. Aweel, we'll have your health again the two of us.

HARE And where does this one live now? *(to JANET)*

JANET I'll take her home with me. Come on, Mary. Come on awa' hame wi' me.

MARY P. Hame wi' you, ye fushionless wee besom? Hame wi' you, ye slut? 'Deed, and I'll no come hame wi' you.

JANET *(catching BURKE's eye as he peers round the settle)* See here, I'm awa'.

MARY P. Then awa' ye go.

HARE Don't you bother with her, sweetheart. Let her go her own way and be damned to her. Dirty little slut. Never heed her. Come over here till you meet me mate. It's he's the right playboy with the girls. Come on over and we'll have such a time that you'll feel like kickin' the stars.

JANET Mary!!

MARY P. The deil harle ye through hell. Give owre skirling like a pea-hen.

JANET Mary, Mary, I'll never see you again.

(MARY sits on BURKE's knee and kisses his forelock)

MARY P. My heart! You're an ugly old dog. You're uglier than your black-faced mate. I'd be blithe to see that ugly phiz grinning at the hangman. *(JANET steals out)* 'Deed an' I will, ae day!

BURKE Be me sowl that's what you'll never see. It's courting and courting the two of us will be from now till the Judgment day. *(To HARE)* What the hell are you gapin' at, you black-faced omadhaun? Away with ye and get me sweetheart another drink.

(He kisses her. She strikes him and springs up.)

MARY P. You stop that. I'll take no familiarity from you or any man.

BURKE Aisy now. Aisy, alannah. I meant no harm. It's great strength you have in them pretty arms of yours. An' a figure that's fine enough to make Venus herself go back into the say. And it's great joy I'd have pullin' you to pieces the way I'd see if you're as beautiful inside as you are out.

MARY P. I'm – I'm feelin' no weel. I'll awa' hame with me.

HARE Ye'll not stir a foot till you drink this. Go on now, it'll put new life into ye.

BURKE An' as for goin' home you'll do nothin' of the kind. It's meself that will take you with me to the grand hotel I'm stoppin' at in West Port. There's beds there fit for a queen to be sleepin' in. An' you can sleep there quiet an' easy till the morning.

MARY P. You're gey gentle to a puir orphan lassie.

BURKE Nebby, Nebby.

LANDLORD Aye.

BURKE Will what's left of that note I gave ye pay for a demijohn?

LANDLORD It will.

BURKE Then give it us quick. We want to be gettin' on to West Port.

(HARE gets the demijohn, and the two of them help MARY up the steps. The LANDLORD polishes the bar with a dirty rag.)

HARE Easy now, me darlin'. We'll help you along. We'll take care of you. Don't you worry, you'll sleep sound this night.

CURTAIN

Scene Two

DR. KNOX's rooms at 10, Surgeons' Square. Four or five hours later. A door at either side and one at back to the right. One window with a broken blind. The grey light of morning is filtering in.

PATERSON, in a leather apron and a sailor's cap with a leather peak, is reading the Bible at a small table on which an oil lamp is set. His skinny arms are bare. He follows the print with his finger and reads aloud in a low, mumbling voice in which the nasal whine of the religious Scot is perceptible.

PATERSON "And if you despise my statutes, or if your soul abhors my judgments, so that ye will not do all my commandments, but that ye break my covenant: I also will do this unto you: I will even appoint over you terror, consumption and the burning ague that shall consume the eyes and cause sorrow of heart . . ." Guid save us, that's an awfu' curse . . . "and ye shall sow your seed in vain, for your enemies shall eat it. And I will set my face against you . . ."

(A key turns in the lock)

What's that?

(KNOX comes in)

(Rising) Ye frichtit me, Dr. Knox. You're early aboot the day.
KNOX Yes. *(He hangs his hat and cloak on a peg and takes off his gloves)*
PATERSON I was expecting twa callants wi' a corpse.
KNOX Good.
PATERSON They was wantin' twelve pound for it, Doctor.
KNOX They were, were they?
PATERSON I'm feart we'll hae to pay.
KNOX Well, pay them, damn it.
PATERSON I havenae the siller by me.
KNOX You can get it from Dr. Anderson or Dr. Wharton Jones. Which is on duty to-night?
PATERSON Dr. Jones is awa'. I was expectin' Dr. Anderson any minute.
KNOX Then what the devil do you mean by bothering me? What's that you're reading? *(Picking up the Bible)*
PATERSON It's lonely for me here. I was reading the Book. It's bread and meat to me is the Book.
KNOX You're a canting humbug, Paterson. There is poetry and philosophy here, but what do you know of poetry and philosophy?
PATERSON There's God's Word in it, Doctor. There's religion.
KNOX If they could cut out the religion it would be a more useful book.

(KNOX goes out, R., slamming the door behind him)

PATERSON Aye. Bang the door. Ye blasphemious bitch!

(A knock)

Wha's there? What's your wull?

WALTER *(outside)* It's all right, Davie. Open.

(PATERSON opens the door. Enter WALTER and RABY. WALTER is sober but haggard.)

PATERSON Oh, Dr. Walter, I'm richt glad to see ye. Are ye all richt noo, Doctor?

WALTER Oh, yes, I'm all right. Raby gave me a corpse-reviver at his lodging, and we walked to Queensferry and swam in the Forth. It washes the troubles off a man, the old Firth of Forth. Have you tried it, Davie?

PATERSON Watter on my skin aye gives me the bronchitis. But I'm real joco you're better. The Chief was askin' for ye.

WALTER The Chief? What's he doing here at this hour?

PATERSON He would be on the randan too yestre'en. He'll have his lectures to get ready. There's times in the early days he would go into the lecture-hall and gesture and rant to naebody but the auld skeleton in the cauld o' the morning. A gey queer thing yon.

WALTER *(sitting down)* Heavens, I'm tired. You tired, Raby?

RABY Oh, so-so.

WALTER You should go away home to your bed. Raby wants to see daybreak in the Chamber of Horrors, David. He has a gruesome mind.

PATERSON The Chief's the only horror I ken here. Do ye ken what he said?

WALTER No. What did he say?

PATERSON Och, it's no' charity to repeat it. It was about the Book.

WALTER What book?

PATERSON The Book of Books. The very Word of the fairest amang the ten thousand of the altogether lovely.

RABY Who is she?

PATERSON She? Young man, take thought. It were more tolerable—

WALTER That's enough, Paterson.

PATERSON While I have a tongue, I will not cease to testify—

WALTER Yes, you will. I'm going to take a nap on the bench. Raby, you'll do so too if you take my advice.

RABY I couldn't sleep here, sir. It's – it's – I couldn't sleep here.

WALTER You're not feared, are you? You're here day after day.

RABY It's all right in the day-time, and it might not be so bad in the night-time, if you understand me; but it's this half-way time is so uncanny.

PATERSON I've been here ten year wi' old Dr. Barclay and two wi' Dr.

Knox, and I've never got ower the eerie feeling o' the half-licht. It's as if the deid men stirred.

(A knock)

RABY What's that?
PATERSON It's a' richt, sir. It'll be a corp I was expectin'.

(He opens the door)

HARE *(without)* Are ye there, janitor?
PATERSON Aye, I'm here. Hae ye got the parcel?
HARE *(To BURKE)* He's here. *(To PATERSON)* We've got it.
PATERSON Bring it in then, and carry it ben.

(BURKE and HARE, drunk, stumble in with a large tea-chest carelessly roped. They drop it on the floor with a heavy thud, and stand near the door.)

WALTER What is your name, my man?
BURKE William Burke, your honour.
WALTER What do you work at?
BURKE I'm an ould soldier, your honour.
WALTER That's not work. What else do you do?
BURKE I'm a shoemaker, your honour.
WALTER I see. This is the body, I presume?
BURKE It is, your honour.
WALTER How did you come by the body?
BURKE It's a young woman, a cousin of Mrs. Hare – this gentleman's good lady, your honour. She come over from Belfast three days back and was took badly in Hare's lodging.
WALTER Took badly with what?
BURKE Wid the colic, your honour.
WALTER What name?
BURKE The name of the young lady, sir?
WALTER Yes, yes.
BURKE Euphemia Brannigan, your worship – I mean, your honour.
WALTER You have been here before with subjects?
BURKE Sure, your honour, I have. Mr. Paterson knows me well.
PATERSON I know him. A very honest man, Dr. Anderson.
WALTER No doubt. Well, shift the box into the mortuary.
BURKE If you please, sir, we'd be afeared to go into a place the like of that. It's bad enough having to bring them here at all. And beggin' your pardon, will you give us our seven guineas and let us be gone out of this?
PATERSON Guineas! You Irish thief. *Guineas!* You cannae trust them, Dr. Anderson, ye cannae really. Pounds it is, sir.

BURKE Holy St. Patrick and all the Saints, will you listen to him? Did you ever hear the like of that, Hare?

HARE I can't believe me ears. Guineas you said, Mr. Paterson. *Seven guineas*, them were your very words.

PATERSON Don't gie them a penny more than they bargained for, Dr. Anderson. Seven pounds it was.

WALTER Oh, damnation. Let them have their pieces of silver. Here's the seven guineas for you, Burke. *(Gives money)*

BURKE May the Lord Almighty watch over you, sir, and keep you in the palm of his hand for your great kindness to honest hard-workin' poor people the like of ourselves.

WALTER *(to HARE)* Here, you. Move that box in there.

HARE In there, is it? Don't ask me to do it, sir. On me two bended knees I'll ask you. It 'ud frighten me out of me seven senses so it would, the Lord be between us and all harm. Come along, Will, we better lose no time or we'll be late for early Mass.

(Exit BURKE and HARE)

(PATERSON is making an entry in his ledger. WALTER throws off his coat and, with RABY, lifts the box towards the door at the back.)

WALTER By George, it's heavy! Easy there. I can't compliment you on your friends, Davie.

PATERSON You should have had a keek at the corp before you paid them. And seven guineas! I never heard the like.

(RABY and WALTER carry the box out of sight)

WALTER Oh, it will be all right. They know which side their bread's buttered on, these hounds. *(From the room)* Bring a tack-hammer, Davie; they've nailed down the lid.

PATERSON Verra weel, sir.

(He goes out. WALTER leans on the door-jamb, waiting for him and talking over his shoulder to RABY.)

WALTER Wait a minute, Raby. He's getting a hammer. Light a candle.

RABY They – they've nailed a lock of red hair between the lid and the sides.

WALTER Eh? What do you say? Lord, my head aches!

RABY They've nailed a lock of red hair between the lid and the sides. Six inches of it. It's very pretty hair.

WALTER It's nice to have an eye for the beautiful, Raby, even in Davie Paterson's dead-house.

RABY The – the lid's fairly loose. I – I think I could . . . Yes, that's it. The lid's off now, sir.

WALTER Oh! Davie, never mind the hammer. *(He goes into the mortuary)* Bring that candle over here.

(Enter PATERSON, with a hammer)

(A pause)

WALTER *(screaming)* My God!

(He rushes into the ante-room, white and shaking. He carries the candle.)

(RABY's scared face appears in the doorway)

PATERSON God save us! What's the matter, Doctor?
WALTER Raby, did you see what I saw? Am I still drunk? Did you see that face?
RABY Yes.
WALTER Have you seen it before?
RABY I think I have.
WALTER You *think?* You *think?* Take the candle and go and look at it again.
RABY Not for a thousand pounds.
WALTER Did I see that girl last night?
PATERSON Hoots, toots, you were in nae condition to see anyone last night.
WALTER Damn you, be quiet, you! Raby, was that the girl I spoke to in the Three Tuns?
RABY Yes.
WALTER And she's dead! *(He sits down on the bench)* She was so beautiful, a man's heart stopped when he looked at her. . . .
RABY She looked in excellent health, I must say.
WALTER *(Springing up)* There's been foul work here. Raby, Paterson, get after those men.

(He rushes to the door and fumbles with the lock)

(Enter KNOX)

KNOX May I ask what is all this?
WALTER Dr. Knox, there's been murder done.

(He is on the edge of collapse. RABY catches him by the arm.)

Let go, Raby. Dr. Knox, there's been murder done. We must get them. They can't be far off. They left a moment ago. Let go, Raby.
RABY You won't catch them now, sir. Wait a bit. There's plenty of time.
KNOX Has Dr. Anderson been drinking, Paterson?

PATERSON Weel, sir, as you might say . . .

WALTER I'm not drunk. I swear I'm not. Go in there, sir. Look for yourself. She's dead! She's dead!

KNOX You are a very foolish young man. You've been drinking spirits. You're reeking of stale spirits. Go home to your bed.

WALTER Dr. Knox, a very few hours ago I was in conversation with a young woman in the Three Tuns public-house. She was brought up here ten minutes ago by two Irish ruffians. Rigor mortis had set in, but the body was still warm. I believe to the bottom of my soul that she has had foul play.

KNOX Sit down. Give me the candle. Come with me, Paterson.

(He goes into the mortuary)

WALTER Oh, Raby, what shall I do? What shall I do? And this may not be the first time, either. You heard that man? They've brought bodies here before. I may have seen them. I forget . . . Mary! That was it. Mary Paterson. Her soft, cool hands on my head! . . .

RABY I shouldn't take it so much to heart. I expect it's all right, really.

WALTER All right! She was so full of life, and they've let the life out of her. Oh, the bloody murderers!

(Re-enter KNOX and PATERSON)

KNOX What are you raving about, man?

WALTER Dr. Knox, don't you realise? That girl was murdered!

KNOX How the devil do you know? There isn't a mark of violence on her body.

WALTER She was murdered, I tell you!

KNOX Dear, dear, dear, dear, dear. What a pity! Murdered, eh? And suppose she were, Dr. Anderson? Do you imagine her life was so significant that we must grue at her death? She looks to me to have been some common trull off the streets.

WALTER Don't you dare say that!

KNOX Sit down, sit down, sit down. I see. I understand you, my dear lad. *Et ego* in Arcadia. But it is past the hour for sentiment. At four in the morning cold common-sense creeps into the chamber, and it is now after half-past five. You must not sentimentalise, if you please, over my anatomy-room subjects. You owe them at least that respect.

RABY Sir, he thinks he recognises the girl.

WALTER Thinks!

KNOX Ah! . . . It will be perhaps a satisfaction to you to know that your friend will be improving the minds of the youth of the town in place of corrupting their morals. . . . Come, my dear lad, I perceive you have had a shock. You must not mind my rough tongue. It is a defect in me as sentimentality is in you. The life of this poor wretch is ended. It is surely a better thing that her beauty of form should be at the service of divine science than at the service of any drunken buck with a crown in his pocket. Our emotions, Walter, are for ever tugging at our coat-tails lest at any time we should look the Truth in the face. . . .

WALTER The truth is she was murdered. You know she was. You are as bad as a murderer yourself. Worse. You pay blood-money!

KNOX You've been drinking.

WALTER This is what all your fine words come to! This is your passion! This is your religion! You hire murderers to choke the life out of poor, handsome girls! You pay blood-money!

KNOX You paid the money, Mr. Anderson, I think.

WALTER God help me, so I did!

KNOX That fact seems to me pertinent, if we are talking of blood-money. Another point that may interest you is this: that if I did not think you a drunken young fool, in no way responsible for his words, I would call you out and shoot you like a dog at twenty paces.

WALTER You mean a duel?

KNOX You are very intelligent.

WALTER Then I'll fight you. You know to what address to send your friends. After I have reported this matter to the police I shall be at my lodging for the rest of the day.

KNOX Can you shoot the pips out of a cinq of hearts at forty paces? If you can, it is strange that I had not heard of your accomplishment. I can perform that feat. You are a good prosector in your sober moments. I have no wish to be compelled to maim you.

WALTER You are a coward and a murderer. Take that. (*He strikes at KNOX, who catches his wrist*)

KNOX Mr. Anderson, I shall not require your services this forenoon. In the afternoon you will present yourself at my private room and apologise to me. In the meantime you will go to bed. In the future I advise you to abstain from alcohol. Now take yourself off.

(*After a pause, WALTER turns about and goes*)

RABY Would you like me to go down to the police-station, sir? I know where it is.

KNOX You do, do you, you gaby? You poroncephalic monstrosity! You will keep quiet, imbecile! You will gabble of nothing you have seen or heard or thought this morning. You will forget with that Lethe-like forgetfulness you apply to your studies. Do you understand?

RABY I understand, sir.

KNOX Then go and help the janitor to prepare the subject. I shall demonstrate it to the class this afternoon.

RABY Very well, sir.

(KNOX *throws a piercing glance at him, and goes out, R.*)

(PATERSON *pulls up the blind. It is broad daylight.*)

PATERSON It's a nice morning, Mr. Raby.

RABY Yes. . . . I say, he's a cool fish, the Governor.

PATERSON Robert the Devil they call him.

RABY Deep, ain't he?

PATERSON As deep as the pit.

RABY What do you think? Does he think they knocked that girl on the head?

PATERSON His Maker only kens what yon man's thinking.

CURTAIN

ACT THREE

The same scene as in Act One. It is early afternoon on 28th January, 1829.

The DISHARTS are from home and the furniture is covered with dust sheets; the curtain is drawn and the blinds are down.

The key is heard turning in the door and enter JESSIE ANN, the maid, precipitately. She is in outdoor dress and is obviously excited. She carries a taper and a basket.

MAID Guid save us! A' the fiends of hell are louse the day!

(She lights the fire and goes to the window, throwing off the dust sheets as she goes. She draws the curtain and pulls up the blind.)

Michty, what a day of days! And there's the chaise and me no ready!

(A bell rings. She rushes out, grabbing some of the remaining dust sheets. After a pause the maid returns with the MISSES DISHART, who are in travelling dress. The MAID has taken off her bonnet and shawl.)

If you'll come awa' in here, Miss Dishart. I've just lit the fire.

AMELIA So I see, Jessie Ann. Just!

MAID Michty, this is a bonny like home-coming frae foreign parts. But it's a God's mercy you're safe. I'll hae a tassie o' tae ready for ye in a jiffy. It's on in the kitchen, and I brocht some griddle scones for ye, Miss Amy.

AMELIA But what possessed you to be so late? I told you to be here at six.

MAID Six! I was feart to cross ma Auntie's door-step. Did ye no see the crood? Did ye no hear them?

AMELIA We heard a noise up at the road end. What is it? An election?

MAID An election! Did ye no ken they were hanging Burke the murderer this morning?

AMELIA Burke the murderer?

MAID Aye. Now, if I didna forget ye wouldna' hear tell!

MARY Oh, Amelia! The vinaigrette we thought we'd lost at Dover!

AMELIA You startled me. What about it?

MARY It's here! It's been standing here all the time!

AMELIA How odd, darling. Jessie Ann, if they had been hanging the General Buonaparte it would be no excuse for being late.

MAID But it was the croods, Mem. A' the gangrel buddies in the toun raging roun' the streets crying, 'Gie us Hare! Gie us Hare!'

AMELIA Give us whose hair? Do compose yourself, Jessie Ann.

(MARY has taken off her travelling cloak and is tidying herself before the mirror. RABY appears at the door carrying a heavy cabin trunk. He stands gaping and breathing heavily.)

AMELIA Mr. Raby, I am so sorry. You should not have brought that heavy case up here. Do put it down.
RABY Indeed, it is all right, ma'am. It's nothing. Nothing whatever.
MARY I'll help you, Mr. Raby.
RABY Not at all. Not at all.

(They lower the trunk between them)

MARY It is heavy! I believe Amelia has killed the courier and brought him home to stuff him. He was so fat and so funny with his beautiful moustachios. Is he in the box, Amelia?

(RABY stares at her)

AMELIA Mary, how can you say such things?

(MARY completes the drawing of the blinds and curtains)

How ungrateful we are, Mr. Raby! And it was so kind of you to meet us at the stage.
RABY *(staring after MARY)* What! Oh, I beg your pardon, ma'am. Yes. Oh, yes! It was nothing. Dr. Anderson will be here presently. The new demonstrator has arrived, you know. Dr. Anderson was showing him the – the ropes.
AMELIA What new demonstrator?
RABY Dr. Anderson is leaving Edinburgh, ma'am. Didn't you know?
AMELIA No. He has not written since we left Dover. Why is he leaving Edinburgh?
RABY Well – ah – perhaps you had better ask him yourself, ma'am. I mean, ma'am, he is sure to know, isn't he? I am no hand at explaining. He'll be here presently. He said he would. But he made a point of somebody meeting you. And I happened to be about.
AMELIA That was very thoughtful of Walter and very kind of you.
RABY Oh, not at all. Not at all. It's of no consequence. Only the streets are not over-safe to-day.
AMELIA Really? I didn't see anything to be alarmed about. Oh! what was that you were telling us, Jessie Ann? I am afraid I didn't listen very attentively.
MAID The riots, Mem. Ower the heid o' the hanging. Burke, Mem. I saw them hang him wi' my own eyes, Mem. Fornenst my Auntie's hoose in the High Street. Faces on a' the causies and faces at a' the windies. And oh, ye should ha' seen him, Mem. He'd a naipkin ower his heid. And a big fellow in a black surtout took awa' what he was staunin' on, Mem. And he played

paw paw for it wi' his feet and syne birled roond three times. And syne he gied a kin' o' a hunch wi' his shouthers and syne he hung still. And oh! I was feart, Mem!

AMELIA How perfectly horrible!

MAID He was drunk, they say, Miss, when they choked him. And then a' them that was there begood tae cry: 'Knox neist! Hang Knox.'

AMELIA Good God, girl, what you do mean?

MAID Knox, Mem, Dr. Knox. *(Proudly)* *Our* Dr. Knox.

AMELIA *(sitting down)* Mary, what is all this about?

MARY I haven't the remotest notion. Dearest, you look ill. Take my smelling-salts.

MAID I've been telling you, Miss Mary Belle. They broke all his windows yestreen. He's in a ballant too. A'body's singing it:

"Up the close and doon the stair,
Ben the hoose wi' Burke and Hare.
Burke's the butcher, Hare's the thief,
Knox the boy who buys the beef."

That's our Dr. Knox, Miss Mary Belle.

AMELIA Mr. Raby! What has happened? You never told us!

MARY We hadn't heard . . .

RABY Well, you see, of course, it was just after you sailed for Dieppe. It was all a frightful scandal. And we've certainly not heard the last of it yet.

AMELIA But who is this Burke and what has he to do with Dr. Knox?

RABY Well, you see it's this way . . .

AMELIA Is Dr. Knox in danger?

RABY Well, yes, ma'am, in a way. But you don't know Dr. Knox. He can fight. They'll catch a Tartar in Dr. Knox.

MARY Can't you see you are upsetting my sister? What has happened, man?

RABY Well, ma'am, it's very difficult to explain. But it was this way. – Oh, thank God, here's Dr. Anderson.

(Enter WALTER)

Well, here you are, Dr. Anderson. I met the ladies all right. Here they are all right.

WALTER Good-afternoon. You shouldn't have left the door open. Anybody might have come in, and all the bad characters in the city are abroad to-day.

AMELIA Walter, what is all this about?

WALTER Hasn't Raby explained?

RABY Yes, Doctor, but they didn't seem to cotton on to what I was saying.

MARY Do tell us, Walter. Go away, Jessie Ann. Have you nothing at all to do?

(The MAID goes away reluctantly)

AMELIA Sit down, Mr. Raby.

WALTER You left to go on the Grand Tour on Hallowe'en?

AMELIA Yes, yes.

WALTER That night, an old vagrant Irishwoman was found murdered in Burke's lodging in the West Port. This man Burke and his associate Hare had inveigled her into a trap and smothered her in cold blood. An artisan called Gray gave the alarm.

AMELIA Go on. Where does Dr. . . .? Go on.

WALTER At the trial Hare turned King's evidence. And he told an appalling story. November a year ago, Burke and Hare sold the body of an old pensioner to the anatomy-room to recoup themselves for his rent. They were paid five pounds ten. They had some plausible cock-and-bull story. The rooms to which they took the body were those of Dr. Knox. Paterson, the janitor, and Wharton Jones bought the body. We – we were very short of subjects at the time.

MARY Oh, Walter!

AMELIA Don't, Mary. Go on.

WALTER Their next lodger was a woman. She was an unconscionable time in dying, and they – they put a pillow over her face. They sold her body to Paterson. They killed about sixteen people – they are not quite certain of the numbers.

AMELIA What a dreadful thing! And Dr. Knox . . .?

WALTER *(rises)* Dr. Knox never in his life set eyes on either of these men. I swear to that. He left the supply of subjects to – others.

MARY To whom did he leave it?

WALTER Oh, to – to his assistants and his porter. He never – he never would deal with known resurrectionists, and that made it difficult. He . . .

MARY Oh, Walter, did you buy bodies from these men?

WALTER Yes, I did.

(Silence)

AMELIA Go on.

WALTER Burke was hanged this morning. There has been an outcry against Knox. They are preaching against him from every pulpit. Christopher North is lashing him with lies in the Press. Every man's hand is against him. The other surgeons have deserted him. The mob is mad for his blood.

AMELIA But I thought— Surely he has fled the town?

WALTER No. He is facing it out.

AMELIA What is he doing?

WALTER He is delivering his lectures as if nothing had happened. He is too proud even to answer his persecutors. God knows I admired and loved him, but never so much as at this hour.

AMELIA Is he in danger?

WALTER They broke his windows last night and tried to set fire to his house. He came out and faced them with two pistols in his hands. The mob hadn't the courage to go on. He is a dead shot, you know.

AMELIA But the constables? Have they not given him a guard?

WALTER He won't have a guard.

RABY He's lectured every day since the trial. Nobody can stop him. We all carry life preservers and take turns to mount guard. He's afraid of nothing. He's a hero, that's what he is.

AMELIA Forgive me, Walter. Your news is a little overwhelming. I – I think I shall lie down for a little. I should like to see you before you go.

(She goes out)

RABY Do you want me, Dr. Anderson?

WALTER No . . . At least . . . Why do you ask?

RABY Dr. Knox's lecture is in twenty minutes.

WALTER And do you want to miss it?

RABY I would rather die. *Au revoir*, Miss Mary Belle. I shall see you again, sir.

MARY *Au revoir*, Mr. Raby. *(He goes)* Mr. Raby says that you are leaving Edinburgh, Walter.

WALTER Yes, I am leaving Edinburgh.

(Pause)

MARY Amelia and I were surprised to see you to-day.

WALTER You were Scottish enough not to show it. In the circumstances I had to come. You see why I hesitated at first. *(Pause)* I am glad I came.

MARY I am glad you came too, Walter. . . . Walter!

WALTER Yes!

MARY It is nearly six months since we saw each other.

WALTER Six months. Yes.

MARY Six months is a long time.

WALTER I found it long, but you had new places and the stir of travel. Did you enjoy your journey?

MARY No. Oh, no, no! It's no use pretending. I missed you dreadfully.

WALTER Did you? Oh, did you? Heavens, how I missed you too! There was never a time when I needed you more.

MARY Walter! Then why didn't you write? Were you too proud? Oh! I'm a beast. That night, that night, that night! I acted like a madwoman. I drove you into the street . . .

WALTER You? Oh, my beautiful, no, no! You were right. God knows how right you were. . . . But something else happened that night. It shook me to the depths. I have the horror of it still in my bones.

MARY Darling, you are ill and unhappy.

WALTER I suppose I am. What does unhappiness matter?

MARY It is terrible to see you unhappy. Darling, forgive me. We'll forget it all. We'll begin again.

WALTER Dearest, dearest, there is nothing to forgive.

MARY Then I'll wait for you for ever and ever. And you can stay in Edinburgh and help Dr. Knox to fight it out. And everything will be as if it hadn't been.

WALTER I can't stay in Edinburgh. I can't stay in Scotland.

MARY But why? Dr. Knox is in need of friends. I . . .

WALTER Dr. Knox understands. I wanted to go before. But he persuaded me to stay. I must go to London now.

MARY Is there a better Anatomy School in London?

WALTER No. Not so good. Not nearly so good.

MARY Then I don't understand. Walter . . . you said something just now . . . about something horrible . . . that happened. . . . What did you mean?

WALTER You mustn't ask what happened. That shadow mustn't fall on you, too, my dearest one, my darling . . . You must trust me. I am taking this step because I must. There is no other way.

(Pause)

MARY Very well, Walter.

WALTER You will marry me no matter what happened?

MARY It is nothing to me what happened. I love you. Oh, Walter, I thought of you every step of the tour.

WALTER Did you? Did you?

MARY I cried my eyes out at my cruelty to you.

WALTER Oh, you weren't cruel. You were just.

MARY I was cruel. It was because I loved you. All lovers are cruel. Kiss me again. Is the pain at your heart well again?

WALTER Almost well again.

MARY Walter, what happened on that night?

WALTER Mary Belle, I can never tell you that. You must help me to forget it.

MARY But how can I help you to forget it if I don't know what it is?

WALTER This way.

(Enter AMELIA)

AMELIA Walter! Mary Belle!

MARY Oh, Amy!

AMELIA What has happened?

MARY Don't ask such silly questions.

WALTER Mary Belle is coming to London with me. She has forgiven me.

AMELIA I think you yourself have more to forgive, Walter.

MARY Yes, hasn't he? And he doesn't realise it. Isn't he a darling?

AMELIA You are both my darlings. What's that?

(An approaching rumour of voices is heard. WALTER goes to the window.)

WALTER Some of the rioters are coming this way. Keep back from the window.

MARY Are they after you? Is that your secret?

WALTER No, no. I'm too small a fish. No. Hare and Knox will satisfy them. . . . I can't see them yet.

(The voices are louder. Cries of 'Hang Knox' predominate.)

Here comes someone. He's walking briskly. Nearly a run. By Jove, it's the Chief. They're after him. I must let him in.

(He rushes out. MARY looks out of the window, biting her handkerchief.)

AMELIA Oh, where shall we hide him?

(There is a roar as the mob rushes past. Enter KNOX. He wears a military riding cloak, and a brace of pistols in a belt strapped round his middle. His bald head is bleeding from a slight graze. WALTER follows. The noise dies away.)

KNOX By Heaven, they stone me! They stone me! They stone me! Pigs! Offal! *Canaille!* Rot their souls! I'm no mealy-mouthed saint and martyr, as they shall very soon find. I'm not the sort of man to die in a night-shirt looking like an angel. Not I, by God! I'll break a few heads first.

AMELIA Doctor, don't. Stand back from the window. You are beside yourself.

KNOX Beside myself. Then, faith, I am in better company than I've been during the last five minutes. . . . I beg your pardon, Miss Amelia. It is somewhat a heady business to be embroiled with a mob. I forgot my notoriously polite manners.

(The noise dies away)

MARY *(at the window)* They have gone.

KNOX I have given them the slip, it appears. Good-afternoon, Miss Dishart; your servant, Miss Mary Belle. You look both of you in excellent health. You have returned early. I expected to see your house still closed. I am glad it was not for more than one reason. I must hurry on now, or I shall be late for my lecture. I hope to pay my duty to you this evening – if I am still welcome.

AMELIA Doctor, your head is hurt. We must get bandages.

KNOX No, no. It's nothing.

AMELIA Is it safe for you to go out?

KNOX Safe? Oh, I think so.

AMELIA Don't show yourself at the window.

KNOX Ah! Someone has told you that I am unpopular? Never mind, they are more afraid of me than I am of them.

MARY Do sit down, Dr. Knox, and rest yourself. You have been running.

KNOX I running? Nothing of the sort.

WALTER Dr. Knox, I don't think it would be wise for you to go out again till nightfall.

KNOX I have said that I will lecture. It will take more than the riff-raff of Auld Reekie to prevent me.

WALTER The public dissection of Burke is going on now and the rioters are blockading Surgeons' Hall. It will be impossible for you to get near it.

KNOX I shall get through somehow.

WALTER Very well, sir. But you had better wait a moment or two. There are organised bands out after you. It is better to know beforehand how the enemy is disposed. Let me go and find out, sir. I shall only be a few minutes.

KNOX Very well.

AMELIA Is it safe?

WALTER Perfectly safe. I am not so kenspeckle as Dr. Knox, I am afraid.

AMELIA Then do be careful, dear Walter.

WALTER I shan't be long.

(He goes)

AMELIA Do be seated, Dr. Knox.

(KNOX takes off his cloak and sits down)

KNOX Thank you, ma'am.

(A silence. KNOX looks at his watch.)

KNOX It is twenty minutes to the hour. I thought so. That is my only superstition, Miss Amelia.

AMELIA This is a terrible time, Dr. Knox. My sister and I have just heard of the monstrous things that are being said against you. We are so sorry.

KNOX You waste your sympathy on me. I find all this inexpressibly exhilarating. It is like swimming in a storm.

MARY Dr. Knox . . .

KNOX Signorina?

MARY No, it doesn't matter.

KNOX You were about to ask a question.

MARY Dr. Knox, you and I have never been friends.

AMELIA Oh, Mary! Candid, rather quarrelsome friends, but still friends!

MARY No, not friends at all; but please believe that I and my sister will listen to nothing that anybody says – says against you in this frightful business.

KNOX I am sincerely grateful. I expected nothing less of you.

MARY Only . . .

KNOX You make a reservation?

MARY No, no. But . . . Doctor, why is Walter going to London?

KNOX I should say because of some essential and ineradicable strain of vulgarity in his nature. It is this that drives many of our most promising young men to these provincial towns. They shiver in the snell east wind of Modern Athens. London! Pompous Ignorance sits enthroned there and welcomes Pretentious Mediocrity with flattery and gifts. Oh, dull and witless city! Very hell for the restless, inquiring, sensitive soul. Paradise for the snob, the parasite and the prig; the pimp, the placeman and the cheap-jack. The women chatter like parakeets, the men fawn like jackals. On my soul, vulgarity or no vulgarity, I cannot tell you why Walter Anderson is going there. Or what there is in London to awaken in a realist any feeling but loathing and contempt. Yet she entraps great men and sucks their blood. Her streets are littered with their bones.

MARY Dr. Knox, six months ago, Walter left this house in a rage. You remember. He has not been back till to-day. Something happened that night. What was it?

KNOX My dear young lady, even if I ever knew, it is not likely I should remember.

MARY Whatever it was, it drove him from us and from Edinburgh. Our quarrel wouldn't have done it. We have quarrelled again and again. Tell me.

KNOX I know what you mean now. Yes. He was excited, poor boy. He felt you had treated him ill. His imagination was ready for all manner of phantasmagoria. A subject was brought into the anatomy rooms by some of our middlemen. He thought he recognised her – a girl, I think it was; I am nearly sure it was a girl – and would have it that she had been murdered.

AMELIA Murdered!

MARY But had she been?

KNOX How can I tell? I know enough now to be sure that I can trust nobody.

AMELIA Dr. Knox, what did you do? What did he do?

KNOX If you want to know, he told me I had murdered her.

MARY What did you say to him?

KNOX I told him not to play the fool. If it was anybody's duty to probe into the source of our supply – and I stoutly deny that it was – the responsibility was his. He apologised to me that same afternoon for his wild words.

MARY And that was all?

KNOX That was all.

MARY And he said he must leave Edinburgh?

KNOX Yes, something of the sort. I could not possibly allow him to do so.

MARY Why not?

KNOX My dear young lady, do you realise the pains and patience I had spent in making Mr. Anderson into some semblance of an anatomist? Do you realise that I have a class of 400 students to whom my honour compels me to do my duty? Do you realise that Mr. Anderson was my demonstrator? Have you any conception of the trouble and time it takes to replace a demonstrator? I simply could not spare him. I have another demonstrator now and Walter can go to London or Jericho if he likes. If he remembers a tenth of what I have taught him he will be a great man there in a twelvemonth.

MARY I understand. Dr. Knox, will you excuse me?

KNOX Certainly, my dear. You should marry him after all. They will make him a knight. You see if they don't. You will be Lady Anderson and drive in your carriage to visit fat duchesses.

MARY I intend to marry him, Dr. Knox.

(MARY goes out)

KNOX *(to AMELIA)* You see I am the same as ever. Adversity has not taught me to bridle my unfortunate tongue. I had better go.

(He rises and puts on his cloak)

AMELIA You must wait for Walter to return, Doctor.

KNOX He is taking a very long time. Miss Amelia, I cannot help this jeering vein of talk. But it is a poor reward for loyalty.

AMELIA My sister needs no rewards to be loyal to you, Dr. Knox.

KNOX And you?

AMELIA I think you need hardly ask.

(Pause)

KNOX Miss Amelia, in this quiet house I have known the only happiness I have ever known. You will never know what you have done for me.

AMELIA Your visits have been a great happiness to us. We are proud of your friendship.

(Pause)

KNOX You understand me so well, so well. You see the little pink shivering boy crouching within this grotesque, this grisly shell of a body. You are sunshine to me, Amelia. You are safe harbourage in storms. I love you. You are everything to me. I love you.

AMELIA Doctor, you mustn't—

KNOX Say only the word and I'll strike my flag. In the light of your presence I see this battle as so much foolish bombast and vanity. Come with me to Italy. Will you come? We'll forget this squalid, torturing farce. We can only live once. Come with me. I love you.

AMELIA And how is Mrs. Knox? These times must be very trying for her.

KNOX Oh, how can you! Mrs. Knox, madam, enjoys her usual ill-health.

AMELIA I am sorry she keeps so poorly. I have so looked forward to meeting her some day.

KNOX God forbid that you should.

AMELIA You can hardly expect me to go to Italy with you without having the benefit of Mrs. Knox's advice. It would be most valuable.

KNOX Woman, have you no heart? Have you no manners? You must know that no real lady would make her lover talk about his wife. It embarrasses him beyond bearing.

AMELIA I know that. (A knock) Ah, here is Jessie Ann with the tea. Come in.

KNOX I shall not drink tea with you . . .

(Enter JESSIE ANN with tea-things)

AMELIA Sit down. Take off your cloak. I feel very much inclined to whip you. That will do, Jessie Ann. (The MAID goes out) Now try to be a man and not a barn-storming tenor.

KNOX I will try.

AMELIA Do you take sugar? How absurd of me to forget.

KNOX No.

AMELIA No what?

KNOX No, thank you.

AMELIA That is better. Would you like one of Jessie Ann's griddle scones?

KNOX No, thank you. One thing and another have impaired my appetite.

AMELIA But Jessie Ann will be very disappointed. She was so proud when you used to commend her griddle scones. For Jessie Ann's sake. Please.

KNOX A hundred thousand devils take Jessie Ann and her griddle scones; and with the deepest regret you also, madam.

AMELIA Doctor, you are becoming quite heated again. You must . . . Oh, what a callous wretch I am! Your poor head. Does it hurt? It must be bandaged.

(She rings the bell)

KNOX No, no, it is nothing. A glancing blow from a stone.

(Enter JESSIE ANN)

AMELIA Jessie Ann, have you been listening at the door?

MAID No, no, Mem, honestly, Mem.

AMELIA Go and get some bandages and hot water, and be quick.
MAID Yes, Mem.

(She goes)

AMELIA *(at the window)* I do hope nothing has happened to Walter.
KNOX I think it unlikely. He is an active fellow, and the mob are cowards to a man.
AMELIA Their hatred is a dreadful thing.
KNOX Dreadful? It is the only compliment they can pay me.
AMELIA You will stay in Edinburgh?
KNOX Yes, ma'am. No man shall threaten or bully or talk me out of Edinburgh. I do my little dog's tricks for you, ma'am. I love soft voices and sugar, but I do not brook the whip.
AMELIA You will talk yourself out of Edinburgh. You are a very injudicious man.
KNOX That's as may be, ma'am. I shall do what I believe to be right, as I have always done.
AMELIA As you have always done?
KNOX What do you mean?

(Re-enter MAID with a bowl and some bandages)

AMELIA Thank you. Put them down there. Now you may take the tea-things. I shall not need you after that. You have brought the lint? Ah, yes, here it is.

(Exit MAID with tea-things)

Now let us have a look at the wound. Am I hurting you?
KNOX Not at this moment, ma'am. But you have the capacity to hurt me.
AMELIA It is not very deep. Am I not the clever surgeon? Why don't you let the ladies be surgeons, Dr. Knox? Are you afraid of them?
KNOX I am afraid of them. Miss Amelia . . . I find myself at a loss . . . Do you think that I am a murderer?
AMELIA Heavens! What a question! Keep still.
KNOX I must know what is in your mind.
AMELIA Keep quite still. Doctor, it is terrible that you should be put in this position. I think of you galloping on a crusade with your eyes to the front, fixed on your goal. How could you know that your horses' hoofs were trampling poor crushed human bodies? You don't realise it yet.
KNOX Good God, ma'am, do you think that of me! Do you think because I strut and rant and put on a bold face that my soul isn't sick within me at the horror of what I have done? What *I* have done. Do you hear?
AMELIA No, no, you didn't mean to . . .
KNOX Didn't mean to? What a beast's excuse. Do me the justice to believe that I would never make that excuse even to myself. No, I carry the deaths

of these poor wretches round my neck till I die. And perhaps after that. Perhaps after that. . . . But I tell you this, that the cause is between Robert Knox and Almighty God. I shall answer to no one else. As for the world, I shall face it. I shall play out the play till the final curtain.

AMELIA Doctor. Oh, poor Doctor! What will you do?

KNOX That is easy. I have acquired certain knowledge of benefit to mankind. It is my duty to pass that knowledge on. I shall lecture at Surgeons' Square as long as I have strength. And nobody on earth shall prevent me. That is clear. That is simple. The things that will trouble me in the night are not so simple.

AMELIA Is the bandage comfortable?

KNOX I thank you, it is.

AMELIA *(suddenly kissing him)* Oh, Robert, you are not the only one who has to fight battles.

(KNOX kisses her hand silently. Enter MARY.)

MARY Amelia, Walter has not come back yet.

KNOX I will go and find him.

MARY You are sure your value to Science is not too great for you to hazard yourself so?

KNOX Miss Mary Belle, you may use me as you like. I am not the monstrous fine fellow I thought I was half an hour ago.

MARY You are not a monstrous fine fellow at all.

KNOX Oh! . . . You think I am a murderer, do you? A murderer! Or worse than that, a sneaking *souteneur* of assassins – too great a coward to strike the blow? You think well of me, by Heaven!

MARY I think you are a vain, hysterical, talented, stupid man. I think that you are wickedly blind and careless when your mind is fixed on something. But all men are like that. There is nothing very uncommon about you, Dr. Knox.

KNOX Indeed, ma'am? I shall leave posterity to judge of that.

MARY Posterity will have to be very clever to judge you justly, Dr. Knox.

KNOX At least it will have the facts before it.

MARY But the excuses will be hard to find.

KNOX I make no excuses. You will do me the justice to say that.

MARY You are too pig-headed.

AMELIA Mary Belle!

KNOX I shall take my leave of you.

MARY You are sulking now.

KNOX *(to AMELIA)* Madam, have I your permission to withdraw?

AMELIA Nothing of the sort. You will stay here till Walter comes back.

KNOX Ladies, I will not consent to be treated like a naughty schoolboy. Do you know who I am? Do you know that I am the apostolic successor of Cuvier, the great naturalist? Do you know that, although I am a comparatively young man, much of my work is already immortal? Do you know that I brush aside that snarling pack of curs, strong in the knowledge that the name of Knox will resound throughout the ages . . .

MARY Yes, for bullying and blustering at poor Mary of Scots. Don't be absurd, Dr. Knox.

(She goes to the window)

KNOX Absurd! I congratulate you on your sense of humour.

MARY Oh, if you prefer to be sinister, you are welcome. . . . Oh! Thank God, there is Walter at last!

AMELIA Doctor, you must not mind her. She is naturally very – very discomposed. She does not mean half she says.

KNOX I see, she is merely making conversation. To put me at my ease. . . . Have I shrunk visibly, Miss Dishart?

AMELIA What do you mean?

KNOX I feel as if I were two feet high and still dwindling. I never felt so small in my life.

AMELIA It will do you good. It must be so dull always to be a giant.

(Enter WALTER)

MARY *(running to him)* Walter!

WALTER My love, my darling! *(Embrace)*

AMELIA Mary Belle, darling.

KNOX You have settled your difficulties then?

WALTER What difficulties? . . . Oh, Dr. Knox, I had almost forgotten. It isn't safe for you to go out yet. There is a crowd two thousand strong outside the Surgeons' Hall. I couldn't get through, sir, but I saw Raby, and he said he'd try. They have broken the windows and are very threatening. There are patrols all over the town, too. One of them is doubling back on the trail. Someone may have seen you come in, sir.

KNOX Then they will break your windows too, Miss Amelia. I had better go.

AMELIA But they will kill you.

KNOX What will that matter? I am a nobody.

AMELIA No, no, no, Doctor. I am sure you are a – a very good anatomist. Isn't he, Walter?

WALTER He is a great anatomist.

MARY We are not discussing Dr. Knox's proficiency, but his immediate safety. Will they be watching the back of the house?

WALTER I don't know. It is probable. The lane opens into the main street.

MARY If he went that way now . . .

KNOX Do you still take sufficient interest in this vain, careless, stupid person to . . .

94

MARY For God's sake don't be a fool. I'll give you an old gown and shawl and a market basket. We could go out like mistress and maid going shopping.
KNOX Or you could carry me out in the buck basket, buried in dirty linen. No, thank you, ma'am. I have my pistols and I will fight if necessary.
AMELIA You are gesturing again, Dr. Knox. I thought we had cured you of that. . . . Hush!

(An approaching rumour of voices is heard)

Here they come.
KNOX I'll go to meet them. *(He assumes his cloak.)*

(The two women throw themselves at him)

MARY No, Dr. Knox.
AMELIA You must stay here.

(The din becomes louder. A hunting horn is heard.)

KNOX Ladies, ladies! Don't you realise? There may he bloodshed. I could never forgive myself if . . .
MARY It will be all right. They may not know you are here.
WALTER I do think you had better stay, sir.

(Crash at the door. Enter the MAID as if shot from a gun.)

MAID Oh, Miss Amelia, Miss Amelia!
AMELIA Compose yourself, Jessie Ann. What is it?
MAID A wheen o' ruffians at the door. They want Dr. Knox to hang him.

(KNOX throws back the flaps of his cloak and looks to the priming of his pistols. A stone crashes through the window. Someone in the street calls for a battering-ram.)

MARY Dr. Knox, you must come upstairs to my room. You can escape along the roof.
AMELIA Yes, do, Dr. Knox.

(The hunting horn sounds again. WALTER takes up a poker.)

WALTER There isn't much time. Give me one of your pistols, and I'll hold them at bay from the steps.
KNOX I'll speak to them myself. I'll tell them what I think of mobs.
WALTER No, no, sir.

(KNOX fires a pistol through the window. A loud crash is heard. The voices become louder.)

They've broken down the door.
MAID They're in the house. Oh, mercy me, they're in the house.

KNOX Get behind me, everyone. Do you hear me?

(He sweeps the women behind him, and stands facing the door. WALTER, with his back to the window, stands on guard with the poker. After a short pause RABY rushes in. His clothes are torn. With one hand he holds a handkerchief to a bleeding nose, and with the other a bludgeon. A dozen or more STUDENTS, variously armed and battered, follow him.)

KNOX Stand back, you! . . . Oh, it's you, is it?

RABY Are you all right, Dr. Knox? Are you all right, sir?

KNOX Yes, I am all right. What has happened?

RABY We heard they were after you. We came down, hell for leather. They had the door down before we reached 'em. We gave 'em hell, sir. *(To his bodyguard)* He's all right, Knoxites. Three cheers for Dr. Dox. Hip, hip, hip . . .

STUDENTS Hooray, hooray, hooray!

RABY *(to AMELIA)* Oh, I beg your pardon, ba'ab. Knoxites, three cheers for Biss Dishart. Hip, hip, hip . . .

STUDENTS Hooray, hooray, hooray!

RABY It's all right now, sir. You're quite safe now. We gave them hell, sir – beg pardon, Miss Dishart, I'b sure. You can't see the seats of their small-clothes for dust. I'b sorry about by dose, Miss Dishart. A great heavy cad got it a clout with his bludgeon. I settled his hash. You're all right now, sir.

KNOX Well then, gentlemen, if you are ready I shall lead you to Surgeons' Square.

STUDENTS But it can't be done, sir.

RABY We'll never bake our way through that mob, sir, not without cannon, sir.

KNOX Well. What the devil does it matter where we lecture? I'll lecture in the Grassmarket. I'll lecture on the Calton Hill. I'll lecture on the steps of St. Giles.

WALTER *(aside to AMELIA)* For God's sake don't let him go. He'll be killed.

(More STUDENTS have drifted in. The room is full.)

AMELIA Dr. Knox, if it doesn't matter where you lecture, why not lecture here?

KNOX Here, ma'am?

AMELIA Why not?

KNOX The place is unsuitable, ma'am.

AMELIA For lectures, Doctor? You've given so many here.

RABY Why not give the lecture here, sir? It's past the time for starting anyhow.

AMELIA Oh, do, Dr. Knox. And may we listen? It is on a subject to which ladies may listen?

KNOX Eminently so, madam. It is on the Heart.

AMELIA How charming! Do say you will.

KNOX *(looking hard at MARY)* Very well.

(The STUDENTS, chattering loudly, begin to arrange the room as a lecture theatre. The travelling trunk is used as a rostrum for KNOX. The ladies are accommodated with chairs in front. The STUDENTS keep asking KNOX for instructions. WALTER, a little distrait, wanders to the spinet and keeps gazing at MARY BELLE, who is giving instructions to the STUDENTS.)

RABY Shall we shift the spinet out of the way, sir?

WALTER Eh! . . . Oh, yes, I suppose so.

(They bring the spinet down stage)

KNOX No, no, you fool! I want the rostrum over there. No. Over there.

(During the bustle and noise, WALTER, still standing, picks out MARY PATERSON's lullaby with one finger on the spinet. The verse portion is only heard vaguely through the noise. When the theatre is ready there is a silence. WALTER, miles away, plays the refrain.)

KNOX Mr. Anderson, when you have completed your overture I will commence my lecture.

(Laughter)

WALTER I am dreadfully sorry, Dr. Knox. My mind was wandering.

KNOX You compose a love-lyric?

WALTER No. It is an air that came into my head. I can't remember what it is.

(He drifts to the window)

KNOX *(wagging his head at MARY BELLE)* Ah, Cyprian, thou who makest strong men mad.

(MARY BELLE bridles. WALTER looks at RABY. They both recognise the tune. WALTER buries his face in his hands.)

KNOX And now, gentlemen, I should say ladies and gentlemen, I am humbly obliged to you. You are well aware that every sneaking scribbler in this intellectual Gomorrah who can smudge an ungrammatical sentence employs his miserable talent to scratch venom on the public news-sheets; that, for the benefit of those worthy citizens who are unable to read, gap-toothed mountebanks scream and splutter at ever street corner. And I, gentlemen, I am the unworthy occasion of all this. I have argued with the

97

great Cuvier in the Academies of Paris. I shall not profane the sacred gift of human speech by replying to these people in any other language than that of the cudgel. With you I shall take the liberty of discussing a weightier matter . . . 'The Heart of the Rhinoceros.' This mighty organ, gentlemen, weighs full twenty-five pounds, a fitting fountainhead for the tumultuous stream that surges through the arteries of that prodigious monster. Clad in proof, gentlemen, and terribly armed as to his snout, the rhinoceros buffets his way through the tangled verdure engirdling his tropical habitat. Such dreadful vigour, gentlemen, such ineluctable energy requires to be sustained by no ordinary forces of nutrition . . .

(While he is speaking the curtain slowly falls. The STUDENTS are listening with a passionate intentness which will, it is hoped, communicate itself to the audience.)

THE END OF THE PLAY

NOTE. – If a more rapid curtain is desired, KNOX should pause for applause after the phrase 'the language of the cudgel'. He then should continue:

KNOX With you, gentlemen, I shall take the liberty of discussing a weightier matter . . . the human Heart. The Heart of Man, we are told, is deceitful and desperately wicked. However that may be, it consists of four chambers, the right ventricle, the left ventricle, the left auricle, the right auricle. . . .

CURTAIN

A SLEEPING CLERGYMAN

A PLAY IN TWO ACTS

Dedicated to Henry Kiell Ayliff

PERSONS

193–
A Sleeping Clergyman
Dr. Cooper
Dr. Coutts
Wilkinson

1867
Charles Cameron the First
Mrs. Hannah
William Marshall
Harriet Marshall

1872
Aunt Walker
Cousin Minnie

1885
William Marshall
Wilhelmina Cameron
John Hannah

1886
William Marshall
John Hannah
Wilhelmina Cameron
Mrs. Hannah

1907
A Sergeant
A Constable
Charles Cameron the Second
William Marshall

1916
Sir Douglas Todd Walker
Lady Todd Walker
Hope Cameron
Donovan
Charles Cameron the Second
William Marshall
A Prostitute

193–
Dr. Purley
Lady Katharine Helliwell
Sir Douglas Todd Walker
Hope Cameron
William Marshall
Donovan
A Medical Student
Dr. Coutts

SCENES

Chorus to Act One
A Club in Glasgow.

ACT ONE:
Scene One.   A lodging near the High Street, Glasgow.
Scene Two.   A Victorian bedroom.
Scene Three. A sea-side cliff near a lighthouse.
Scene Four.   Dr. Marshall's consulting room.

Chorus to Act Two
A Club in Glasgow.

ACT TWO:
Scene One.   A police station in a country town.
Scene Two.   Dr. Marshall's drawing room.
Scene Three. A flat in London.
Scenes Four and Five. The Hotel Paradise, Northumberland Avenue, converted into the Walker Institute.

CHORUS TO ACT ONE

SCENE – *A reputable Club in Glasgow. The smoking-room at six o'clock. Three vast shabby armchairs are arranged in front of the fire. In the left-hand chair a huge, white-bearded clergyman is asleep with the* Spectator *spread on his abdomen. The middle chair is empty. In the right-hand chair a Specialist in Diseases of Women is sitting. Gentlemen of this profession have been classified as shopwalkers and greengrocers. DR. COOPER is a shopwalker. A Neurologist enters. He is an undistinguished but fluent person called COUTTS. He is dressed for a funeral.*

COOPER (*suppressing his voice so as not to wake the clergyman*) Oh, hello! Good evening, Dr. Coutts.
COUTTS Good evening, Dr. Cooper. Club's empty tonight. (*He sits down*)
COOPER Yes. (*He rings a bell*)
COUTTS Isn't it cold . . . ? Oh, you're ringing, I see.
COOPER Yes. I wondered whether a glass of sherry might not do me good. Will you join me?
COUTTS No, I think not. A wee drop of the auld Kirk for me. I find it suits me better. I always think sherry's a little liverish at this time of year.

(*A Waiter appears*)

COOPER Good evening, Wilkinson; a glass of dry sherry for me and a whisky and soda for Dr. Coutts.
WILKINSON Very good, Sir. (*He disappears*)
COOPER The Rev. Gentleman looks as if he'd sleep like that till the Day of Judgment.
COUTTS Yes. Do you remember the Red King?
COOPER What Red King?
COUTTS Haven't you read *Through the Looking Glass*?
COOPER By Harold Begbie, isn't it?
COUTTS No, no . . . Horribly cold, isn't it?
COOPER It *is* horribly cold. Have you been . . .
COUTTS Yes.
COOPER Not a relative, I hope? I didn't see . . .
COUTTS No, no. Old Marshall's funeral. I was representing the Faculty.
COOPER Marshall? Marshall? Was he in practice hereabouts?
COUTTS No, no. Not for years. *You* remember. Old Bill Marshall. He was ninety-seven. They brought him up from Harrogate.
COOPER Of course. I know where you are now. He was a Visiting Physician at the Royal. Years ago. When I was a first-year student.

COUTTS That's right. A fine old boy. I only knew him slightly. My father and he were great friends.

COOPER He was buried in the country?

COUTTS Yes. In a little place on the Ayrshire coast. I don't suppose you know it. Duthie Bay.

COOPER Yes, I know it. I did a Caesarean and a round of golf there last week.

COUTTS Bonny little spot. A skylark was singing. I was quite affected.

COOPER I thought you were hardened to funerals.

COUTTS I am. I hate them. But it was nice, in a way, to see the old fellow home. He had a hard passage all his life.

(Enter WILKINSON with alcoholic drinks)

COOPER Ah, here's Wilkinson. Say when.

COUTTS Stop, stop. You'll drown it. Thank you.

WILKINSON Thank you, Sir.

COOPER Good God, Wilkinson, you've actually brought the drink I asked for!

WILKINSON I do my best, Sir.

COUTTS Of course you do, Wilkinson.

WILKINSON Will there be anything else, Sir?

COOPER No, thanks.

WILKINSON Thank you, Sir. *(Exit WILKINSON)*

COUTTS Well, here's happiness.

COOPER And yours . . . Marshall . . . No, I can't recall much about him.

COUTTS No? He kept very quiet for the last twenty-five years. . . . You knew he was Cameron's uncle, of course?

COOPER Cameron?

COUTTS THE Cameron. Sir Charles Cameron, the Bacteriologist, my old chief.

COOPER Was he, by Jove? Well, well. Funny, one doesn't, somehow, associate Cameron with relations.

COUTTS Cameron owed a lot to the old boy. He was there with Lord Duthie, old Douglas Walker, you know . . . he's a relation too . . . they were both at the funeral.

COOPER Was he? A first-chop funeral, then. Cameron isn't often seen in these parts.

COUTTS No. He's a little sensitive about it. He . . . Oh, well.

COOPER Don't bother about his Reverence. He's dining here, and the Day of Judgment wouldn't wake him before half-past seven. You were saying . . . ?

COUTTS Cameron's a by-blow, you know. An illegitimate child.

COOPER Yes. I knew that. His father was supposed to be . . .

COUTTS No, he wasn't. I've heard that story. Extraordinary what people will say. I know the true story, but I've always kept my mouth shut.

COOPER Oh, but I was told absolutely circumstantially . . .

COUTTS Well, you were told wrong. Cameron's the grandson of old Bill Marshall's sister. She died in childbirth away back in the 'sixties. That was a kind of tragic story, too. You see, about 1867, it would be, the Marshalls had a house at Duthie Bay, and a very jolly sort of crew they were, my old father told me. Marshall had started practice and was doing very well when he took a fancy to a damned rascal called Cameron, a proper sweep of a fellow, a medical student. Marshall was always a bit of a lame-dog fancier . . .

(COUTTS stops articulating, but his lips still move, and COOPER appears to be following a story. The lights fade out and, as they fade, the snores of the sleeping Cleric become louder and louder till they are taken up and carried on by a bass viol playing a solemn march. If a rapid change of scene is practicable here, the lights go up almost immediately on CAMERON's lodging. If not, the curtain may fall and the orchestra develop the bass viol's rumblings into an interlude.)

ACT ONE

Scene One

Time, 1867. CAMERON's lodging near the High Street of Glasgow. The dirty frippery of its decoration displays the soul of its landlady; the hell of untidiness, the habits of CHARLIE CAMERON himself. He is smoking in bed and reading a big book, and, although it is four o'clock in the afternoon, he is drinking neat whisky. He is twenty years old, and wears a fluffy little moustache and whiskers like young feathers. He is dying of phthisis. A microscope, some razors and obscene things in jam jars and glass tubes are among the litter on the table.

CAMERON *(coughing painfully)* Tyach. . . . The cough . . . it's got me by the throat like a garotte. . . . How can I work? How can I work? How can I work when it's tearing the lungs out of me, Hell blast it!

(He buries his face in the foul pillow. The door opens a little way. The face of a hard-bitten hag of about forty appears. She is carrying a loathly trayful of food.)

MRS. HANNAH Mr. Cameron? D'ye hear me speaking to ye, Mr. Cameron?

CAMERON What the devil do you want?

MRS. HANNAH I thought you were sleeping. You'll be wanting your tea, Mr. Cameron?

CAMERON What have you got?

MRS. HANNAH I've brought you a tasty bit of cold sausage and a nice bit of rice pudding.

CAMERON You have, have you? Let my eyes behold them. Oh, mine old familiar! O sausage that speakest to my heart. There's poetry and romance in that sausage, Mrs. Hannah.

MRS. HANNAH I'm glad you think so.

CAMERON I am glad that you are glad. And all this gladness, all this ecstatic beatification, does it give you the seeing eye, Mrs. Hannah? Can you see beyond that piebald guttapercha skin to the truths that lie within that sausage, Mrs. Hannah?

MRS. HANNAH See, I've got my work to do, and . . .

CAMERON There's metaphysics in that sausage, though, God knows, metaphysics are only a sort of joke. But there's biology in that sausage, and that's no joke. Is it, Mrs. Hannah, is it? Don't go away.

MRS. HANNAH Tuts. I don't know what you're speaking about.

CAMERON I'm speaking about a yearning, mange-bitten tom-cat under an inscrutable moon. Hungry for scraps and for blood and for love. For love, Mrs. Hannah. Have you ever had immoral longings in you, Mrs. Hannah?

MRS. HANNAH Now, then. You know I'm not used to that kind of talk.

CAMERON No. You haven't had 'em. You were got by a Presbyterian on a Presbyterian, and so was your mother and hers and hers and . . . But you've heard the passionate song of the tom-cat? The dreadful midnight scream of his breaking heart. It broke, Mrs. Hannah. He died, poor Diamond. *Hic jacet*, Mrs. Hannah. Here he lies in his jacket. . . . The end, do you think? Ah, no, no, no, no! Look at these little islands of blue and grey. These are moulds, Mrs. Hannah. These lovely little fungi are LIFE. Get me a microscope slide from that boot beside the cuspidor and I'll show you. I'll show you how a poor, dead, minced, boiled cat may have life, and have it more abundantly.

MRS. HANNAH See here. You take that sausage or leave it. There's many's the one would be glad to have it.

CAMERON Dear Mrs. Hannah, don't think I'm ungrateful, now, for all your thwarted mother-love. You are a mother to me, Mrs. Hannah.

MRS. HANNAH The Lord forbid.

CAMERON Yes, yes, you are. Your son, Johnny, even, is a brother to me. What a feat, Mrs. Hannah! You have made me feel a brother to that whining, thieving, cringing, wet-nosed, lying brat your little son, the apple of your . . .

MRS. HANNAH Just you keep your tongue off my Johnny, do you hear? You hold your tongue, see. If I thought he would grow up to be the like of you I'd thraw his neck like a pullet's, so I would.

CAMERON Keep your mind easy, my Spartan ma. He won't be like me. He'll never be anything but a sneaking little hound all his . . .

(A fit of coughing interrupts him)

MRS. HANNAH Look you here. . . . Pity me, what a hoast.

CAMERON Take your damned trash away. Do you hear me? Take it away. And yourself too.

MRS. HANNAH If you would smoke less of that tobacco-pipe. Dirty like tricks, sitting up smoking like a chimney, and drink, drink, drinking, read, read, reading all the night through.

CAMERON I pay for the candles.

MRS. HANNAH See, there's your tea. I canna trust myself to speak to you.

CAMERON You are safe with me, my dear beldame. Take your virtue out of this.

(She slams down the tray and goes out. CAMERON gets up unsteadily and examines part of the sausage under the microscope, muttering to

himself. MRS. HANNAH reappears ushering in DR. MARSHALL, a fine young man of twenty-six, nobly whiskered and frock-coated.)

MRS. HANNAH Just step this way, Doctor. Your patient's having his tea.
MARSHALL Well, Charlie?
CAMERON Hello, Marshall. How are you?
MRS. HANNAH You're not working too hard, Doctor?
MARSHALL Oh, no. I'm in excellent health, thank you, Elspeth.
MRS. HANNAH It's strange, looking at you, to think you are the same bairn I used to wash his face for, lang syne.
MARSHALL Hey? I can feel your hard knuckles on the back of my neck, still.
MRS. HANNAH Heh! heh! . . . A wee bit hardness was what you were needing. Ye were aye a steering wee smatchet. . . . You'll excuse the state his room's in, Doctor. I'm at my wits' end with him.
MARSHALL I don't wonder. He's an awful one. . . . And who the devil told you you could get out of your bed? Come to the window and let's have a look at you? . . . Great heavens, man, you're like a corpse. Get into bed at once. Why didn't you send for me?
CAMERON I didn't want to bother you. I felt better.

(He gets into bed)

MARSHALL Better!
MRS. HANNAH There's no getting him to do a thing you tell him. I try to do my best for him. If only for your sake, Doctor Willie.
MARSHALL I feel sure you do, Elspeth. He's a dour, difficult patient.

(He examines CAMERON's throat)

MRS. HANNAH I'll never forget how kind you were to me and to my John that's in Heaven, you and your dear father between you . . .
MARSHALL Hush! Don't talk while I'm auscultating.

(MRS. HANNAH sniffs)

Say "onetwothree" . . . again . . . again. . . . Whisper it. . . . Now, breathe. Um. Yes. . . . What were you saying, Elspeth?
MRS. HANNAH I was saying how often I tell our wee Johnny that's all that's left to me what we owe to you and yours and your great loving-kindness to the widow and the fatherless, and I'm sure I don't see anything to laugh at in that, Mr. Cameron, God forgive you.
MARSHALL He wasn't laughing at you, Elspeth. Of course, he wasn't. Now, will you leave us for a little? I want to talk to this young man.
MRS. HANNAH Surely, Sir, surely. And don't pay any heed to what he says about me. Poor lad, he's not responsible.

(She goes out)

CAMERON Take off that archiepiscopal face. I'll warstle through, don't you fret.

MARSHALL Warstle! I never saw the like of it. The place reeks like a quayside pub. Inspissated putrescence. . . . Get under the blankets and I'll open the window. . . . Damn it, I can't get about for your old junk. What the devil do you mean by working when you're in a state like this?

CAMERON I wasn't working. I was dreaming.

MARSHALL If you'd been thinking it would have been more to the point. Have you thought over my proposal?

CAMERON Which one?

MARSHALL *Ach Himmel*, man, the only one. Will . . . you . . . come . . . down . . . to Duthie Bay and stay with my people for a month or so?

CAMERON It's no use talking. I can't.

MARSHALL You mean you won't?

CAMERON If you like.

MARSHALL But why, why, why? Don't you realise? . . . Look here, Charlie, the sea will be the life of you. It's a grand tonic. You'll come back to your work fit and able for it . . . and you're far from that just now.

CAMERON Don't I know that as well as you do? . . . And I'm only a puir diseased body of a medical student, and you're a rising star. But I won't go.

MARSHALL But think, boy, think. . . . See here. I'll tell you what I haven't told you before. Maybe I shouldn't, but I will.

CAMERON Well?

MARSHALL This is your last chance. If you don't go, you'll die. That's it plump and plain.

CAMERON Oh, I don't know.

MARSHALL But I know, Charlie; your right lung is away with it and your left is going fast.

CAMERON Yes. I suppose that's true. And I'll die. And that will be the end of that.

MARSHALL But, Charlie, it must NOT end that way. You must get well. You must take your degree and make a name for yourself. Good Lord, you've got brains. You've got more native ability than all the Faculty put together. You have it in you to make your mark . . . to be a great man, even. Everybody says so. . . . Joe Lister was asking for you only this morning.

CAMERON Lister? Was he? What did he say?

MARSHALL He's a bit of a crank, too, but he knows genius when he sees it.

CAMERON Did Lister say I was a genius?

MARSHALL No, not exactly . . .

CAMERON No, I should think not exactly. Good old Holy Joe.

MARSHALL He spoke very highly of you, very highly indeed. . . . You must go to the sea, Charlie. You owe it to all of us.

CAMERON Lister's a fine fellow. Benign-looking cove, too. Made in the image of God – like me and Mrs. Hannah.

MARSHALL Never mind Mr. Lister just now. Listen to me.

CAMERON I could work with Joe Lister. I'd like to sit behind him and tell him what to do. Some one will, some day. Joe's a force of nature. It'd be like harnessing the Tides.

MARSHALL Well, ask him. Ask him. Perhaps he'll make you a dresser this autumn. Only you must – get – well – first. Come down to Duthie for a month.

CAMERON And a month would cure me?

MARSHALL It would give you a chance.

CAMERON A chance, only.

MARSHALL Well, you've none here. Not a dog's chance. Come, Charlie. My mother and the girls will be delighted. Harriet is particularly keen that you should come.

CAMERON Did your sister – did Miss Harriet say so in so many words?

MARSHALL Of course she did. We drove up together this morning. I left her at my aunt, Mrs. Walker's at Pollokshields; she's staying the night there. She said I *must* get you to come. She'll be dreadfully disappointed if you don't.

CAMERON She said that, did she?

MARSHALL Yes. And she really meant it. Charlie, you're a bit of a reprobate – you've not always been very – very wise; but we've all got a soft side to you.

CAMERON Including Harriet?

MARSHALL Harriet more than any of us. She admires your intellect tremendously.

CAMERON She admires my intellect, does she? Doctor, I can't go.

MARSHALL Why not, man, why not?

CAMERON How long will I live if I stay here?

MARSHALL You want a straight answer?

CAMERON Yes.

MARSHALL You can live two months. Three at the outside.

CAMERON A month will do.

MARSHALL What do you mean by that?

CAMERON You know what I'm after, Marshall.

MARSHALL Your mean this? *(He indicates the microscope.)* Oh, I've got a rough notion. You'd be far better sticking to your books. I'm not saying there isn't *something* in it, but . . .

CAMERON Everything's in it. For me, at any rate. Look here, listen . . .

MARSHALL Yes, I know, I know. You've told me. But . . .

CAMERON Have you ever heard of Pasteur?

MARSHALL No. Yes. The French chemist.

CAMERON Do you know his work on ferments?

MARSHALL What? . . . Oh, yes. He believes in spontaneous generation, doesn't he?

CAMERON Oh, my God! Spallanzani killed that a hundred years ago. Do you ever read your Voltaire?

MARSHALL Voltaire was not a man of science.

CAMERON And you are, I suppose? And you don't know what Pasteur's doing. Neither does he, for that matter. But you know what Joe Lister's doing.

MARSHALL Yes. Poisoning his patients with carbolic. And why? Because of germs, ha, ha! Because of germs he pretends to see floating in the air. Lister's a fine fellow, but that kind of thing isn't far removed from delusional insanity. Like old Blake seeing the air full of angels. Well, damn it, the angels may be there, but they won't bite you.

CAMERON Won't they?

MARSHALL Look here, young Cameron, you stick to facts. Our profession has been storing facts since the days of Hippocrates, and they're good enough for me and good enough for you. You leave Lister to people the circumambient ether with infusorial animalcula. You let them alone. And put on your shore-going clothes and come down with Harriet and me to Duthie this very evening, and let the west wind blow the infusorial animalcula out of your skull.

CAMERON Listen to me. You're to imagine that you are ten thousand years old cocked up on the edge of the firmament looking at the world through a monstrous telescope.

MARSHALL Oh, Lord, you've been at the bottle again. Now, Charles, I told . . .

CAMERON You see a green and blue world for a bit. Then parts of the green become patchy with brown and grey. Then little tuberosities appear on the dark patches and they become hacked and fissured and distorted; and, maybe, in a few hundred years they become green again. What conclusions would you draw, eh? What would you think about it all?

MARSHALL I suppose you want me to say I would be looking at cities growing up and dying.

CAMERON Yes, yes, yes. But suppose you'd never heard of a city?

MARSHALL Well . . . it would look like a disease process.

CAMERON Wouldn't it? Wouldn't it? And would you ever suspect that it was caused by a form of life; parasitic; intensely active; made up of millions of units; capable of reproduction; destroying; building up; killing and dying themselves in turn?

MARSHALL I suppose so, yes.

CAMERON Look at me. Get up on the edge of the firmament and look at me. Look through me. Look through those barrel girds of ribs into my lungs.

MARSHALL Charlie, I see what you're after, but you can't argue by analogy. You . . .

CAMERON If I say that a parasitic race is making me what I am? If I say that when I'm hot with fever at night, they're working, and when I'm cool in the morning, they're resting? If I say they are using my body to fulfil their damned destiny – to build tubercle towns? If I say that every stage in my disease is a stage in the history of my parasites? The wee beasts Leeuwenhoek saw, ages ago.

MARSHALL I should say you were making a very violent assumption. But don't let us . . .

CAMERON Violent assumption! I should say so. And I tell you, too, that every corrupting wound, every fever, every ill the body is heir to is the expression of the life of these little enemies. Each after his kind. A different race for each disease. Do you believe me?

MARSHALL My dear boy, if you showed me the enemies you speak of, and . . .

CAMERON That's it. I will, I'll show you them. In a month, I will.

MARSHALL How?

CAMERON I'll transplant them. I'll colonise them. I'll make them grow in colonies. Outside the body. On gelatine. On broth. On – on sausages. I'll show you the beasts themselves, individually, under the microscope. I'll put them back in the body of a mouse and they'll build their cities. I'll show you.

MARSHALL Tuts, man.

CAMERON I'll stain them with dyes. Blue for the alkaline beasts and red for the acid beasts – or plants. Maybe they're plants.

MARSHALL I see. Why not tie blue and red ribbons round their necks?

CAMERON But I've stained them. I've done it. I could show you.

MARSHALL Oh? Let me see.

CAMERON I won't let you see. Not yet. And if I die I'll never let you see. So you had better keep me alive. You wouldn't understand the only notes I'd leave behind. Joe Lister might. But then, he's a genius too.

MARSHALL Oh, he's a genius *too*, is he? You've got a guid conceit of yourself.

CAMERON That's not conceit, you fool. Do you want me to smirk and blush and bite my handkerchief and pretend to be something else? I KNOW I'm a genius.

MARSHALL I don't want you to do anything but come to Duthie Bay.

CAMERON Well, I won't.

MARSHALL See here, I'm sure your work is all very important and interesting. You can come back in a couple of months to it, a well man again.

CAMERON I'm not going to gamble on that. I'm going ahead. If I die, the world will have to do without, that's all.

MARSHALL Then that's your last word?

CAMERON That's my – (*coughs*) – last word.

MARSHALL I've a good mind to throw up your case altogether.

CAMERON All right, dear whale, throw up your little Jonah if he makes you sick. You'll have to in a month anyway.

MARSHALL Charlie . . .

CAMERON Well?

MARSHALL Is there any reason . . . any other reason . . . any reason you haven't told me?

CAMERON Haven't I given you reason enough?

MARSHALL No. You haven't.

CAMERON Then you'll have to be content. I'm too tired to argue. Good-bye.

MARSHALL I'm not going to give up. I'll see you to-morrow. Are you taking your medicine?

CAMERON I am. You'll count that in my favour?

MARSHALL Au revoir, then.

CAMERON Good-bye. . . . Mrs. Hannah!

MRS. HANNAH *(in the passage)* What is it?

CAMERON Show the Doctor out. And, Marshall . . . lend me a couple of pounds till to-morrow, will you? . . . Thank you. I love your bedside manner of lending money. I'll pay it back. Good-bye.

MARSHALL No hurry, my dear boy. And do behave yourself.

(MARSHALL goes. CAMERON struggles to his feet; watches stealthily from behind a curtain as MARSHALL goes down the street; returns to the microscope, coughing. MRS. HANNAH comes in.)

MRS. HANNAH Here. The Doctor said you was to stay in bed.

CAMERON He likes to hear himself talk. You would too if you had a beautiful voice like him.

MRS. HANNAH You haven't touched your high tea.

CAMERON No. Nor would with a barge-pole. Take it away.

MRS. HANNAH But you haven't etten a bite for days.

CAMERON Take the damned muck away, and don't stand there yammering.

MRS. HANNAH See here. You'll not kill yourself in my lodgings. I've had enough trouble with you as it is.

CAMERON I'll keep alive to please you, Mrs. Hannah. *(A bell rings)* Who will that be now?

MRS. HANNAH It'll be the bookseller's man again. I'm not going to be bothered telling him any more lies. Are you or are you not going to pay him?

CAMERON I hate riddles. I give it up. But that isn't a dun's ring. It's a wee, gentle, excited ring. A lady's ring.

MRS. HANNAH Well, if it's another of your fancy tarts, she'll not cross my door.

(She goes out. CAMERON gets into bed again and lights a foul clay pipe.)

CAMERON Of all the girls that are so smart
There's none like Mrs. Hannah,
But introduce her to a tart
And note her frigid manner.
. . . Ach. The rats have been at my bellows and no mistake.

(HARRIET MARSHALL is ushered in by MRS. HANNAH)

MRS. HANNAH It's Miss Marshall to see you, Mr. Cameron. I haven't had time to tidy the room yet, Miss. What with getting Johnny out to the school and what not. I'm black affronted at it.

HARRIET And how is Johnny? He must be getting a big fellow now.

MRS. HANNAH He is that, Miss Harry. Never misses a day, and aye at the top of his class.

HARRIET How splendid!

CAMERON Miss Marshall came to see me, Mrs. Hannah . . . Though she hasn't said "Good-afternoon" yet.

HARRIET Oh – good-afternoon.

CAMERON Good afternoon. Get out, Mrs. Hannah.

MRS. HANNAH Oh, I'm not the one to intrude. Two's company, I suppose.

(She goes)

HARRIET Charlie!

CAMERON Well, Harriet?

HARRIET My dear, my dear, how are you?

CAMERON I? Ask your brother. He has just gone. . . . This is not very wise of you, Harriet.

HARRIET I know, I know. But I couldn't help it. I had to come. Oh, Charlie, I'm in terrible trouble.

CAMERON So am I. My trouble is deadly. So your brother told me in his bright, breezy fashion.

HARRIET Oh, my darling, I don't want to bother you and distress you when you are so ill, but . . .

CAMERON I told you not to come. Why do you disobey me?

HARRIET I'm trying to tell you, Charlie. Charlie, it's . . . I won't be able to keep it from them . . . Charlie, what will I do? What will I do? You'll have to marry me, dear.

CAMERON You mean you are going to have a child?

HARRIET Yes.

CAMERON Then why the devil can't you say so?

HARRIET But, but . . . oh!

CAMERON My fault, this prospective arrival?

HARRIET Darling, what do you mean?

CAMERON Oh, I suppose it is. . . . You want me to marry you?

HARRIET Dearest, you must. You must. You . . . your manner's so funny to-day, I thought. . . . Oh, but you will. You mean to, don't you? I'd kill myself if you didn't.

CAMERON It's damnably unfortunate.

HARRIET Look at me, Charlie. Look at me.

CAMERON Well? I'm looking at you.

HARRIET Don't you love me? Any more? Not any more?

CAMERON Oh, yes. I suppose so. Better than any of the other young ladies who have been obliging to me.

HARRIET Oh, my God!

CAMERON I won't marry you, though. I won't marry anybody. My soul's my own. I won't have your big, reproachful eyes prying into it. And bombast apart, I won't be any rich woman's kept man. I've some self-respect left. But not much life. It doesn't matter anyhow. I'm dying.

HARRIET No, no. You're not, my love. You're not. You're trying to make me think badly of you; but I know. You're mine. I'll nurse you. I'll save you. I'll do what you like. I'll be your slave. Charlie, you must marry me.

(A pause)

CAMERON I seem fated to spend the rest of this day being badgered and bullied by the Marshall family. . . . Yes. I'll marry you. It'll save you from being hounded to death by your Christian friends and relations. We'll hop over the tongs. We'll join hands in the sacred edifice like a couple of God's comedians. It will be something to laugh at in the grey days.

HARRIET We could get married in the Scots form. All we need is two witnesses. I could bring Bessie, one of Aunt Walker's maids, and Mrs. Hannah could be the other. She'd do anything for half-a-crown.

CAMERON You prescribe the necessary mumbo-jumbo. . . . I'll take you, Harriet Marshall, to be my wedded wife. . . . No, no, no. . . . No! Every bit of me is in revolt against it. Every drop of my poisoned blood. Let me die alone – like a gentleman.

HARRIET Gentleman? You are a pretty gentleman. You vain, selfish, blackguardly hound.

CAMERON Hold your tongue, you fool. You might have jockeyed me into it with your snivelling, but I won't marry a damned fishwife.

HARRIET I wish God would kill you.

CAMERON He's doing His best. Let Him alone. Don't improve on His work by fretting me into a fever. I won't sleep to-night.

HARRIET I don't believe you're ill at all.

CAMERON Oh, I'm not so ill as they think. If I were sure I was going to die, I believe I'd marry you all right. But I'm not going to die. I'm going to fight and work and live, and I'm going to fight without any long-haired, soft-skinned, piping-voiced bag of whims and vapours hanging round my neck. And you can make up your mind to that – you "recreation of the warrior".

HARRIET I didn't believe there could be people like you. You low, sordid beast. You drunken, treacherous beast.

CAMERON Be quiet, you slut.

HARRIET You're proud of your brains. Very proud. You're a genius. You'll put everybody right, won't you? You're a great scientist, aren't you? You said so yourself. You go into all the public-houses and say it, and all the sots and the potboys and the girls of the street admire you – oh, immensely, don't they?

(CAMERON is half out of bed. His face is disfigured with rage.)

Now you're going to strike me, aren't you? You Highland gentleman. You genius.

(He strikes her in the face. She falls back against the table.)

CAMERON Take care of those culture tubes!

HARRIET *(knocking the rack of tubes to the floor)* There they go. Now, kill me.

(CAMERON looks for a moment as if he would, but he staggers and falls exhausted face downwards on the bed)

Oh, my dear. What have I done? What have I done?

CAMERON Nothing. It's all right. Nothing. I'm a little . . . it's nothing. Help me into bed.

HARRIET Oh, my blessed, my sweetheart. What is it? What can I do?

CAMERON Don't worry. I'm sorry I hit you, Harry. You'd better go now. I'll be all right in a wee while.

HARRIET I'll send Mrs. Hannah for Willie. You look dreadfully ill.

CAMERON I tell you I'm all right. Don't keep on at it. Don't be such a Marshall. Go now, dear. Don't tell Will anything about this.

HARRIET But I must.

CAMERON No. Do as I tell you. Go away. . . . Wait. . . . Give me some whisky. . . . That's better; I think I'll sleep now . . . Harry . . .

HARRIET Yes, my darling?

CAMERON You mustn't tell your brother. It'll be all right. I'll see you through this, old girl. Kiss me. No. On the forehead.

HARRIET Oh! . . . There's blood on your forehead now. From my mouth. Where you hit me.

CAMERON Leave it alone. Leave it there. You've forgiven me?

HARRIET Yes, yes, yes.

CAMERON Come to-morrow then. At eleven. And bring a witness. I like

Scots marriages. The word of honour of the contracting parties. Nothing more. We're an honourable race, aren't we, my dear?

HARRIET Yes. To-morrow morning?

CAMERON At eleven. Your brother doesn't come till the afternoon. Good-bye, Harry.

HARRIET Good-night, Charlie. Are you sure you are all right?

CAMERON I'm all right – now.

(She tucks in his bedclothes and goes. The room is growing dark.)

Most touching. Most affecting. What memories to weep over, my dear, twenty years ahead. Your miserable, begrutten face! And now I'm going to die. I've bilked you, you bitch.

(After a short pause, enter MRS. HANNAH)

MRS. HANNAH That's fine carries on. My certes, that's fine carries on. What would old Mr. and Mrs. Marshall think if they knew of the like of this? And look at my carpet!

CAMERON Get the Doctor.

MRS. HANNAH Indeed and I will not get the Doctor. You'd think I had nothing to do morning, noon and night but run after you. And my carpet. My good carpet. It's a bad end you'll come to, aye, and your children and your grandchildren if you have any. Bad all through. Bad to the bone.

(She goes out and returns clattering a dustpan and brush)

You'll go out of here to-morrow, so you will. How I'll ever let this room again, I'm sure I don't know. A perfect pig-stye. I'm sure I don't know what sort of home you come out of. And that young lady, too, that I was in the house of the day she was born. I little knew, I've kept myself decent and my premises decent till the black burning day you came, Mister Cameron. Never mind. Out you go to-morrow's morning. And you'll pay for the carpet, and the clock you broke, and the holes in the mantelshelf you burned with your pipe, and the antimacassar you tore. You'll pay. And you needna pretend to be asleep. You know as well as I do . . . as I do . . . Jesus, Mary and Joseph. He's dead.

CURTAIN

ACT ONE

Scene Two

Night in the Second Best Bedroom at Bella's Choice, Pollokshields, Glasgow, in 1872. A YOUNG LADY is retiring for the night. A knock is heard.

YOUNG LADY Oh! . . . Oh, yes! It's you, Aunt Walker. Do come in. Excuse my déshabille.

(Enter an OLD LADY)

OLD LADY Well, here you are, Minnie, dear. I looked in to see if you were comfortable. You must be tired. All that long journey and then . . .

YOUNG LADY Oh, I'm not a bit tired, Auntie.

OLD LADY You've got everything you want?

YOUNG LADY Oh, yes. Everything.

OLD LADY It was so good of you to come to little Wilhelmina's birthday party.

YOUNG LADY Not at all. It was so good of you to have me here at all, with Little Douglas's whooping cough and the whole house upset.

OLD LADY Poor little Douglas Todd Walker! He's sleeping like an angel. He's next door to you. I hope he doesn't have an attack and disturb you during the night.

YOUNG LADY Oh, I don't mind. . . . At least . . . Well . . . It's such a pity. He must be so disappointed. I suppose his little cousin and he are great friends?

OLD LADY Hm. . . . Well . . .

YOUNG LADY Living right away at Pollokshields, I don't suppose you often see her.

OLD LADY Poor little thing!

YOUNG LADY So precocious, too. Some of the things she said quite frightened me.

OLD LADY No wonder. . . . Of course, you hadn't seen her before.

YOUNG LADY No, Aunt Walker. You forget how long I've been an exile. I hadn't even seen Cousin Will since I was a little thing with my hair down my back. He used to pull my pigtails.

OLD LADY A nice fellow, Will Marshall. A clever fellow. You're sure you're not tired, Minnie, dear?

YOUNG LADY No, no. Not a bit. It's been lovely.

OLD LADY I wondered what you must think of me – rushing you off to a children's party when you had hardly got off the London train.

YOUNG LADY Oh, we do much more terrible things than that at home in Putney.

OLD LADY It sounds so funny. Putney. Home.

YOUNG LADY Oh, I'm quite acclimatised now.

OLD LADY I suppose you have a very gay time. Concerts and balls and parties. Bless me, I haven't had time for a single word with you since you arrived.

YOUNG LADY No. It's been awful. I was quite at sea among all these Marshall and Walker cousins. I didn't know t'other from which. I'd have been better of a little coaching beforehand.

OLD LADY I think you did very well, dear. They were all terrified of their swell London cousin.

YOUNG LADY That's all right, then. But I did feel a fool.

OLD LADY You were the belle of the party.

YOUNG LADY I can't get that child's face out of my mind. What she said was curious enough, but she looked as if she had all the wisdom of the ages, bad and good, in her little round head.

OLD LADY Poor wee soul!

YOUNG LADY She was Harriet's child, wasn't she?

OLD LADY Yes.

YOUNG LADY I never knew Harriet very well. She was too terribly clever to have anything to do with us little brats. A very proud girl, wasn't she?

OLD LADY Yes.

YOUNG LADY A little stuck up, we thought her. Tragic, dying like that. . . . What sort of man was this Cameron?

OLD LADY We don't talk about him, darling. It was a bad business.

YOUNG LADY Rather fast, wasn't he?

OLD LADY Yes.

YOUNG LADY Oh, Aunt Walker, I wish you wouldn't be such an old clam.

OLD LADY Minnie, darling!

YOUNG LADY I can't get a thing out of you.

OLD LADY Well, darling, you're not very old yet.

YOUNG LADY But we talk about all sorts of things now. Socialism and everything. And physiology. Don't be so old-fashioned.

OLD LADY Well. . . . I suppose. . . . In Putney.

YOUNG LADY We were frightfully excited when the baby arrived. We'd never heard of the marriage, you see. I suppose it was a runaway match.

OLD LADY There was . . . Oh, well . . . I suppose you'll have to learn the facts of life some day. . . . There wasn't any marriage.

YOUNG LADY How awful!

OLD LADY We're apt to think, we who have been decently brought up, that marriage is really an essential preliminary to, to all that sort of thing, and that only scullery-maids and royalty . . . well, you see what I mean?

117

YOUNG LADY Yes.

OLD LADY I mean royalty in the old days and abroad, of course.

YOUNG LADY Of course.

OLD LADY Well, that's how it was. It was really very kind of Cousin Will to take the little girl.

YOUNG LADY But what a frightful risk!

OLD LADY (*sighing*) Yes. It is a risk. I've often worried and worried and worried about it. I've talked to your Uncle Walker about it; but your Uncle Walker, with all his fine gifts of character and integrity, is just a little stupid, my dear. Don't say I said so.

YOUNG LADY No, Aunt.

OLD LADY This man Cameron was almost a maniac. He was bad through and through, body and soul. He had consumption. He drank. He stole money from Will. He had all sorts of unmentionable associates. The kindest thing to think was that he was insane. And there you are. You see what I mean.

YOUNG LADY I see. Heredity.

OLD LADY And added to that, this unsuspected weakness of Harriet's. She was actually staying with us when the terrible man died. And poor Will is so wrapped up in the child.

YOUNG LADY What does he think of it? The heredity, I mean. I mean, I've read a lot about it, and it's awful. You have it running through generation after generation. A lot of us think something ought to be done – oh, well – to prevent people like that getting married at all. But, then, they didn't get married.

OLD LADY Of course I can't very well speak to Will about it, directly, you know. But he's got some strange ideas about it. The Marshalls always were a little queer.

YOUNG LADY What does he say?

OLD LADY I think he thinks that the good characteristics are just as likely to be handed down as the bad ones. Though what good he saw in that awful man I am at a loss to know. He said to me once that social impulses in a person sometimes harness the strong anti-social impulses, and then we see some fun, he said. I didn't follow quite. He said he had faith in God.

YOUNG LADY What an odd thing to say!

OLD LADY Oh, I don't think so. We all ought to have.

YOUNG LADY Oh, yes, of course, in a way. But I don't see what it's got to do with this. I mean she's sure to go to the bad anyhow. And he's so wrapped up in her. It'll be simply tragic. It's all very well to be religious.

OLD LADY But he isn't religious. That's the funny thing. Last time we dined there your Uncle Walker said to me afterwards that he'd never enter that house again. He did, of course, but it shows you. And your Uncle Walker is quite a broadminded man. Very advanced and broadminded.

YOUNG LADY But it isn't a question of religion at all. It's a question of fact.

OLD LADY Yes. And doesn't the Bible say, "The fathers have eaten sour grapes and the children's teeth shall be set on edge"?

YOUNG LADY Yes. It's all very difficult. But, then, his own sister's child. What could he do?

OLD LADY He should have boarded her out. In a case like that, he wasn't responsible. Before God and man, he wasn't responsible.

YOUNG LADY No.

OLD LADY I don't know why we're talking like this. Tell me about the shops and the Opera and the Row. I suppose you go out a great deal.

YOUNG LADY Well, to tell you the truth, not very much. We have formed a little circle – just a few friends – to study the works of Mr. and Mrs. Browning.

OLD LADY Ah! . . .

DOUGLAS TODD WALKER (*without*) Ach. . . . Ach-achachachach. . . . WHOOOOOP!

OLD LADY Oh, mercy! I must run. Oh, dear, the poor lamb! It's little Douglas!

YOUNG LADY The poor lamb! Is he very bad?

OLD LADY No, no. Very mild, the doctor says. And the nurse is there, of course, and she's so good and patient. . . . You'll think it's silly, but little Douglas Todd Walker is all in all to me. I know he'll get over it, of course. It's his destiny. That boy, Minnie (*solemnly*), was born under a good star as surely as poor little Wilhelmina was born under a bad one. And that's a fact.

YOUNG LADY Oh, do you think there's really anything in that? *Really*, I mean. You see, I always think . . .

DOUGLAS (*without*) WHOOOOOOP!

OLD LADY Oh, dear. I must run. Good-night, darling. Happy dreams. They'll call you at seven.

YOUNG LADY Good-night, Auntie.

(*OLD LADY goes*)

Fat little pig. I hope he chokes!

CURTAIN

ACT ONE

Scene Three

A cliff-top near Duthie Bay on the Ayrshire coast. It is a Sunday afternoon in the summer of 1885. MARSHALL and WILHELMINA are picnicking. WILHELMINA is HARRIET's daughter.

WILHELMINA *(singing in an undertone)*
        Oh, the days of the Kerry dancing,
        Oh, the clang of the wooden shoon,
        Oh, for one of those hours of gladness
        Gone, alas! like our youth, too soon.
. . . That's a little sad, isn't it, Uncle Will?
MARSHALL Eh? What's that, Wilhelmina? What is?
WILHELMINA That is. What I was singing just now. 'Gone, alas! like our youth, too soon.' Gone, comma, alas, point of exclamation, like our youth, comma, too soon, full stop.
MARSHALL Too soon? Nothing of the sort. Youth's a silly-sickness. It's grand to get over it.
WILHELMINA I can see that. But, O God, O God, I want to grip it and hold it and never let it go. I suppose that's part of the sickness?
MARSHALL Yes. When I came of age I felt that the rope had broken and there was I going tapsalteerie into the abyss. It was all nonsense. I've no wish to be a boy again, and I was happier than most boys. Where did you put the fusees?
WILHELMINA Catch.
MARSHALL *(lighting a cigar)* I smoked my first when I was fourteen, and the world suddenly turned very grey for me.
WILHELMINA Give me one.
MARSHALL I lay for an hour with my brow on the cold scullery floor.
WILHELMINA Give me one. Give me a cigar.
MARSHALL Why?
WILHELMINA I want to try it.
MARSHALL There's a lot of things you'd better not try on your journey through life, my dear. Cigars, for one thing.
WILHELMINA We ought to try everything.
MARSHALL Well, try and behave yourself. That'll keep you busy. And you've had enough of that Barsac – a wee girl like you.
WILHELMINA It makes me feel as if I were one of a great sleepy crowd swimming in an enormous slow river in hot sunshine – me, and my mother and my grandmother and my great-grandmother and my great-great-grandmother and my . . .

MARSHALL Hi. Give me that bottle. You have had too much. You're tipsy.

WILHELMINA No. I'm not. I've been tipsy, and I know what it's like.

MARSHALL When were you tipsy? This is news to me.

WILHELMINA Never mind. There's lots of things you don't know about me. Why can't we call John Hannah over and give him some?

MARSHALL John Hannah's a teetotaller. And quite right, too.

WILHELMINA It must be dull for him having nobody but the pony to talk to.

MARSHALL John knows his place. He wouldn't be comfortable picnicking with us.

WILHELMINA Why shouldn't he be? He's as good as we are.

MARSHALL In the sight of Heaven, maybe.

WILHELMINA We're in the sight of Heaven now. Call him over, Uncle Will.

MARSHALL Don't be a damned radical.

WILHELMINA I'm not a radical. He'll be a doctor soon. Just like you.

MARSHALL When he is a doctor, I'll be pleased to receive him at my table. For the present he's my handyman, working his passage through College. He recognises what, for the present, is his place. I'll be much obliged if you will, also.

WILHELMINA That's silly.

MARSHALL It may be, but it's my wish. You're just a shade too familiar with that lad.

WILHELMINA I'm not.

MARSHALL You are. He's a decent fellow, but he's young. You'll give him ideas.

WILHELMINA What ideas?

MARSHALL Never mind. It's easiest for us all if we remember our stations.

WILHELMINA Oh, easy, easy, easy, easy! It's easy all the way with you, Uncle Will! You'd like to be a cabbage in a garden. You're an old three-toed sloth.

MARSHALL And you're an impudent besom. . . . *Ach Himmel*, fancy being a Nihilist on a glorious day like this. Sit at peace and enjoy the sunshine.

WILHELMINA All right. . . . Dearest, why am I so ugly?

MARSHALL You're not ugly.

WILHELMINA Yes. I'm pretty ugly. Not bonnie, anyhow. Not that there isn't something about me.

MARSHALL Away with you. You're fishing for compliments.

WILHELMINA (*sitting up abruptly*) That's an insult, and a damned insult. Why do you spoil a delicious day like this by insulting me?

MARSHALL I'll insult you as much as I like. And keep your temper. Listen.

WILHELMINA Listen to what?

MARSHALL Just listen. What do you hear?

WILHELMINA The waves on the beach and a bee on the clover and a lamb on the hill-side calling to its mother.

(A silence)

But there is something about me, Uncle Will, don't you think?

MARSHALL Yes. There is.

WILHELMINA You know the daft things girls think about. . . . Are you really my uncle?

MARSHALL Oh, yes.

WILHELMINA I'm not a bit like you. I suppose . . . it's fancy. . . . I sometimes have the feeling there's a sort of greatness in me. Almost as if I were a sort of royalty. I suppose there's nothing in that.

MARSHALL Nothing whatever.

WILHELMINA Not even on the wrong side of the blanket.

MARSHALL No. You're middle-class. Right away back.

WILHELMINA I was afraid of that. What sort of man was my father?

MARSHALL He was as God made him. It's time we were getting home.

WILHELMINA Why won't you talk to me about my father?

MARSHALL Because it would make you unhappy and me unhappy. There's no mystery about him. He was a poor fish, and that's all there is to it. You pack up. I'll take the milkcan back to the lighthouse. I – I've got something to tell Macalister up there.

(He gets up abruptly and walks off. He stops.)

John! . . . He's asleep.

HANNAH *(off)* No, Doctor, I'm not.

MARSHALL You're not, aren't you? You've a sharp pair of ears, anyhow. Come over here and help Miss Cameron with the basket. I'm away up to the lighthouse.

(As HANNAH enters, he goes)

WILHELMINA What were you saying to the pony all afternoon?

HANNAH I wasn't speaking to the pony.

WILHELMINA What were you doing?

HANNAH I was doing equations in my head.

WILHELMINA Wasna that breakin' the Sawbath, doin' equations in your heid?

HANNAH No, Miss. It's quite permissible to work in abstractions on the Sabbath.

WILHELMINA I see. . . . Look! You've got a spider on your coat. Heavens, how fast he runs! Let me catch him. Got you, you young rascal! Now say, "Thank you, Miss Cameron."

HANNAH I'm sure I'm much obliged to you, Miss.
WILHELMINA Then say, "Thank you, Miss Cameron."
HANNAH Thank you, Miss Cameron.
WILHELMINA "Thank you kindly, Miss Wilhelmina Cameron."
HANNAH Thank you kindly, Miss Wilhelmina Cameron.
WILHELMINA Isn't that arch of me?
HANNAH I don't know, Miss.
WILHELMINA Do you like girls to be arch?
HANNAH I've not right considered it, Miss.
WILHELMINA I suppose not. But the really important point is, arch or not arch, do you like me?
HANNAH That's a funny sort of thing to ask.
WILHELMINA Is it? I don't think so. But never mind whether it's funny or not. Do you like me?
HANNAH Well, yes, Miss. I do.
WILHELMINA Then why are you so sulky?
HANNAH I wasn't aware that I was sulky, Miss.
WILHELMINA You've got nice hair, but I don't like your eyes.
HANNAH Is that so?
WILHELMINA Yes. They're too close together.
HANNAH They're as the Lord made them, Miss Wilhelmina.
WILHELMINA That's what Uncle Will said about my father a few minutes ago.
HANNAH Aye? Did he now?
WILHELMINA You said that in a queer tone.
HANNAH I don't think so, Miss.
WILHELMINA Don't contradict, please. What did you mean by saying it in that queer tone?
HANNAH Nothing, Miss. Leave go of me, please. Your uncle'll be back in a minute and the packing not done.
WILHELMINA You're older than me. Did you know my father?
HANNAH Och, I was only a wee boy at the time.
WILHELMINA Did you know him?
HANNAH I did and I didn't.
WILHELMINA What like was he? Tell me.
HANNAH Oh, a pleasant spoken sort of gentleman. Now, Miss, please.
WILHELMINA (fawning on him) Tell me about him. Tell me all about him. Tell me. Dear John. Please.
HANNAH Now, Miss. Really, Miss.
WILHELMINA Please, John darling. Please. I'd give anything to know. Please . . .

(He kisses her roughly)

Oh, you swine! How dare you? Don't do that. . . . Oh . . . you . . .

HANNAH And that's what you get and what you'll get again.
WILHELMINA I'll tell my uncle.
HANNAH No, you won't. Pass those cups.

(She stares at him)

You can stop gaping at me. Come along. Pass that cup.

(She passes it with a trance-like movement)

That'll maybe learn you that a common servant's made of flesh and blood like the rest of folk.

(He closes and lifts the luncheon basket)

WILHELMINA Nothing like that ever happened to me before.
HANNAH It's a wonder.
WILHELMINA Put down that basket . . . I want to . . . Why did you do that just now?
HANNAH That's asking.
WILHELMINA But I want to know.
HANNAH Fine you know already.
WILHELMINA I don't. Honestly, I don't. Not really. Tell me.
HANNAH I'll tell you all right – some time.
WILHELMINA When will you tell me?
HANNAH Here's your uncle coming back. Pull yourself together.
WILHELMINA When will you tell me?
HANNAH There's times I take a walk up by the old summer-house at the top of the glen. Maybe about half-past eleven. Before I go to bed. Just for a walk. I might and I might not. . . . I think that's everything, Miss. I'll take this over to the phaeton and yoke the pony.

(MARSHALL is heard approaching, singing "The Kerry Dance" in a cracked baritone. Exit HANNAH.)

MARSHALL *(entering)* Well. Time to bundle and go. What are you gazing at?
WILHELMINA It's something about John Hannah's back and the funny stiff way he holds his shoulders – like a highwayman on the scaffold.
MARSHALL You let John Hannah's back alone and chuck me that rug. I'll carry it.
WILHELMINA You carry everything, dear Uncle Will. Am I great responsibility?
MARSHALL Yes. You've been out too long. You're looking quite white. Are you feeling all right?
WILHELMINA Yes. I'm all right.

124

(MARSHALL clears up what is left of the impedimenta, humming "The Kerry Dance" as he does so. He goes out on the line, "Oh, for one of those hours of gladness.")

WILHELMINA Gone, alas, like our youth, too soon.

(She picks up her hat and runs out)

CURTAIN

ACT ONE

Scene Four

Midnight in the winter of 1886. WILLIAM MARSHALL's consulting-room at his house in Woodside Place, Glasgow. Mahogany and horsehair furniture, oil paintings of grim Highland mountains and battling fishing-boats, black marble and embossed wall-paper give the room a hideous dignity. Part of the big bookcase contains medicine bottles and a few medical instruments. MARSHALL, who is now forty-five, sits by the fire. He wears a velvet jacket and a smoking-cap. He is drinking port wine and smoking a cigar. JOHN HANNAH, aged twenty-five, is writing at a desk. Twelve o'clock strikes. MARSHALL starts. He has been more than half asleep.

MARSHALL Bless my soul! I was nearly asleep. That's not midnight, is it?
HANNAH Yes, Sir. It is.
MARSHALL Are there any more letters to write?
HANNAH Yes, Sir. One, Sir. To Dr. Appleringie, Sir.
MARSHALL That scoundrel. What about?
HANNAH About the patient he sent to see you this afternoon. Mrs. McKirdy from the Balgrayhill.
MARSHALL Mrs. Mac . . . Tuts! I can't remember anything about her, except that she had a red nose. Always take careful notes, Hannah. A cautious clinician always takes notes. And now, what the . . . ?
HANNAH She was a case of nervous dyspepsia, Sir.
MARSHALL Oh, one of those? Right. Take thy pen and write quickly:
  Mr. Appleringie. My Dear Sir, I am greatly obliged by the opportunity of examining your patient, Mrs Thingummybob, and – ah um – feel bound to agree with your diagnosis of – ah um, dash it all! Oh yes – diagnosis of asthenia of hysterical origin. I imagine that the exhibition of – ah um – Blaud's Pill and Valerian – fill in the dosage, Hannah – continued over a period will conduce to that happy issue we mutually desire. With most respectful regards to your amiable wife, and the deepest feelings of esteem for yourself, my dear sir, I have the honour to remain and so on. . . . Was I asleep?
HANNAH No, Sir. Just dovering, every now and then.
MARSHALL You didn't hear my niece come in?
HANNAH No, Sir. I didn't.
MARSHALL She's abominably late. Her chaperone should be ashamed of herself. Girls didn't stay out till past midnight in my young days except on special occasions. I tell you what it is, John Hannah, this generation is getting clean out of hand.

HANNAH Yes, Sir. They are that.

MARSHALL And what the devil do you know about it? You haven't the cut of a ladies' man.

HANNAH No, Sir. I hope not, Sir.

MARSHALL You don't practise the minor amatory exercises in your spare time?

HANNAH I have no spare time, Sir.

MARSHALL That's right. Don't you get tangled with the petticoats. Plenty of time for that when you are well set on the road you are going.

HANNAH Not much time for it even then.

MARSHALL Maybe so. Maybe so. We get our passions before we get sense, and by the time we get sense they've left us. And if we do our work we lose all the fun. And if we don't do our work we can neither appreciate the fun nor pay for it. That's the way of it, Johnny, isn't it?

HANNAH I haven't thought of it. It seems to me we weren't put here just for fun, begging your pardon, Sir.

MARSHALL Eh? What d'you think we were put here for? Have a glass of port wine.

HANNAH No, thank you, Sir. I'm an abstainer.

MARSHALL Quite right. (He drinks) What were we put here for?

HANNAH To fulfil a Purpose, I suppose.

MARSHALL I wish the purpose were a little clearer.

HANNAH It's clear enough to me, Sir.

MARSHALL Then you're damned lucky. You're a Catholic, aren't you, by the way?

HANNAH No, Sir. You're thinking of my mother, Sir. I've seen the light.

MARSHALL That's nice. Heigho! I'll awa to my bed. . . . Oh, that reminds me. Did you remember that prescription for your mother?

HANNAH I was going to ask you, Sir.

MARSHALL Take it down: Sodii carbonati, granas 120; Acidi Hydrocyanici Diluti, minimes 30; Compound infusion of gentian, quantum sufficit ad six ounces; misce ut fit haustus; signitur a table-spoonful ter in die after meals.

HANNAH I've got that, Sir.

MARSHALL Right. Here's the key of the poison cupboard, in case you want to make up the prescription now. You'll need it for the hydrocyanic acid.

HANNAH Thank you, Sir.

MARSHALL You believe in God, do you?

HANNAH I do.

MARSHALL So do I. . . . And, by God, I would need to.

(He checks himself on the way to the door and returns to the table for another glass of port. He leans against the mantelpiece, drinking his wine.)

How old are you, Hannah?

HANNAH Twenty-five this week, Sir.

MARSHALL So? It's latish to be starting medicine.

HANNAH I know. It took me too long to realise I was wasted in the shop. Playing for safety's all very fine, but it's best to keep an eye open for bettering yourself.

MARSHALL Playing for safety. Yes. . . . Never trust anybody too much, Hannah.

HANNAH No, Sir. I won't.

MARSHALL Or love anybody too much. . . . And yet it all comes right if you wait, Johnny. It all comes right if you wait. . . . You don't know what I'm talking about? Never mind. Tell Miss Cameron when she comes in that I'm very seriously annoyed with her, bless her heart.

HANNAH Very well, Sir.

MARSHALL Hannah, I know quite well what you think of me. They say there's no fool like an old fool, but a middle-aged one is a good imitation. Life's pretty simple to you young seagreen incorruptibles. It's not such an easy matter when you're older. . . . You think I'm soft with my niece, eh?

HANNAH It's not for me to say, Sir.

MARSHALL Damn it, say what you think, for once.

HANNAH Well, Sir, they say a young growing girl needs a strong hand to guide her, these days.

MARSHALL That's what they say, is it? Well, they don't know what they're talking about. . . . John, that girl means to me everything I believe in and everything I hope for. If anything happened to her my whole universe would burst like a bomb. "The substance of things hoped for. . . ." You know what happened in my family. It killed my mother and my elder sister, and it sent my two brothers to the ends of the earth. But I know that my redeemer liveth. I know. I know. She has . . . she is . . . *Ach Himmel*, I've had too much to drink. Good night. And don't forget to put the gas out. And don't forget that to make for righteousness is a biological necessity. . . . Ach, I'm havering. I'm at the theological stage of inebriety. Stick to your principles, my boy, if they're only teetotalism. Good night to you.

HANNAH Good night, Sir.

(Exit MARSHALL. HANNAH lights a cigar, helps himself to wine, and leisurely collects materials for making up a stomachic mixture. The door opens gradually and WILHELMINA CAMERON, in a ball dress, enters stealthily.)

WILHELMINA Hullo!

HANNAH I didn't hear you come in.

WILHELMINA That's a mercy, anyhow. I nearly bumped into Uncle Willie. Is he angry?

HANNAH Yes.

WILHELMINA Are you angry?

HANNAH Well, what do you think? You never see me going to a ball with another young lady and stopping out till all hours.

WILHELMINA You! You're not a party man, are you, Johnny? Wasn't it clever of me to find out what a passionate little person you really were? . . . What are you doing?

HANNAH Making up a prescription for Ma.

WILHELMINA How is she?

HANNAH Badly. She's getting old.

WILHELMINA *(reading a label)* Acid Hydrocyan Dil. Poison. What's this, Johnny?

HANNAH Put that down; it's prussic acid.

WILHELMINA Are you going to poison your Ma?

HANNAH No. We only put thirty drops in the whole bottle, and she only gets two and a half in a dose.

WILHELMINA But suppose she drank the whole bottle?

HANNAH My mother's not such a fool.

WILHELMINA Would it kill her?

HANNAH It might. A teaspoonful of that diluted stuff would. Don't go playing about with it.

WILHELMINA You're very grumpy tonight. Just when your Mina wants such a friendly talk with you. You can do that afterwards. Sit down and rest, Mina's own sweetheart.

HANNAH I'm wearied. I've got to work hard all day, if you haven't.

WILHELMINA Mina knows the poor thing's wearied. Sit down in the nice big cosy chair and let Mina stroke her dear animal's hair and soothe all her dear animal's weariness away, away.

HANNAH Och, well. For five minutes. Shove over the decanter.

(He sits in the armchair. WILHELMINA fills his glass and pours out another for herself. She sits on the arm of his chair. The decanter and glasses are within easy reach.)

WILHELMINA The dear animal doesn't ask his Mina how she enjoyed the party.

HANNAH De'il ha'e't I care how she enjoyed her party. You'd be with yon great Mr. Sutherland most of the night, I don't wonder.

WILHELMINA Well? If I was?

HANNAH Of course, he's a gentleman. A soft goods warehouse, no less. Wholesale. A gey improvement on a rough tyke of a medical student. A Captain in the Volunteers, they tell me. Quite the gentry. Would he be in his uniform, maybe?

WILHELMINA Yes. He was in his uniform.

HANNAH The soldier's lass. Just that. Imphm. Real handsome, with his whiskers and moustachios. A dashing cavalier. The shauchly, weaver-kneed brock!

WILHELMINA Oh, mercy, gracious, goodness me, what a jealous wee animal we have tonight!

HANNAH Jealous! Of a Jessie the like of that? I'll wager you'd sooner dance with your auntie, you wee besom. Eh? ha, ha! I'm not angry with you. Give us a kiss.

(She kisses him)

How did you get on? Did he touch your elbow and then beg your pardon. Hey? Haw, haw!

WILHELMINA Haw, haw! What sparkling, polished, satisfying wit! Let me tell you, if you were half as good a man as Mr. Sutherland . . .

HANNAH Captain Sutherland.

WILHELMINA Do stop trying to be funny. I hate you when you try to be funny. You're like a cart-horse in tights. And particularly, please, will you refrain from making coarse jests about my friends? I dislike it intensely.

HANNAH Oh, quite the Madam, now! We're to be very respectful to the great Captain Sutherland after this.

WILHELMINA I should prefer you to be so.

HANNAH You should prefer me to be so. Now maybe, you'll be so good as for to oblige your most humble and obedient servant with a reason as to why he should restrain his risible faculties at the thought of a wabbit gomeral the like of yon?

WILHELMINA You want a reason, do you?

HANNAH I'd be humbly obliged and eternally grateful.

WILHELMINA Very well, then. Mr. Sutherland is my future husband.

HANNAH *(springing from his seat)* What?

WILHELMINA He proposed to me tonight. I accepted him.

HANNAH You did, did you?

WILHELMINA Yes.

HANNAH And may I most respectfully inquire, Miss Wilhelmina Cameron, where I come in?

WILHELMINA You don't come in at all. You keep out. I don't belong to you.

HANNAH You don't, don't you? You have, more than once.

(A pause)

WILHELMINA It makes me sick to think of it.

HANNAH If you think I'm the sort that gives up his girl without a fight, you're wrong.

WILHELMINA What can you do?

HANNAH You'll see what I can do. Marry you, for one thing.

WILHELMINA Marry me?

HANNAH Aye. Make an honest woman of you.

WILHELMINA No, you won't. You'll never marry me. I'm a lady. You came from the gutter. Do you hear me? From the gutter. You still stink of the gutter. Do you hear?

HANNAH Aye, I hear. The whole house'll hear, too. Sit down and be sensible.

WILHELMINA No.

HANNAH Then I will.

(He sits down with his back to the desk. WILHELMINA fidgets nervously with the bottle on the table.)

We'll see, my lassie, we'll see.

WILHELMINA We'll see what?

HANNAH We'll see what your uncle and Mr. Sutherland have to say to one or two things.

WILHELMINA What things?

HANNAH Oh, about one or two of those letters I got from a certain weel-brocht-up, pure-minded young lady of high degree. Man, I'm surprised at ye, Wilhelmina. It's not everybody could bring a blush to the cheek of a gutter brat, but there were things in yon epistles . . .

WILHELMINA I told you to burn them. You said you had burnt them.

HANNAH Did I, now? Did I really? . . . Dod, it's an awful thing to have a bad memory. . . . And forbye, there's that most interesting story of the night I went down to Duthie Bay with some papers. If I told that, weel, it might give the Captain some bonnie hints for his honeymoon.

(He drinks, reaching behind him for his glass and replacing it on the table. WILHELMINA grows very still and follows every action with her eyes.)

Very enjoyable, yon. Very enjoyable. . . . And, there's the time you were supposed to be staying with your auntie, and the time I came knocking in the night at the ground-floor window . . .

WILHELMINA Stop that. . . . Johnny, you burned the letters. Didn't you? Say you burned them.

HANNAH The ground-floor window. Aye. Very handy. And only ten days ago. Dod, you're a hard-hearted baggage.

WILHELMINA Johnny, I was only joking. Johnny, you wouldn't tell; Uncle would kill you.

HANNAH Maybe, maybe. He'd find me gey hard to kill.

WILHELMINA You haven't got the letters.

HANNAH I've got the letters all right.

(He takes a bundle from his pocket)

"My darling, my darling lover – A thousand thousand kisses. . . ." Keep back.

WILHELMINA You're hurting my arm –

HANNAH I'll have it off at the shoulder if you play your monkey games with me.

(He puts the letters back in his pocket and buttons his coat; refills his glass; gulps it and refills again, drinking half and replacing the glass)

Dr. John Hannah, son-in-law of the great Dr. William Marshall, Physician to the Royal Infirmary, Glasgow; author of *Marshall on Fevers*. The industrious apprentice leads the blushing niece of his friend and teacher to the altar. And after that . . . and after that . . . no more cantrips for you, my lassie. I'll sort you. No fears. Sutherland!! Ha, ha!

(WILHELMINA pours the contents of the medicine bottle into his glass)

Gimme another drink. . . . Do you hear me, Mrs. Hannah? Give me another drink.

(She pours a little wine on top of his prussic acid cocktail and hands it to him. He takes it off without heeltaps.)

Hey! What's this?

(He wrenches himself round to glare at her horribly, and then falls dead on the hearthrug. He is hidden from the audience by the chair. WILHELMINA, after a moment of shrinking, unbuttons the coat and retrieves the letters. While she is doing so, enter MARSHALL. They face one another.)

MARSHALL What's the matter?

WILHELMINA I've killed him.

MARSHALL John Hannah?

(She hands him the letters. After a glance he tosses them into the fire and kneels beside the body examining it for signs of life.)

When did you come in?

WILHELMINA He is dead, isn't he? About ten past twelve. Is he dead?

MARSHALL Quite dead.

(He gets up and examines the bottles on the table)

I see. Go and fetch Dr. Coutts.

WILHELMINA Oh, I can't. I can't. Oh, Uncle Will, I can't . . .

MARSHALL Do as I tell you. And tell him you had just come in and don't know what it is all about. Merely that I want him urgently. Hurry.

(WILHELMINA goes. MARSHALL turns back the hands on the Presentation Black Marble Clock to twelve ten. Enter MRS. HANNAH in night attire.)

MARSHALL Go to bed, Elspeth. Do you hear me, go to bed!

CURTAIN

CHORUS TO ACT TWO

The scene is the same as in the introduction to Act One. The light grows. The Waiter has just brought two more drinks and is leaving the Stage as the lights go up. The Clergyman still sleeps.

COOPER Good health.
COUTTS Thank you.
COOPER Nasty business that.
COUTTS An awful business.
COOPER Do you think she killed the fellow?
COUTTS I know she killed him.

(Pause)

COOPER How do you know?
COUTTS Well, it's been a sort of a family secret, but . . . Well, I don't suppose it matters now. . . . My father was called in.
COOPER Yes?
COUTTS Our young madam woke him up in the middle of the night looking like a ghost in her white ball dress. She would say nothing but, "Come, come quickly. . . ." He found old Bill sitting in the armchair looking down at the body as if he wished it were alive again and he could kill it all over again. I don't think old Bill ever hated anything in his life but that one corpse. . . . Then he got up and said "Good evening," quite calmly, and began systematically pulling the wool over my father's eyes. The cheek of him! My father said, "Bill, your clock's slow." And Bill said, "Jamie, your watch has aye something the matter with it. That clock's never missed a minute for years." That was true. I think he sent for my governor because he knew his watch was always wrong and because he knew about the clock. And while my father was standing with his foot on the fender and his watch in his hand, looking at the watch and then at the clock, old Bill knocked the watch out of his hand on to the stone hearth.
COOPER And your father held his tongue about that?
COUTTS He held his tongue about that. If the old woman hadn't informed the police, there would have been no trouble. She heard Wilhelmina come in and heard them quarrelling. But the young Sutherland fellow she was engaged to – he swore to the hour she got out of his cab, and my governor swore to the time on the clock. It was a good alibi.
COOPER But the old woman carried conviction enough to get her brought to trial?
COUTTS My father said she was just one old wizened lump of malignity. Counsel for the Defence made her contradict herself every second word. The judge said straight out that she must have been daft or dreaming, but she held

134

to her point, and the jury brought a verdict of Not Proven. A good verdict, my father said.

(The Clergyman stirs in his sleep)

Hush! He's waking.

COOPER No, no. Go on. What became of her?

COUTTS It's a queer thing . . . that what I'm going to say should sound sort of funny. Man, it was no joke for anybody concerned. . . . Six months after the trial she had twins! A boy and a girl. They were registered in Duthie Parish under her own name – Cameron. I've seen the entry.

COOPER And this Sutherland man? He didn't marry her, of course?

COUTTS He wanted her to, but she wouldn't. A month later she went over the cliff, near the lighthouse at Duthie Bay. In her sleep, they said. . . . I don't know about you, but I'm getting hungry. I had no lunch and . . .

COOPER Go on with your story. It's too early for dinner. Go on.

COUTTS We'll wake the Doctor, there, and we'll have him dining at our table for our sins. . . . Or we might go out bang. Like a candle.

COOPER No. He won't wake. Go on.

COUTTS Well, Marshall took charge of the twins. Strange thing to do. Collecting babies like that. The girl developed a lung, and he sent her to Switzerland with a governess when she was ten. He enrolled the boy as a medical student; he was a bit of a handful then. He's a handful now. I remember when I worked with him in the Great Epidemic. . . . You know. The Walker Institute.

COOPER A bad time that. A bad time. Extraordinary to think it was only three years ago. The Great Sickness!

COUTTS Yes. I say, come in to dinner. I'll tell you the rest there. I'm sure he's going to wake up.

COOPER Come along then.

(They go. The lights fade out.)

ACT TWO

Scene One

The Police Station at a small town near Glasgow. The time is two o'clock in the morning. A SERGEANT is writing at his desk, to him, a CONSTABLE.

The Scene takes place during the summer of 1907.

CONSTABLE Your tea's ready, Sergeant.

SERGEANT Just a minute. I've this bit to do. How do you spell "accommodation"?

CONSTABLE Which bit of it is sticking you?

SERGEANT I never can mind if it's two "c's" or one "c".

CONSTABLE Ah, well, I don't know. I'd just be putting you wrong if I guessed.

SERGEANT We'll try one "c". It saves extra work, anyhow.

CONSTABLE He's an awful one that.

SERGEANT Who is?

CONSTABLE Him, in by.

SERGEANT Tyach, aye. I've no patience with that sort.

CONSTABLE It was kind of funny, too.

SERGEANT I see nothing funny in it.

CONSTABLE You being a sergeant, maybe you wouldn't see anything funny in it; but I was hard put to it to keep from smiling, mysel'.

SERGEANT You're soft!

CONSTABLE Was that his right-enough address he gave?

SERGEANT Aye. The old block's coming down. He'll be here any minute.

CONSTABLE The doctor?

SERGEANT Aye, Marshall, they call him. It's him that's a Professor in the Royal at Glasgow. Away and have your tea, Lachie.

CONSTABLE Him that looked after Willie Johnstone when he had the gastric stomach?

SERGEANT The same. You surely don't think if I hadn't known him I would have rang him up on the 'phone?

CONSTABLE No. There's that.

SERGEANT Our young Lord would have had a clout on the head to sleep off, forbye all that beer. But he's a fine old body, the Doctor.

CONSTABLE And you're sure this lad's his nephew?

SERGEANT Aye, he's his nephew right enough. And how the mischief am I to get writing my report with you standing havering there? Run away in, like a good lad.

136

CONSTABLE A fine man, the Professor, Willie Johnstone said.

(A noise of hammering is heard)

Pity me! there he is again. . . . Hi! Haud your peace!

(More hammering is heard)

Be a good lad, now. Your uncle will be here soon.
SERGEANT Tyach!
CONSTABLE Now then, Mr. Cameron, now then.
SERGEANT *(disdainfully)* Now then! *(In a bellow like a bull's)* Stop you
that noise or I'll put you upstairs.

(Louder hammering)

Away and see what he wants.

(Exit CONSTABLE. Hammering stops)

CONSTABLE *(re-entering)* He wants a cigarette. Can I give him one?
SERGEANT Oh, anything for peace.

*(Exit CONSTABLE. Enter DR. MARSHALL. He is alert and vigorous
at sixty-six.)*

MARSHALL Good evening, Sergeant.
SERGEANT Good evening to you, Sir. It'll be Professor Marshall, will it
not?
MARSHALL Yes. What's all this?
SERGEANT Oh, he's a foolish young man, Sir. A foolish young man.
MARSHALL Good God! I know that. But what's he done this time?
SERGEANT Well, I didn't just know what to charge him with, Professor.
I'm thinking it's larceny, you see, Sir; but that's a kind of serious matter, and
when he said he was your nephew . . .
MARSHALL Larceny? What did he steal?
SERGEANT Ducks, Sir.
MARSHALL What?
SERGEANT Ducks. Thirty-seven ducks. A serious business, Sir.
MARSHALL But how in all the world did he contrive to steal thirty-seven
ducks?
SERGEANT Ah, that's just it, Professor. You see, he was here for the Races,
Professor, and he had a beer or two, Sir. . . . That's what he's charged with,
Doctor – "drunk and disorderly." It's more respectable, like. The last record
of his movements we had, Sir, before the depredation, he was in the "Cross
Keys" standing drinks all round to a lot of riff-raff, and drinking "The King
over the Water" – that's Prince Charlie, Sir, him that's dead long syne –
and making speeches about Big Business and Private Enterprise, Sir. That
would be at half-past five, Professor. And at half-past eight, there was him

and a lot of wee boys driving a cleckan of ducks down the London Road, and a crowd after him.

MARSHALL I see. Is he sober now?

SERGEANT I wouldn't wonder, Sir. Lachie, there, gave him a cup of nice strong tea.

MARSHALL You'll take bail for him, I suppose?

SERGEANT Oh, yes, Professor, surely. Three pounds, it'll be, if it's all the same to you.

MARSHALL He didn't assault the police this time?

SERGEANT No, no. Lachie didn't give him the chance.

MARSHALL That's something, anyhow.

SERGEANT I'll make you out a receipt.

MARSHALL I'm not sure that I'll stand bail for him.

SERGEANT Och, now, Sir. He's had his lesson.

MARSHALL He hasn't. He's never out of trouble.

SERGEANT Och, it's just high spirits. Just youth and high spirits.

MARSHALL It's more than that, unfortunately, Sergeant. Can I see him?

SERGEANT Certainly, Professor, certainly. Lachie and me'll away in for our tea. You can tell him your private opinion of his conduct, sotto voce, as the saying is. . . . Lachie!

CONSTABLE (*without*) Right you are, Sergeant.

(*Enter with CHARLES CAMERON, a lad of twenty-one – a little dissipated-looking, with a shy manner and a pronounced but variable stutter. He is sober.*)

SERGEANT You can give your parole for him, Professor. We'll be just next door.

(*The POLICEMEN go out*)

MARSHALL Well, Charlie?

CAMERON Well, Uncle Will?

MARSHALL Here you are again.

CAMERON Here I am again.

MARSHALL And that's all you've got to say.

CAMERON N-no. Oh, no. I'm s-s-s-s-sorry. I sh-shouldn't have bothered you with this. Only the Final's to-morrow.

MARSHALL You propose to sit your Final Examination to-morrow.

CAMERON Yes. They start to-morrow. You're examining, aren't you? I'm in the first batch.

MARSHALL And what sort of a shape do you expect to make at your examination with your head humming from a debauch?

CAMERON It w-w-w-wasn't a debauch, Uncle Will.

MARSHALL I don't want any argument. I'm asking a question.

CAMERON Well, it's a s-s-s-silly question. Like "Have you stopped beating your wife?" I haven't got a wife, and I n-never began beating her.

MARSHALL Charlie, if you had any sense you'd see I'm in no mood for facetiousness.

CAMERON Neither am I, Uncle Will. I'm d-d-dead serious. I've got to get to Glasgow by nine tomorrow. And I can't break out of the cell. I've tried. It'd take a week. So I had to touch you for bail. You're the only man I could trust.

MARSHALL I wish to Heaven I could trust you.

CAMERON You can, Uncle Will. I'm going to get Honours. I've got distinction in every d-darned thing up till now and m-medals in every class but Midwifery – and it's so damned silly . . .

MARSHALL Will you be good enough to stop your damned impudence and stick to the point?

CAMERON B-but it is the point, Uncle Will. The point is, am I an efficient member of society or am I not? I am.

MARSHALL The point is that this is the seventh time you've dragged the family into the police court, and I've some respect for my own professional and social status, if you haven't. And I'm simply not going to stand it.

CAMERON Uncle Will, it's very friendly of you to keep me in bed and board and to turn out in the middle of the night to deliver me from my ch-ch-ch-chains; but I must insist that it gives you no right to dictate my course of action. You know you're as proud of me as a d-d-dog with two tails, and I think that pretty well meets m-most of my obligations to you. Moreover . . .

MARSHALL Look here, you young hound . . .

CAMERON Please let me finish. I'm sorry you've had all this trouble. But even you must see that I've got to get my degree. I don't expect they'd send the examiners out here, so I've got to get to them. You m-must be reasonable.

MARSHALL (*with iron self-control*) Do you know, you're the most impudent dog I ever met?

CAMERON Throwing mud isn't arguing, Uncle Will.

MARSHALL I'm not arguing.

CAMERON I know that. I'm just telling you you aren't.

MARSHALL Look here, Charlie; do you know what I'm going to do?

CAMERON Wicked Uncle now assumes initiative. No, Uncle Will, I am all ears.

MARSHALL I'm going to get into my car and drive away.

CAMERON Leaving me to dree my w-weird?

MARSHALL Leaving you to dree your weird.

CAMERON Wait a minute, Uncle Will.

MARSHALL What is it?

CAMERON If you try that, I'll butt you in the tummy and bolt.

MARSHALL You will, you whiskyfied, pasty-faced lump?

CAMERON I'll have a try. Don't you understand? I've got to sit the F-final. I've got to go into the Western next week as Sir Billy's house surgeon. I've got to be in Bobby's laboratory by this time next year. I've got the next five years of my life all arranged. You don't want to upset it all, do you?

MARSHALL That's your responsibility, not mine. It's high time you had a sharp lesson, and I'm going to give you one.

CAMERON I take sharp lessons from no man. Not even you.

MARSHALL Don't talk like a fool. Sit down there. I've never been a stern guardian to you!

CAMERON That's true.

MARSHALL I never beat you when you were a kid, though the Lord knows you needed it.

CAMERON If you had, I'd have killed you. Go on.

MARSHALL I've always tried to go alongside you, and not to sit up in the clouds and throw thunderbolts at you. I've tried to make you feel that I'm an old friend, ready to help you when you're up against problems . . .

CAMERON I'm up against one now.

MARSHALL Let me speak. I took that course because I know better than you, perhaps, what fights with the Devil you've had and will have. . . . I've never talked to you about your parents.

CAMERON No-no. B-but I wasn't at school very long before I had to look up the dictionary for the word "bastard".

MARSHALL Then you know?

CAMERON Yes.

MARSHALL I didn't realise that.

CAMERON Oh, I don't mind. It gives me a hell of a fine freelance feeling. It must be rotten to be somebody's son.

MARSHALL You're a son to me, Charlie.

CAMERON No, I'm not. I love and admire you, but you haven't got me by the leg that way, Uncle Will. I'm my own son.

MARSHALL Laddie, you're the son of a bad man and a foolish girl. And it gets worse as it goes back. If I had been one of those eugenic madmen I'd have drowned you when you were a pup. It would be better I had you by the leg than your heredity.

CAMERON Heredity's all rot.

MARSHALL Is it? You've your grandfather's eyes and ears and hands and mouth. You've your mother's trick of tossing your head back. Thank God I see little of your father in you but your obstinacy and your infernal love of an argument . . . though he was a methodical brute, too, damn him! and so are you. . . . It's not that we're like our fathers and mothers. We *are* our fathers and mothers. And, by Heaven, that's a solemn thought, when I stand in this dirty police station and look at you.

CAMERON I've played the game. I've worked like a nigger. I've hurt nobody but myself. It isn't fair to cast up my parents to me.

MARSHALL Don't talk like a licked bairn. I'm not casting up to you, and you know it. I didn't speak to you like this before because I didn't want the smallest hint or suggestion to turn you into a sense of irresponsibility. Charlie, I want to keep a grip of you. I'm a simple old man, and not clever. But I know life and I know your danger points. You must let me guide you for a bit. I know where you're strong and I know where you're weak. You're only a boy. You must let me guide you. . . .

CAMERON They say you kill a lot of pneumonias that way.

MARSHALL Who say? What are you talking about?

CAMERON Yes. They say you hump them about once or twice a day to percuss their backs and sicken them with digitalis and knock out their livers with whisky and stupefy them with paraldehyde and flood their bronchi with expectorants and poison them with . . .

MARSHALL *Ach Himmel!* I do nothing of the sort.

CAMERON You do. I've seen you at it. In the c-clinique.

MARSHALL You're an infernal liar. I sit at the bedside of a case of pneumonia, in no way attempting the impossible task of controlling the tempest, far from it; but I lay the hand of experience on the tiller in the hope that, under Providence, I may bring the frail vessel . . .

CAMERON ". . . storm-tossed and shattered, it is true. Leaking at every seam. But still afloat. Safe to the desired haven." I've heard all that.

MARSHALL How dare you burlesque my lectures? You're not fit . . .

CAMERON *You're* not fit to manage another man's life. Not you nor any man. It's all my eye, this wise-guidance business. A pneumonia dies or he gets better. Nothing you do makes a tuppen'orth of difference except for the worse. Is that true, or isn't it?

MARSHALL Of course it's true. Damn it! I taught you that myself. But . . .

CAMERON But you like to feel you're driving the gig, like the drunk man in the story. Well, you're not holding the reins. And you'll have to trust my beast's instinct to take me past the ditches. You say I'm a mixture of b-blackguards and idiots. Well, you'll have to let the mixture be, and hope for the best.

MARSHALL But there's genius in the mixture too, Charlie. We mustn't let that . . .

CAMERON Let it be, then? What sort of a man are you t-to bring genius to heel and teach it d-dog's tricks?

MARSHALL There's one thing I'm sure of about you.

CAMERON What's that?

MARSHALL You could talk yourself out of the inmost circle of the pit of Hell. Have you a hat and coat?

CAMERON I had a hat somewhere. Oh, there it is.

MARSHALL Sergeant!

CAMERON It's very good of you, Uncle Will. I'm a b-bad egg, but I think you'll find I'm good in parts.

(Enter the SERGEANT, his mouth full)

MARSHALL How much did you say you wanted, Sergeant?

SERGEANT Three pounds, Professor. I'll make out the receipt.

(He sits down at his desk)

Did you give him a good talking to, Sir?

MARSHALL He seems to have done most of the talking. But I don't think he'll bother you again. He tells me he's good in parts, like the curate's egg.

SERGEANT I don't know that I have ever seen a curate's egg. . . . Here's your receipt, Sir. Will you sign here? Thank you.

MARSHALL Thank you. Good night to you, Sergeant. You've been very civil.

SERGEANT Not at all, Sir. You were very kind to one of our lads up bye in the Infirmary. Willie Johnstone. Constable William Johnstone.

MARSHALL Ah! How is he?

SERGEANT He's a bit stiff in the left knee, yet, but och, he's fine. It's a quiet place this, for the constabulary. It's not often we get young gentlemen from Glasgow down waking up the town.

MARSHALL A good job too.

SERGEANT I wouldn't say, Sir. There's the things we took from your pockets, Mr. Cameron. Will you sign for them here?

CAMERON Righto.

MARSHALL Good night.

SERGEANT Good night, Professor, and a pleasant journey.

CAMERON Good night, Sergeant. Say good night to Lachie for me.

(The SERGEANT does not answer, but busies himself with his papers. MARSHALL and CAMERON go out.)

CURTAIN

ACT TWO

Scene Two

MARSHALL's drawing-room in Woodside Place, Glasgow. It is the autumn of 1916. The room has some good pictures and furniture, but the pictures are badly hung and the furniture ill-assorted and ill-arranged. A MANSERVANT announces two guests.

MANSERVANT Sir Douglas and Lady Todd Walker. . . . Oh, I'm sorry, Sir Douglas. The Colonel hasn't come down yet.

SIR DOUGLAS That's all right, Donovan. We are early, I think.

MANSERVANT Thank you very much, Sir.

SIR DOUGLAS You haven't been called up yet, I see.

MANSERVANT No, Sir. I have mitral stenosis, Sir. In any case, I should probably be required to drive the Colonel's car.

LADY WALKER Funny to hear Cousin Will called "the Colonel".

SIR DOUGLAS I don't see that it's particularly funny. He is a colonel.

LADY WALKER I know. In a way he is. But . . .

SIR DOUGLAS What do you mean, in a way? A medical colonel is a colonel the same as any other colonel. He holds the King's Commission, therefore he is a colonel.

LADY WALKER Don't let's argue about it, anyhow. How is Colonel Marshall, Donovan? Is he quite better?

MANSERVANT Yes, my lady, I think so. He took the little dog for a walk in the park this afternoon.

LADY WALKER That's nice. And the little dog would be so delighted to go out with him again.

SIR DOUGLAS Cough troublesome?

MANSERVANT The Colonel's? No, Sir, not at all now.

SIR DOUGLAS I remember when I had whooping-cough. Lord! Shall I ever forget it. I was four then. My grandmother nearly killed me. Lethal creatures, grandmothers.

MANSERVANT Yes, Sir.

SIR DOUGLAS That sort of thing leaves a very deep impression. Terrible!

LADY WALKER Has Captain Cameron arrived, Donovan?

MANSERVANT Not yet, my lady.

LADY WALKER Not *yet*? But when did you expect him?

MANSERVANT He was at the Palace getting his medal yesterday, my lady. Colonel Marshall *did* think he would travel over-night and be here for breakfast.

LADY WALKER But didn't he send word?

MANSERVANT I don't know, my lady. I don't think so.

LADY WALKER Ah! . . . Thank you, Donovan.
MANSERVANT Thank you, my lady.

(Exit MANSERVANT)

LADY WALKER *(looking at a photograph)* And there's the dear old soul in his uniform. He looks every inch a soldier, and he must be a long way over seventy.
SIR DOUGLAS Seventy-five.
LADY WALKER And going up to the hospital every day. It seems so funny.
SIR DOUGLAS Why do you keep saying everything seems so funny? Hindenburg's over seventy. Joffre's over seventy. Balfour's over seventy.
LADY WALKER I know, dear. But when it's someone you know it seems funnier.
SIR DOUGLAS Funnier than what?
LADY WALKER *(after sighing in an extremely irritating manner)* And there's Charlie himself.
SIR DOUGLAS Where? . . . Oh, the photograph. I wonder if he *will* turn up.
LADY WALKER Oh, he must. His first leave for two years and getting his DSO from the King, and the dear old soul taking 'flu and not being able to go south for the investiture. Such a disappointment. He's sure to come.
SIR DOUGLAS I wouldn't bet on it.
LADY WALKER You don't mean he might not come?
SIR DOUGLAS I think it highly probable that he won't.
LADY WALKER Oh, Douglas! He couldn't be so heartless.
SIR DOUGLAS Couldn't he? You haven't much idea of that boy's capabilities.
LADY WALKER He isn't a boy any longer. And so brave, too, the papers said.
SIR DOUGLAS Daft, I'd call it. He doesn't care much for anything; even his own skin.
LADY WALKER Now, now. I won't have you being hard on him, especially when the dinner-party's in his honour. . . . That girl Hope's to be here too, tonight. Now, if it had been Hope.
SIR DOUGLAS If what had been Hope?
LADY WALKER If it had been Hope that had let her uncle down like this.
SIR DOUGLAS It wouldn't break my heart if she did. She ought to be in gaol.
LADY WALKER It's going to be an awful dinner. How she lets that dear old soul live in all that loneliness and misery . . .

(Enter HOPE)

HOPE Hello, Aunt Aggie. Hello, Uncle Douglas. How are you?

LADY WALKER Quite well, thank you, dear.

HOPE Sit down.

(They sit. Silence.)

Oh, I forgot. You're Lady Walker now! How does it feel?

LADY WALKER Well, of course, we expected it for some time. I mean, Douglas was sure to be recognised for his services to the country and . . .

SIR DOUGLAS It doesn't make much difference really. . . .

HOPE No. I don't suppose it does.

(Another pause)

SIR DOUGLAS Uncle keeping fairly fit again, Hope?

HOPE I don't know. I haven't seen him for six months.

LADY WALKER Not seen him for . . . ?

HOPE No. Too busy. I had to rush to get through from Edinburgh this evening, and I'd just time to dive into and half out of this piece of silly nonsense. How do you like it?

LADY WALKER I think it's rather sweet, but . . .

HOPE I don't know what's happened to Uncle Bill. I heard him yelling for Donovan just now, but you kept him gossiping in the drawing-room. . . . Oh, here he is with the cocktails.

(Enter MANSERVANT with a tray)

He seems to do every blooming thing in this house. Have one. I've no small talk, so we'd better all get drunk. Tell me, what have you been doing with yourself these days?

LADY WALKER Oh, I've been terribly, terribly busy . . .

HOPE That's a lie, anyhow. What have you been doing, Uncle Douglas?

LADY WALKER He has been . . .

HOPE Let the poor creature speak for himself.

SIR DOUGLAS Well, if you are really interested, I have been back and forward to London twice a week for the last . . .

HOPE The engine-driver and the fireman and the guard do it oftener than that, and don't look like sick haddocks over it. I suppose you've been helping on the War.

SIR DOUGLAS I've been doing my best.

HOPE Then you ought to be ashamed of yourself.

SIR DOUGLAS I never thought to hear a Scotswoman talk like that. You ought to be ashamed of *yourself*.

HOPE I am ashamed – of myself and of everybody else. Have another cocktail.

SIR DOUGLAS No, thank you. This cocktail drinking is all of a piece with the rest of it. Grossly unpatriotic, though I don't suppose that would weigh with you for a moment.

HOPE Not for a moment.

SIR DOUGLAS I see. How is your brother?

HOPE How should I know? I'm not my brother's keeper; though God knows it's a keeper he needs.

(Enter MARSHALL)

MARSHALL Good evening, Agnes. Good evening, Douglas. It was very good of you to come. Have you had cocktails? I'm so sorry for being late. . . . Ah, I see Hope has been doing the honours.

LADY WALKER Hope is a delightful hostess.

MARSHALL You look very nice tonight, dear.

HOPE All for you, dearest. I hate looking nice.

LADY WALKER Is the influenza quite better, Cousin Will? You must be careful, for all our sakes.

SIR DOUGLAS You're not so young as you once were.

MARSHALL Not many of us are. . . . Yes, I'm quite better, thanks. . . . Any word of Charlie, Hope dear?

HOPE No. I wired to him at five different addresses this morning.

MARSHALL What did you say?

HOPE I said, "You beast, you cad, you pig, you brute." He'll understand.

MARSHALL He ought to. You seem to have made your opinion pretty clear. . . . I don't suppose he'll come. He would have been here by this time.

HOPE Yes.

MARSHALL Do you mind if we wait for a few minutes? I've got a feeling that he might turn up at the last minute. . . . And I shouldn't like to start without . . . Do sit down. Is there any news tonight? I didn't see the papers.

SIR DOUGLAS We seem to have got them on the run now. It's a matter of gun-power. We've got the ammunition now we ought to have had two years ago. It cheers the troops enormously to hear them pooping off.

LADY WALKER What a joy it must be to the boys to feel they're making headway at last!

HOPE Oh, rapturous, delirious joy!

MARSHALL Be quiet, Hope. . . . What time is it now? My glasses. . . . I can't see the clock. . . .

HOPE Quarter to eight.

MARSHALL I'll ask Donovan to keep back dinner for a little. You don't mind?

LADY WALKER Oh, not in the least, Cousin Will.

(MARSHALL goes out)

SIR DOUGLAS Enormous expense, all that gunfire. By Jove, we'll have to make them sweat blood to pay for it, after the War.

HOPE Make who sweat blood?

SIR DOUGLAS The Boches.

HOPE I see.

LADY WALKER Don't let's talk about the War any more.

HOPE Yes. It's a dull subject, isn't it?

LADY WALKER It's not that, but it's all so terrible. Of course, Hope, you're so strong and efficient and hard, dear, that you can't possibly realise what it all means to really sensitive people. But sometimes I can hardly bear it.

(MARSHALL returns)

. . . What *can* be keeping your soldier boy, Cousin Will?

MARSHALL I don't know. I know he had to see them at the War House about a report he made on a phosgene protection scheme. Perhaps they've kept him. It's very unfortunate.

LADY WALKER Wonderful what our family has done for the War. There's Douglas getting his KBE, and you a colonel, and Charlie winning the DSO on the battlefield, and poor David's two boys getting killed at Suvla. It just shows you that a good stock always tells, doesn't it? Heredity.

(HOPE goes to the piano and plays desultorily through the dialogue which follows)

MARSHALL Eh? I didn't hear what you were saying just now, Agnes. I was thinking of something else. . . . Have a cigarette, Douglas.

SIR DOUGLAS Thank you.

LADY WALKER I was just thinking, it's all very well, but where would they have been without people like us?

SIR DOUGLAS Who would have been? Like us? What do you mean, people like us?

LADY WALKER Oh, I mean our sort. People with decent parents and grandparents. I mean, when you see these wretched people in the slums having huge families and handing down disease and all sorts of things. . . .

SIR DOUGLAS All sorts of what things?

LADY WALKER All sorts of criminal tendencies. All sorts of everything.

MARSHALL There aren't many diseases they can hand down very far, Agnes; and "criminal tendency" is a very vague expression.

LADY WALKER Well, insanity.

MARSHALL That's another very vague expression.

LADY WALKER You can't bamboozle me that way, Cousin Will. I read all about it in a book. Two bad people getting married can go on and on till, after two or three generations, you've got thousands of criminal lunatics.

And that sort of people ought not to be allowed to have children. It should be stopped by law.

MARSHALL How?

LADY WALKER There are loads of ways. That's eugenics.

SIR DOUGLAS There's a lot in what Agnes says, I think. We do all sorts of things to get a decent stock in cattle-breeding. Why on earth shouldn't we do the same with human beings? We want a decent stock, and so far as I can see we're taking steps to provide the exact opposite.

LADY WALKER It's a horrid way of putting it, and the two things aren't exactly the same, but I do think Douglas is right. You, as a medical man, should know what a terrible lot of harm is done by people having children who aren't fit to have children.

MARSHALL When you're breeding a strain of cattle you know what you want. They've got to be big and fat and good to eat. Like you and Douglas.

LADY WALKER Really, Cousin Will! Well, if that's what you think of us . . . !

MARSHALL I don't think that of you. Who am I to judge my fellow creatures?

SIR DOUGLAS But you can't get over the fact that there are bad hereditary tendencies. They stare you in the face.

MARSHALL What are they, then? There's a thing we used to call the phthisical diathesis. That means that some of the children of some consumptive parents look like Keats and Shelley and die young. But they write like Keats and Shelley too.

SIR DOUGLAS Oh? And you'd like to see thousands of people dying of consumption every year because an odd one or two of them writes a book of poetry, eh?

MARSHALL Quite a number of us die of something sometime. And I think sometimes we'd be better with fewer old folk and more books of poetry.

SIR DOUGLAS That's all very well. That's all very well. But that's only one bit of it. What about families of drunks, eh? And families of thieves, eh? Aye, and families of murderers?

LADY WALKER Oh, Douglas. . . .

MARSHALL In this year of grace, 1916, we'd be in a bonny pickle if we hadn't a few murderers to keep us from being bossed by a lot of brachycephalic, potbellied, doctrinaire North Germans.

SIR DOUGLAS Well, if that's what you think of our lads in the trenches. . . .

MARSHALL What sort of parents have they got? Any sort, damn it! And if you set them to a proper big job, all their inherited characteristics, all of them, bad and good, combine and sublimate, and you get something like heroism. Mankind aren't so bad, Douglas. What you and your eugenic friends should turn their minds to is breeding a type that'll find them something decent to do. . . . If you ask me what kind of characteristics you want for *that* type, I can't tell you. There's a certain kind of energy and – and vitality you'll find oftener in cripples and epileptics and poor bodies with chronic dyspepsia than you'll find it in heavy-weight boxers and eupeptic stockbrokers and amateur policemen. But I think probably your best plan is to leave it to God Almighty. Whoever He is, He's got some notion of the principles of Biology, I find.

HOPE I know more about inherited characteristics than any of you.

MARSHALL Do you, now, lassie?

HOPE Yes. I am full of Marshalls and Walkers, and I love good food and good clothes and solid houses and fresh air and lots and lots and lots of money and to be respected by my neighbours and dead from the neck up. I am also, on my father's side, a liar, a hypocrite, a thief, a seducer and a blackmailer. On my mother's side I am a harlot and a murderess.

MARSHALL Hope. That's not the way to speak.

LADY WALKER Oh dear, oh dear!

HOPE And my grandmother Marshall was a sensual fool, and my grandmother Hannah was a corpse-fed maggot, and my grandfather Cameron was a whisky-sodden blackguard. . . .

MARSHALL Hope. I can't sit and listen to this. You're mad.

(HOPE strikes a few noisy chords to silence him)

HOPE But my father could work and slave and eat dirt and have patience and wait. And my mother had the courage to do what was to be done and the courage to kill and the courage to die. And my grandfather had the key to all the mysteries. . . . And Charlie's their child, and I don't know what's become of him nor what is to become of him. And I'm their child and I want my dinner.

LADY WALKER Oh! oh! I don't know how we're going to get through dinner after all that. I never heard . . .

HOPE Dear Aunt Aggie, if the Apocalypse comes at a meal-hour, thousands of Marshalls and Walkers will be found seated and expectant; and the vials are yet to pour.

(She rings a bell)

Do you think we need wait for Donovan to announce dinner?

MARSHALL No, I don't think so. You've rung? He'll go ahead.

HOPE Very well, then. Uncle Will, will you take Lady Walker down? . . . And now, Uncle Douglas, you will tell me all about how they gave you a KBE for making all those delicious little shiny shells . . .

(They go out)

CURTAIN

ACT TWO

Scene Three

The morning following the previous scene. A room in a North-West London flat. The profession of its lady tenant is sufficiently obvious from its garnishings. From one of its two doors comes CAPTAIN CHARLES CAMERON, now a rather hard-faced but young-looking man of thirty. He is dressed in a khaki shirt, breeches and socks. He hunts for the rest of his uniform, which has been thrown about into all sorts of places on the previous evening. He puts on his boots, leggings and spurs, cursing continuously under his breath and hurting his fingernails on the buckles. He walks over to a mirror and gazes at his tousled hair and unshaven chin.

CAMERON Captain Charles Cameron, RAMC, made in the image of his Maker!

(He gives a harsh laugh, fastens his necktie with a vicious tug, and goes in search of his tunic. This is seen to be hung with the Distinguished Service Order, the Military Cross, the Croix de Guerre and the Médaille Militaire. He jingles the medals between his fingers and laughs again. He puts on his tunic and feels in the pockets. He finds three unopened telegrams. He reads them, tears them into small pieces, and throws them over his left shoulder. He looks pretty glum. The telegrams are from his sister, Hope. He finds his Sam Browne belt and his cap; straightens himself up; salutes his reflection in the mirror. He puts a couple of Bradburys on the mantelpiece. He puts on a disreputable and ragged British Warm coat.)

A VOICE FROM THE DOORWAY Oi!
CAMERON Oh, you're awake, are you?
VOICE Yes. You're not going away?
CAMERON Yes. I've got to run. I didn't mean to waken you. Go to sleep again.
VOICE But looky here, lovie . . .
CAMERON Stay where you are. I've left a little present on the mantelpiece.
VOICE Righty-oh. God, I'm so sleepy! Oh, I say . . .
CAMERON What?
VOICE What about a souvenir?
CAMERON A what?
VOICE A souvenir. I'm a sentimental little thing. I like to have something to remember my friends by.

CAMERON I see.
VOICE Just an eeny wee collar badge, or somep'n.
CAMERON All right.

(Grinning like a fiend, he pulls the DSO from his tunic)

Here. Like this?

(He throws the medal through the doorway)

VOICE Oh, I say! But that's your DSO, Scottie.
CAMERON I know that.
VOICE But you didn't ought to do that. I mean . . .
CAMERON You're welcome to it.
VOICE 'Ere! Oi! Do you reelise . . . ?
CAMERON I realise what it means all right. I won the damned thing. But I've bigger things to do than that. N-n-now sh-shut up and go to sleep. Cheery-oh.
VOICE Cheery-oh, then. Don't get killed.
CAMERON No. I won't get killed.

(He goes. Shortly afterwards a young creature comes yawning into the room with the DSO in her hand. She polishes it listlessly on the sleeve of her kimono and chucks it into a drawer. She takes the pound notes off the mantelpiece and puts them rather more lovingly into the drawer too. She takes in the morning milk, drinks a little of it out of the bottle and trails off to bed again.)

CURTAIN

ACT TWO

Scene Four

It is a room in the Hotel Paradise, though you wouldn't recognise it. It is in the spring of 193–. There is no carpet on the floor, and the room is furnished with filing cabinets, kitchen tables, and a few incongruous chairs. A sort of war map of London hangs on the wall, with a number of graphs and tables of statistics roughly executed in coloured chalk. There is a huge blackboard covered with figures. A big ultra-microscope stands under a lamp in the corner near a wash-hand basin. On the same table there is a litter of bacteriological instruments and material. A soiled white coat hangs near. Huge lamps of radiological machinery, some of them wrapped in sacking, lie about anyhow. The general effect is of a strangely purposive earthquake. A rather wintry view of Northumberland Avenue is seen through the big window. A young man in horn-rimmed spectacles and a khaki drill overall is typing copies of some notes. To him a smart, tailor-made young lady carrying a large box of flowers.

LADY KATHARINE HELLIWELL Hello!

DR PURLEY Hello, you!

KATHARINE Had your lunch?

PURLEY Lunch? Lunch? What do you mean by lunch? Do you think the bloody Spartans at bloody Thermopylae worried about their bloody lunch?

KATHARINE God! At least it splits the day into two. And your language is filthy.

PURLEY I'm sorry, Lady Katharine. You see that.

(He indicates an empty chair)

KATHARINE Oh no! Harry Williams! But he was there when I went out. Not an hour ago.

PURLEY He fell out of his chair before you were across the street. The great sickness doesn't give you much time.

KATHARINE Oh poor, poor, devil! Does the Chief know?

PURLEY Yes, I 'phoned him.

KATHARINE What'd he say?

PURLEY Asked me what the hell I meant by bothering him. His second assistant, mind you, snoring out his soul with acute encephalitis. Told me to give him a dose of the 595 antivirus. Before the damned thing's been tried out, mind you. There's not much of the milk of human what's his name in Doctor Charles Cameron, Fellow of the Royal Society.

KATHARINE How is Williams?

PURLEY He's for it, and he's damned lucky. His work's done, all right, all

152

right. Now I'm the Pooh-bloody-bah of this joint. And now shut up. If this graph's not ready for C. C. he'll be worse than the Pandemic. Gosh! See what the wind's blown in.

(Enter DR. COUTTS in a mackintosh and bowler)

KATHARINE Hello, Dr. Coutts.
PURLEY Where the devil have you been?
COUTTS Was the Chief asking for me?
PURLEY No.
COUTTS Williams downstairs?
PURLEY Yes.
COUTTS In the lab?
PURLEY No. In a ward. In a bed.
COUTTS *(whistling concernedly)* Strong fellow too. I suppose we've all got to take our chance. I say! that looks bad.

(He is looking at a chart full of curves: mounting ones)

PURLEY Bloody. What's it like outside?
COUTTS As bad as it could be. The epidemic's gaining ground. I've been round to Guy's, Bart's and the London collecting reports. Heavens, what a mess! How they cope with it at all I don't know. They're all out, I tell you. All out. Half of their staffs are down with the Great Sickness and the rest look like ghosts. They're beaten, Purley, beaten. They think we're done for.
PURLEY It's up to us, eh?
COUTTS It's up to us.
KATHARINE Do you want to see the Chief? He's gone to the Middlesex to raise some sort of Hell about something.
COUTTS No. I've got nothing important for him. There's a new cerebellar type coming up from Berkhamsted. I took a chance of seeing him. My taxi's ticking up. I've got to rush off to see about a *cordon sanitaire* round Hoxton – though a fat lot that will do.
PURLEY You're lucky.
KATHARINE Yes. We've got to sit still here.
COUTTS My God, you're *doing* something here. I'm blowing about like a straw hat in a gale. It's maddening to be so helpless. Any news?
KATHARINE Well . . .
PURLEY Never mind about news, Doctor; when will you be back?
COUTTS In an hour or so.
PURLEY I hope we'll have something sensational for you then.
COUTTS I must go. Say I looked in, Lady Katharine.

(Enter a MEDICAL STUDENT)

Oh! Hello, young fellow!
STUDENT Hello, Dr. Coutts.

PURLEY What do you want?

STUDENT Dr. Harris would like the Chief to look at these two o'clock cultures.

PURLEY Right ho. Put them on the table and hop it.

(STUDENT goes)

COUTTS *(looking at the cultures)* Lord, these look pretty hot.

PURLEY You wouldn't like these crawling up and down your cerebro-spinal system.

COUTTS I would not! Oh, damn! I must run. Cheerioh, Lady Katharine. Cheerioh, Purley.

(Exit COUTTS)

PURLEY Cheerioh . . . Fussy little old person! What are you doing, K.?

KATHARINE I've brought some flowers. I thought if something wasn't done about it, I'd just definitely die.

(She arranges the flowers in a ten-litre jar)

PURLEY You will anyhow. We all shall, in a week or so.

KATHARINE My darling child, don't say things like that. . . . Gosh! I wish C. C. would hurry.

PURLEY Why? The work's going on all right even when he isn't here.

KATHARINE I suppose so, but I don't believe it. I feel as if the moment he goes out a wind might get up and blow the Hotel Paradise . . . I beg its pardon, the Walker Institute. . . . Oh, by the way . . .

PURLEY By the way what? I wish you'd shut up and let me get on with these . . .

KATHARINE Talking of the Walker Institute, the generous benefactor and founder of the Walker Institute is coming round after lunch.

PURLEY What for?

KATHARINE He's got cold feet.

PURLEY What's he got to get cold feet about?

KATHARINE Well, we all have a little, darling.

PURLEY Speak for yourself.

KATHARINE And in addition to being afraid of – of what we're all afraid of, he's about two millions shy over this racket already. He says Charlie Cameron talked him into founding the Institute against his better judgment. He says . . .

PURLEY Of course he did. He filled the old boy with Napoleon brandy and played unscrupulously on his blue funk.

KATHARINE It's nothing to the funk he's in now. You can't turn the Hotel Paradise into a huge hospital laboratory for fourpence.

(Telephone bell rings)

Hello. Yes, yes, I know. No, Dr. Cameron is not in yet, but he's expecting Sir Douglas. Ask him to come up.

(Hangs up receiver)

PURLEY Funny, getting all hotted up about money when the whole habitable globe will be swept clean of human beings in a month.
KATHARINE *(looking at the charts)* It looks a little like it.
PURLEY It looks exactly like it. And a damned good job too.
KATHARINE *(shivering)* Oh, I don't know. . . . I do definitely think it's a thoroughly disappointing Day of Judgment.
PURLEY No, no, no. I always dreaded the Day of Judgment because of the infernal fuss I thought there was bound to be. I never expected anything so charmingly business-like as a pandemic of acute polio-encephalitis. It's as if the Angel of Death were going round in a quiet gentlemanly fashion bumping us one after another on the head with a humane killer. I think it's quite fun, myself.
KATHARINE Don't you dare say that!
PURLEY What's the matter?
KATHARINE I'm sorry, Bugs. Nerves. Wash that out. I *walked* to the office this morning.
PURLEY You shouldn't do that.
KATHARINE I know, Bugs. I'd been reading *The Journal of the Plague.* You know. They wrote "The Lord have mercy upon us" on their doors, and the heavy carts kept rumbling all night long with the men on the carts calling, "Bring out your dead." Oh, dreary!
PURLEY I think the silence now is a bit more devilish.
KATHARINE Yes, isn't it? The big still houses with their blinds drawn and somebody dead in every one of them.
PURLEY Probably.
KATHARINE I met a dozen undertakers' vans going quietly and quickly like hungry crows. . . . It's a nasty, bad dream.
PURLEY I hear they are expecting riots to-morrow.
KATHARINE Really? I was in the last big one in Hyde Park. I got a black eye and a rousing kick on the behind that left me limping for weeks.
PURLEY Served you right.
KATHARINE Oh, I loved *that* all right. . . . It's this . . . this stealthiness. How do you like the flowers, Bugs?
PURLEY They're ruthlessly terrific; but you don't suppose the Chief's going to admire them, do you?
KATHARINE Don't you think he will?
PURLEY What a hope!

(Enter SIR DOUGLAS WALKER. He is a baronet now, and about

twenty years older. He has grown by that the more glorious, but he looks harassed and there is terror at the back of his eyes.)

KATHARINE Oh, good afternoon, Sir Douglas.
PURLEY Good afternoon, Lady Katharine. Good afternoon, Dr. Purley.
PURLEY Afternoon.
SIR DOUGLAS What delicious blooms! Cameron not in yet?
KATHARINE No. We are going through a few moments of sinister calm before the next hurricane bursts.
SIR DOUGLAS I see. I want to see him most particularly. It's a matter of – of most particular importance.
KATHARINE Yes?
SIR DOUGLAS It's very chilly for the time of the year.
KATHARINE Yes. Isn't it?
SIR DOUGLAS I wonder if a few days of good, heavy rain would improve matters.
KATHARINE It might and it might not.

(She is opening letters and separating them into boxes)

SIR DOUGLAS I spent the morning with the PM and the Minister of Health. They're extremely interested in the work of the Institute. They think it's marvellous how we've managed in the short time at our disposal. I was glad to be able to cheer them up a bit. They didn't seem too optimistic. The Medical Research Council had been quite encouraging, but then they always are. They're on our side now, anyhow, and that's a mercy.
KATHARINE Yes. It's jolly, isn't it? Gives the whole thing a sort of Christmassy air.
SIR DOUGLAS Well, I did feel a bit uneasy, until we got Official Recognition. . . . Cameron's so difficult, isn't he? And one never knows. I'm not interrupting your work, am I?
PURLEY Not at all.
SIR DOUGLAS I hope something comes of it all. I hope so. I don't mind telling you, Lady Katharine, it's pretty well ruined me, whatever happens. Not that I complain. After all, it's a matter of life and death, isn't it?
KATHARINE Yes.
SIR DOUGLAS Three thousand cases and nine hundred deaths yesterday in the Westminster area alone. It's awful! Awful! And it's world-wide. You can't escape it. My wife and I thought we . . . well, we went to our house in Lewis – the Hebrides, you know – and three of the household staff died on the morning of our arrival; it was an eye-opener. We're just as safe here as anywhere, don't you think, Dr. Purley, eh?
PURLEY Oh, yes.
SIR DOUGLAS And if they do find something, there'd be less loss of time, wouldn't there, eh? Getting treatment. . . . I've taken a room here. They say

there's not much danger of infection. I use my own entrance. . . . You think you're getting nearer finding something, eh?

PURLEY It's difficult to say. I suppose we're on the right lines.

SIR DOUGLAS But it's imperative. You *must* get a move on. The death-rate's going up and up. It might – it might attack any of us. Any one of us. It's pretty desperate. We've got to keep our nerve, of course, and take what precautions we can. . . . But it's like living on a volcano. I can't sleep. I have to take medinal every night. . . . And there's to be a big demonstration to-morrow. Against the Government. I hope they've got the guts to prohibit it. I'd shoot them down. I'd clear the streets with machine guns. A strong hand's necessary in a crisis like this. . . . I hope nothing's happened to Cameron. He's later than usual, surely.

KATHARINE It's only five past two. . . . Oh, here he is!

(Enter CAMERON. He nods to WALKER, puts on the white coat and sticks a cigarette in his mouth.)

CAMERON Matches. Matches. Who the Hell's got matches?

(LADY KATHARINE obliges with a cigarette lighter)

CAMERON (to SIR DOUGLAS) Well? Wh-what do you want?

SIR DOUGLAS I want a few minutes' private conversation with you, Charlie.

CAMERON Oh, to Hell with that! I've got work to do. Say your piece here and then clear out.

SIR DOUGLAS Well. . . . Stevenson tells me you've scrapped the infra-red camera you got last week and ordered a new one.

CAMERON Well?

SIR DOUGLAS It's only an item, but a lot of items of that sort amount to a great deal. Have you any idea what these instruments cost?

CAMERON You'd better ask Stevenson. I can't be bothered with price-lists. What you had better get into your head is that I will not work with inferior tools. . . . If I'm going to be p-palmed off with m-muck and asked to account for the bloody petty cash, I'm going to chuck it.

SIR DOUGLAS No, no. There's to be no question of that. But it's only right to tell you, here and now, that I'm at the end of my resources.

CAMERON Then you'll have to get someone to back you. I'm not going to try to put out this fire with a garden hose.

SIR DOUGLAS Do you realise that this Institute has cost me eight hundred and fifty thousand pounds?

CAMERON Is that all? Now, if you don't mind. . . . What the Devil are those?

(He indicates the flowers)

KATHARINE I thought you might like . . .

CAMERON Will you kindly realise that this is my work-room, and not a damned amateur Bloomsbury brothel?

(He throws the flowers out of the window)

KATHARINE You're a swine!

CAMERON You k-keep a civil tongue in your head or out of this you go. My dear Uncle Douglas: the Institute is greatly obliged to you for forgoing your cigarettes and tram fares in the great cause of scientific research; but I, as its head, b-beg to remind you that every minute wasted in this shopkeeper haggling increases the probability that you and many others will be attacked by polio-encephalo-myelitis acute, pandemic variety before I and my able assistants have found out what to do about it. So go away and gargle and spray and make slooching noises with your nose, or, better still, go to bed. You don't look well.

SIR DOUGLAS Oh . . . Do you think so . . . ? How . . . ?

CAMERON Oh, damn, if you think you've got it, run downstairs and get one of the interns to examine you. They seem to have nothing to do but make lascivious advances to the nurses. There's your hat. Good-bye. Give my love to Aunt Aggie if she's not dead of funk. Good-bye, good-bye, good-bye, good-bye.

(He hustles SIR DOUGLAS through the doorway)

Why did you let that old fool in here?

KATHARINE After all, C. C., he's got a right to be in here.

PURLEY I was just telling her he hadn't.

(He gathers up some papers and goes out)

KATHARINE And you needn't have been such a pig about my flowers.

CAMERON Did you want me to stick them in my hair and do a spring dance?

KATHARINE No. But I'd rather you kept your Neanderthal play-acting within limits.

CAMERON It is probably your idiotic upbringing that leads you to assume that what you'd rather have or rather not have is of as much interest to me as the reflections of one of the laboratory guinea-pigs. And talking of guinea-pigs, if your dear mama, the Marchioness, sets any of her anti-vivisection gang on me again, I'll send Purley to murder her. If your imbecile set want to live in a world of their own, let that world be Heaven.

(The telephone bell buzzes. LADY KATHARINE answers it.)

KATHARINE Yes? Yes? Oh, yes. Very bright, thank you. No. Yes. He's here, but he's busy. Hold the line, will you? . . . That's the Medical Research Council, C. C.

CAMERON What do they want?

KATHARINE I'll ask them. . . . Hello! I say, Walter. . . . He wants to know what you want . . . Yes . . . I'll tell him . . . *(to CAMERON)* . . . The Minister has been badgering them again. Walter would like to come round to see you.
CAMERON *(busy with papers)* Tell him to go to Hell.
KATHARINE He says you're to go to Hell. There's no more news. Yes. He'll let you know. At once, yes. Bless you. Bye-bye. *(Hangs up)* And what were we talking about when we were interrupted?
CAMERON I don't know and I don't c-care. We've no time to talk, here. . . . Oh, by the way . . .
KATHARINE What?
CAMERON I did want to talk to you.
KATHARINE How nice!
CAMERON You've always b-been a pretty fit sort of girl, haven't you? I m-mean you were in the Open Golf Championship or something, weren't you?
KATHARINE Or something. Yes. Why?
CAMERON No fits or insanity in your family?
KATHARINE What is this questionnaire? Are you doing a little life insurance on the side?
CAMERON No. I want to know.
KATHARINE We're a very healthy family. Hundreds of years of us.
CAMERON I know. I thought of that. It's an advantage to have records. *(Looks at his watch)* I've got time. . . . I say, K., I'd like you to marry me, if you would.
KATHARINE Gosh!
CAMERON I want . . . well, you see I'm fifty now. And if I want any descendants I'll have to get a move on, it occurred to me.
KATHARINE Oh, it occurred to you, did it?
CAMERON Yes. I mean to say . . . You've got a small head and long legs and an eye like a good race-horse. I thought with your breeding and my . . .
KATHARINE That'll do. I'm not dressed up for this. Are you approaching me as a lover or as a dog-fancier?
CAMERON No, no! I'm quite serious. I – I've been too busy all my life to pick up the technique of lovemaking. I've not been celibate by any means, but I've always left the hard work to be done by the other party.
KATHARINE This is the most *nudest* proposal I have ever had in my life.
CAMERON I know. I feel awful. I think I'm afraid of you. But do you think? . . . Between ourselves? I'm damned well preserved in spite of the life I've led and . . .
KATHARINE Oh, don't! or I'll have the first fit in our family for five hundred years.

CAMERON You look funny, certainly. You'd better lie down. Or put your head between your knees. I'll get you something.
KATHARINE No, no. I'm all right now. Don't bother. . . . Look at you. You've come all over D. H. Lawrence yourself.
CAMERON What do you mean?

(She bursts into a yell of hysterical laughter)

Don't laugh at me, damn it! Don't laugh at me. You mustn't laugh at me.
KATHARINE Oh, dear! Oh, dear! Oh, dear!
CAMERON I say, pull yourself together and listen. Do you think . . . Could you love me and all that sort of thing?
KATHARINE Of course I love you! Do you think I'd let a cad like you kick me round the room week in and week out unless I adored you?
CAMERON Good! That's settled then!

(He goes irresolutely to his work table)

KATHARINE Come here. . . . Come here!
CAMERON Oh, Katharine.

(They embrace)

You d-don't mind it . . . that I'm f-fifty, I mean?
KATHARINE Shut up.

(Enter HOPE CAMERON. She is a good-looking, well-preserved creature of fifty. Her hair is white and her bearing active and imperturbable.)

HOPE Hello! Ought I to cough, or anything?

(CAMERON and KATHARINE separate rather sheepishly)

Good-afternoon, Charlie. The newspapers say you are on the edge of a great discovery.
CAMERON Where did you come from, Hope?
HOPE *(varying her intonation to convey her contempt, weariness and maternal love)* Oh, Geneva, Geneva, Geneva.
CAMERON Ext-extraordinary woman. . . . By the way, Lady Katharine, this is my sister. She's principal secretary over there, you know. She saved them from tumbling to bits in '33. Hope, Lady Katharine and I are engaged to be married.
HOPE Yes?
KATHARINE Yes. . . . I say, you don't think this sort of thing goes on all the time here, do you?
HOPE I shouldn't be surprised. Charles is an incontinent devil.

KATHARINE He's not. He's been strictly professional all the time – even when he was proposing to me. I never heard of such a strictly professional proposal.

HOPE I see. And what is *your* profession, may one ask?

CAMERON Look here, Hope. I don't ask you to behave yourself. You never could, and you're too old to change. But will you kindly keep a civil tongue in your head when you're talking to my girl?

KATHARINE Be quiet, C. C. Hope's not making rows; it's you who are making rows . . .

HOPE Congratulations, both of you. . . . You look as if you had some backbone, my dear. And that's better than having sense, any day. . . . Have you discovered how to stop the epidemic?

CAMERON We'll see very soon. You've turned up quite appropriately for that, too, Hope. You're maddeningly appropriate.

HOPE They sent me over *(she laughs)* to tell you to hurry up.

CAMERON The League did?

HOPE The League did.

CAMERON They chose their emissary well. If they'd sent Mussolini or even Hitler I'd have kicked him downstairs.

KATHARINE I believe he would, Hope. He's created an international situation already by the way he treated the American Ambassador.

HOPE I know. Such a good job too. It keeps the poor dears busy writing notes. It takes their minds off the facts. . . . Well, I've delivered my message, Charlie.

CAMERON Thank you. And now, why did you come? You can't help me. You don't know this kind of game. You'll only madden me by being as good as me. I've c-collected a lot of tame rats to work for me. I don't work with equals.

KATHARINE What the devil do you mean?

CAMERON Hold your tongue. I'm not speaking to you.

HOPE If you butt in when he's speaking he makes these beastly sounds. That's all they are. They don't mean anything, dear.

CAMERON What? . . . Oh, darling, yes, that's right. . . . K. knows me b-by this time, Hope.

HOPE I thought that sort of love-talk might sound a little strange to her.

CAMERON Of c-course, K., darling, I'm dreadfully sorry. You see, I get rather absorbed when I'm speaking to an equal, and I've always looked upon Hope . . .

KATHARINE I adore you, you foul brute!

HOPE *(rapidly)* Now then, now then. You were asking why I came. I came because I know now that you are going to win out. And to see that when you have won out you won't stop.

CAMERON How do you know I am going to win out?

HOPE I had a letter from Uncle Bill. He told me.

CAMERON And what in God's name does he know about it?

HOPE He knows more, perhaps, than we think.

CAMERON Well . . . that may be . . . And if I d-do win out, I shall have vindicated the Walkers and the Marshalls and Uncle Douglas; and saved the world from something worse than the Black Death. I shall have discovered the virus of a killer disease. I shall have done the neatest, prettiest bit of research since Koch discovered the tubercle bacillus. I shall have laid down a new, four-square, water-tight Law of Immunity. Isn't that enough? Won't that satisfy you?

HOPE No, no, no.

CAMERON Listen. . . . And hold your tongue about this, please, that I'm going to t-tell you. I'm going down to the Wards at three o'clock. This morning at seven o'clock twelve moribund cases and twelve early cases received injections of my new serum against twenty-four controls. I fully expect to find that at least forty of the forty-eight are already on their way to the mortuary. If not . . .

HOPE If not? If it works?

CAMERON Well. It's a simple technique. Every laboratory and drug house in the world will have it by tomorrow morning. By the end of the week we shall have stopped the epidemic.

HOPE Why?

CAMERON Why? Why? Why? I don't know.

KATHARINE Darling, you don't know?

HOPE Of course he doesn't know. There are too many people in the world.

KATHARINE There aren't too many people in the world.

HOPE Oh, there aren't too many to feed and clothe and shelter. We could do all that for fifty times as many if we had any sense. I'm thinking of the formidable growing mass of people with nothing to do. Nothing. A great pot of emancipated, uncontrolled, uncontrollable life. Billions of units of mankind's dreadful energy. I'm not easily frightened, but it frightens me.

KATHARINE And you want to kill it?

HOPE My dear, I've no say in the matter. But it seems to me, as an impartial observer, that the laws of biology are exercising a little common sense for once in a way.

CAMERON I suppose I've got the ordinary human objection to knuckling under to the laws of biology. In any case, I'm damned if I will.

KATHARINE Perhaps you're a law of biology yourself, C. C.

CAMERON Gosh, you lovely thing, I almost think I am! . . .

HOPE If you are determined to save the surplus race, you'd better get busy and find a way of using them.

CAMERON I'll do one thing at a time, you nagging harridan.

HOPE One thing at a time. That's rather good. That's extremely rich.

(Big Ben strikes three. CAMERON makes for the door, but stops. He gives a short, weak, hysterical laugh. Hope looks from one to the other.)

. . . I say! I know what this room wants besides a vacuum cleaner. Give me a little jug and some water.

(CAMERON fills a beaker and gives it to her. HOPE takes a bunch of violets from her lapel and puts it in the water.)

You see . . . we are blethering . . . and quarrelling . . . and falling in love . . . because we are all excited beyond bearing by one of . . . the most exciting things . . . that has ever happened in history. And flowers are such dear little soothing nincompoops. I'm rather surprised at Katharine. She should have thought of that. . . . Oh! . . . Doesn't it show you? . . . I nearly forgot to ask for Uncle Bill. It's a week since he wrote me.

CAMERON I'd forgotten all about him myself. He's p-pretty fit, I think.

HOPE He's ninety-five. What a monstrous age. Like William Blake's Jehovah.

CAMERON Here's a letter from him. I haven't had time to read it. . . . K., while I remember, will you make a copy of young Harris's protocol and file it in B cabinet? And correct his spelling. I've been over his arithmetic myself. . . . No, I forgot, I missed this table . . .

(He stabs at a sheet with a blue pencil. KATHARINE begins to work again.)

HOPE *(reading the letter)* What a beautiful hand he writes! . . . Oh, how lovely! A bit of Latin. . . . What does this mean, Charlie?
    "Te semper anteit, saeva Necessitas."
What an ignorant old beast I am!

CAMERON Eh? I don't know. Ask K.

KATHARINE It's a tag from Horace. It means, "Ever before thee goes implacable Necessity."

HOPE I see. Dear old Uncle Bill.

KATHARINE Oh, God! I can't go on with this. What's happening? What's happening down in the Wards? Woman, how can you stand there cooing over a letter when the whole world's in the balance?

CAMERON Pull yourself together, K. I'm near breaking point, too. I daren't go down to the Wards, and that's the truth. I daren't.

(HOPE disregards CAMERON's outburst and walks quickly across to KATHARINE and catches her by the wrists)

HOPE That's enough of that. Are you the sort of woman that takes the heart out of her man? Go on with your work.

KATHARINE All right. Let me go. I lost my nerve for a second.

(She goes on with her typing, and CAMERON with his corrections. HOPE watches him. The scene is held as long as possible, and then PURLEY bursts in, frenzied with excitement. He stands at the door quite unable to utter more than inarticulate babblings.)

PURLEY Doctor . . . C-C- . . . Sir. . . . I say . . .

CAMERON What's the matter?

PURLEY The serum. . . . I've just come from Ward Eleven. . . . The patients . . . all twenty-four of them . . . they were dying or in coma this morning. . . . They're better . . . they're well. I – I spoke to them. It's a bloody miracle.

(A bunch of men and women in white coats appear in the doorway, dumb with emotion)

CAMERON What are these people doing there?

PURLEY They came up, Sir. They're mad with excitement, they can't speak. The whole nursing staff has gone off its head.

CAMERON Get back to the Wards. Tell them to behave like human beings. We'll have it all over the town if we're not careful. I'll be down presently. Get out.

(Exeunt PURLEY and the Others)

HOPE I'm glad, dear.

CAMERON Thanks, dear. So am I. Damnation, K., don't go to bits *now*. Look here. Get the MRC on the 'phone. Tell them it's all right, but not to go ahead till I tell them.

(He goes out. KATHARINE is too overcome to telephone. HOPE takes the receiver.)

HOPE Hello! Get me the Medical Research Council, please . . .

CURTAIN

ACT TWO

Scene Five

The same room as in Scene Four, five days later. It is tidier. There are some comfortable chairs and a divan. The lumpish bits of machinery have gone and the kitchen tables are pulled against the wall. There are flowers. The microscope is still there, and CAMERON's laboratory jacket still hangs beside the basin. A bright summer day is seen through the windows. An occasional sound of cheering is heard and, at intervals, a distant band. HOPE, dressed, with very slight alterations, as she was in the last scene, is reclining, hatless and jacketless, on the divan, dipping into a sort of running buffet of papers and bluebooks and smoking a cigarette. A burst of cheering annoys her and she gets up and shuts the windows. Enter DONOVAN. He is now sixty years old and looks it.

DONOVAN I beg pardon, Miss Hope.

HOPE Granted, Donovan. What can I do for you?

DONOVAN Dr. Marshall has awakened, Miss Hope. He asked if Dr. Cameron had returned yet.

HOPE No. He's not back yet. Indeed, there isn't a soul in the place but you, me and that old, old man. I am absolutely at your mercy.

DONOVAN Yes, Miss. Shall I wheel his chair in here?

HOPE Do. . . . You must have been a good-looking fellow, Donovan, when you were younger. I wonder why I didn't try to turn your head – long ago.

DONOVAN Would you like me to open the window, Miss?

HOPE No. I wasn't feeling the heat – it was just a thought that came into my head. Leave the window. I've just shut it. I couldn't stand the row.

DONOVAN No, Miss? Highly gratifying demonstration, I call it.

HOPE It doesn't gratify, me. It has been going on since Monday. Is Uncle Bill ready?

DONOVAN Quite ready, Miss. I'll wheel him in now. Thank you, Miss.

(He goes out, but returns in a moment)

Are you at home to Sir Douglas Todd Walker, Miss?

HOPE I suppose so. Show him in.

(DONOVAN ushers in SIR DOUGLAS WALKER and retires)

SIR DOUGLAS Well, Hope? What do you think of us now, eh?

HOPE That's a difficult question to answer offhand. I think you are wonderful. Will that do?

SIR DOUGLAS Only five days, and we've got the whole thing well in hand.

165

We've stopped it dead. All over the world. In five days. It seems years. It's colossal.

HOPE Yes. It's a very big thing.

SIR DOUGLAS It's been worth all the sacrifice and all the anxiety. At times I nearly gave up hope. But I set my teeth and told myself, "It's neck or nothing." And I've done it, by Jove! We've done it, I should say. Where's Charlie?

HOPE He has taken Katharine for a ride on the top of a 'bus.

SIR DOUGLAS What a funny thing to do!

HOPE Lots of people do it. He'll be back presently. Uncle Bill is here.

SIR DOUGLAS Is he? Is he? That's splendid! He'll be pleased at all this.

HOPE He is very pleased.

SIR DOUGLAS We've pulled it off all right this time, Hope, eh? I had my dose of the prophylactic on Monday night, and got a dose down to Agnes by Tuesday morning. Quick work. They're turning the stuff out by the ton from Reykjavik to Cape Horn; and, incidentally, there's a fortune in it. Cast your bread upon the waters, eh?

HOPE Yes.

SIR DOUGLAS I never regretted founding the Walker Institute, and I've little reason to now. Charlie'll get his whack out of it too. I'll see to that, though he wouldn't sign a contract. I look on it as an obligation of honour.

HOPE Of what, Uncle Douglas?

SIR DOUGLAS Of honour. Charlie'll be a rich man, Hope. And by Jove he deserves it.

HOPE No. He doesn't deserve that.

SIR DOUGLAS Now, now, Hope. Come, come. You mustn't be down on Charlie now that he's a great man. I've a bit of news for you, but you must promise not to repeat it.

HOPE I won't repeat it, Uncle Douglas.

SIR DOUGLAS I've just come back from Downing Street.

HOPE Very well, Uncle Douglas. I shall tell nobody where you've been. Your secret is safe with me.

SIR DOUGLAS Oh, you can tell anybody that! Everybody knows I've been in and out of the place all week. No. This is the point. Charlie's to get a knighthood, and they're talking of the Order of Merit. What do you think of that?

HOPE I think Charlie will be extremely interested.

SIR DOUGLAS And – well – it struck me all of a heap – I didn't expect more than a simple recognition – but – well – in point of fact they're giving me an earldom. A bit of a jump from a baronet. It means I've got three titles to think out. They'll have to make me a baron and a viscount, too. A bit of a bore.

HOPE A dreadful bore. Have you decided on your designations?

SIR DOUGLAS No. Not yet. It's a pity Earl Walker sounds a bit funny.

There's the Institute called after me, and one gets lost and out of sight behind a territorial title. Uncle Will should be very tickled, having an earl in the family. I can see him, I suppose?
HOPE I suppose so.
SIR DOUGLAS You don't seem wildly enthusiastic about the whole business, Hope.
HOPE I'm so utterly possessed with the thought of the great thing my brother has done that I can't trust myself even to kill you. Here's Uncle Bill.

(DONOVAN enters, wheeling MARSHALL in an invalid chair)

SIR DOUGLAS Good afternoon, Uncle Will. How are you?
MARSHALL That you, Douglas? I'm very well, thank you.
HOPE Have you had pleasant dreams, dear old man?

(She kisses him)

MARSHALL I never dream these days, bless you.
SIR DOUGLAS You're looking very fit, Uncle Will.
MARSHALL How is Agnes?
SIR DOUGLAS Oh, fine. She sends her love. I'm on my way to see her now. I just dropped in for a moment.
HOPE Uncle Douglas has got such wonderful news, sweetheart. They're going to make him an earl.
MARSHALL Eh? What for?
SIR DOUGLAS For stopping the epidemic.
MARSHALL But Charlie did that, didn't he?
HOPE He only did the technical side of it, darling. It's Uncle Douglas's Institute – the Walker Institute – this – that we're in now.
MARSHALL I don't follow that. . . . Donovan, that's all, I think. I won't want you for a bit. Go out and listen to the band. It will be a treat for you.
DONOVAN Thank you, Sir.

(He goes)

SIR DOUGLAS I think I had better be going, too. I've a lot of things to do, and I want to tell Agnes in person. By the way, Hope will tell you, Charlie's to get a knighthood.
MARSHALL In what particular order of chivalry?
SIR DOUGLAS Eh? Oh, it's a KBE, I believe. I'm glad they've recognised his work.
MARSHALL I am glad, too. You must hurry away?
SIR DOUGLAS Yes.
MARSHALL Good-bye. I congratulate you heartily.
SIR DOUGLAS Thanks very much. Good-bye, Hope.
HOPE Good-bye.

(Exit SIR DOUGLAS)

MARSHALL Aye, aye. So they're going to offer Charlie a knighthood. Do you think he'll take it?

HOPE He might. For fun.

MARSHALL He still thinks life is funny?

HOPE I don't think he does, now.

MARSHALL I'm glad of that. . . . You have shut the window. Is it cold?

HOPE No, darling. But the crowds are cheering and making such a noise.

MARSHALL Open the window, dear.

HOPE You want to hear them cheering Uncle Douglas when he goes out?

MARSHALL I had an idea I would like to.

HOPE *You* haven't given up thinking that life is funny.

MARSHALL I don't believe I have. I'll maybe get more sense as I grow older.

(HOPE opens a window)

HOPE I hate that sound. It would be very nearly the same sound if they were howling for Charlie's head on a pike.

MARSHALL Charlie's not well. I wish I could get him to go to Duthie Bay for a month. . . . Poor fellow! He doesn't give himself or his lung a chance. He works too hard. He has a mad idea about germs. Like Joe Lister. Harriet dear, I wish you'd write to him and ask him to . . . and ask him . . . *Ach Himmel*, I'm wandering. You can close the window, now.

HOPE *(shutting the window)* Disgusting Whipsnade noises.

MARSHALL You never liked people in bulk, did you, Hope dear? I've noticed that people who deal with the human race in bulk don't think much of them. . . . Where is Charlie?

HOPE Out with K. They'll be back any minute.

MARSHALL I hope he isn't getting into trouble again. Poor devil, his whole life is a running battle with his – with his . . . I shouldn't be telling you all this. . . . Sing me that song you used to sing. I can't get it out of my head.

HOPE What song, darling?

MARSHALL That infernal, sloppy, sham-Irish thing you used to sing. . . . You remember; sentimental thing, "The Kerry Dancing". "Oh, the days of the Kerry dancing." *You* know.

HOPE I don't know it, old man.

MARSHALL Neither you do. I was forgetting. Never mind.

HOPE You haven't wakened up properly after your sleep.

MARSHALL I muddle up the years and the generations a little, these days.

HOPE It's strange that you should hold three generations in the hollow of your hand.

MARSHALL It is strange. . . . You had a bad parentage, Hope dear. A bad start.

HOPE No. They lived in a time when what their neighbours thought and said could kill them utterly. And yet they saw what they had to do and did it. We don't live in those times now, Uncle Bill.

MARSHALL No. The world's ready for you.

HOPE Are you happy, old man?

MARSHALL Yes. Charlie Cameron the First had the spark in his poor diseased body. Now lettest thou thy servant depart in peace. I did my best to keep the spark alive, and now it's a great flame in Charlie and in you. Humanity will warm its hands at you.

HOPE Oh, Uncle Will, I'm a barren old woman.

MARSHALL Charlie's your brother and your lover and your son. You will make him do great things for the world . . . if the world is worth it.

HOPE Whether the world is worth it or not.

CURTAIN

END OF THE PLAY

MR. BOLFRY

A PLAY IN FOUR SCENES

Persons in the Play

Cully
Cohen
Jean
Morag
Mr. McCrimmon
Mrs. McCrimmon
Mr. Bolfry

Scene One

A parlour in the Free Kirk Manse at Larach, in the West Highlands of Scotland. It is Sunday afternoon. The furnishing is austere. Two walls are occupied by bookcases full of forbidding-looking books. On the other wall are signed engravings of elderly clergymen. There is a presentation black-marble clock on the mantelpiece. There are no further concessions to decorative art. A lanky man in battle-dress is lounging in the only comfortable chair, with his slippered feet on the mantelpiece. His name is CULLY. When he speaks, it is with an "educated" accent. He wears large horn-rimmed spectacles. Through the window is seen an autumnal Highland landscape, illuminated, for the moment, by a watery beam of sunshine. A second soldier enters. He is small, sturdy, Hebraic and disconsolate. His name is COHEN.

COHEN *(singing, dirge fashion)* "Roll out the barrel; we'll have a barrel of fun. . . ." Not half, we won't.

(He finds a dishcloth in his hands and throws it back through the open door)

CULLY *(in what he imagines to be Scots)* Hoots mon! Don't ye no ken, you cannot sing on the Sabbath Day?
COHEN Don't I know it!
CULLY Where have you been, my dear Mr. Gordon Montefiore Cohen?
COHEN Cleaning up the crimson dinner dishes. That's where I've been.
CULLY Don't you get enough polishing to do at the Camp?
COHEN You've said it.
CULLY Then what's the matter with you? Gone balmy?
COHEN Not yet.

(He sits down and absently takes out a cigarette)

CULLY You can't smoke in here, cocky.
COHEN Hell, no. *(He puts his fag away)* Cor, stone the crows, what a dump! What a billet! Cor darn my socks!
CULLY You've only got your lousy ambition to thank for it.
COHEN What do you mean ambition? Did I have any ambition to get drafted up North to this perishing cold doorstep of a country? Did I have any ambition to be billeted on an old holy, sour-puss, praying bloody preacher? Tell me, I'm asking you.
CULLY You were ambitious to be the cleanest, best-behaved man in the battery, and that's why they picked you.
COHEN Oh, indeed. And why did they pick you?
CULLY God knows. They thought I needed a bit of religion, I expect.

COHEN What's the good? Lord love me, what's the good?

CULLY They'll make you a bombardier all right. This is only a small spot of purgatory, before they receive you into everlasting glory.

COHEN Bombardier? Not me, they won't. Not with a nose my shape and that old Nazi of a BSM anti-semiting all over the ship. Tin-eyed old beer-tank. What you reading?

CULLY *Meditations among the Tombs.*

COHEN So help me, there isn't a decent cemetery to go to, let alone a cinema.

CULLY Why did you wash the dishes?

COHEN Something to do. Just to pass the time.

CULLY Damned liar.

COHEN Well . . . I thought there might be a bit of fun in it.

CULLY Was there?

COHEN No fear! They made her go to the matinee – the afternoon service, whatever you call it – the minute I offered. The nasty minds these holy blokes has.

CULLY Bad luck.

COHEN I'll be more careful next time. A bit unsophisticated but quite a pretty little bit of stuff. And a skirt's always a skirt. And I ain't seen many round hereabouts.

CULLY I thought you were a respectable married man.

COHEN Hell, chum, I wouldn't be a married man if I didn't like a bit of skirt. Be reasonable. There ain't no harm in it. Read us a bit. I'm right browned off, and that's a fact.

CULLY "Indulge, my soul, a serious pause. Recollect all the gay things that were wont to dazzle thy eyes and inveigle thy affections. Here, examine those baits of sense. Here form an estimate of their real value. Suppose thyself first among the favourites of fortune, who revel in the lap of pleasure; who shine in the robes of honour; and swim in tides of unexhausted riches; yet, how soon would the passing bell proclaim thy exit; and, when once the iron call has summoned thee to thy future reckoning, where would all these gratifications be? At that period, how will all the pageantry of the most affluent, splendid and luxurious circumstances vanish into empty air? . . ."

COHEN I ain't got that. Who's supposed to have murdered who?

CULLY Nobody's murdered anybody.

COHEN Who's this bloke supposed to be talking to?

CULLY To anybody. To you.

COHEN He is, is he? Then he don't know me! Swim in tides of unexhausted riches! He don't say anything about skirts, does he?

CULLY Oh, yes. There's a lot about blokes dying and skirts howling over them. Would you like me to read you a bit?

COHEN No, I thank you. I thank you kindly, I am much obliged, but I should not think of troubling you. I don't like howling skirts, I like joyful skirts. I'd give a week's pay to see one this moment.

CULLY You damp down your libido, cocky. There aren't any skirts around here.

COHEN No. And if there were, there ain't much to make them joyful.

(He goes to the window)

What a country!

CULLY Well, the sun was shining last time I looked out.

COHEN Yes. You can see across the loch. They say hereabouts when you can see across the loch it's going to rain, and when you can't see across the loch it blooming well is raining.

(JEAN, a tall, cheerful-looking young lady in a dressing-gown appears in the doorway)

JEAN Hello!

CULLY Oh, hello!

JEAN *(to COHEN)* Hello! you too.

COHEN Hello! Miss.

CULLY Who are you?

JEAN A joyful skirt.

COHEN You heard us talking?

JEAN Yes. I heard you. I hesitated for years. I was too shy to come in, till you said what you liked. So then I came.

COHEN I'm sorry, Miss. I'm not that sort of a chap at all. I'm not really. But you know how it is, when two blokes gets chinning together.

JEAN Oh yes. That's all right. May I have a book?

CULLY Oh, yes. Please.

JEAN I didn't mean to interrupt you.

COHEN Not at all. It's a pleasure.

JEAN I'm the Meenister's niece.

CULLY No. Really? Are you?

JEAN Yes. My name's Jean Ogilvie. What are your names?

CULLY Cully's mine.

COHEN Gunner Cohen, Miss.

JEAN What are your first names?

CULLY Tom.

COHEN Gordon.

JEAN Do sit down, Tom and Gordon. I won't be a minute. Are you from the gun position on the hill?

COHEN Yes.

JEAN I heard you were billeted here. It must be pretty dull for you.

COHEN You have said it.

JEAN Where do you come from? London?

COHEN Yes. Little shop in the Borough Road.

JEAN You too?

CULLY More or less, yes.

JEAN So do I. I'm a typist and teapot carrier at the Ministry of Interference. I was blitzed about a bit, and they sent me for a week's holiday. That's why I'm still in bed.

CULLY I see.

JEAN I only came yesterday. The hills are nice, don't you think?

CULLY Very nice.

JEAN How do you like my uncle?

COHEN He seems a very nice gentleman.

JEAN And there's no doubt about my aunt being nice, so it's all very nice together – only dull. I must try to see about getting you cheered up a bit. But my uncle's so damned strict.

COHEN He is a bit, isn't he?

JEAN Yes. It's funny. He's very intelligent too. I'm no match for him. Are you intelligent?

CULLY I used to think I was. Cohen certainly is.

JEAN Then we must tackle him tonight after evening service.

CULLY It will be a pleasure.

JEAN Will it be a pleasure to you too? . . . I say, look here, I can't call you Gordon. Haven't you another name?

COHEN The boys sometimes calls me Conk.

JEAN May I?

COHEN Yes, if you like.

JEAN Conk, will you help me with my uncle?

COHEN Well, if it's not too much of a liberty in the gentleman's own house.

JEAN But it's for his good. There's lots of things we could teach him.

COHEN I shouldn't be surprised.

JEAN Then that's settled. I must run now. . . . What's this book? . . . Oh, Greek, damn. Never mind. I feel much better. I think I'll get up.

COHEN Won't you stay and talk to us?

JEAN No, Conk. My uncle doesn't think naked women are good for soldiers. He'll be back any minute now. Cheers. I'll see you later.

(She goes out before the SOLDIERS have time to get to the door-handle. They make polite rushes and get to the door opposite one another.)

COHEN After you, Claude.

CULLY Not funny. How do you like her?

COHEN What do *you* think of her?

CULLY I don't know. I haven't really seen her yet.

COHEN It seemed to me like you had a good look.

CULLY She was putting on an act. She needn't have troubled. I didn't come

175

all the way up to the Heilans to be sparkled at. I'm like old Wordsworth, Mr. Conk. I am one of them as likes a solitary Highland Lass to be a solitary Highland Lass. I can get plenty "Come on, you chaps" stuff where I come from.

COHEN A bit hard to please.

CULLY *(resuming his chair and his book)* Yes.

COHEN Looked a very high-toned bit of stuff to me. You could see she was a lady.

CULLY There are no ladies nowadays.

COHEN In that case, I'll mizzle up to the canteen. Coming?

CULLY No. Remember you've got to be back for supper at eight.

COHEN Hell, yes . . . *(at the window)* . . . and there's the soft refreshing rain coming. And there's the church coming out. And there's his holiness coming up the path. I can't make it. No dodging the column this time, chum!

(He sits down beside the table with a gesture of hopelessness)

A fatalist. That's me.

(McCRIMMON enters. He is a handsome, serious man of about fifty. He wears a turnover collar and a white bow tie. He carries a silk hat carefully in his hand. Behind him come MRS. McCRIMMON, a pretty little woman of forty, and MORAG, the serving-maid, a girl of seventeen.)

McCRIMMON Morag! Put my hat in the box, girl. And take you great care of the nap this time.

(MORAG takes the hat and goes out)

MRS. McCRIMMON Oh, Mr. Cully! The Minister's chair!

CULLY Sorry, Mrs. McCrimmon.

McCRIMMON Oh, it is all right. It is all right, dear me. A man who defends my country is at liberty to sit in my chair, I'm sure. Sit ye down.

CULLY No thank you, Sir. Cohen and I were thinking of going out for a walk.

McCRIMMON It is a nice thing, a walk. You would be too tired maybe to attend the afternoon diet of worship? But I forgot. I am the stupid man. You do not belong to our communion.

MRS. McCRIMMON It's raining now, Mr. Cully. Maybe you'd be better to stay in beside the fire. I'll put some peats on it, and the Minister will be in his study at his evening sermon, and I'll be in the kitchen with Morag, so you needn't be bothering yourself.

McCRIMMON Oh, there is no harm in the young men going for a walk. No harm at all. You were reading?

CULLY *(showing him the book)* Yes.

McCRIMMON Well, well. Hervey's *Meditations among the Tombs*. An improving kind of a work in its way, but to my mind he was a greeting bit body, that. And not very sound in his doctrine. But he's dead longsyne, and no doubt he has done you little harm with his greeting.

(MRS. McCRIMMON is busy with the peats. COHEN is helping her.)

CULLY He makes very soothing Sunday-afternoon reading.
McCRIMMON The Lord did not give his Day that you should he soothed, young man.
CULLY Oh? I was always told he did.
McCRIMMON Those who told you so did you no service. The Day was given for rest of the body, improvement of the mind, and the ordinances of public and private worship.
CULLY Oh, but, Mr. McCrimmon, surely . . .
McCRIMMON Marget, will you bid Morag put my cup of gruel in the study? You will excuse me, Sir? I have to make some meditations of my own before my sermon.
CULLY At least I was trying to improve my mind.
McCRIMMON Indeed, I hope so. And now will you excuse me?

(MRS. McCRIMMON and COHEN leave the fireside)

(Exit McCRIMMON)

MRS. McCRIMMON Now, there's a clean fireside, and I think there's nothing nicer in the whole wide world. Don't you think so, Mr. Cohen, and you a family man?
COHEN You're right. Not that I won't say them turf fires take a bit of getting used to.
MRS. McCRIMMON If you handle them kindly you get a fine steady glow. And the smell of the burning peat is grand.
CULLY Like a burnt offering on the family altar.
MRS. McCRIMMON You're making fun of me, and that's fine; I wouldn't make jokes of things like that, Mr. Cully. Not of sacred subjects.
CULLY I didn't think a good Presbyterian would think altars particularly sacred.
MRS. McCRIMMON Maybe not, but they are no subject for levity.
CULLY I wasn't trying to be funny.
MRS. McCRIMMON That's all right, then.
CULLY I'll go up and get my boots on. What about you, Conk?
COHEN I've got my boots on.
MRS. McCRIMMON If you're going for a walk, I wouldn't go anywhere you might be seen during the evening service. There might be talk, and you living with the Minister.

CULLY Right ho.

MRS. McCRIMMON And you'll be back for supper at half-past eight, will you not? It's only pease brose, but there will be a wee bit of cold ham for the pair of you.

CULLY Fine. I'll remember.

(*CULLY goes out*)

MRS. McCRIMMON He seems kind of vexed. I hope I was not too sharp with him.

COHEN Keep your mind easy. He's been on the mat before sharper-tongued people than you.

MRS. McCRIMMON Maybe he's not very used to the ways of a minister's house, only being here three days; and none of them the Sabbath.

COHEN That's it. He's not used to it.

MRS. McCRIMMON He's a fine young fellow. It's a pity he's an episcopalian.

COHEN He's not that, Mum, whatever else he is. He's C. of E.

MRS. McCRIMMON Ah, dear me, now, he cannot help his upbringing. . . . Look, the fire's glowing fine. It's a homey looking thing, a fire.

COHEN It is and all.

MRS. McCRIMMON And it growing so dark and gloomy out bye. I think we will have a storm. It is not a nice walk you will be having at all.

COHEN It helps to pass the time.

MRS. McCRIMMON Och, dear me, with me the time passes without any help. You would think there was scarcely enough of it.

COHEN It hangs a bit heavy when you're used to city life.

MRS. McCRIMMON And what would you do, now, if you were in the city at this very moment?

COHEN Well, now you ast me, I shouldn't be surprised if I sat down by the fireside and went to sleep. I'd have read all the Sunday papers by this time.

MRS. McCRIMMON Tuts, tuts! Sunday papers!

COHEN But it'd be a comfort knowing there was places I could go, if I wanted to.

(*COHEN heaves a deep sigh and suddenly takes a pocket-book out and pushes a snap-shot at MRS. McCRIMMON as if it were a pistol*)

MRS. McCRIMMON Oh! What's that?

COHEN Me and the trouble and strife. Down at Southend. That's the kid she's holding up to get took.

MRS. McCRIMMON What a lovely boy!

COHEN He's a bit of all right; but he isn't a boy. He's a girl.

MRS. McCRIMMON Amn't I the stupid one! I should have known.

COHEN Don't see how you could, with all them clothes on.

MRS. McCRIMMON She's a bonny wee lass. How old is she?

COHEN Eleven months there. Had her third birthday last week. There she is. Sitting in the park with her blooming dawg.

MRS. McCRIMMON My, my, how they grow! She'll be the great chatterbox now.

COHEN She's like her ma. Got a lot to say and says it.

MRS. McCRIMMON She's got a look of you too.

COHEN Cor blimey! I hope not.

MRS. McCRIMMON It's about the eyes.

COHEN She's a way of laughing with her eyes before the rest of her face gets going.

MRS. McCRIMMON What's her name?

COHEN Gladys. Same as the old lady.

MRS. McCRIMMON You must miss them sorely.

COHEN Not half, I do. Roll on the time.

MRS. McCRIMMON Roll on the time.

(A pause)

COHEN No news yet from North Africa?

MRS. McCRIMMON Not yet. He'll be twenty next month. Ninth of November.

COHEN You don't look like you'd a grown-up son.

MRS. McCRIMMON There's whiles I'm surprised myself.

(They turn and look at a photograph of a Seaforth Highlander on the mantelpiece)

MRS. McCRIMMON That was taken the day he got his commission.

COHEN You'd be proper and proud of him that day.

MRS. McCRIMMON What's it you say? Not half I wasn't!

(She laughs)

You'll have us all speaking the fine, high English before you've finished with us.

COHEN You speak first-class English. There's a bit of an accent, if you don't mind my saying so, but I can understand every word you say.

MRS. McCRIMMON Ah, well, now, am I not glad of that? You will be finding us a wild uncivilised lot in the Highlands?

COHEN I wouldn't go as far as that. You don't get the same chanst as what we get up in London, but I wouldn't call you uncivilised – except on Sundays.

MRS. McCRIMMON Well, well, we've all got our ways of doing things, I suppose. Is it a nice place, London? It'll not be all wickedness with eight million folk in it.

COHEN I wish you could see our little place in the Borough Road. Above

179

the shop, it is. Nice and handy. And Gladys, she keeps it a treat. Pots and pans shining and a couple of budgerigars in a gilt cage. And always something tasty after we puts up the shutters.

MRS. McCRIMMON She still keeps the shop open?

COHEN You bet she does. Twicet she's had the window blown in, but what does she care? Out with the old broom and bucket and on with the job. Cor stone the crows, I shouldn't have the nerve. And I'm supposed to be a soldier.

MRS. McCRIMMON Och, now, you're a very brave soldier too, I'm sure.

COHEN Not me. I get the willies, sometimes, imagining what's going to happen to me if the Gerries get busy on my gun.

MRS. McCRIMMON You'll be like us up here. You've a strong imagination. There's whiles I can frighten myself more than Hitler and Goering and that lad Rommel could do if they were all in this room waving their pistols and making faces at me. I'll be lying awake at night with my head under the blankets thinking there's devils and bogles and kelpies coming down the chimney, though fine I know there's no such thing. But when they dropped a big bomb on Aberdeen and me at a shop door and knocked over with the blast with all my messages flung mixty maxty, I wasn't afraid at all, at all. I was just angered.

COHEN That's right. It's the same with Gladys.

MRS. McCRIMMON Not but what I put up a wee prayer, the minute I could think about it.

COHEN The way you'd hear Gladys howling about the War, you'd think old Hitler got it all up for her benefit. But there's no more howling when it comes to the bit.

MRS. McCRIMMON It's our imaginations. They're an awful nuisance our imaginations.

(Enter JEAN – now fully dressed)

My sorrow and my shame! What are you doing up and about, you bad girl?

JEAN I'm cured, Aunt Maggie. It's the Highland air.

MRS. McCRIMMON You should think shame of yourself. I told you to stay in bed till I said you could get up.

JEAN You know quite well that I never did what you told me.

MRS. McCRIMMON And that's a true word. You've always been little better than a wayward wee rascal.

JEAN But I'm interrupting you.

MRS. McCRIMMON *(in some confusion)* Oh, I was just having a wee talk with Mr. Cohen. You'll not have met Mr. Cohen. He's one of the two gentlemen who are billeted with us.

JEAN I've met Mr. Cohen and Mr. Cully too.

MRS. McCRIMMON Dear me, when would that be, now?

JEAN Never mind. And go on with your wee talk. I'll go and speak to Morag and try to work up a bad cough for next time I come back.

MRS. McCRIMMON You are just terrible, and that's the only one word for you. She has no respect for her elders, Mr. Cohen. I'm real sorry for her poor mother. And you'll just stay here and cheer Mr. Cohen up, and I'll away ben to the kitchen.

(Enter CULLY in his boots)

Now, Mr. Cully, you're surely not going out on an evening the like of this.

CULLY It does look pretty black.

MRS. McCRIMMON And there's the mists coming down from the ben. I have seen me lost a hundred yards from the Manse door.

COHEN I'm not going out, you can bet your life on that.

CULLY I'll go myself, then.

JEAN I'll go with you if you aren't going far. Mr. Cohen can lend me his waterproof cape.

MRS. McCRIMMON Jean!

JEAN Well, Aunt Maggie?

MRS. McCRIMMON You're just out of your bed.

JEAN I told you I was all right now.

MRS. McCRIMMON And apart from all else, do you remember what day it is?

JEAN Yes. Quite well.

MRS. McCRIMMON What will people think? What will your uncle say?

JEAN I haven't the least idea what people will think, and Uncle Mac can say what he likes, and I'll be delighted. He has a beautiful, thrilling voice.

MRS. McCRIMMON Oh, but, Jean . . .

JEAN If you like, I'll promise you one thing. If Gunner Cully attacks my virtue, I shall defend it heartily. I am feeling very virtuous tonight.

MRS. McCRIMMON Oh, Jean, that's awful talk! And it's not like you at all. I don't know what's come over you.

JEAN Get your mackintosh cape, Conk, will you?

(COHEN goes out)

MRS. McCRIMMON I've half a mind to fetch your uncle.

JEAN Yes. Do. I haven't seen him today.

MRS. McCRIMMON Oh, Jean! . . . It's all right in England, dearie, and there's no harm in it, I suppose; but surely you know what sort of place this is?

JEAN Yes. It's got the best record for church attendance and the highest illegitimacy rate in the Kingdom. I don't respect it for either of these records much. I'm not very keen on going to church, and I rather like behaving myself decently. So I propose to do exactly what I like. I hope you don't mind.

MRS. McCRIMMON Well. . . . Don't go too far away, and see and be back in time for supper. I think I'll let Morag get the supper ready and go and lie down for a wee bit. I've a kind of a headache coming on, and it's still an hour and a half to the evening service.

JEAN Oh, poor soul! Would you like an aspirin? I've got dozens.

MRS. McCRIMMON No, no. It's only a wee headache. Don't be late.

JEAN No. I won't be late. We won't go far.

MRS. McCRIMMON *(going)* I hope you have a nice walk.

JEAN Please forgive me, Aunt Maggie. I'm an ill-tempered beast. I must be a bit nervy.

MRS. McCRIMMON Yes. You would be after all those experiences.

JEAN I wish I weren't going for that walk, but you see I've got to now, don't you?

CULLY I say, really, I'm not frightfully keen . . .

JEAN Shut up. . . . You see, Aunt Maggie, don't you?

MRS. McCRIMMON Now don't be asking me if I see or if I don't see. Away for your walk and don't bother me.

JEAN But we're friends, aren't we?

MRS. McCRIMMON Och, I've no patience with you. Away with you and your havering.

(She gives JEAN a tearful smile and goes out)

JEAN The fool I am, fighting about nothing.

CULLY I don't know. I couldn't see what all the fuss was about.

JEAN This is a Wee Free Parish. They think it's a mortal sin to be seen on the road with a strange young man – especially on the Sawbath.

CULLY I gathered that.

JEAN That's why they stick to hedges and ditches for their – social occasions. Disgusting, superstitious pigs. And they're not only immoral and hypocritical. They're Devil-Worshippers.

CULLY I'd hardly put it that way.

JEAN They are. I don't want particularly to go for a walk in the rain with you, but I'm not going to knuckle under to Devil-Worship.

CULLY What do you mean by Devil-Worship?

JEAN Have you read any of these books?

(Indicating the bookcase)

CULLY Two or three. They're very interesting. I've just been cooling off a bit with Hervey on the Tombs.

JEAN Have you heard any of my uncle's sermons?

CULLY No. I've denied myself that pleasure.

JEAN They don't worship God. They worship the Devil. They call him

God, but he's really the Devil. All this holiness and censoriousness is to save their skins from boils and leprosy and their souls from damnation. They think if they flatter this fiend and go through a few – rites of propitiation, he'll let them alone. They're like savages tying red rags outside their caves to keep away demons. I know them. I've lived among them. I'm one of them.

CULLY You may be right about the particular deity these people believe in, but I think you're wrong about the Devil.

JEAN How wrong?

CULLY Anybody who has thought a lot about the Devil has a great respect for him.

JEAN You mean they cringe to him. That's what I'm saying.

CULLY No. They don't cringe. None of the fellows I'm thinking about knew how to cringe.

JEAN Who are they?

CULLY Milton, Goethe, William Blake, your own Bobbie Burns.

JEAN Robert Burns to you, please. Well?

CULLY Even in the Old Testament all they could find against him was that he was rebellious and had a proper pride in himself and tried to educate people.

(Enter COHEN with soldier's waterproof cape)

JEAN Oh, thank you, Conk.

CULLY Conk's ancestors made exactly the same charges against Christ himself.

COHEN Never mind about my ancestors. What was your ancestors like in those far-off times? Painted blue, they was.

CULLY They still are. Come along, Jean, let's get some cold, damp, fresh air.

COHEN You don't want me to come with you, I don't suppose?

(He helps JEAN on with the cape)

CULLY You can come if you like.

JEAN Yes, do. I've got my own mackintosh upstairs.

COHEN No, thank you. I'll settle down to a good book.

JEAN Oh, yes. Good. Do read the Institutes of Calvinism. We want your opinion on them.

COHEN I've already got my opinion of most of these here books, lady. I hope you have an enjoyable swim.

JEAN Gosh, yes. It's raining cats and dogs. Still, we must get out sometime. Come on, Cully. We'd better face it. See you later, Conk.

COHEN Cheery bye.

(Exeunt JEAN and CULLY. When they are well away, COHEN opens the door carefully, leans against the jamb and whistles low and

melodiously with his eyes on the passage ceiling. After a few bars, MORAG comes in the door in some trepidation.)

MORAG What is it you want?
COHEN Me? I was just whistling.
MORAG You cannae whistle on the Sabbath. The Minister'll be hearing you.
COHEN Come in the office.
MORAG Oh, I couldna.
COHEN The Missus has gone to lie down. The other two are out. Come in a minute.
MORAG Well, just for a wee minute.
COHEN I got something for you.
MORAG Dear me, what can it be?
COHEN Packet of chocolate.

(He gives her a packet of chocolate)

MORAG Now, are you not the kind man, man, no indeed yes.
COHEN Like chocolate?
MORAG Och, I'm most terrible keen on the chocolates. I could be sitting there eating the like for all eternity, whatever.
COHEN You're pretty easy on the eye.
MORAG Och, I don't know what you're saying, easy on the eye.
COHEN Got a boy friend?
MORAG What would I be doing with boy friends, away up here in Larach? I've no patience with them at all, with their ignorance.
COHEN What's the matter with me, then?
MORAG Nothing doing.

(She pronounces this "Nuthun DOOOOun," with a dignified coyness unusual in most uses of the phrase. After a brief attack and a token defence, COHEN succeeds in kissing her expertly. They disengage.)

Dear me, aren't you the awful man, and a great danger to the neighbourhood.
COHEN Not me, and thank you very much. Do you know what that was worth to me?
MORAG It would not be much to a gallus rascal the like of you.
COHEN It was as good as a hundred Players, four pints of mild and bitter, and a gallon of Rosie Lee. And now you better hop it. I don't want you to be getting into no trouble.
MORAG Deed yes. This is not the thing at all.

(Exit MORAG)

(COHEN registers mild satisfaction and then goes to the bookshelf. His

spirits drop. He wearily chooses a book, without very much hope; takes it to the table and begins to turn over the leaves with a rather disgusted air. Noise of CULLY and JEAN in the passage.)

JEAN No. Wait. I'll take them into the kitchen. You'd better take your boots off before you go into the parlour.

(COHEN listens, is about to get up, but returns to his book. Presently JEAN comes in, a little bedraggled about the head and carrying her muddy shoes in her hand.)

JEAN Hello, Conk.

(She puts her shoes at the fireside)

Thank God there's somebody in the British Army with a little sense. What possessed that man to go out on a day like this, I do not know.
COHEN You didn't go far.
JEAN Quite far enough. What a day! It's getting dark, too. Another ten minutes and we'd have been hopelessly lost. We couldn't see a yard in front of us.

(She takes off her stockings and hangs them on the fire-irons, while she is speaking)

I asked Morag to bring in a nice cup of tea. She was very doubtful. She rather thought she'd go to Hell if she did. I told her there was nothing in the Bible about having tea between one o'clock and half-past eight. I don't suppose there is, is there?
COHEN What of it if there is? All that stuffs a lot of hooey, if you ask me.
JEAN Are you an atheist?
COHEN I'm an agnostic.
JEAN Good. We'll make Uncle pull his socks up tonight. Talking of socks, I'd better go up and "put cla'es on my feet," or I'll be excommunicated.

(CULLY enters, wearing his slippers)

JEAN Oh, hello! You've been very quick. I'm just going to tidy up. You'd better dry your shins at the fire.
CULLY Yes. Thanks.

(Exit JEAN. CULLY dries his shins at the fire.)

COHEN Any luck?
CULLY What do you mean by "Any luck"?
COHEN Garn! Errcher!

CULLY I've told you what I think of the young person. I haven't had time to change my mind. She's not my type.

COHEN Any skirt's anybody's type in a place like this. You're a Cissy. That's what you are.

CULLY If you call me a Cissy, I'll fetch you a skelp on the jaw that'll make your teeth rattle.

COHEN No offence.

CULLY Take care that there isn't, you cock-eyed guttersnipe.

COHEN All right, all right.

CULLY And if you want to make offensive remarks, you'll kindly keep them strictly impersonal, if you understand what that means.

COHEN Keep your hair on. Who's making offensive remarks?

CULLY You were winding yourself up into your most facetious vein. You'd better unwind yourself. I find your facetiae offensive.

COHEN Ah, shut up and let me read. It gives me a pain when you talk like a gory dictionary.

CULLY What are you reading?

COHEN Never mind.

CULLY Why can't you keep your temper?

COHEN I like that. Who lost his temper? You did.

CULLY I asked you a perfectly civil question and you answered like a sulky kid.

COHEN A bloke's got to be careful what he says to the great Goramity Mister Cully – him what writes to the Reviews. . . . What the Hell's biting you, chum?

CULLY Nothing. I'm sorry. It's funny how chaps begin yapping like terrier pups when the weather changes. Forget what I said.

COHEN I accept your perishing apology. . . . It's five o'clock. Five stricken hours till bedtime.

CULLY Oh, as it's turned out, it may not be so bad.

COHEN Not so bad as what? A blinding Gerry concentration camp at the blazing North Pole?

CULLY I think we'll see some sparks flying.

COHEN What sparks?

CULLY Wait and see. Our young lady seems to think she has a mission to assault thrones, dominations, princedoms, virtues, powers, and crack their forced hallelujahs.

COHEN She seems to think what's it?

CULLY She's spoiling for a row with his Reverence.

COHEN I don't see much good in that myself.

CULLY No more do I.

COHEN Live and let live, I always say.

CULLY She says that too. Only she says his Reverence won't let live.

COHEN Cor blind me, you got to make allowances. If you come to a place where there's niggers what likes bowing down to idols because it does them good, cor blimey, let them get on with it. They didn't ask you to come. They don't want your blooming interference.

CULLY You're probably right, but she doesn't think so. I think we'll have quite a pretty fight.

COHEN *He* won't fight. He's too blinking self-satisfied. He's got the Commanding Officer on his side.

CULLY If he does, she won't have a chance.

COHEN Yes, she will.

CULLY You underrate his Reverence. I think you'll find he packs a pretty heavy punch.

COHEN I never saw a skirt yet get the worst of an argument. All in, of course. No holds barred.

CULLY We'll see. It might be quite a Pleasant Sunday Evening after all.

(MORAG comes in with a teapot and three cups and a section of black bun. She is very nervous about it all.)

MORAG Oh, dear me, I wish to thank goodness Miss Jean would go away back to London. We'll all have our heids in our hands.

CULLY What's the matter?

MORAG Oh, where is she? Drink your tea now quick like good lads, before the Minister finds out. My sorrow, you cannae say, "No", to her, she's that birsey.

(Enter JEAN. She has changed her stockings, shoes and skirt and rearranged her hair.)

JEAN Oh, thank you, Morag. You are a Highland seraph.

MORAG I may be a seraph or a geraffe or a camomile, but haste ye now, Miss Jean, before the Mistress finds the dirty cups and teapot.

JEAN Awa wi' ye, you chittering oinseach! There's nobody going to eat you.

MORAG I wouldna be over sure of that, Miss Jean. Ochonorie! It's a weary day for me.

(Exit MORAG, lamenting. The OTHERS sit round the table.)

JEAN Gather round, chaps. Do you both take sugar?

CULLY ⎫ Yes, please.
COHEN ⎭

JEAN What a lot of sugar! I suppose the Army's the generous donor.

COHEN They get our ration, you see, and neither of them takes it.

JEAN Thank the Lord for our gallant defenders. Here's mud in your eye.

COHEN And in yours, Miss.

JEAN *(picking up the book COHEN has left on the table)* The Discoverie of Witchcraft, by Reginald Scot. You been reading this, Conk?

COHEN *Glancing at it.* The spelling seems a bit cock-eyed to me.

JEAN When I was a kid I used to stay here for the holidays. I sneaked in when nobody was about and read this book. I didn't notice much wrong with the spelling then. It frightened me out of my wits. My uncle found me reading it and gave me the telling off of my life. I still feel beautifully frightened when I only look at the book.

COHEN Tells you how to raise the Devil and that.

JEAN Oh, does it? I never got so far as that. You draw cabalistic signs and repeat a spell, don't you?

COHEN I shouldn't be surprised. Like the old boze in the opera.

JEAN It would be quite fun to try.

COHEN A waste of time, if you ask me.

JEAN I don't know. He might tell us why the Wee Frees behave in that extraordinary fashion.

COHEN He might if there was any such things as devils.

CULLY What about the good old Battery Sergeant-Major?

COHEN Cor stifle me, don't you go calling him up now. He's bad enough in the old monkey kit, but think what he'd be like in red tights! Old Mestify-toffles!

(He laughs and chokes on his tea. JEAN thumps him on the back.)

JEAN Take it easy, Conk.

COHEN I'm sorry. I had to laugh. Think of him blowing out flames instead of beer, with his fore and aft hanging to his near side horn. "Battery, tails up!"

(He coughs again. Both JEAN and CULLY take a hand at thumping him on the back.)

JEAN Oh dear, oh dear; the man'll choke himself.

CULLY Pull yourself together, Conk.

COHEN Easy on. Easy on. It's having a sense of humour. It'll be the death of me.

(These lines are spoken simultaneously. As they are being spoken, McCRIMMON enters without being noticed and watches the scene with an enigmatic expression on his face. JEAN sees him first; knocks the book off the table onto the floor; picks it up and hides it on a chair. Silence falls.)

JEAN Oh, hello, Uncle Jock.

McCRIMMON Good evening, Jean. Your aunt did not tell me that you were up and about.

JEAN I got up this afternoon. I'm ever so much better.

McCRIMMON That is a blessing.

(He sits down at the table)

JEAN Will you have a cup of tea?

McCRIMMON No. I thank you.

JEAN It has turned into an awful night. Cully and I were out in it for a little.

McCRIMMON Indeed?

JEAN Yes. It didn't seem to like us. It drove us in after a very few minutes. I suppose it was a lesson to us to do as the Romans do.

McCRIMMON What Romans?

JEAN You know. When you are in Rome, you should do as the Romans do. I don't agree with that, do you? I mean, you couldn't do as the Romans do even if you wanted to. And they'd like you much better if you were just yourself. We used to laugh at the Japanese for wearing bowler hats and trying to talk slang. I think we were quite right. They were much nicer in those lovely silk dressing-gowns.

McCRIMMON No doubt.

CULLY Of course, there's got to be some sort of compromise, hasn't there? You can be yourself, I hope, without offending the local customs and prejudices.

JEAN Naturally.

McCRIMMON We have a very peculiar local prejudice, Mr. Cully, in this part of the country. We have a prejudice against desecrating the Lord's Day.

JEAN Is that remark intended for our benefit?

McCRIMMON Indeed, I hope that if you conseeder it seriously you may indeed benefit by it.

JEAN How have we desecrated the Lord's Day, as you call it?

McCRIMMON Your consciences will tell you that. And it isn't I who have called it the Lord's Day.

JEAN Look here, Uncle, let's get this straight. What are we supposed to have done?

McCRIMMON You are my guests, and it is unbecoming that I should rebuke you; but, since you ask me, I have found you eating and drinking at unsuitable hours and indulging yourselves in unseemly levity and in that laughter that is like the crackling of thorns under a pot: and this on a day that we are enjoined to keep holy.

JEAN Uncle Jock, there are nearly seven hundred millions of Christians in this world, and nearly seven hundred millions of them wouldn't see an atom of harm in anything we've done today.

McCRIMMON To be called a Christian is not to be a Christian. You will find in the Gospel according to St. Luke the words, "Why call ye me, Lord, Lord, and do not the thing which I say?"

JEAN When and where did the Lord tell us not to have tea on Sunday afternoon?

McCRIMMON In the Fourth Commandment.

JEAN The Fourth Commandment says nothing about tea.

McCRIMMON Tea is included.

JEAN And buns. Like a Sunday School Trip.

McCRIMMON I have no inclination to listen to blasphemy.

JEAN It isn't blasphemy.

McCRIMMON It is blasphemous to mock at the Ten Commandments.

JEAN The Ten Commandments are a set of rules for a wandering desert tribe. And not very good rules either. An American girl said they didn't tell you what to do. They only put ideas into your head.

McCRIMMON She would find elsewhere plenty of instructions what to do. And the ideas were there already.

JEAN Anyhow, they tell us to keep Saturday holy, not Sunday.

McCRIMMON If you were in a proper frame of mind, I would explain to you why.

JEAN What do you mean by a proper frame of mind?

McCRIMMON A state of humility and reverence.

JEAN You mean I'm to swallow everything I'm told?

McCRIMMON When you were a child you were not allowed to argue about your medicine.

JEAN I'm not a child now.

McCRIMMON Ah, well, now, I'm not so sure of that.

JEAN I'm nearly thirty.

McCRIMMON If you were Legion, you'd still be a bairn. You have all the signs and symptoms of infancy.

JEAN I'm glad to hear it, then. But there's something about out of the mouths of babes and sucklings, isn't there?

McCRIMMON Hath He perfected praise. I did not observe that you were in the exercise of Praise, when I entered just now. And since then I have not been aware of any high spirit of reverence.

JEAN I can't revere things I don't believe in.

McCRIMMON You do not believe in the Word of God as it is revealed in His Holy Scriptures?

JEAN Oh, I believe lots of it, and I'd like to believe lots of it, but when you put on that hangman's face and that awful voice and call it "The Word of God as it is revealed in His Holy Scriptures", I go all shivery down to my stomach and I don't believe a word of it.

McCRIMMON (*with a bland seriousness*) Well, now, I have observed the same thing in my conversations with the atheists and infidels from England who come up for the fishing. If I employ the sacred and beautiful words appropriate to the subject, they flinch and flee from my presence. I must even abandon plain English and descend to their baby talk. And yet I find that they have the presumption to set their opinions against the Gospel with not even an educated schoolboy's vocabulary to support them. It is very peculiar. They are so ignorant that their own episcopalian meenisters, poor bodies, in ministering to them have well nigh lost the power of human speech. I have to wait till I see Father Mackintosh, the priest from Strathdearg, before I can converse in a civilised language forbye the Gaelic.

JEAN *(helplessly)* Do listen to that, Cully. If anybody dares to speak back to him, he makes a beautiful little speech showing that they're fools and ignoramuses – or ignorami or ignoramae – which is it, Uncle Jock? You know I can only talk baby talk. What am I? An ignorama?

McCRIMMON The wee bit of Latin I once taught you has gone by the board. Mr. Cully will tell you that ignoramus is not a noun.

CULLY Oh, isn't it?

McCRIMMON It is not. But I will talk to you in any language you please. What is it you want to know?

JEAN I don't want to know anything. At least, I don't want to know anything about religion. At least, I don't want to know anything about religion that you can tell me. Because I think you're all wrong. Absolutely and entirely wrong.

McCRIMMON That is your opinion, is it?

JEAN It isn't my opinion only. It's the opinion of all decent sensible people. You contradict your own book of words by making your holy day Sunday instead of Saturday; and by denying that it was made for man and not man for it; and by preaching original sin and election and predestination . . .

COHEN Stop the horses a minute. I like a good argument. It's like the Brains Trust. But I like to know what you're talking about.

JEAN Original sin means that a baby is damned to Hell Fire even before it's born. Election means that only a little clique will ever get into the kingdom of Heaven and the rest haven't a chance. Predestination means that it doesn't matter two hoots what you do, because it was all fixed long ago. It's all a pack of nonsense.

COHEN It sounds funny, all right.

McCRIMMON You do not believe in these doctrines?

JEAN I do not. I think your premises are wrong and your evidence is phoney. There's nothing in the whole thing that appeals to my reason. And if you don't appeal to my reason, you need no more expect me to believe you than to believe a man who tells me he's a poached egg. There might even be some sense in *that*. Some men look like poached eggs.

COHEN That's the stuff to give him. Reason all the time.

McCRIMMON How far away is the sun?

JEAN I don't know.

CULLY About ninety million miles.

JEAN Yes. That's it. I'd forgotten.

McCRIMMON Who told you?

JEAN I don't remember. I read it in some book.

McCRIMMON And you believed it?

JEAN Yes. I suppose I did.

McCRIMMON Did your reason tell you to believe it?

JEAN Yes. Because it can be checked. If it's a lie any expert could disprove it.

McCRIMMON And when an expert had disproved it you would believe that it was a lie. Very well, then. I will tell you a wee story.

COHEN But if you don't believe experts, who are you to believe?

McCRIMMON I will tell you, with your permission, a wee story: Once upon a time there was a wee wee fellow with the finest set of whiskers that ever you saw and his name was wee Stumpie Stowsie.

COHEN Cor blimey!

JEAN Shut up, Conk.

McCRIMMON If there was one thing he was fond of it was a good swim. He would be down in the pond every day and all day swimming with his whiskers.

One day he was swimming and thinking about nothing at all and up comes a snail as big as a whale. "I'll swallow you as if you was Jonah," said the snail. "Come on. Do it," says the bold Stumpie Stowsie. So the snail swallowed him, and it was peaceful and warm in the insides of the snail, and Stumpie was quite joco, like a tourist passenger on a steamboat sailing round the Western Isles. But a time came when he thought and better thought, "Now am not I the silly one, dozing away in the insides of a great big snail when I might be settling down in a house of my own with a growing family to keep me cheery?" So he made a great to do in the insides of the snail till the snail was for no more of it, and he ups with Stumpie Stowsie and his whiskers into a forest that ran down to the seashore. So Stumpie he looks and he looks, and the verdure was that thick he could see nothing. So he climbs up a big palm tree to spy out the land.

COHEN So along comes his Fairy Godmother on a magic carpet. Good night, children, everywhere.

McCRIMMON No. It was a kangaroo ass big ass a post office. But I am wearying you, with my havers.

JEAN No. Honestly. We're enjoying it. It's like old times. Do you remember telling stories to Colin and me, on Saturday nights when we were wee tottums?

McCRIMMON I do, I do.

JEAN You tell them so well! I believed every word.

McCRIMMON You don't believe this one?

JEAN Of course I do, in a way.

McCRIMMON In what kind of a way? Would you put your experts on to prove it or to disprove it?

JEAN No, of course not.

McCRIMMON But they would be very pleased, whatever, your experts. Indeed, now, a whole clacking of experts have been at that very story, proving it and disproving it till they were nearly black in the face.

CULLY I see what you mean.

JEAN I'm afraid I don't.

CULLY He's been telling us the story of the Liver Fluke. It swims about in pools until it's swallowed by a water-snail. And then it's puked up onto a blade of grass. And a kangaroo eats the grass and the Fluke lays its eggs in the kangaroo's liver. Unless he does all these things the Fluke can't live. He seems to be very well named.

McCRIMMON So we are told.

JEAN What a cad's trick!

McCRIMMON Are you referring to the *Distoma hepaticum* or to your humble relative by marriage?

JEAN To you. I call it cheating.

McCRIMMON But you believe my story now, I think.

JEAN Yes, I suppose so.

McCRIMMON In both ways?

JEAN How in both ways?

McCRIMMON When I took you into a world outside this world you readily suspended what you call your reason and believed in Stumpie Stowsie. When Mr. Cully brought you back to earth and told you the story in another way, you believed it in another way without stopping to think. Your marvellous power of reasoning hadna much say in it either way, I'm thinking.

(He gets up, but stays at the table)

It comes to this, that you wish to have the eternal world outside our wee temporal world explained to you in the language of the tuppeny-ha'penny general knowledge text-books. Such language is neither adequate nor exact. But I'll do my best. Use your eyes and look round you. Mr. Cully and Mr. Cohen, you'd be bonny-like soldiers if you had no discipline. For three hundred years Scotland disciplined itself in body, brain and soul on one day of the week at least. The result was a breed of men that has not died out even in this shauchly generation. You don't believe in Original Sin, Jean, you are telling me? Well, now, you could easily have had ten babies by this time if you had not preferred talking and sentimentalising about them. Then you would have found the truth that a baby has every sensual vice of which it is anatomically capable with no spirituality to temper it. You do not believe that mankind is divided into the sheep and the goats – the Elect and the Damned? Use your eyes and look around you. You may pity the Damned – and indeed it is your duty so to do. But you cannot deny that they exist.

You do not believe in Predestination? That is because you do not like it. If you only believe what is nice and comfortable, our doctrine is of no service to you. If I give you a crack on the head with a stick, you need not believe it; you need not believe in your dentist's drill or in the tax-gatherer's demand. Go on. Believe what is agreeable to you. I do assure you that you will be in such a continuous state of surprise that your eyebrows will jump off the top of your head. Even your heathen philosophers *knew* that Predestination was a fact, like Ben Nevis. You can go round it. You can go over it. But you are foolish to ignore it.

Do you believe that the body rises from the grave on the Great Day?

JEAN I believe that the spirit does.

McCRIMMON In all my days I have never seen the interment of a spirit. You do not believe that the body can rise again, though every spring and every day in a myriad forms you see that actual thing happening. But it is folly to talk to you. The Lord gave you a spiritual mind with which you might see the truth of these things. But you are afraid of your spiritual sight. And 'deed I can hardly blame you. Yet it is with that sight alone that you can apprehend spiritual truths. Reason is a poor instrument for such a purpose.

CULLY The Fathers of the Church cultivated the spiritual mind?

McCRIMMON I believe some of them did.

CULLY They found in the world outside reason a lot of unreasonable phenomena. They believed in transubstantiation and miraculous liquefaction and the remission of sins by priests and the efficacy of prayers for the dead. They found warrant for all these things on the spiritual level. Yet they are outside reason. Do you believe in them?

McCRIMMON No.

CULLY Why? Because your reason rejects them?

McCRIMMON When I said that reason was a feeble instrument I did not refer to my own reason. But I must ask you to excuse me. My evening diet of worship is in ten minutes. It is in the Gaelic; and I must think for a little in the Gaelic before I am ready to speak it. In the meantime I would feel very obliged if you would respect my serious and conseedered opinion that today is a sacred day and should be observed, within these walls at least with all due decorum.

CULLY Oh, yes, of course, but . . .

McCRIMMON I thank you. That is all I wished of you. I shall see you at the evening meal.

(Exit McCRIMMON)

COHEN *(with the gestures of one drowned or dizzy)* Help! Throw me a lifebelt, somebody.

JEAN I think you scored a hit, Cully. His eyes flashed for a minute, but he broke off the engagement very quickly.

CULLY And very neatly. He won handsomely on points.

JEAN Why didn't you chip in earlier?

CULLY What's the good? He's a professional and we're only drivelling amateurs. We're apt to forget that parsons are professionals. Our English parsons are a bit like your professional soldiers. They want us to forget that they know their job.

COHEN Why don't you shout him down, like you used to do in the barrack room?

CULLY He'd beat me at that too. He's a chest on him like a bull.

JEAN He'd talk the hind leg off the Devil himself.

CULLY Would he?

JEAN I suppose so. And he's so utterly wrong. It kills everything that's gay and decent in life. The other churches let you alone. They sometimes go haywire and burn a few heretics, but most of the heretics are Calvinists, so it doesn't matter.

CULLY He made it look so damned logical for a bit. It's his infernal totalitarianism I can't stand, though.

JEAN They seem to have a sadistic love for persecution for its own sake.

COHEN A lot of Nazis.

CULLY I don't know.

COHEN What do you mean, you don't know?

CULLY Do you know who invented modern democracy?

COHEN The thing we're fighting for? No. Lloyd George?

CULLY No. Calvin.

JEAN I don't believe it.

CULLY You can look it up. His system was a theocracy; but all its officials were elected by vote and responsible to God and to the electors. And everybody in the community voted, so long as he behaved himself.

JEAN You're on his side?

CULLY I'm on nobody's side. I'm a sort of Devil's Advocate.

JEAN I wish we could raise the Devil and get him to speak for himself.

COHEN You seemed to me to be doing your best.

JEAN Conk! Your book!

(She finds Reginald Scot on the floor)

We'll follow the printed instructions and have a shot.

CULLY That's an idea. It will help to pass the time for Conk.

JEAN They are all in bed before ten. We could sneak down quietly and try at, say, about midnight.

CULLY I'm on.

COHEN What's this? A séance?

JEAN Yes. A sort of a séance.

COHEN I went to a séance. Spoke to my grandfather. Cor blimey, the poor old perisher had gone off his head. Said he was happy.

JEAN But what about your beauty sleep?

CULLY That's all right. Four hours' sleep's enough for the likes of Conk and me.

JEAN That's a date, then. We'll have to be very quiet.

(At door)

CULLY Where are you going to?
JEAN I'm going to church.
COHEN Cor blimey.

(Exit JEAN)

END OF SCENE ONE.

THE CURTAIN IS LOWERED TO DENOTE THE PASSAGE OF SIX HOURS.

Scene Two

The same. Darkness, except for the dull glow of the fire. Enter CULLY, commando fashion, in gym shoes. He lights the oil-lamp and turns it low. To him, JEAN.

JEAN *(in a whisper)* Hello.
CULLY Hello.

(He suddenly embraces her with some violence)

JEAN Damn you, what do you think you're doing?

(She disengages forcibly and gets in a rousing slap to CULLY's cheek)

CULLY Sorry.
JEAN I should damn well think so.
CULLY I thought you wanted me to. I didn't know. I'm sorry. You see, I'm not much of an expert at amatory exercises. I never know whether they want to make love or not.
JEAN What do you mean by "they"?
CULLY Oh, anybody.
JEAN Well, I'm not just anybody. I'm a friendly sort of creature; and when I pass a fellow-creature a cheery-oh I don't intend it as a mating call. Do you appreciate that?
CULLY Yes. I think so.
JEAN And do you think you can manage to be friendly with me in a civilised fashion without getting into a continual state of excitement – or pretending to get into one?
CULLY Yes, of course.
JEAN That's all right, then. Sit down.
CULLY Thanks.
JEAN I'm not a puritan. I suppose I've got the ordinary appetites. But I think it's absolutely disgusting to go cuddling or guzzling one's way through life. Do you agree, or are you just the ordinary pig-man?
CULLY Yes. You're perfectly right. I made a mistake. I've said I'm sorry. I suppose it was a sort of compliment to your general attractiveness.
JEAN It's not a compliment at all. It's a squalid insult. It always has been, until the last few years. Never mind. You know now that "I'm not that sort of girl." Forget about it. Where's your friend?
CULLY I don't know. I suppose he's making his own arrangements.
JEAN How beastly! Go and fetch him.
CULLY I shouldn't think he'd like that.
JEAN Whether he likes it or not, do as I tell you. If you mean what I think

197

you mean, the sooner you two learn to behave yourselves the better. You're my uncle's guests, and you must behave as if you were. Where is he?

CULLY I think he said something about the wash-house.

JEAN Wait. I had better go. I know my way in the dark; we mustn't wake everybody up. You wait here and keep cave.

CULLY You'll get wet.

JEAN There's a cape in the lobby and it's only a few yards.

(She goes out. CULLY fetches the DISCOVERIE OF WITCHCRAFT and opens it on the table. The clock strikes twelve. Re-enter JEAN with COHEN and MORAG. They are both fully dressed. MORAG is in some confusion of spirit, but is inclined to brave it out.)

JEAN Come in and sit down here.

MORAG I'll away to my bed, Miss Jean.

JEAN You will not. Do as I tell you.

(All sit down at the table)

I'm surprised at you, Morag.

COHEN Aren't you surprised at me?

JEAN Not a bit.

MORAG There was no harm in it. No harm in it at all. He was telling me about the wee talking birds he has got in a cage down in London.

JEAN Well, he can go on telling you here. Cully and I don't mind.

MORAG This is not the thing. This is not the thing at all. Sitting in the parlour and the Minister upstairs in his bed. It is you that is the surprising one, Miss Jean, I am telling you. Now like a good lady, be letting me away to my bed. I have my washing to do, tomorrow's morning.

JEAN Sit still. Maybe you'll hear something for the good of your soul.

MORAG Oh, dear me, let you my soul alone. It is two minutes past twelve, and not the Sabbath day now at all, whatever.

JEAN That clock is ten minutes fast. It's still the Sabbath day. Sit still and be quiet.

MORAG Oh, dear me. My sorrow and my pain!

(She mumbles a little in Gaelic and relapses into silence)

JEAN You were going to tell us about the birds, Conk.

COHEN *(grunts)*

JEAN Oh, very well, then. We'll get on with the business of the meeting. Have you the book, Cully?

CULLY Yes.

JEAN Have you found the place?

CULLY Yes.

JEAN Let me see. I've got a bit of chalk. . . . Oh, but this is terribly complicated! We have to go out and bathe in a spring; and we've got to have a lion-skin or a hart-skin girdle; and we've got to have chest protectors with words on them; and we've got to have a knife. . . .

CULLY That's all right. We've all bathed quite recently, and a tap's as good as a spring. I've made myself a chest protector and Conk and I have both got magic belts with brass devices on them. You can have them if you like. Conk, give the lady your belt.

COHEN I can't. It's keeping up my respectability.

JEAN You're sure they will do?

CULLY Yes. I know the drill pretty well. I've written Agla and the mystic signs on my jack-knife. There it is.

(He opens his jack-knife and throws it on the table)

JEAN Hush! Don't make a noise. You're wonderful, Cully.

CULLY You go ahead and make Solomon's Circle. That's it – on page 244. I'll read a sort of condensed version of the exorcism. It should do well enough. Get cracking, now. Give me a bit of chalk. I'll do the central diagram on the table.

(JEAN draws a circle round the table and adds certain cabalistic signs. CULLY makes marks on the table itself.)

JEAN Whom shall we call up, Cully?

CULLY It'll have to be a Duke of the Infernal Regions. They are free from midnight till four a.m. I should think Bealphares would be the best. He's the Golden Devil and a great talker.

COHEN I thought you sat in a circle with your hands on the table and played "Lead Kindly Light" on the gramophone.

CULLY We'll do that too, except the gramophone. Are you ready, Jean?

JEAN Nearly. What's this word? AGLA . . . EL . . . YA . . . PANTHON.

(Standing up)

Righty-ho.

CULLY Give me the book and sit down. Turn down the light, Conk. Not too far, you fool.

(COHEN lowers the light)

COHEN Do we sit with our hands touching?

CULLY Yes. Are you ready? Now keep very quiet.

(He takes up the knife and points it at all in turn)

Fugiat omne malignum
Salvetur quodque benignum. . . . Say Amen.

OMNES Amen.

CULLY Homo . . . sacarus . . . musceolameas . . . cherubozca: I exorcise and conjure Bealphares, also called Berith, also called Beall and Bolfry, thou great and terrible divell, by the sacraments and by the unspeakable name TETRAGRAMMATON. I conjure and exorcise thee, Bealphares, by the virtue of all angels, archangels, thrones, dominations, principats, potestats, cherubim and seraphim that thou do come unto us, in fair form of man or womankind, here visible, before this circle and not terrible by any manner of ways; and that thou do answer truly without craft or deceit unto all my demands and questions. Lemaac, solmaac, elmay, gezagra. Josamin, sabach, ha, aem, re, sepha, sephar, semoit, gergoin, letes. Amen. Fiat, fiat, flat. Amen.

OMNES Amen.

(The light turns blue. MORAG begins to whimper softly. There is a crash of thunder and the door swings suddenly open, revealing an elfish little gentleman in a glistening black mackintosh and a tall silk hat. His umbrella is open and dripping with water. He closes it. MORAG stands up to her full height and gives a piercing scream, which she checks by biting on the back of her hand.)

MORAG It's unchancy to bring an umbrella into a hoose and it open. It's unlucky.

COHEN For Gord's sake put up the light.

(He turns up the lamp with a shaking hand. The GENTLEMAN takes off his mackintosh and hat and gives them to MORAG, with the umbrella. MORAG gingerly puts the umbrella upside down at the edge of the fireplace. He is dressed, to the astonishment of everybody, in exactly the same way as the REV. MR. McCRIMMON. His face is amiable and his hair is a silky black. He comes into the room with a light, springy step and takes his stance in front of the fireplace, beaming on the conjurors.)

THE GENTLEMAN Well, ladies and gentleman, a most disagreeable evening.

(He lights a big cigar by some sleight of hand and then looks at the clock)

Your clock is slow, I think. It is just after twelve o'clock, as I happen to know.

(He smiles benignantly, tucking his hands under his coat-tails. Enter McCRIMMON, in nightshirt and dressing-gown. MRS. McCRIMMON behind.)

Ah, Mr. McCrimmon, I believe? I am Dr. Bolfry. How do you do?

McCRIMMON *(shaking hands uncertainly)* How do you do?

BOLFRY I am very well, thank you.

(He stands smiling on McCRIMMON)

THE CURTAIN FALLS

Scene Three

The same, an hour later. The fire has been stoked up to a cheery glow, and illuminates BOLFRY with just a suspicion of red light. He is reclining in the Minister's chair, with his feet on another chair. A bottle of "medicinal" whisky is on the mantelpiece, and he is obviously enjoying himself. McCRIMMON, still in his dressing-gown, sits bolt upright at the far end of the table with a dazed expression on his face. MRS. McCRIMMON, with her back to the Audience, sits beside him. JEAN is on his other side. They both appear anxious about McCRIMMON, who is certainly looking very strange. CULLY is next MRS. McCRIMMON, COHEN next JEAN, MORAG, completely pixilated, is just within reach of BOLFRY, and he is able to lean over and pat her hand or her knee affectionately from time to time.

CULLY I see. Yes. That's very interesting. But, you see, Mr. Bolfry, we have got a little away from the conceptions of Good and Evil that were prevalent in . . . well, in your time. We have rather a different orientation, if you see what I mean.

BOLFRY I see exactly what you mean. Your generation is not what you call orientated at all. Your scientific gentlemen have robbed you of Time and Space, and you are all little blind semi-conscious creatures tossing about in a tempest of skim milk. If I may be allowed to say so, it all comes of thinking yourselves a little too good for your priests. You went prancing away from your churches and schoolrooms. And the first thing you did with your emancipated state was to hand yourselves over body and soul to a number of plain-clothes priests whose only qualification was that they were good at sums. That was very foolish of you. *(To MORAG)* Wasn't it, my dear?

MORAG Yes, Sir.

BOLFRY You can't organise and expound the sentient Universe simply by being good at sums, can you?

MORAG No, Sir.

BOLFRY Just as I thought. And then you found that even sums were a bit too difficult. If you can't do a quadratic equation, all these pages of incomprehensible figures are too much of a strain on simple Faith. You went to a new sort of old gentleman who said to you, "Life, my dear brethren, is one long smutty story."

"Aha!" you said, "This is a bit of all right. Why wasn't I told this before?" But no amount of licentious conversation with serious-looking professors could cure the ache and restlessness in your souls. Could it, my darling?

MORAG Whatever you say yourself, Sir.

(He helps himself to another drink)

BOLFRY That's an admirable whisky you keep, Mrs. McCrimmon.

MRS. McCRIMMON We only keep it as a medicine. Mr. McCrimmon is a teetotaller.

BOLFRY Everything is a medicine, Mrs. McCrimmon. Everybody in this world is sick. Why is everybody in this world sick? A most profitable line of enquiry. Why are we all sick, Morag?

MORAG I think it is because we're all a bit feared of you, Mr. Bolfry.

BOLFRY Feared of me? Feared of me? Dear, dear. Come, come. You're not afraid of me, are you, McCrimmon?

McCRIMMON Get thee behind me, Satan!

BOLFRY What did you say?

McCRIMMON Avoid thee. Get thee behind me, Satan!

BOLFRY Perhaps I should not have allowed you to get within that comfortable ring of chalk. You must not speak to me like that.

McCRIMMON *(throwing over his chair as he stands up)* This is nonsensical. It is an evil dream. Presently I will be waking up. What do they call you, you masquerading fiend?

BOLFRY I have told you, Sir. My name is Bolfry. In the days of sanity and belief, it was a name not unknown to men of your cloth.

McCRIMMON You are dressed like a minister. Where is your kirk?

BOLFRY In Hell.

McCRIMMON Are there kirks in Hell?

BOLFRY Why not? Would you deny us the consolations of religion?

McCRIMMON What I would deny you or grant you is nothing to the point. You are a liar and the Father of lies. There cannot be a kirk in Hell.

BOLFRY *(twisting suddenly round to look at the portrait of a clergyman hanging on the wall)* Who is that?

McCRIMMON That is the worthy Doctor Scanderlands of Fetterclash.

BOLFRY How do you know?

McCRIMMON It is an engraving of a portrait taken from the life.

BOLFRY The portrait was bitten into a plate with acid and printed in ink on paper. The black ink and the white paper were arranged according as the light and shadow fell on the Doctor's face and bands and gown; so that the Doctor's friends cried in delight: "It is the very lineaments of the Doctor himself that we behold!" Would you recognise it as the Doctor if it were all black ink or white paper?

McCRIMMON If you came here, Sir, at the back-end of night to give us a lecture on the Art of Engraving, I can only observe . . .

BOLFRY Keep your herrings for the loch, and do not drag them across my path. Without this black and that white, there would be no form of Doctor Scanderlands that we could see?

McCRIMMON Maybe you are right.

BOLFRY The Artist could tell us nothing about the Doctor without them?

McCRIMMON He could not.

BOLFRY And neither you nor I nor anyone else can tell anything about Heaven or Hell, or this very imperfect makeshift of an Earth on which we stand, without our blacks and whites and our greys, which are whites mixed with black. To put it in simple words, we cannot conceive the Universe except as a pattern of reciprocating opposites – *(to MORAG)* – Can we, my love? No, of course we can't. Therefore when I tell you that there are kirks in Hell, I am telling you something that is at least credible. And I give you my word of honour as a gentleman that it is true.

McCRIMMON What do you preach in your kirks?

BOLFRY Lend me your pulpit and I will show you a specimen.

JEAN Oh, Uncle Jock, do! You may never get such a chance again.

McCRIMMON Sleeping or waking, dream or no dream, I'll have no blasphemy in this parish.

BOLFRY Blasphemy? I should never think of committing blasphemy. I think I may say that I know my position better. I am a Duke and a General of Legions. Only gutter devils are impertinent to the Deity. . . . But won't you sit down?

McCRIMMON *(sitting)* I can make nothing of this.

BOLFRY You disappoint me. You are a Master of Arts. You are a Bachelor of Divinity. You are a theologian and a metaphysician and a scholar of Greek and Hebrew. What is your difficulty? Don't you believe in the Devil?

McCRIMMON He goeth about like a roaring lion.

BOLFRY Not when I am sober. Answer my question.

McCRIMMON I believe in a personal Devil.

BOLFRY And in Good and Evil?

McCRIMMON Yes.

BOLFRY And in Heaven and Hell?

McCRIMMON Yes.

BOLFRY And Body and Soul?

McCRIMMON Yes.

BOLFRY And Creation and Destruction?

McCRIMMON Yes.

BOLFRY And Life and Death?

McCRIMMON Yes.

BOLFRY Do you believe in the truth and inspiration of the Bible?

McCRIMMON Yes.

BOLFRY Have you read the Book of Job?

McCRIMMON Yes.

BOLFRY "Now there was a day when the sons of God came to present themselves before the Lord, and Satan came among them."

McCRIMMON The Devil can quote Scripture for his own purpose.

BOLFRY An entirely suitable purpose in this case. . . . Mr. McCrimmon, I believe also in the things of which I have spoken.

McCRIMMON And tremble.

BOLFRY Not infrequently. But the point is this: Why, if we hold all these beliefs in common, do you find anything odd in my conversation or my appearance here?

McCRIMMON I don't know.

BOLFRY Tuts, tuts, man. Pull yourself together. If the Creator Himself could sit down peacefully and amicably and discuss experimental psychology with the Adversary, surely you can follow His example?

McCRIMMON Mr. Bolfry, or whatever you call yourself, it is plain to me that you could talk the handle off a pump. If you have a message for me, I hope I have enough Highland courtesy to listen to it patiently, but I must ask you to be brief.

BOLFRY Mr. McCrimmon, I am not charged with any message for you. Indeed, I think it will turn out that you and I are in agreement on most essential points. But these young people have summoned me on a cold and dismal night from my extremely warm and comfortable quarters. If you had instructed them properly, all this wouldn't have been necessary. But we'll let that pass. Do you mind if we go on from the point at which you rather rudely ordered me to get behind you?

McCRIMMON Go you on from any point you like. You are whirling about like a Tee-to-tum.

BOLFRY Highland courtesy, Mr. Cully.

McCRIMMON And keep your tongue off the Highlands.

BOLFRY Mr. McCrimmon, I may be only a Devil, but I am not accustomed to be addressed in that fashion.

JEAN Mr. Bolfry . . .

BOLFRY One moment, please. *(To McCRIMMON)* Unless, Sir, you are prepared to exercise a little civility, I must decline to continue this discussion.

McCRIMMON The discussion, Sir, is none of my seeking – no more than is your intrusion into my house and family circle. So far as I am concerned, you are completely at liberty to continue or to sneck up.

MRS. McCRIMMON Oh, John! That's an awful like way to speak to a guest.

McCRIMMON He is no guest of mine.

BOLFRY That is true. I am Mr. Cully's guest. Why did you send for me, Mr. Cully?

CULLY I'm blessed if I know, now you come to ask.

BOLFRY The likeliest reason was that you were unhappy and afraid. These are common complaints in these days. Were you crying for me from the dark?

JEAN No. We weren't. My uncle thinks he has got divine authority. And he was using his confidence in that and his learning and his eloquence and his personality to bully us. We wanted a little authority on our side.

BOLFRY I see. Thank you very much.

JEAN He's got the advantage of believing everything he says.

BOLFRY A great advantage.

JEAN You can't meet a man like that on his own ground if you think he's talking nonsense.

BOLFRY You can't discuss what brand of green cheese the moon is made of unless you accept the possibility that the moon is made of green cheese. I see. In what *do* you believe, Miss Jean?

JEAN I believe that the Kingdom of Heaven is within me.

BOLFRY Is that all?

JEAN That's practically all.

BOLFRY So far as it goes, you are quite right. But you are the receptacle of the Kingdom of Hell and of a number of other irrelevances left over in the process of Evolution. Until you can reconcile those remarkable elements with one another, you will remain unhappy and have the impulse, from time to time, to raise the Devil.

JEAN Then we ought to study these what-do-you-call-'ems – these elements, and try to reconcile them?

BOLFRY I didn't say you *ought* to. I said you won't be happy till you do.

JEAN Then we ought to, oughtn't we?

BOLFRY If you want equilibrium. If you want happiness.

CULLY But surely the pursuit of happiness . . .

BOLFRY Yes, yes. The pursuit. A very different thing from catching your electric hare. The happiest man is a general paralytic in Bedlam. Yet you do not envy him. He is in a state of death in life. You naturally prefer life in death – probably because you are used to it. . . . You are not favouring me with much of your attention, Mr. Cohen.

COHEN Sorry, Sir.

BOLFRY Why not?

COHEN Well, Sir, if you want to know the honest truth, I'm bored bloody stiff.

BOLFRY You say that with an air of some superiority. You must not be proud of being bored stiff. Boredom is a sign of satisfied ignorance, blunted apprehension, crass sympathies, dull understanding, feeble powers of attention and irreclaimable weakness of character. You belie your lively Semitic countenance, Mr. Cohen. If you are alive, Mr. Cohen, you should be interested in everything – even in the phenomenon of a Devil incarnate explaining to you the grand Purpose in virtue of which you live, move and have your breakfast.

COHEN It's all hooey, that. There's no such thing as a Purpose. It's a tele – teleo – teleological fallacy. That's what it is.

BOLFRY Dear me! *Dear* me! Mr. McCrimmon, you are an amateur of blasphemy. What do you say to that?

McCRIMMON The man is wrong.

BOLFRY Another point on which we are agreed.

COHEN I can't help it. I'm entitled to my opinion.

McCRIMMON In what sort of a world have you been living, man?

COHEN In the Borough Road. Do you know it?

McCRIMMON Even in the Borough Road, do you find no evidence of Eternal Purpose?

COHEN Not a bit.

BOLFRY My dear goodness gracious me, I know the place very well, and it's simply bursting with Eternal Purpose.

McCRIMMON There's not one brick laid on another, there's not one foot moving past another on the dirty pavement doesn't tap out "Purpose, purpose, purpose," to anybody with the ears to hear.

BOLFRY Every one of your higher faculties is bent to some purpose or other. You can't make anything happen without a purpose. There are things happening all round you on the Borough Road. How in the world do you think they happen without a purpose behind them?

McCRIMMON Do you deny to your Maker the only respectable faculty you've got?

COHEN All I can say is, if I've got a Maker and He's got a purpose, I can't congratulate Him on the way it works out.

BOLFRY and ⎫ But my dear good chap, you can't possibly sit there
McCRIMMON, ⎬ and . . .
talking together ⎭ How can you have the presumption to sit there and . . .

BOLFRY I beg your pardon.

McCRIMMON No, no. Excuse me. Please go on.

BOLFRY Not at all. After you.

McCRIMMON It is not for you to congratulate or not to congratulate. Who is able to judge the Creator of Heaven and Earth?

CULLY Well, who is?

COHEN Yes, who is? Mind, I don't admit there's any such person. But if there is and he give us a critical faculty, we got to use it, see?

JEAN Conk's absolutely right. You tell us to praise Him. What's the good of praise when you've no chance of blaming? It doesn't mean a thing.

CULLY What happens to your reciprocating opposites, Mr. Bolfry, if we can't be anything but a lot of sanctified Yes Men?

COHEN Hallelujah all the time. Not much encouragement to the Creator to stick to His job.

JEAN That's the stuff to give them, Conk! And I thought you were too much the gentleman to open your head.

COHEN No offence meant, of course.

McCRIMMON Young man, do you realise that your foolish words are jeopardising your immortal souls?

COHEN That's all tinky-tonk with me. We ain't got any immortal souls.

BOLFRY I begin to believe it. Mr. McCrimmon, it seems to me we cannot begin our battle for the souls of these persons until they realise that they have souls to battle for.

McCRIMMON It is terrible indeed. Our duty is plain. We must wrestle with them. We must admonish and exhort them.

BOLFRY It is my duty no less than yours.

McCRIMMON But stop you a minute. I know that this is a dream, but there must be logic, even in dreams. I understand you to say you are a Devil.

BOLFRY But I am also, like yourself, a servant of One whom I need not name.

McCRIMMON I am a very distressed man. You must not quibble with me nor use words with double meanings.

BOLFRY I am bound by my contract with our young exorcist here to tell nothing but the plain truth. My distinguished relative is in the same position as I. I am the same Instrument of Providence as he who smote Job's body with boils for the good of his soul.

McCRIMMON That is a way of looking at it. Certainly it is a way of looking at it, whatever.

BOLFRY More than that, if it is of any interest to you, I am an ordained Minister of the Gospel.

McCRIMMON Do you tell me that? Where were you ordained?

BOLFRY In Geneva in 1570.

McCRIMMON What did you say?

BOLFRY In Geneva, I said.

McCRIMMON But in what year?

BOLFRY The year is immaterial. I can't swear to it within two or three years. But ordained I am. And I have preached, among other places, in the High Kirk at North Berwick, to the no small edification of the lieges.

McCRIMMON Will you swear to that?

BOLFRY Mr. McCrimmon, my Yea is Yea and my Nay is Nay.

McCRIMMON It is a most remarkable thing, but from what I have heard from your lips so far, your doctrine appears to be sound.

BOLFRY None sounder. And now that you are satisfied, I have a proposal to make.

McCRIMMON What is you proposal?

BOLFRY I propose that we adjourn to the adjoining edifice and there admonish and exhort our brothers and sister in a place suitable for these exercises.

McCRIMMON You mean in my kirk?

BOLFRY Where else? Is it not the place most suitable for a conversion?

McCRIMMON It is suitable. But all this is very strange.

BOLFRY All life is very strange. Shall we go?

McCRIMMON I cannot enter the kirk in my nightshirt; though it is true that I have dreamed that same more times that once.

BOLFRY Go upstairs then and change. I shall wait for you.

McCRIMMON Well, well. Come with me, Marget. . . . And in case I wake up before I come down again, Mr. Bolfry, let me assure you that it has been, upon the whole, a pleasure to meet you. I hope I have not passed the stage of learning . . . even from a – a Being of your – your Nature.

BOLFRY Sir, you are most polite. I hope to reciprocate the compliment.

(Exeunt MR. and MRS. McCRIMMON, BOLFRY holding the door open for them)

JEAN I never heard the like of that!

BOLFRY *(mildly)* Of what, my dear?

JEAN You're on his *side*!

BOLFRY What did you expect?

JEAN I don't know. I certainly didn't expect such a pious Devil!

BOLFRY My dear young lady, you don't know everything, as you are very shortly to find out.

JEAN If you want to know my opinion, I think you're drunk.

BOLFRY Drunk? Dear me! Tut tut, tut tut!

(He helps himself)

CULLY Well, I don't know what you chaps feel, but I'd feel the better of a drink myself.

MORAG No!

CULLY What do you mean by No?

MORAG Don't leave the circle. He'll get you if you leave the circle.

BOLFRY She's quite right. Quite right. You are a percipient little slut, my darling.

JEAN But . . . I mean, it's all nonsense . . . but what happens on the way to church?

BOLFRY Nothing. Nothing. The Holy Man will protect you. They have their uses, Holy Men. Not that I am really dangerous. But we are mischievous a little, and fond of experiments. Eve and the apple was the first great step in experimental science. But sit down, Mister Gunner Cully. There is plenty of time. Let us continue our delightful conversation. Let me see. Where were we?

JEAN Does it matter very much? You're the most inconsequent character I ever met.

BOLFRY Oh, no, no. I follow the pattern. If there is one. Perhaps that's what's wrong with you young people. You don't seem to have any pattern The woof, as it were, is flying loosely about in space. There is no drama about your associations. Now, I am very fond of the Drama. I have done a little bit in that way myself. To my mind the really interesting life is that which moves from situation to situation, with character developing naturally in step with that orderly progress. Now what is the matter with the four of you is that you haven't a situation among you. You are a quartette that has forgotten its music. We must do something about it. Let me see. Mr. Cully.

CULLY Well?

BOLFRY Here we have a common soldier who . . .

CULLY I'm not a common soldier. I'm in the Royal Artillery.

BOLFRY Here we have a young intellectual . . .

CULLY There's no need to use foul language. Call me what you like, but not that.

BOLFRY Very well, then. Here we have a product of our Universities and Public Schools. I know I am correct there.

CULLY How do you know?

BOLFRY Because you can't listen patiently and because you have no manners. Here we have this delicately nurtured youth cheerfully bearing the rigours of the barrack and the bivouac. Why? Has he a secret sorrow?

CULLY No, I haven't. And I'm bearing the rigours because I've blooming well got to. I was stuck for a commission on my eyesight, but I'll be in the Pay Corps within a month with any luck. And then good-bye rigours of the barrack and the bivouac.

BOLFRY None the less, an interesting character. A philosopher. An observer of Life. Obviously the juvenile lead for want of a better.

CULLY Thank you.

BOLFRY Don't mention it. There is about him a certain air of mystery which we shall presently resolve. The leading woman, on the other hand, is cast along more stereotyped lines. She is what happens in the third generation after one of the many thousand Movements for the emancipation of Women. So is Mr. Cully, by the way.

JEAN What in the world do you mean by that?

BOLFRY You are only faintly feminine and he is only slightly masculine. All these Women's Movements tend to have a neutralising effect on the Human Race. Never mind. It will make our little drama interesting to the psychologist, and we are all psychologists nowadays. We come now to what used to be called Comic Relief.

COHEN That wouldn't be me, I don't suppose?

BOLFRY Yes. There is nothing dramatic about the Poor unless they are very funny or very tragic.

COHEN Wotjer mean by the Poor? I ain't never had a bob I haven't worked for.

BOLFRY That is what I mean by the Poor. As for the extremely charming little person on my right, I haven't decided whether she is funny or not. As she is an unsophisticated savage she is probably significant of something which will no doubt emerge.

CULLY What about the Minister?

BOLFRY He will provide Personality. The drama will revolve about him and . . . ah, yes . . . his lady wife. As I had nearly forgotten all about her, she is probably the key to the whole business. There, my dear friends, are the Dramatis Personae. We have now . . .

COHEN Where do you come in?

BOLFRY I am the Devil from the Machine. Here we have our Persons in the Play. We know very little about them, because, so far, there is nothing much to know. We cannot imitate the old dramatists and describe them as Cully, in love with Jean, Conk, in love with Morag, Jean, in love with Cully, Morag . . .

MORAG Now, I am not, Mr. Bolfry, no indeed at all. And you needn't be saying it.

JEAN Nobody's in love with anybody else. Not here, anyhow. Why should they be?

BOLFRY The animals went in two by two for a very particular reason. And when a drama has no other especial interest, it would be unkind to deny it a Love Interest. I think the least you can do is fall in love as quickly as possible. You are wasting time.

JEAN Except Conk and Morag.

MORAG Now, Miss Jean! . . .

COHEN We told you before we was only talking about budgerigars.

BOLFRY Budgerigars! Love Birds! Brilliant images of tenderness and desire with every delicate feather-frond alive with passion! We taught them speech that they might teach us their mystery. And what did they say: "Cocky's clever. Cocky's clever. Chirrup, chirrup. Good morning, good evening." That's all. And yet how much better do you express the primeval urgencies within you? "Cully's clever. Jean's clever. Chirrup. Good evening." I must teach you how to express yourselves better, young enemies of Death. Come, then. Why don't you tell Miss Jean what you think of her, Cully? She would be extremely flattered.

JEAN No, I wouldn't. He's told me already what he thinks of me, and I've slapped his face. You're a silly old ass. If you've come here to talk about repressions and inhibit personalities, I wish you'd stayed in Hell. You know perfectly well that if it weren't for inhibitions every living thing on this earth would run down in a few minutes.

BOLFRY Of course it would. And how shockingly you misunderstand me. I love repression. You repress your passion to intensify it; to have it more abundantly; to joy in its abundance. The prisoner cannot leap to lose his chain unless he has been chained.

JEAN Then what *are* you talking about?

BOLFRY About you. Come. I'll marry you.

JEAN But I don't want to marry you.

BOLFRY No, no. I mean, I'll marry Cully and you. I'll bind you by the strongest and most solemn contract ever forged in heaven. Think of the agonising fun and excitement you'll have in breaking it.

JEAN No. Thank you very much.

BOLFRY But why don't you do something? Why is the blood galloping through your not unsightly limbs? Why are the nerve cells snapping and flashing in your head if you are to wrap this gift of life in a napkin and bury it in a back garden?

JEAN We are doing something.

BOLFRY Indeed?

JEAN We're fighting Hitler.

BOLFRY And who is Hitler?

COHEN Blind me, I'd've thought if anybody knew the old basket, it'd be you.

CULLY Do you mean to tell me that we've all gone to the trouble of fetching a damned medieval hypothesis out of Hell to tell us what life is all about, and now we have to tell *him*?

JEAN Mr. Bolfry, dearest, Hitler is the man who started the War.

BOLFRY Is he? I thought I had done that. How is the War getting on? . . . No. Don't tell me. I'll try to guess.

(BOLFRY helps himself to another drink)

I should think some lunatic has been able to persuade his country that it is possible to regiment mankind. I should think the people he has persuaded are my old friends the Germans. They are sufficiently orderly and sufficiently stupid so to be persuaded. I should conjecture that mankind has risen in an intense state of indignation at the bare possibility of being regimented. I should think that the regimenters will succeed in hammering their enemies into some sort of cohesion. Mankind will then roll them in the mud for a bit and then pull them out and forget all about them. They will have much more interesting things to attend to – such as making money and making love. . . . Ah, there you are, McCrimmon.

(Re-enter MR. and MRS. McCRIMMON. MRS. McCRIMMON is carrying a Minister's gown and white Geneva bands.)

Well, my dear Sir, time is getting on. Shall we adjourn to the kirk?

McCRIMMON No.

BOLFRY No? But, my dear fellow, I thought it was all arranged.

McCRIMMON No. This is a dream, of course; but there must be decency even in dreams. Waking or sleeping, I will have no phantasmagorical equivocator preaching in my kirk.

BOLFRY A dream, eh? You think this is all a dream?

McCRIMMON What else can it be?

BOLFRY What is the difference between a dream and a supernatural happening?

McCRIMMON The question does not arise. This is nothing but a highly circumstantial dream. I shall laugh at it in the morning.

BOLFRY The sign of a supernatural event is that it obeys all the laws of Nature except one. You will find that true of every event from the Burning Bush to the Resurrection.

McCRIMMON There is truth in that.

BOLFRY Has your room changed? Have the people around you changed? Does the clock go on ticking? This is not a dream, Mr. McCrimmon.

McCRIMMON I am troubled in my mind, but I can yet hold fast to what there is to grasp. I will have no spectre or Devil preaching in my church.

BOLFRY *(in a low and sinister voice)* By the Throne of Thunder and the Canopy of Eternal Night . . .

MRS. McCRIMMON Now, now, then, Mr. Bolfry, there's no need to excite yourself. You can preach here quite well. See, here's the wee reading-desk, and I've brought the Minister's second-best gown and bands. Put the desk on the table, Mr. Cohen.

(COHEN puts a small reading-desk on the table)

There now, that's fine. For Sabbath after Sabbath we had the diet of worship in this wee room when the kirk was being done for the dry rot. We'll pull the chairs round, and Mr. Bolfry will give us the grand sermon, I'm sure.

JEAN Yes, Mr. Bolfry. It would be better. Give me the gown, Auntie.

BOLFRY What is there in Creation or beyond it that cannot be wheedled by women?

(JEAN and MRS. McCRIMMON close in on him and invest him in the gown and bands. He is a little tipsy. The others arrange the furniture for the Sermon.)

MRS. McCRIMMON Well, well, that's no' very polite talk. Put your arm through here and content yourself.

JEAN *(with the bands)* How does this go, Auntie?

MORAG There's a wee thingummy that catches behind the collar. Look you, I'll do it.

(MORAG fastens the bands, while JEAN walks round for a front view. MRS. McCRIMMON smooths the robe.)

JEAN You look absolutely beautiful.

(BOLFRY goes to the fireplace and surveys himself in the picture-glass. The others sit down round the table in silence. BOLFRY turns and goes to the makeshift Pulpit.)

BOLFRY You will find my text in the Gospel according to William Blake, that Poet and Prophet who walked to the edge of Hampstead Heath and put his finger through the sky. "Now is the dominion of Edom and the return of Adam to Paradise."

CULLY Ha! Ha!

BOLFRY What are you laughing at?

CULLY Paradise! I can't help it.

BOLFRY You must not laugh at Paradise.

CULLY Have a look at your Paradise. . . . Hunger and filth and disease and murder.

BOLFRY Have a look at your Bible and don't interrupt my Sermon. You sit there in your squalid, drab, killer's clothes, with your squalid, drab mind and see nothing but your little bodily rough-and-tumble in your little thieves' kitchen of a world. Look up! The real War is beyond and about it. The War between Good and Evil. The Holy War. It is a War not to destroy, but to create. It is like the war between man and woman. If there were no war, God would go to sleep. The Kingdom of Heaven would wilt and wither. Death would conquer both Good and Evil and there would be Nothing. It is unbearable that there should be nothing. The War must go on.

For what, you ask me, do these forces fight? Their War Aims are plain. My Führer fights for the New Disorder; for disorder is perpetual movement and movement is life. The Enemy has stated clearly his Ten Points, from Mount Sinai in a thunder storm.* [We must not allow our reverence to stray from one single object. We must not create works of Art, nor devote ourselves to them. We must not conceive or propagate any idea about God that is not strictly true. We must do no work on the seventh day of the week. We must respect the Family. We must not destroy life. We must be faithful to our first love and desire no other woman. We must not live on another man's efforts. We must not lie about our neighbours. We must want nothing that another man has.]

To these are added two more powerful commands, spoken quietly on a hot and dusty day. We must love the Holy Spirit with all our strength and we must love Tom, Dick and Harry as ourselves.

To effect these things is impossible. It is admitted by the teachers that to do them is impossible to man; and man is the cleverest thing we know. But to the Holy Spirit, they say, everything is possible. By its Grace, they say, and by forcing the soul through Fire and Water up to Crucifixion itself man will at last achieve the impossible, which will be Victory.

I, the Devil, am Fire and Water. I hoist the gallows and drive the pike between the ribs. Without an enemy, there can be no Victory. Honour me, then, for my part in your triumph. Honour me for the day when you spurn the clouds written with curses, when you stamp the stony laws to dust, "loosing eternal horses from the dens of night".

McCRIMMON Rhetoric! Rhetoric! Rhetoric! The Fathers have confuted you hundreds of years back.

BOLFRY So much the worse for them.

McCRIMMON You are talking a parcel of old-fashioned Dualistic sophistications. You are a Manichæan.

BOLFRY You are a liar.

---

* The lines within brackets may be omitted.

COHEN Order, order!

McCRIMMON I do not take issue with you for that word, because you are my own heart speaking in a dream. But it is sorrowful I am that it should be so.

BOLFRY You are better than your neighbours, Mr. McCrimmon. They would say that because a truth was sorrowful or distasteful, or inconvenient, it was therefore not a truth. That is why they will not believe what I have come to tell you; that Victory may go the other way.

McCRIMMON What do you mean?

BOLFRY That the Gates of Hell may prevail against the armies of the Cherubim. That Disorder may win the day. If that were not possible, why do you wrestle and pray?

McCRIMMON God forbid that it should be so.

BOLFRY God forbade Adam to eat an apple.

JEAN What will happen if you win this War?

BOLFRY Man's genius will burst its bonds and leap to meet the sun. The living, glorious animal in you will riot in the fields, and the soul will laugh for joy, naked but not ashamed. Your Self will be triumphant.

When I win, Man will be an individual. You may love your neighbour if you like, but all that is highest in you tells him to keep his distance. You don't know him. You will never know him. You are no longer a thing in a herd, crouching against your neighbour's wool to keep you from the cold. You are a man. You are a woman.

Onward, Christian Soldiers, shuffling along shouldered with your heavy packs, and your blistered feet, and the fear of Hell in your eyes. It's a rocky road to Zion, and what will you find when you get there? Your officers lash you on with curses and punishment and flatter you with Hope. There is no Hope in my country. No man hopes for what he has.

What are the virtues that keep you going? Courage? Honesty? Charity? I have them too. Courage is the reaction to Fear. You are more afraid than I am. Honesty is the reaction to lies. Charity is the reaction to hate and suspicion. My honesty spurns your superstitions. My charity embraces both the sheep and the goats.

My flags are the Pride of the Eye and the Lust of the Flesh. Their other names are Art and Poetry, and where they wave the abomination of desolation can never be.

How long, O Lucifer, Son of the Morning, how long? How long will these fools listen to the quaverings of impotent old priests, haters of the Life they never know?

How long will they swaddle their strong limbs in dusty parchments? How long will they shut out the sky from their eyes with prisons of cold stone?

I tell you that all you have and all you know is your Self. Honour your Self and set him free; for the Soul and the Body are one, and their only home is the World, and their only life is the Flesh and their only friend is the Devil.

Let the wild horses loose!

McCRIMMON *(rising)* In nomine Patris Aeternis, Filii et Spiritus Sancti, conjuro te, Sathanas . . .

BOLFRY Latin, eh? You've gone Papist, have you? You don't know your own regiment, my man.

McCRIMMON Away with you! Away with you out of my house!

BOLFRY Take care, McCrimmon.

McCRIMMON *(quietly)* If you are, as I think you are, a bad dream and the voice of my own heart speaking evil, I will tear you from my breast if I die for it.

BOLFRY Stay where you are. You said there was truth in what I told you – "The sign of a supernatural event is that it obeys all the laws of Nature except one." Think of that before you act too rashly.

McCRIMMON You said you were here to free the Self from its shackles. I am my Self, and myself is a Minister of the Gospel. I will follow my inclination, look you. And what is my inclination? It is to have the thrapple of you out by the roots.

(McCRIMMON suddenly takes up CULLY's knife. The WOMEN scream. BOLFRY backs out of his pulpit and towards the door.)

BOLFRY You are not very wise, McCrimmon. You are not very wise.

MORAG Stay in the circle. He will have you. He will have you.

JEAN Uncle, don't be a fool.

MRS. McCRIMMON Oh, no! Oh, no!

CULLY Let him be. It's all right. Conk and I will look after him.

BOLFRY You will have it, will you? Come along, then. Let's see you hunt the Devil over the moor.

(McCRIMMON breaks from CULLY and COHEN and makes for BOLFRY. BOLFRY throws the gown over McCRIMMON's head and makes for the door. In a moment McCRIMMON recovers himself and, flinging the gown over his shoulder like a cloak, follows BOLFRY through the doorway.)

COHEN Come on, Cully. There'll be murder done.

(He runs through the doorway)

CULLY Murder? Of what?

(He follows COHEN)

MRS. McCRIMMON Oh, such a like night to be out! And in his slippers, too. Well, well. We'll away to our beds.

JEAN But, Auntie . . . But . . .

MRS. McCRIMMON Och, we're dreaming all this. And I've a hard day's work before me tomorrow when I wake up. And moreover, when I do wake up, I'd like it to be decent-like in my bed. Away to your bed, Morag, girl.

MORAG You're sure, now, we're only dreaming?

MRS. McCRIMMON What else would we be doing, you silly creature? Away with you to your bed.

MORAG Well, dear me, good night, then, Mem.

MRS. McCRIMMON Good night, Morag.

JEAN Good night, Morag.

MORAG Good night, Miss Jean.

(Exit MORAG)

JEAN Do you think . . . ? I mean to say . . .

MRS. McCRIMMON Och, that girl's head is such a mixty-maxty of nonsensicalities, it'll be all the same to her in the morning, dream or no dream.

JEAN What will be all the same in the morning? Do you think we *are* dreaming? Are you dreaming the same dream as I am, or are you just part of the dream? Is she dreaming too?

MRS. McCRIMMON I thought you knew enough about the Highlands to know that it is all one whether we are dreaming or not.

(She begins to tidy up the room, moving the reading-desk to its proper place and shifting the chairs)

JEAN I don't think I'm dreaming. I'm sure somebody has been here. It was so absolutely real. It's real now.

MRS. McCRIMMON Maybe Aye, maybe No.

(She dusts off the chalk marks)

JEAN But there was a wee minister – you saw him too.

MRS. McCRIMMON Oh, aye, may be.

JEAN What are they doing out on the moor? Uncle Jock went after him with a knife.

MRS. McCRIMMON As likely as not your uncle is up in his bed snoring.

JEAN Why don't you go upstairs and look?

MRS. McCRIMMON What difference would that make? Here or there, it's all one in a dream, if a dream it is. And it's gey like one, I must say. Forbye, I'm going up the stair this minute. I'm blind with sleep. We can tidy up in the morning, if there's anything to tidy.

JEAN I'll wait and see if they come back.

MRS. McCRIMMON Please yourself.

JEAN But, Aunt Marget . . . if it's a real man . . . if he's chasing a real man, with a real knife . . .

MRS. McCRIMMON Your uncle never did the like of that in his life.

That's why I know fine it's a dream. Don't you fash yourself . . . and put out the lamp when you come up.

JEAN But if it's not a real lamp, what does it matter whether I put it out or not?

MRS. McCRIMMON It's unlucky to set the house on fire, even in a dream. Good night.

JEAN Good night, Aunt Marget.

(Exit MRS. McCRIMMON. JEAN rubs her eyes, pinches herself, picks up the DISCOVERIE OF WITCHCRAFT, looks at it for a moment, slams it shut, and puts it back on the shelf. JEAN starts and turns around as McCRIMMON enters followed by CULLY and COHEN. All three look dazed. McCRIMMON throws the knife on the table and the gown on the chair and stares into the dead fire. COHEN picks up the knife, rubs his thumb along the edge and shows it to CULLY.)

COHEN No blood. He can't have used it.

CULLY Yes, but . . . the Name I wrote on it. Agla. It isn't there.

COHEN Rubbed off, I expect.

CULLY It's damned funny.

COHEN It's all damned funny. Do you think we're crackers or what?

CULLY I don't know what to think.

JEAN Where's Bolfry?

COHEN He grabbed his hat and his coat and away he went across the moor like an electric hare with his old Battle of the Nile on his head. His Reverence caught up with him on the edge of the cliff. Then he hit him. With Cully's jack-knife, I thought. Anyways he . . . the . . . Bolfry, I mean . . . he took a leap like a circus acrobat straight out and down into the sea. A 'undred blinking feet down. Into deep water. We couldn't do nothing about it.

CULLY And where he dived, the water boiled like a pot. You saw it. Why not say so?

COHEN I won't swear as how I didn't see it. But it might have been anything. Atmospherics or a squall or something.

CULLY The sea was as calm as a millpond. And the steam rose to the cliff's edge. Damnation, we've all gone mad.

(He takes up the knife, rubs it vigorously on his sleeve, closes it, and puts it in his pocket. JEAN has been staring at them and automatically straightening the furniture.)

JEAN Cully, what's happened? What do you think has happened? What do you think, Cully?

CULLY I'm doing no thinking tonight. Come along, Conk. Let's get down to it. If I stay in this room any longer . . .

COHEN Look at him.

(He indicates McCRIMMON. All three watch him as he slowly picks up the bottle and pours the heel of it into BOLFRY's glass. He swallows the whisky neat at one gulp.)

COHEN That's right, Guv'nor. You need it. Do you a world of good, that, eh?

McCRIMMON What did you say?

COHEN I said it'd do you good.

McCRIMMON *(picking up the empty bottle and looking at it in a mournful, puzzled sort of way)* Do me good, do you think? . . . Well, well.

(He turns to CULLY and COHEN)

Gentlemen, I must ask your forgiveness. It seems that I . . . that I have forgotten myself. When I was a Divinity student there was a time when I was over-addicted to alcohol. It is many years ago. I thought I had conquered the vice. Indeed, I thought it. But it seems I was over-confident. I have been too confident about too much.

JEAN Perhaps you should go to bed now, Uncle.

McCRIMMON No doubt but you are right. I cannot conceive how it happened. My head is not yet clear, but my legs seem to be doing their duty. I will go to bed. It is the black disgrace of a fellow I am, and me a minister. . . . Stop you, though, am I right or am I wrong? Was there another person here?

JEAN How could there be? There's only Cully and Conk and me, Uncle Mac.

McCRIMMON Dear me, that is so. It is a terrible thing this weakness of mine. I thought for a moment . . . I will go to bed. You will put away this . . . evidence?

JEAN All right, Uncle Mac, I'll get rid of the dead man.

McCRIMMON The dead man? . . . Ah, the bottle. Do, like a good girl. I would not like to think . . .

COHEN That's all okey-doke. We know how to keep our traps shut. We've forgotten all about it already. That's right, Cully?

CULLY That's right.

McCRIMMON Tell me, was I violent at all? I seem to recall a lot of noise and rushing to and fro.

COHEN Nothing out of the ordinary. You were a bit excited, but always the gentleman. My old grandfather used to get a bit that way, but Lord bless you, he meant no harm by it, and he was all right in the morning.

McCRIMMON There was something I wanted to say.

JEAN It will do in the morning, Uncle Mac.

McCRIMMON I will go to bed.

COHEN Need any help, Guv'nor?

McCRIMMON No, I thank you. You have been very kind and very forbearing. Good night. Indeed, I am ashamed.

(Exit McCRIMMON)

JEAN Oh, dear? I wonder. Should we have explained?
CULLY Explained what?
JEAN I see. There's that in it.
CULLY If you can explain, I wish you would.
COHEN If you ask me, I think we'd best forget about all this. Unless it's a blooming murder and we're all in it.
CULLY If it's not a murder, I'm damned if I know what it is. But it's not a murder.
JEAN Are you sure?
CULLY I'm not sure of anything in the whole Universe.
JEAN I'm a bit frightened.
CULLY By God, so am I.

(He puts an arm round JEAN)

COHEN Oh, I don't know. A cousin of the wife's went to one of them spiritualist meetings and seen a trumpet flying through the air. But I says to her, "If you started worrying about things the like of that, you'd fetch up in the Silly House," I says.
CULLY You think there are . . . ? Gosh, I nearly said it.
COHEN Said what?
JEAN That there are more things in Heaven and Earth than are dreamt of in our philosophy, Conk.
COHEN Oh, I don't know. Depends on what your philosophy is. Seems to me if there *was* SOMEONE up top-sides – and I'm not saying there is and I'm not saying there ain't – he wouldn't tell the likes of you and me what he was up to. Nor we wouldn't have much idea of what he was gabbing about if he did. . . . Do you see the time?
CULLY Yes, by Jove!
COHEN Only three hours to good old Wakey-Wakey. Good night, Miss. You waiting up a bit, Cully?
CULLY No.
COHEN Okey-doke. Good night, Miss.

(COHEN goes. JEAN and CULLY have separated and stand looking at each other.)

CULLY Cully's clever, Jean's clever, chirrup-chirrup, good evening. Only not so damned clever.
JEAN I'm still frightened.
CULLY May I kiss you now? Would that help?

JEAN Oh, no, no, no, no! It would make it worse. But thank you all the same.

CULLY Good night, then.

JEAN Good night, my dear.

(They shake hands and CULLY goes. JEAN puts out the lamp.)

BLACK OUT

Scene Four

The same. The following morning. Bright sunshine. JEAN, in a spectacular dressing-gown, and MRS. McCRIMMON have just sat down to breakfast. MORAG has just brought in a cover and coffee.

JEAN Good morning, Morag.

MORAG Good morning, Miss Jean. It's fresh herrings and bread-crumbs, Miss Jean.

JEAN Isn't that splendid! There's nothing I'd like better. Did you sleep well last night, Morag?

MORAG Yes, Miss Jean. I slept like a top all night, thank you very much. Coffee, Mrs. McCrimmon.

MRS. McCRIMMON Thank you, Morag.

    (MORAG goes)

For what we are about to receive, the Lord make us truly thankful.

JEAN Uncle Mac isn't down yet?

MRS. McCRIMMON No. He had a disturbed night, your uncle. I wanted him to have his breakfast in bed, but he's coming down. It's a beautiful day.

JEAN How do you mean a disturbed night?

MRS. McCRIMMON Oh, well. He has the indigestion whiles. And it's an awful thing for not letting you sleep very well. That's a beautiful dressing-gown you're wearing. Have I seen it before?

JEAN No, Auntie. Didn't Uncle Mac sleep, then?

MRS. McCRIMMON It is very nice. But, mind you, it is hardly what we are used to up in these outlandish parts. I don't say your uncle will make a remark. He may and he may not. But he may not think it just quite the thing for breakfast. Mind, I'm not saying. But even on my honeymoon I always dressed for breakfast. It was just the way we had. Not that it's important.

JEAN I'm sorry. I didn't sleep too well either.

MRS. McCRIMMON Did you not, now? You shouldn't have got up. We'd have brought you your breakfast. Are you sure you're feeling all right?

JEAN Oh, yes. Fine now. But it was a most peculiar night.

MRS. McCRIMMON Was it so? You would be dreaming, maybe. I never pay any attention to such things. Will you be well enough to come down to the village with me today?

JEAN No. Yes. I think so. Have the two soldiers gone?

MRS. McCRIMMON Ah, yes. They have to be out for their runnings and their jumpings. They have breakfast up at the guns, poor souls. Nice lads, too. We are very lucky, whatever. Mrs. McLean up by Offerance, she got some gey funny ones. But these are nice quiet lads.

JEAN Aunt Marget . . . how did you sleep last night?

MRS. McCRIMMON Oh, very well, I thank you. But nothing puts me up or down, from the moment I put my head on the pillow.

JEAN I was wondering. I . . . You . . . I had an eerie dream last night, Aunt Marget.

MRS. McCRIMMON Had you, dear? It was a wild night. It is a strange place up here in Larach, but, och, you get used to it. It might be something you ate.

JEAN That's what I said to Morag. I mean . . .

MRS. McCRIMMON I hope you won't be putting daft ideas into that lassie's head. It's full enough of daftness already.

JEAN All right, Aunt Marget, I won't. Oh, good morning, Uncle Mac.

(McCRIMMON enters. He is very solemn.)

McCRIMMON Good morning, Jean.

(He sits down)

Heavenly Father, we thank thee for all these mercies. Sanctify them to our use. Amen. Well, that's a fine day.

MRS. McCRIMMON Yes. Isn't it a beautiful day?

McCRIMMON It's not often you'll see Larach all over smiles the like of this, Jean. It's a great compliment to our visitor. It can be a wild place, Larach.

MRS. McCRIMMON Indeed, that is so. I hope you don't object to the herring. There wasn't a single egg this morning. I don't know what came over the hens. It would be the storm, maybe.

McCRIMMON Aye, yes. The storm.

MRS. McCRIMMON And now you two will have to excuse me. We're a wee thing late, and I have to check over the linen for the washing before I go down for the messages.

McCRIMMON Certainly, my dear. Certainly.

(MRS. McCRIMMON goes out. She turns at the door and makes mysterious signs to JEAN from behind her husband's back. He is not on any account to be worried. JEAN nods.)

McCRIMMON A man is a very curious thing.

JEAN Yes, isn't he?

McCRIMMON Dear me, I did not think that I would behave like that at this time of day. It is a lesson to me.

JEAN Oh, it was nothing, Uncle Mac. Nothing, really, at all.

McCRIMMON Nothing? That one who should be an example to the flock should give way to strong drink like a beast?

JEAN Beasts don't give way to strong drink. Besides, it wasn't your fault.

McCRIMMON A bottle of whisky! Mind you, it is not everybody who could drink a bottle of whisky and go up to bed as straight as a die. Pre-war whisky too.

JEAN But you didn't . . .

McCRIMMON I must have. It was full on the Lord's morning, because I happened to notice. Forbye it is not the first time, the Lord forgive me. But, Lord helping me, it will be the last. It comes on me about every five years. But never like this time.

JEAN How? What happened?

McCRIMMON That's the queer thing. I don't know. I had a whirling vision that I was disputing with Beelzebub himself in this very room and racing over the moor with a knife in my hand. And then I found myself leaning against the mantelpiece finishing off the bottle with the two lads tidying up the room. I aye throw the furniture about a wee. Or I did when I was that way.

JEAN It was a strange dream.

McCRIMMON Never have I had a dream so real. I could see Beelzebub as plain as could be – in that chair and then uttering blasphemies in my ears as if he were in the pulpit – in my gown and bands. I mind every word I thought he said.

JEAN (breathlessly) What did he say?

McCRIMMON I thought you and Marget and the lads were here too. He was telling you all to stamp the ancient Law into dust and revolt against the Armies of the Lord.

(He laughs)

Very plausible and persuasive he was, too. I had an answer for him, but he never heard it. I was that angered I struck him with my dirk and threw him into the Firth. It wasn't a bad answer, but I had a better.

JEAN What was your answer? I mean, what would it have been?

McCRIMMON (ignoring her question) It was my own mind speaking. We've got the queer, dark corners in our mind and strange beasts in them that come out ranging in the night. A sophisticated black beast yon. I never knew of him. I wonder, now, did I kill him? If I did it was worth it all. Mind you, there were points where he nearly had me.

(He has been thinking aloud, but he becomes again aware of JEAN and turns to her)

Of course, this was all a dream or a delirium, I canna right say which. But you learn things in these states. It's a kind of a twisted inspiration. I learned one thing.

JEAN What was that?

McCRIMMON That mankind turns to Almighty God as a nettle turns to the sun. And if the nettle had a fine, argufying brain in it and a spacious command of words, it could do little better and maybe a good deal worse. We've a thing called Faith in us, Jean, and we've no more command over it than we have over our lungs. Mind you, we can develop our lungs and we can develop our Faith. Maybe, I've neglected that a bit. I was over proud of my head. But in the middle of all the talk it rose up within me and told me to strike the Devil dead . . . in my delirium, mind you. But it was awful like the real thing. A lesson to me.

(*MRS. McCRIMMON re-enters, ushering in CULLY and COHEN. CULLY wears a brand-new Lance-Bombardier's stripe. COHEN carries a postbag. He lays it down near the door.*)

MRS. McCRIMMON Isn't this a nice surprise? Come in, boys, and have a cup of tea.

COHEN Look at him. Lance-Bombardier Cully, Non-Commissioned Officer in charge of his Majesty's Mails, and the same old Gunner Cohen, Lance-Bombardier's stooge to same.

JEAN Oh, congratulations, Cully.

CULLY Thanks very much.

COHEN We thought we'd pop in. No good getting a dog's leg if you don't give the skirts a treat.

CULLY How are you, Mr. McCrimmon?

McCRIMMON I am well, I thank you. Indeed, remarkably well. And you?

CULLY I couldn't sleep. Look here, Mr. McCrimmon, it's no use pretending and telling lies. It's not fair to you. It's not fair to any of us. You weren't drunk last night.

MRS. McCRIMMON Oh dear me, what a thing to say! As if the Minister would be!

McCRIMMON (*rising*) What do you mean?

CULLY Something happened last night that I don't understand, and we've got to thrash it out somehow.

McCRIMMON Do you mean that the – the – the – experience I had last night was shared by the whole of you?

(*McCRIMMON sits down again in great perturbation of mind. MRS. McCRIMMON goes to him to soothe him. JEAN sits rigid.*)

MRS. McCRIMMON Now, now, now, now. The best thing is to forget all about it.

COHEN I told you that, Cully. You can't do any good.

CULLY No, we've got to get it straight. There must be an explanation. We can't leave things that way. Look, Mr. McCrimmon, do you know anything about Mass Hypnotism? I know they don't think there's much in it, but you know about the Indian Rope Trick, don't you? And the old necromancers who thought they were raising the Devil, they *did* induce a sort of suggestible state. I mean they sat down and deliberately hypnotised themselves with their spells and magic circles. I mean, what do you think? . . . Of course, you and Mrs. McCrimmon weren't here at the beginning of the séance, but it's the only explanation that seems to me natural.

JEAN You mean there was really nobody here?

CULLY Yes. There must be a natural explanation. I know the other one's wrong.

JEAN What other one?

McCRIMMON That I killed a man. I did not kill a man. How I know, I do not know, but I know it. I did not kill a man.

MRS. McCRIMMON Of course you didn't, now.

CULLY I'm sure you didn't. It's mass suggestion. Nothing happened. Look at the room. There are no signs of anything happening in this room.

McCRIMMON It is a peaceful room. Everything is natural. Everything obeys the Laws of Nature. It is the sign of a . . . let me see . . . it is the sign of a supernatural event that everything obeys the Laws of Nature except one thing. No doubt you are right.

JEAN *(suddenly screaming)* The umbrella!! It's Bolfry's.

(All look towards the umbrella on the hearth. There is a tense pause. Then the umbrella gets up and walks by itself out of the room.)

MRS. McCRIMMON Well, now, isn't that the queer like thing? And with all this havering, I was forgetting about your cups of tea. It isn't long infused, or have you time to wait for some fresh?

(The OTHERS are too astonished to react to this. MRS. McCRIMMON pours hot water into the teapot and pours out cups. She talks all the time. COHEN and CULLY, in a trance-like state, take their cups.)

Well, well, it seems you had a kind of a tuilzie with the De'il, after all. You're not the first good and godly man who did the like of that. Maybe you didn't kill him, but I'm sure you'd give him a sore dunt. And you're none the worse yourself.

It's a funny thing we should be surprised at seeing the Devil and him raging through the skies and blotting out the sun at this very hour. We're all such a nice kind of lot that we've forgotten there's any such person. Poor soul, him roaring away like a raging lion and nobody paying any attention to him with their fine plans to make us all the happy ones.

Will you be having another cup of tea, dear, now? You're looking quite white and peely-wally, and no wonder, dear me.

McCRIMMON I have nowhere seen such great Faith, no, not in Israel.

MRS. McCRIMMON Drink you your tea.

Och, well, dear me, a walking umbrella's nothing to the things that happen in the Bible. Whirling fiery wheels and all these big beasts with the three heads and horns. It's very lucky we are that it was no worse. Drink up your tea.

(McCRIMMON smiles and takes her hand)

CURTAIN

END OF THE PLAY

DAPHNE LAUREOLA

A PLAY IN FOUR ACTS

For Edith Evans

THE CHARACTERS

MR. WATSON, a fat man
TWO SPIVS
A BORED and SLEEPY MAN and WOMAN
MAISIE ⎫
BILL ⎪
       ⎬ Four Young People
HELEN ⎪
BOB ⎭
GEORGE
ERNEST
LADY PITTS
GOOCH
VINCENT
SIR JOSEPH PITTS
MANAGER of Le Toit Aux Porcs

THE SCENES

ACT ONE: Le Toit Aux Porcs, a London Restaurant, Evening.
ACT TWO: A Summerhouse in a Suburban House.
ACT THREE: The Same. A Week Later.
ACT FOUR: Le Toit Aux Porcs. Six Months Later.

ACT ONE

A London restaurant. Soho or somewhere. It doesn't matter. It is not very smart and not very shabby. It is called "Le Toit Aux Porcs". Part of the floor, as will be explained, is dangerous and is covered with a sheet, downstage. The walls are half painted with a playful design and half new plaster. A ladder and a ceiling sheet make it obvious that the place is undergoing repairs. But it is in use.

Upstage, a wall seat and three small tables are arranged, the tables set pretty close together. Two larger tables (for four) are arranged on either side, downstage.

An archway, R, leads into another restaurant. Service tables and part of a bar are seen.

A tall, elegant woman is sitting at the righthand upstage table. She has finished her meal. An empty bottle of Tokay stands in front of her and she is drinking a large brandy and staring gloomily in front of her. From left to right the downstage tables are occupied by: (1) a FAT MAN eating heavily, with his face to the audience; (2) a couple of SPIVS in earnest conversation; (3) a SLEEPY MAN and a BORED-LOOKING WOMAN, who is manicuring herself; (4) four YOUNG PEOPLE who have just finished dining.

The boys and girls at table 4 whisper and giggle casting "don't look" glances at the solitary lady at the cross table.

MAISIE I'm dead certain I've seen her photograph somewhere. But don't look now.

BILL Don't look? You've been gazing and gazing at her for the last half-hour.

MAISIE No, I haven't, and I'm positive I've seen her photograph.

BILL She's an actress, probably.

MAISIE No, she's not. I know all the actresses.

HELEN Shut up! She'll hear you.

BILL She is older than the rocks among which she is seated; like the vampire she has been dead many times and has learned the secrets of the tomb; and she has dived into the deep seas and still bears about her their ruined day. . . .

MAISIE Or words to that effect?

BOB Or words to that effect.

BILL She knows how to knock 'em back, anyhow.

MAISIE That's her fifth double brandy.

HELEN Be quiet, I tell you!

MAISIE She's not an actress. But I know that face. I wish I could remember. . . .

BOB It's a complex. She probably reminds you of the nurse who let you fall out of your pram.

MAISIE I never fell out of my pram.

BILL Oh yes you did! On your head. That's the only thing that could account for you.

MAISIE Oh, you think so, do you?

BILL Yes. It's cause and effect.

MAISIE Cause and what's-it?

BILL Yes, you see something in the woodshed and then years after . . .

MAISIE I saw something in the woodshed once.

(She bursts into a fit of uncontrollable laughter)

Oh hit me on the back! Not too hard.

(BILL hits her on the back)

BOB What did you see in the woodshed?

MAISIE You beast, you've made me swallow my tonsils.

BILL Not unless they're black market tonsils. Not in this dump.

MAISIE That's silly. Whoever heard of black market tonsils? Besides, I forgot. They're out.

HELEN Who are?

MAISIE My tonsils.

HELEN Oh, when?

MAISIE When I was a kid. I don't remember.

HELEN I had mine out last year.

BOB They grow again, often.

HELEN Oh hell! Do they?

BOB Yes. Often. *(A pause)* My God, it's ten o'clock.

HELEN We'd better be going then, hadn't we?

MAISIE Yes, if we can. I'm tight.

BILL No, you're not. Hi, waiter! George!

HELEN Don't call him George. They don't like it.

BILL His name's George. Look, you can go if you like. Well meet you at the door.

HELEN All right. Come along, Maisie. I believe you *are* tight.

MAISIE No, I'm not.

(The GIRLS get up and collect their paraphernalia)

BILL Gosh, what a lot of things you carry about with you! At the door, then. Tell George to hurry up if you see him.

HELEN All right.

(The GIRLS go out through the archway. They meet GEORGE, leading in a man called ERNEST. ERNEST is a shy young man of about twenty,

229

with a sort of Middle European look about him. He carries a big book under his arm. GEORGE is something short of a hundred years old and looks moribund.)

MAISIE Hurry up, George. They want you.
GEORGE Very good, miss. All right.
MAISIE And oh, George, thank you very much for a lovely dinner.
GEORGE Thank *you*, miss. I'm glad you enjoyed yourself.
MAISIE Oh, I did, I did. I'm tight.
HELEN Oh, do come along, Maisie.
GEORGE I should not have noticed it. Good evening, miss. Good evening, miss. *(To ERNEST)* This way, sir.
BILL Garcon, l'addition, s'il vous plait.
GEORGE A l'instant, monsieur. *(To ERNEST)* This way, sir.

(He guides ERNEST to the table next but one to the lady)

ERNEST Thank you. Thank you very much. This will do very well. Thank you.

(He sits down, lays his book on the table and begins to study the menu. Exit BOB as GEORGE brings the bill to BILL. While BILL is settling up the SPIVS are heard for a moment.)

1ST SPIV Yes. . . . Look, I just had an idea. Could you do anything with 250 tins of steak and kidney pud?
2ND SPIV Me?
1ST SPIV That's right.
2ND SPIV Look, I don't want to talk business tonight.
1ST SPIV But use your imagination . . . 250 tins of steak and kidney. . . .
2ND SPIV Ah, put a sock in it. I'm tired.
1ST SPIV Please yourself. At the same time the business of the Country's got to go on, tired or not tired.
2ND SPIV Right, Sir Stafford, I heard you. What did you say to Maurice?
1ST SPIV I says "Look, Maurice . . ."

(BILL pays and gets up)

BILL There you are, George, you old hold-up man. There go my month's wages.
GEORGE Thank you very much, sir. Good night, sir.

(The LADY upsets her glass, but does not appear to be herself upset by this incident. GEORGE goes to her assistance. BILL has a good look at her as he goes out.)

Tut, tut! Dear, dear! What an accident! Fortunately there wasn't much in it.

LADY Please bring me another double brandy.

GEORGE Are you sure, madam?

LADY Perfectly sure.

GEORGE Very good, madam. A double brandy. *(He rejoins ERNEST)* Some nice hors d'oeuvres to start with, sir? We have some very nice beans and chopped turnip and a bit of beetroot, with a little Russian salad.

ERNEST No, please. I think I should like some Vienna steak and pommes sautés.

GEORGE You couldn't do better, sir.

ERNEST Oh? It is very good, then?

GEORGE I didn't say it was very good, sir. I said you couldn't do better.

(Exit GEORGE. Table 3 begins to show some signs of life.)

BORED WOMAN Your coffee's getting cold.

BORED MAN I like it cold.

BORED WOMAN You kick up hell in the morning if it's cold.

BORED MAN This isn't the morning.

BORED WOMAN I know it isn't the morning. I never said it was the morning, did I?

BORED MAN I don't know whether you did or not.

BORED WOMAN No. You never listen to what I say.

BORED MAN I listen to nothing else.

BORED WOMAN Well, it isn't the morning, and it's getting late and we won't get a taxi. What about going home?

BORED MAN What for?

BORED WOMAN What do you mean by what for? After all, home's home.

BORED MAN Is it?

BORED WOMAN That's right. Start an argument. We can't come out for a quiet evening together but you start a horrible argument. I work my fingers to the bone with no help trying to make things comfortable for you, and then when we go out for an evening together you deliberately spoil it all.

BORED MAN Spoil what all? You would insist on coming out. You would insist on coming to this damned awful restaurant. Look at it. I wouldn't be surprised if it tumbled down about our ears.

BORED WOMAN You used to like coming here, and is it my fault if it's tumbling down? You know perfectly well how difficult it is to get permits. If you had to do the shopping these days you'd have a little more understanding.

BORED MAN Now don't start on that again . . . Hi, waiter!

(During this delightful conversation ERNEST has been reading his book and stealing glances at the lone LADY who stares straight in front of her. Enter GEORGE with tray.)

GEORGE Coming, sir.

(GEORGE serves the LADY with a glass of brandy, ERNEST with Vienna steak, the FAT MAN with Dundee cake and port, and the SPIVS with coffee, clearing away as he does so. He goes out past table 3.)

BORED MAN I want my bill.

GEORGE Directly, sir.

BORED MAN Then look sharp about it. *(Exit GEORGE)*

BORED WOMAN He's coming as fast as he can. Besides, you weren't in such a hurry a minute ago. You haven't even finished your coffee. I must say you're extremely difficult to please. Anyhow, my father always told me that it was a sign of a gentleman to be polite and courteous to servants.

BORED MAN Hell of a fine gentleman your father was.

BORED WOMAN I'm not going to discuss my father with you.

BORED MAN I should think not.

BORED WOMAN At least he always treated my mother as if she was a lady.

BORED MAN Perhaps she was.

BORED WOMAN No perhaps about it. What d'you mean by perhaps? I should think you'll admit that I knew my own parents.

BORED MAN Go on. Let's have a row about nothing.

BORED WOMAN I don't think it's nothing when you say unkind and insulting things about my parents. I was very fond of my parents.

BORED MAN That must have been nice for them.

(Re-enter GEORGE with bill. BORED MAN settles up in silence. ERNEST is on the point of speaking to the lone lady, but thinks better of it and returns to his book.)

GEORGE Thank you, sir. Thank you very much. Good evening, sir. Good evening, madam.

(The BORED MAN and WOMAN go out without speaking. A SPIV calls GEORGE's attention. SPIV signs the bill, and they too go out, also in silence. The FAT MAN goes on eating reflectively. GEORGE clears the empty tables. A radio in the next room begins to play softly a nostalgic air blending with the clatter of the dishes and the FAT MAN's heavy breathing. As GEORGE is going out ERNEST gives a cough to attract the lone LADY's attention. She does not appear to notice. Almost immediately a jovial, middle-aged man comes in with GEORGE. His name is GOOCH.)

GOOCH Well, well, well! So you're still alive, George?

GEORGE Sometimes I'm not very sure.

GOOCH By gum, you've made a dog's breakfast of this place since I saw it last. What's the floor cleared for? Going to have a dance?

GEORGE No, sir. The big beam that kept up the floor was worm-eaten. They're going to prop it up with steel girders, but they can't get the girders. It's safe enough round the walls so we're using this place as an overflow.
GOOCH We're on the lip of the pit, eh?
GEORGE Yes, sir. In a way of speaking. It's all right if you don't walk on it.

(He has GOOCH's hat and coat and pulls out the middle table at back to allow him to get in between ERNEST and the LADY)

GOOCH *(sitting down)* Well, we've got darned good seats for Hell if it does give way. *(To ERNEST)* What do you think, sir, eh?
ERNEST Yes, excellent. *(He reads his book)*
GOOCH Never mind the menu, George. Bring me what you've got and a pint of mild and bitter.
GEORGE Certainly, Mr. Gooch. I think we have a nice portion of chicken en casserole.
GOOCH Your special, particular, long-eared chickens, hey?

(He laughs uproariously. GEORGE does not respond.)

GEORGE And some Marmite to begin with, Mr. Gooch?
GOOCH I leave it to you, partner.

(Exit GEORGE)

(to ERNEST) Pretty cold out.
ERNEST Yes, it is cold.
GOOCH *(to LADY)* Do you mind if I smoke?
LADY No.
GOOCH Some people mind. I always ask permission first.

(He takes out a hideous black cheroot and lights up)

That's better. My nephew is in the Merchant Navy. He brings these all the way from Burma. A good job, too. If I hadn't had these to fall back on I should have died. And that would have been a pity, wouldn't it, sir?
ERNEST A great pity.
GOOCH When I'm in Town I always come here. Old George treats me like a Dutch uncle, and it's quiet. I like quiet places. I'm not one who likes to have his meals in the parrot house at the zoo. A lot of screaming and chatter to try to drown a band. I used to tell my old stocking-mender: "It's bird-seed that lot want, not grub." I like it quiet. A quiet meal and a quiet cheroot. It lets the old tum get down to its work. They know me here, of course. That makes a difference too. Don't they, George?

(Enter GEORGE with soup and beer)

GEORGE Yes, sir.

GOOCH I was telling them, George, that what I like about this place was that even if it's jammed to the door it's always quiet. What's that they're playing on the wireless?

GEORGE Bit of Chopin, I fancy. It's in the private room. Small wedding party.

GOOCH Give them my love.

GEORGE Very good, sir. But I don't suppose they'll need it. . . . Hi! Look out, sir.

(The FAT MAN has got up and is about to cross the floor)

GEORGE *(guiding him)* Round by the edge, sir. Unless you want to go through the floor. On thin ice, you were, sir, there. I suppose we all are, these days. This way, sir. Easy does it.

FAT MAN I forgot. *(Soberly)* You told me. Sorry.

(Exeunt GEORGE and FAT MAN)

GOOCH Makes you think, doesn't it? He might have broken his blooming neck. This soup's quite hot. I don't know how they do it.

(Short interlude of soup-eating and wireless. The radio changes to Massenet's "Elegie".)

LADY *(suddenly in a loud, clear mezzo-soprano)* Ah, doux printemps d'autre fois! Comme tu es. . . .

GOOCH Going to give us a bit of a song? Good.

(The LADY stares at him coldly and falls silent)

GOOCH Go on. Don't mind me. I like it.

LADY Who are you?

GOOCH Me? My name's Gooch. Let me see, I've got a card, somewhere.

(He produces a large card and gives it to the LADY. She flicks it back into his soup.)

LADY I don't know you. It is very impertinent of you to speak to me.

GOOCH *(rescuing his card)* Well, there's nice manners, I must say. Card's ruined. Don't know who some people think they are.

(He sulkily eats his soup, mumbling to himself)

You'd think some people had no feelings. They won't keep their old customers if they let the like of that lot in. Merely passed a civil remark.

(Enter GEORGE with his second course)

Listen, George, shift me over to that table, like a good fellow. It'll give the lady and gent more elbow room.

GEORGE As you please, sir.

(GOOCH is transferred to Table 4)

LADY Bring me another of these, please.
GEORGE Yes, madam.
GOOCH *(sotto voce to GEORGE)* She's had plenty already, if you ask me.

(Re-enter the FAT MAN. He makes his way heavily to Table 1.)

GEORGE Round the edge, sir.
FAT MAN I know. I know. Don't keep telling me. . . . Coffee and Kummel.
GEORGE Very good, sir.

(Exit GEORGE. The ensuing silence is broken again by the LADY. She picks up GOOCH's damp card, which he has left on the table, looks at it absently, and begins to talk in clear level tones.)

LADY My father is dead, I think. He was a mild man, with a great red beard. He wore a beard because shaving hurt him. His skin was very tender. My mother died before him and I was the eldest of seven daughters. I don't know why I am talking about him. He is dead, you see. They are both dead, my father and my mother.
GOOCH He was a clergyman, I should think. And they were giving a garden party at the dear old vicarage. . . .

(He has not intended to be heard, but the LADY overhears him)

LADY Yes, he was a clergyman.

(She looks at the card and again at GOOCH with a puzzled air)

We had a laburnum tree at the vicarage. The pods were poisonous. We were told that we must not on any account eat the pods. It was like the tree of the knowledge of good and evil in the Garden of Eden. Only that was an apple tree. This was a laburnum tree. I ate some laburnum seeds and I was very ill, but I learned no more about good and no more about evil by that act. All that came later. But my father was very angry. He was terrible in his rage. I wore a white sailor suit when I ate the laburnum. My father thought I did it out of badness or to show off. There were several little boys there when I ate the laburnum. But he was wrong. Perhaps God was wrong about Adam and Eve. I only wanted to know about good and evil. That was reasonable enough. That was very, very reasonable. Even God is often unreasonable.

(She sings)

> Pull for the shore, sailor,
> Pull for the shore,
> Heed not the rolling breakers,
> Stand to the oar.

(GEORGE hurries in with his tray. He puts it down on the dumb waiter and goes over to the LADY.)

GEORGE Now, madam! Please, madam! You can't do that sort of thing here.
LADY Why not?
GEORGE Well, madam, it stands to reason.
LADY You do not wish me to sing?
GEORGE No, madam, please, if it's all the same to you.
LADY Very well. Bring me another brandy.
GEORGE Well, it's not for me to say, madam, but don't you think you've had about enough?
LADY Would it be too much to ask you not to argue with me? I've had rather a trying day. I should be very much obliged if you would bring me, quietly and quickly, another brandy.

(All through this scene the LADY's intonation and phrasing have been perfect. Apart from her rapt expression and the curious content of her speeches it would be impossible to say that she was tipsy. Now she speaks with the quiet confidence of one who expects to be obeyed.

GEORGE appears about to resist for a moment, and then gives way)

GEORGE Very good, madam. A small brandy, I think you said, madam.
LADY No. A large brandy.
GEORGE *(to ERNEST)* What would you like to follow, sir?
ERNEST *(starting)* Oh. . . . Nothing, thank you.
GEORGE Some coffee?
ERNEST Yes. Please. Some coffee.

(GEORGE serves the FAT MAN and GOOCH)

GEORGE Your coffee, sir. And your Kummel. Would you like a nice cigar?
FAT MAN No. Don't smoke.
GEORGE I've brought you a nice bit of apple flan. I thought you'd like it.
GOOCH Just what the doctor ordered. *(Whispering)* Giving you a bit of trouble, that one.
GEORGE Oh, no, sir. Not at all, sir.
GOOCH Does she come here often?
GEORGE Not very often, sir.
GOOCH What's this – a cat?

(He feels below the table and produces a large furry glove)

Someone's left this, George. I thought it was a cat.

GEORGE No, sir. No cats here, sir.

LADY I like cats. They do not give one solitary damn.

GEORGE One of the young ladies must have left it. I'll take charge of it, sir.

(MAISIE re-enters through the archway)

MAISIE Oh, my glove. Oh, there it is. I thought I'd lost it.

GEORGE No, miss. This gentleman found it all right.

MAISIE Oh, that's terribly kind of you. I thought I'd lost it.

GOOCH *(politely)* Not at all, miss. A pleasure, I'm sure.

LADY *(in a loud, clear voice)* What is your name?

GEORGE Don't pay any attention to her, miss.

LADY What is your name?

MAISIE Oh, Maisie McArthur, as a matter of fact.

LADY How old are you?

MAISIE Twenty-one.

LADY That is not very old.

MAISIE It's my birthday today, as a matter of fact.

GOOCH Got the key of the door, eh, miss?

MAISIE Well, yes, as a matter of fact.

LADY This is a very bad time to be twenty-one. Perhaps it is always a bad time to be twenty-one. It is a wretched age. Where do you live?

MAISIE Well, as a matter of fact . . .

LADY Write it down and give it to me.

GOOCH I wouldn't, miss, if I was you. You never know these days.

LADY I should like to know where you live. Come here and write it down.

(MAISIE goes to the LADY's table. ERNEST passes along a menu and a fountain-pen.)

GOOCH Ah, well, it isn't the slightest use telling anybody anything. I've learnt that by bitter experience.

(MAISIE writes her address on the menu)

LADY Thank you very much. Goodbye.

MAISIE Oh, well, thank *you*. And cheerio. Thank you. I must run now. And thank you ever so for finding the glove. I thought I'd lost it. It's not so easy to get new ones. I must run. Thank you. Good night, all.

(As she is going through the archway the LADY begins to speak again. MAISIE pauses to listen.)

LADY On my twenty-first birthday my father took me to London for a treat. I'd never before heard the long, subdued, pulsating roar of London. I thought of an enormous beast purring in its sleep. My father took me to this restaurant. He used to come to this restaurant when he was at Cambridge. He was once dining here on the night of the Inter-Varsity Rugby match. He was dining with the Cambridge full-back. He went out into Dean Street and the Cambridge full-back tackled a trotting hansom cab-horse. He tackled it low. The horse fell and the cab fell over on its side. But nobody was hurt except my father. The cabman hit him but he hit the cabman too. My father was a very good boxer. They were all taken to Vine Street. But it was all right and they drank with the cabman till four o'clock in the morning. I've never seen anybody look so happy as my father did when he was telling that story. I cannot imagine why he looked happy. The poor horse might have been seriously hurt. Men have brutality in their bones. There are no exceptions. None.

GOOCH If I may be permitted to say so, madam, you're getting downright insulting.

LADY Our gardener used to beat his wife. He was covered with hair like a monkey. She was worse than he was. She liked being beaten. Our gardener was kind to me because he was a hypocrite. I did not know that at the time. He gave me a piece of cherry-wood once that looked like a doll. I dressed it up in some silk rags and loved it more passionately than I have ever loved anything in my life. I still feel faint when I smell cherry wood. . . . But that isn't what I was going to say. . . . What is it that I was going to say?

ERNEST *(politely)* I do not know, madam.

GOOCH *(muttering)* If you say much more you'll be out on your ear. You've said a damned sight too much already if you ask me.

(The LADY looks at ERNEST in a puzzled sort of way)

LADY I've seen you before somewhere. It doesn't matter. Everything has happened before. The Dark Ages have happened before. The apes have beaten us before when we thought they were feeding out of our hands. I had an old aunt once who opened a gorilla's cage in a menagerie. She couldn't bear to see him in the cage because he was so like her late husband, my uncle. She had managed my uncle by kindness, all by kindness, and she thought everything could be done by kindness. It can't, you know. Have you seen a play called *The Tempest*?

ERNEST Yes, madam.

LADY My father took me to *The Tempest* as a great treat when I was nine years old. It wasn't a great treat; it was a terrible nightmare. It was about an old scientist on an island. He had a daughter who was almost an imbecile. He had a slave called Caliban. He tortured poor Caliban with rheumatism and frightened him with spangled spooks. After twenty years on the island he sailed away and left it worse than it was before. No books, no spooks, nothing but rheumatism and Caliban in a bad temper. Caliban got two new masters. One was drunk and the other was silly. I don't know what he did with them after the liquor went dry. He probably ate them. Thank God the play stopped before that. It always happens. It always happens. "An hundred generations, the leaves of autumn, have dropped into the grave." And again we shiver miserably in the confines of a long winter, as Christendom and the Roman Empire did hundreds of years ago. Again and again and again and again we have covered the face of the earth with order and loveliness and a little justice. But only the face of it. Deep down below the subterranean brutes have bided their time to shake down our churches and palaces and let loose the little rats to sport among the ruins.

GOOCH *(satirically)* Encore!

(Enter GEORGE with brandy)

LADY Oh! Here you are! How very good of you. I'm afraid you spoil me. It's horrible brandy; but I am passionately fond of brandy of any kind. It's like loving children, isn't it? We never realise that all children are different, do we?

GEORGE Your taxi's waiting, ma'am.

LADY Oh, the poor taxi! It is terrible to wait and wait and wait, and often to find that nothing happens after all.

GEORGE May I help you on with your coat, ma'am?

LADY No. That's not what I meant. Give the taxi some money and send it away.

GEORGE He won't be too pleased, ma'am.

LADY My life is not very important, but I find it too important to devote it entirely to pleasing taxis. Be good enough to do as I tell you.

GEORGE Very good, madam.

(As he is going out GOOCH stops him)

GOOCH If you can't deal with her why don't you bring the manager?

GEORGE That's all right, sir. You leave it to me.

(The LADY swallows her brandy at one gulp and undergoes a rapid change of mood. She beams round on the company. Exit GEORGE.)

LADY You must all come to see me in my beautiful garden. I shall tell Vincent to prepare a very special tea-party. I shall write to all of you. To *all* of you. But I haven't got your addresses. I've only two here. There is a gentleman over there who has said nothing at all. He will be a very valuable guest at my tea-party. I am afraid I talk far too much myself.

(She rises from her seat and begins to walk quite steadily and gracefully towards the FAT MAN. GOOCH and MAISIE suddenly realise that she is crossing the dangerous floor and shout simultaneously.)

MAISIE Look out! Go round the edge.
GOOCH You can't cross that floor! It's dangerous.

(The LADY pays no attention to them and crosses to the FAT MAN)

LADY Good evening.
FAT MAN 'Evening.
LADY What is your name?
FAT MAN Watson.
LADY Where do you live?
FAT MAN Me? What's that got to do with you?
LADY Perhaps I didn't make myself clear. Will you please give me your card, if you have one?
FAT MAN Yes, I've got one, if it's any use to you.
LADY You are not ashamed of it, are you?
FAT MAN 'Course not. I've nothing to be ashamed of.
LADY How fortunate you are. Will you let me have your card, please?
FAT MAN Don't see why you should and don't see why you shouldn't. Herey'are.

(He gives her a card)

LADY Oh, thank you. That is so very, very good of you.

(Enter BILL)

BILL *(to MAISIE)* Oh, there you are. Where in the world have you been?
MAISIE Just here.
BILL You look like a hypnotised rabbit.
MAISIE I found my glove.
BILL Well, then, come along then. You're hanging up the whole outfit.
MAISIE All right, Bill.
LADY Will you bring Bill to my tea-party?
MAISIE Yes. Thanks ever so much. Goodbye, then.
LADY Goodbye.

(Exeunt MAISIE and BILL. The LADY again crosses the floor, this time with a slightly strutting gait. As she walks she murmurs a piece from "archy and mehitabel".)

LADY "i know that i am bound
       for a journey down the sound
       in the midst of a refuse mound
       but wotthehell wotthehell
       oh i should worry and fret
       death and i will coquette
       there's a dance in the old dame yet
       toujours gai toujours gai"

(She sits again at her table)

"ours is the zest of the alley cat."
(to ERNEST) What do *you* think, archy?
ERNEST It is not my name, archy.

(He laughs)

LADY You haven't given me your name, have you?
ERNEST No, excuse me, not yet.
LADY But I know you, don't I?
ERNEST I do not think so.
LADY It doesn't matter whether I know you or not. My name is mehitabel.
ERNEST It is an interesting name.
LADY I lurk in the alleys. I am the prima ballerina of the crumbling chimney stacks and the wet slippery slates. Did you drink my brandy?
ERNEST No, madame.
LADY I must have drunk it myself. You look honest enough.
ERNEST It is very kind of you to say so.
LADY Are you a foreigner?
ERNEST Yes, madame. At home I am not a foreigner; but now I have no home.
LADY *(in fluent Polish)* You are a stray cat too? Some other fat cat is lapping at your saucer of milk.
ERNEST You speak Polish, madame.
LADY Do I? I asked you if you were a stray cat too. I asked you if some other fat cat was lapping at your saucer of milk.
ERNEST Yes, madame. You asked that. A fat cat is sitting in my saucer; but there is no milk. My name is Ernest Piaste. I live at the Young Men's Christian Association in Bedford Place.
LADY Piaste? We may have met. I cannot tell. The probability of an event is the ratio of the number of cases that favour it to the number of all the possible cases which ought to occur rather than the others; which renders them for us equally possible.
ERNEST You have read, then, Laplace on Probabilities?
LADY Not I. My father told me that, and I remembered it. We may have met and it may even be probable. You will come to my tea-party?
ERNEST I shall be honoured.
GOOCH I hope there's somebody there to keep the party clean.
LADY What did you say?
GOOCH Merely passed a remark.
LADY Then keep your remarks to yourself, you god-damned, greasy toad.
GOOCH I suppose you call yourself a lady.
LADY I'd be interested to know what you call yourself. I could suggest several names. Oaf, lout, dolt, pig, ass, ape, slubberdegullion, son of a bitch, clown, fool, lickspittle, codface, idiot, imbecile, stinkard. . . .

GOOCH Here, here, here, here; a little less of that.

LADY You louse-bitten tinker's cur, how dare you speak to me?

GOOCH I've no desire to speak to you.

LADY Then keep your blasted trap shut.

(She turns to ERNEST and smiles at him radiantly. GEORGE is heard beyond the archway.)

GEORGE *(without)* Sorry, sir. We're closing now.

VINCENT *(without)* All right. All right. I'm looking for a friend of mine.

(Enter VINCENT, a strongly built man in a chauffeur's overcoat, covering a black jacket and striped trousers. He carries a chauffeur's hat in his hand. GEORGE follows. After a short glance round, he goes to the LADY's table.)

VINCENT Home now.

LADY O, hello, Vincent. I'm not going home. I've found my affinity.

VINCENT He can wait. Here's your coat. By God, you've led me a pretty dance.

(He throws the coat rather roughly over the LADY's shoulders and puts his hand on her arm to lift her up)

LADY Don't touch me. Don't you dare touch me.

VINCENT Get up, then.

ERNEST *(rising)* My friend, you must behave yourself.

VINCENT You keep out of this, see? Keep out of it, do you hear?

ERNEST I hear perfectly well.

(GEORGE goes round to ERNEST to pacify him)

GEORGE It's all right, sir. He's taking the lady home.

ERNEST He is not taking the lady home unless she wishes to go.

LADY How beautiful, Ernest. I do love you!

ERNEST Madame, if you will accept me for your escort . . .

VINCENT You sit down, sir, before you get hurt.

LADY Ernest, take me with you to the YMCA.

(VINCENT crosses and gets between ERNEST and the LADY)

VINCENT I told you to sit down.

ERNEST Get out of my way.

LADY Kill him, Ernest, my darling, my lamb.

VINCENT You keep quiet.

(He thrusts a table napkin into her mouth and holds it there with the flat of his hand. ERNEST hits him on the head with his book and is

rewarded by a snappy uppercut that knocks him over the table and on to the floor.

GEORGE and GOOCH go to his aid and even the FAT MAN is disturbed.)

GEORGE Oh, this is terrible. I never saw the like of this.

VINCENT Sorry, sir; but you asked for it. . . . Come along, now.

LADY Poor Ernest. . . . Yes, Vincent. Perhaps I had better come with you. You have the car?

VINCENT Yes, ma'am. The Rolls. Have you got your bill?

LADY No. Pay it please.

(The LADY rises and adjusts herself at a mirror on the wall. VINCENT calls to GEORGE.)

VINCENT He isn't dead, is he?

GEORGE Fortunately, no.

VINCENT Couple'a fivers cover it?

GEORGE I think so.

VINCENT It had better. Here you are.

(He gives GEORGE two five pound notes)

GEORGE Thank you.

VINCENT Keep the change. If there's no change you can lump it. Tell your boy friend I'm not going to sue him for assault. 'Night.

GEORGE Good night to you.

VINCENT *(to the LADY)* Ready?

LADY Yes.

(She goes out, moving with a steady grace. It might almost seem that she was levitated. VINCENT follows her, quite respectfully. There is a silence as all except ERNEST watch her go.)

GOOCH Feeling better, chum?

ERNEST Yes, thank you.

GOOCH A little drop of something?

ERNEST No, thank you.

GOOCH Glass of water then. George, get the gent a glass of water.

(GEORGE brings a glass of water from the table. GOOCH gives ERNEST a drink.)

GOOCH You hit him first, you know. Mistake, that. Never hit a man first if you don't know him. I've stuck to that all my life and it's saved me a lot of trouble. That guy knows the fighting game. I never saw a neater blow. Didn't hurt you much, I shouldn't think.

ERNEST I don't know. I was conscious of terrible rage and then I knew no more.

GOOCH Feel like getting up? No hurry.

ERNEST I get up. Forgive me. I was foolish.

(GEORGE and GOOCH help him to a chair)

GEORGE Mr. Gooch is quite right. You didn't ought to have hit him, sir.

ERNEST I am very sorry. But you will understand there was not anything else I could do. In my country it would not be permitted to insult a lady.

GOOCH We don't like it much here, sir, either. But it depends a good deal on the lady.

ERNEST If I comprehend you, sir, you are demanding that I should strike you also.

GOOCH Hold your horses, old man. My fighting days are past. No offence meant and none taken, of course, I hope.

GEORGE That's right, sir, we've had enough for the evening. Shall I call you a taxi?

ERNEST No.

FAT MAN Flew at him like a blooming wild cat mad with wounds, he did. He was asking for a clip on the jaw. Lucky that was all he got. A bad type, that fellow. Got any cheese?

GEORGE No, sir.

FAT MAN Might as well be in Germany. Bring me my bill.

GEORGE Certainly, sir.

FAT MAN What the hell we fought the War for, I don't know. It beats me. Be starving in a week or two, I shouldn't wonder. Bed's the only thing.

(GEORGE retires to back and prepares bill)

No law and order, these days. Every second type you meet carries a cosh in his hip-pocket and a razor in his waistcoat. Decent people won't be able to cross their doorsteps for a square meal. Not that they'd find one if they did cross their blooming doorsteps. Gas oven's the only thing, I said to my housekeeper. No grub, no private enterprise, no nothing. Life's not worth living.

GEORGE Your bill, sir. . . . Thank you, sir. I hope you enjoyed your dinner, sir.

FAT MAN Do you? That's past hoping for, these days. Where are the snows of yester-year? Nowhere. Just blooming well nowhere.

GEORGE Mind the flooring, sir.

FAT MAN Oh, yes. Thanks. Goodnight.

(Exit FAT MAN)

GOOCH He's right in a way. But you get to take life as you find it. We only get one life, let's make the best of it. That's right, isn't it?

ERNEST She rose a little from the ground and passed from the room like a ghost.

GOOCH What about fetching a doctor, George?

ERNEST No, no. Forgive me. I am OK.

GOOCH I'll take you home.

ERNEST No. I thank you. It is not needful. I shall pay. I shall go. You are very kind.

GOOCH Have one for the road.

(ERNEST stands up)

ERNEST No. See. I am quite all right.

GEORGE Your bill, sir.

ERNEST Thank you.

(He pays)

GEORGE And thank *you*, sir. Very much. I hope you enjoyed your dinner, sir.

ERNEST Yes. Very much indeed, I thank you.

(Exit ERNEST)

GOOCH Foreigner?

GEORGE I shouldn't wonder.

GOOCH Nice sort of chap, all the same. He can take it. I liked the way he went for that tough. I'd have done the same, in my young days. So'd you, I've no doubt.

GEORGE I don't remember my young days.

GOOCH Well, you can't say we don't see life.

GEORGE The less the better.

GOOCH Oh, I wouldn't say that. Who was the dame?

GEORGE Her? Oh, a pleasant enough lady when she's sober.

GOOCH Been a bit of a looker in her day.

GEORGE No doubt, sir.

GOOCH Her day's past.

GEORGE It probably is, sir.

GOOCH Sad, when they drink. *(Drinks)*

CURTAIN

END OF ACT ONE

ACT TWO

A summerhouse in a suburban garden on a Sunday afternoon. Church bells are heard.

SIR JOSEPH PITTS is asleep covered and surrounded by Sunday newspapers. He is a very old gentleman who carries an acoustic apparatus, but seems to have no difficulty in hearing his wife when she speaks in normal tones. "The LADY" – henceforth LADY PITTS – is knitting and reading. SIR JOSEPH wakes up.

SIR JOSEPH Bells, eh? I think I hear bells.
LADY PITTS Yes, darling. Bells.
SIR JOSEPH What bells? What time is it?
LADY PITTS The Nonconformist Chapel communicants are just going to have an afternoon service. It's nearly four o'clock.
SIR JOSEPH I hope they enjoy it.
LADY PITTS So do I. I suppose they will in their own quiet way. Have you had a good sleep?
SIR JOSEPH Perhaps I have. I was unconscious. I know nothing about it. Are we having tea here?
LADY PITTS Would you like it here?
SIR JOSEPH Is anybody coming?
LADY PITTS I don't think so.
SIR JOSEPH You didn't ask anybody?
LADY PITTS I hope not. I feel a little tired today.
SIR JOSEPH You don't think some abominable bores might take it into their heads to pop in?
LADY PITTS I think I've got 'em trained to stay away when they're not invited.
SIR JOSEPH Still, you might have asked somebody at the hospital board meeting or somewhere and forgotten all about it. You're sometimes forgetful and it's a fine afternoon for October.
LADY PITTS All the more reason why you should banish these morbid thoughts. No, I think we're quite safe.
SIR JOSEPH Good. Just you and me, then.
LADY PITTS Just you and me, darling.

(VINCENT appears. He has been transformed into the perfect manservant. But he looks a little worried.)

Oh, there you are, Vincent. We'll have tea out here – just for Sir Joseph and me. We'll have it now before the afternoon gets any colder.
VINCENT Yes, my lady. . . . Excuse me, my lady, could I speak to you for a moment?

246

LADY PITTS Of course, Vincent.

VINCENT It's a little awkward, my lady. It's a young man who says he wants to see you. I told him you weren't at home, but he won't go away.

(He has dropped his voice so that SIR JOSEPH will not hear, but SIR JOSEPH reaches for his Acousticon and fixes it)

SIR JOSEPH Eh? What's that? What are you blethering about?

VINCENT I was asking about the tea, sir.

SIR JOSEPH Well, fetch it, will you? Fetch it, and don't stand havering there.

LADY PITTS I am afraid we've got a visitor, after all. Who is it, Vincent?

VINCENT A young foreign gentleman, my lady. He says you invited him for this afternoon. Name of Ernest Piaste.

LADY PITTS Piaste? Piaste? I don't remember the name.

VINCENT *(sotto voce and very quickly)* I think I remember him, my lady. I'd have dealt with him but I was afraid he'd make trouble. He showed me your invitation. It is in your handwriting all right.

SIR JOSEPH For God's sake don't mumble. Tell the damned fellow her ladyship is not at home.

VINCENT I told him that, sir.

SIR JOSEPH And is he still there?

VINCENT Yes, sir.

SIR JOSEPH What d'ye say?

VINCENT I said, "Yes, sir."

SIR JOSEPH Then kick him downstairs.

VINCENT Very good, sir. If those are my instructions.

SIR JOSEPH You shouldn't need instructions. I'm afraid you're a bit of a cissie, Vincent.

LADY PITTS Stop. I think I remember. Send him here, Vincent, and make it tea for three.

VINCENT Very well, my lady, if that is your wish. But . . .

SIR JOSEPH What's he waiting for?

LADY PITTS I don't know, darling. What are you waiting for, Vincent?

VINCENT I hope you realise that I'm doing my best.

SIR JOSEPH What's he say?

LADY PITTS He says he is doing his best.

SIR JOSEPH I never want to see him doing his worst.

VINCENT Thank you, my lady.

(Exit VINCENT)

SIR JOSEPH I don't like the fellow. Sulky sort of type. I'll speak to the Doctor and get him to find someone else.

LADY PITTS He does very well.

SIR JOSEPH But do we need a man of that kind – now? You're better, aren't you?

LADY PITTS Yes, dearest. Much better.

SIR JOSEPH Very well, then. I'll speak to the Doctor.

LADY PITTS If you like.

SIR JOSEPH Stands to reason you can't sit on a dozen committees without having a clearer head than most people. And that fellow reminds me. . . . Oh, well.

LADY PITTS I'd rather you didn't remind *me*.

SIR JOSEPH I know. I'm sorry. I can't keep my mouth shut. Forgive me.

LADY PITTS Of course, dearest. . . . And, dearest, you'll have to forgive me too. We've got a visitor after all.

SIR JOSEPH Oh, I say, dammit. I told Vincent to kick him out.

LADY PITTS I don't think that would do. I promise he won't stay long.

SIR JOSEPH Who is he?

LADY PITTS A very charming young displaced person.

SIR JOSEPH Who sent him? The Bracknell Committee?

LADY PITTS Yes, dear.

SIR JOSEPH Then I'm going in. *(Rises)*

LADY PITTS Oh, don't. It's only for a little.

SIR JOSEPH I've some difficulty in following when most people try to speak English – except you, my dear. But I will not bust myself trying to disentangle broken English. Tell Vincent to bring tea to my study.

LADY PITTS You are very naughty. I shall have to punish you.

SIR JOSEPH Not you. Too kind-hearted. Funny thing that, but it's true. Most kind-hearted women have faces like the back of a cab; but you haven't. Can't understand you at all.

(He kisses her and goes out)

LADY PITTS Ernest Piaste. Ernest Piaste. No. I can't remember.

(She makes ready to receive the Unknown. Enter VINCENT with ERNEST.)

VINCENT Mr. Piaste.

LADY PITTS Oh, Vincent? . . . Take barley water to Sir Joseph in the study; and bring tea here.

VINCENT Thank you, my lady. And, my lady, if you don't recall who this young gentleman is, and if he tries any of his blackmailing tricks, you can tell him that *I* know him. I know him very well. Thank you, my lady.

(Exit VINCENT)

LADY PITTS So you and Vincent are old friends.

ERNEST No, madame.

248

LADY PITTS Then you must not mind what he says. He is a little eccentric.

ERNEST He is, then, your servant?

LADY PITTS Yes, of course.

ERNEST I see. . . . You do not think that is why I came – to blackmail you?

LADY PITTS Why should you? And I invited you, didn't I?

ERNEST Yes, madame. It was most kind of you.

LADY PITTS Very well, then. Vincent has simply said something rather extraordinary and we shall pretend not to have heard him. Tell me all about yourself.

ERNEST Yes, madame. But first I do not wish that there should be a mistake. At the commencement of our acquaintance, no.

LADY PITTS It would be a pity to make any mistakes at all. What is troubling you?

ERNEST I read in an English novel this word, Blackmail. You cannot believe it of me that I would do such a thing?

LADY PITTS Naturally. Or I should not have invited you to tea. We agreed to forget all about that foolish Vincent and his strange, insane manner of talking.

ERNEST It is natural that he should not like me; but that is no reason for saying such things.

LADY PITTS I don't understand. I thought you didn't know him.

ERNEST I said that we were not friends. You do not remember, then, the manner in which I made his acquaintance?

LADY PITTS Help me. I'll try to remember.

ERNEST I hit him on the head with *The Wealth of Nations* by Adam Smith.

LADY PITTS You hit him on the head with *The Wealth of Nations* by Adam Smiss? I mean Adam Smith.

ERNEST Yes, madame.

LADY PITTS It comes back to me gradually. Why did you do that?

ERNEST Because his conduct to you was unbearable.

LADY PITTS Oh, poor Vincent.

ERNEST I should do it again.

LADY PITTS You must be a very violent young man.

ERNEST You must never believe that of me.

LADY PITTS Let me think. Where did all this happen?

ERNEST At Le Toit Aux Porcs.

LADY PITTS In Soho?

ERNEST Yes, madame.

LADY PITTS I see. And then I wrote to you asking you to come to tea.

ERNEST Yes, madame. In the Polish language.

LADY PITTS You are a Pole, then?

ERNEST My father was Polish. My mother was Scottish. I have applied for naturalisation. I wish to be a British subject.

LADY PITTS An extraordinary ambition. Are your parents dead?

ERNEST I think they are, madame.

LADY PITTS And you don't want to go back to Poland. Why?

ERNEST I have been back to Poland.

LADY PITTS You found that there was nothing for you in Poland?

ERNEST My father and my mother had disappeared. I fought for a little with the Russian maquis. Not very well, for I was only a boy. I did not like the Russians. I am a Presbyterian.

LADY PITTS A what?

ERNEST I think that the Church should be governed by presbyters and not by bishops. It was the faith of my mother. Pardon me, I think it is the true faith. The Russians and the Polish Government care for none of these things. My mother was very strict. She did not like the Communists because they are atheists. My father did not like them because he was a baron. You know Poland, madame?

LADY PITTS Poland? Yes.

ERNEST I do not wish now to speak the Polish language. I wish to be an English Nonconformist. My mother and I went to the Scottish Church in Cracow. Do you know it?

LADY PITTS I didn't know that it existed.

ERNEST Not now, I think. But we were very strict. In the church to which I go in Kensington, they are not so strict.

LADY PITTS My husband was once a Nonconformist. At least, he got into Parliament on the Nonconformist vote in 1906.

ERNEST He is dead now, no?

LADY PITTS Oh, no. He is very much alive.

ERNEST He lives here, no?

LADY PITTS Yes.

ERNEST Oh.

(There is a pause here. LADY PITTS is trying hard to reconstruct the events in the restaurant and ERNEST has been quite extraordinarily dashed in his spirits by learning that LADY PITTS has a husband. VINCENT brings in tea. ERNEST looks at him doubtfully. He is wondering whether he is LADY PITTS' lover.

VINCENT ignores him.)

LADY PITTS Thank you, Vincent.

VINCENT Will that be all, my lady?

LADY PITTS Yes. *(Exit VINCENT)* Sugar and milk?

ERNEST No, please. Not either. *(Another short, awkward pause)* He has been for a long time your servant?

LADY PITTS Vincent? Oh, yes. Quite a long time. He is quite one of the family.

ERNEST One of the family. Yes.

LADY PITTS Don't let us bother about Vincent. I want to hear about you. You must have led a very exciting and dangerous life.

ERNEST Perhaps. I don't know. Strange things have happened to me; but they have been like a dream. I feel safe in my waking world because I hold fast to the Church of my mother. All the other things have been of great irrelevance.

LADY PITTS Are you going to be a clergyman?

ERNEST Perhaps. I don't know.

LADY PITTS But don't you take any delight in danger?

ERNEST No, not much.

LADY PITTS But you were with the partisans. You must have had times of great exaltation – times when you were living with great intensity.

ERNEST One night I lie awake in a wet ditch for twelve hours waiting to kill a German soldier. When it was between the day and the night I killed him. You may think that then this was life and very intense. Not so. Things like that are not life unless we know how to appreciate what they mean. I was like a stupid cat who killed a rat. Was I better on that morning or worse than one who takes tea in summerhouses?

LADY PITTS But surely it is more exciting to stalk Germans than to take tea in summerhouses?

ERNEST Not so. Unless we are educated. Unless we have education.

LADY PITTS Oh, education!

ERNEST Education is what is told us by those who are better than we are. I do not mean those who teach in classrooms. They are better than nobody. But they sometimes teach to us the words of great men and these words change us from stupid little apes to men and to ourselves.

LADY PITTS I don't understand that. I have been very thoroughly educated. At least I can read and write. It has never done me a bit of good. I have spent hours reading about what other people have done instead of going out and doing things for myself.

ERNEST You cannot do anything for yourself or other people unless you have education. You cannot construct.

LADY PITTS But I don't want to construct. I want to experience things. I want danger. I want to risk something. I want to risk my health and my reputation, my livelihood, my life itself. We can only appreciate what we have by risking it.

ERNEST But even to take risks is meaningless without education. We must understand. We must be conscious.

LADY PITTS But education may be wrong.

ERNEST That is true and that is terrible. But even if it is wrong it makes us different from the beasts.

LADY PITTS Why do you want to be different from the beasts? Beasts are delightful. If they had a sense of humour and the gambling instinct they would be perfect.

ERNEST It is possible that you are a very bad woman. I do not know. My mother told me that some women are very bad, though she took good care that I never met one.

LADY PITTS You've only met good ones?

ERNEST Yes. Only good ones.

LADY PITTS Even with the partisans?

ERNEST With the partisans they were not women at all. They were avenging animals. It is only when we are idle that we realise that women are women.

LADY PITTS At this moment we are pretty idle.

ERNEST Yes.

LADY PITTS And you realise that I am a woman?

ERNEST Yes.

LADY PITTS And you have decided that I am a bad one?

ERNEST I do not say that. I do not know.

LADY PITTS Well, perhaps you'd better go home and look me up in a book.

ERNEST I do not wish to go home yet.

LADY PITTS In that case will you have another cup of tea?

ERNEST Please, yes.

LADY PITTS Why don't you want to look me up in a book.

ERNEST Because this is for me a new situation.

LADY PITTS You find it different from lying in a wet ditch?

ERNEST Quite different.

LADY PITTS I am glad of that.

ERNEST I am not certain that it pleases me.

LADY PITTS It's like a dream, I suppose.

ERNEST No, madame, it is like life. That is why I am unhappy.

LADY PITTS I'm sorry you are unhappy. Try one of these repulsive little cakes.

ERNEST No, please, I thank you.

LADY PITTS I wish I could remember how I met you first. There must have been something interesting about you, or I should not have asked you to tea. But I can't think what it can be.

ERNEST I do not interest you?

LADY PITTS Not very much, I'm afraid. You seem to me to be rather a conceited, argumentative young man.

ERNEST Yes. I was afraid that I should appear so to you.

LADY PITTS You don't mind my saying so, do you?

ERNEST It makes me very sad; but I am not offended. I am conceited, argumentative, and young. You speak only the truth.

LADY PITTS Tell me about our first meeting. My memory plays me the evillest tricks.

ERNEST To me it was most like when spring rain falls and the dead meadows begin to stir and to breathe.

LADY PITTS My dear Ernest! There *is* another side to your character.

ERNEST I tell you simply how it appeared to me.

LADY PITTS But when did this happen?

ERNEST It was on last Tuesday.

LADY PITTS Where?

ERNEST I told you. At Le Toit Aux Porcs.

LADY PITTS Yes. You told me. And you hit Vincent with your book.

ERNEST Yes, madame.

LADY PITTS Did he hit you?

ERNEST Yes, madame.

LADY PITTS Hard?

ERNEST Yes. Very hard.

LADY PITTS I'm so sorry. Were you arguing with him about education? He's rather sensitive about that. He never had very much education.

ERNEST No. I did not argue with him.

LADY PITTS I seem to remember now that there were a lot of other people there.

ERNEST Yes.

LADY PITTS There was a fat man and a noisy man and several cheerful young people. Was it a good party?

ERNEST No.

LADY PITTS I very seldom go to parties nowadays. I have not been very well.

ERNEST I am sorry.

LADY PITTS I ought to remember. Do tell me more.

ERNEST It was at a restaurant. It was not a party.

LADY PITTS I must have drunk an awful lot. Did I?

ERNEST I think you did.

LADY PITTS It was foolish of me. I don't remember writing to you even. What did I say?

ERNEST You said "Dear M. Piaste, It is very seldom in this year of grace that one meets anybody one wants to meet again; but I want to meet you. Will you take tea with me on Sunday afternoon at this address? In case you do not remember me I had dinner beside you yesterday evening. Yours very sincerely, Katherine Pitts." You are perhaps Katherine Pitts?

LADY PITTS No doubt about it.

ERNEST I thought you must be.

LADY PITTS So you came. It was very good of you.

ERNEST I came because it was necessary to come.

LADY PITTS *Necessary*, Ernest?

ERNEST Yes. I had seen you once and all was changed. You were La Gloriosa donna della mia mente. Dante said that about Beatrice. It means the glorious lady of my mind. He knew that as soon as he had seen her walking in Florence with the other two ladies. I saw you drinking in a cafe, but it was all the same. You are the glorious lady of my mind. Of my *mind*, Mrs. Pitts.

LADY PITTS Well. . . . It's Lady Pitts, as a matter of fact.

ERNEST You are, then, noble?

LADY PITTS My husband is a baronet. That is a sort of little baron.

ERNEST It would not have mattered if you were a princess. That you are a little lower in rank does not matter to me. We do not ask for the pedigree of the planets.

LADY PITTS I am beginning to enjoy our little chat.

(Enter VINCENT)

Oh, Vincent, how very tiresome of you! What is it now?

VINCENT There is a Miss McArthur to see you, my lady. She has another young lady and two young gentlemen with her. She says she has an appointment?

LADY PITTS Who in the world is she, Vincent? Do you know her?

VINCENT No, my lady.

LADY PITTS Mr. Piaste has been telling me about this party when you and he came to blows. Was she at the party?

VINCENT I did not see her, my lady.

LADY PITTS Perhaps she's from the hospital.

VINCENT I hardly think so, my lady.

LADY PITTS You mean she doesn't look ill?

VINCENT No, my lady. She looks in excellent health.

LADY PITTS Is she a young person?

VINCENT A young person, my lady.

LADY PITTS I think she'd better come out here. If I go in to her Ernest might run away. You were quite wrong about him, you know, Vincent.

VINCENT I hope so, my lady.

LADY PITTS He says you hit him, but that he hit you first. You wouldn't like to shake hands or anything?

VINCENT No, my lady. *(Exit VINCENT)*

LADY PITTS Vincent is sometimes a little difficult.

ERNEST I have found him so.

LADY PITTS What were we talking about?

ERNEST Have you forgotten already?

LADY PITTS How could I? I only rang that little jingle of words to bring it back again.

ERNEST We cannot talk of such things in the presence of young persons and their cavaliers.

LADY PITTS I know. It's a pity. I wonder who they are? *(She looks off)* Here they come. I have never set eyes on them before.

(Enter MAISIE, HELEN, BILL and BOB, with VINCENT)

How good of you to come, Miss McArthur, and how nice of you to bring your friends. Have you had tea?

MAISIE Well, as a matter of fact, no. Actually, you asked us to tea.

LADY PITTS Of course I did. Will you bring some more tea, Vincent, please?

VINCENT Yes, my lady.

(Exit VINCENT)

LADY PITTS Now, this is *very* nice. It's quite like old times. Do please find seats for yourselves.

(All sit)

You know Mr. Piaste, of course.

MAISIE No. I don't think so. Oh, yes. . . . You were . . . I mean to say, there. Weren't you?

ERNEST Yes.

MAISIE How do you do? This is Helen Willis and Bob Kentish and Bill Wishforth. They're awful fools, really.

LADY PITTS How very unjust of you. I don't think they're a bit awful.

MAISIE It was most terribly kind of you to have us, Lady Pitts. Of course we'd all heard of you. And I swore black and blue I knew you – only by sight, of course. And I was quite right. Wasn't I, Bill?

BILL Absolutely right.

MAISIE I saw you at that film première you were running for the Deaf and Dumb. You remember?

LADY PITTS I don't remember you, I'm afraid.

MAISIE I wasn't anybody, really. But I got a ticket somehow.

BILL I suppose you were representing the dumb?

MAISIE You think you're terribly funny, don't you? And Queen Mary was there.

LADY PITTS Yes. I remember her.

MAISIE And Abbott and Costello. It was terribly exciting. I'd never been at one of these things before.

LADY PITTS So you were all at this party at . . . What's the name of the place?

ERNEST Le Toit Aux Porcs.

LADY PITTS It was such a pity it finished up with a fight, when everything was going so well.

BOB We went away before that.

LADY PITTS Very wise of you.

BILL I don't know.

LADY PITTS Oh! Do you like fighting?

BILL Not me. But Bob, here, was in the commandos.

BOB Easy on. I only trained for them.

HELEN That was bad enough, training. He broke his leg.

LADY PITTS Did he?

HELEN Yes. Compound fracture.

LADY PITTS Mr. Piaste shot a German once.

MAISIE Gosh. That must have been awful. I've seen them brought down, but shooting one's different.

HELEN Oh!

LADY PITTS What's the matter?

HELEN Nothing. I had a funny feeling.

LADY PITTS What kind of a funny feeling?

HELEN It was nothing. It was silly. It was a dream I had. . . . It's nothing to do with this really.

LADY PITTS But what was your dream? I love people who tell their dreams.

BOB I wouldn't, if I were you. It's probably Freudian.

HELEN I was skating round and round in narrowing circles, and I knew somehow that the ice was as thin as tissue paper in the middle and if I went through I'd go down and down and down. Nothing was ever deeper. And I couldn't stop.

BILL What's that got to do with what Maisie's just said?

HELEN I don't know. It's funny.

MAISIE Do you remember the floor at the Twa O'Pork? You probably dreamed about that without knowing it. You walked over that, Lady Pitts.

LADY PITTS Did I?

MAISIE Yes. You walked on the floor. It was funny.

LADY PITTS It would have been funnier if I had walked on the ceiling, wouldn't it?

MAISIE No. I mean the floor was dangerous. George said so.

LADY PITTS George?

MAISIE The waiter.

LADY PITTS Oh, the waiter.

MAISIE I'd never have dared to walk over that floor. George told you; but you paid no attention. I'd never have dared.

HELEN When was that?

MAISIE When I came back for my gloves.

HELEN Oh! I didn't know what you were talking about, so I couldn't have dreamed *that*, could I?

BOB I don't know. I'd a feeling that night we were all on the edge of a precipice. Perhaps it was telepathy.

MAISIE It was when you started talking, Lady Pitts. . . .

BILL *(in a hoarse whisper)* Shut up, will you.

MAISIE Oh. I'm sorry. I mean. I mean I don't mean . . .

LADY PITTS I was talking, was I? What was I talking about?

BILL It was nothing. You were all right, really.

LADY PITTS What was I talking about?

MAISIE Oh, about yourself and when you were young and so on. It was awfully interesting, really, and I think really we ought to go, now. It was terribly nice of you to have us.

LADY PITTS I can't allow you to do that. You've had no tea. And we haven't got to know each other yet.

MAISIE Oh, I don't think we'll bother about tea, honestly. I'm not really hungry, are you, Helen?

HELEN No, not really. And it was very kind of you to ask us, Lady Pitts, and thank you very much.

LADY PITTS But here *is* the tea.

(Enter VINCENT with tray)

MAISIE Oh, well.

VINCENT There are two gentlemen here, my lady. They say you were expecting them. A Mr. Gooch and a Mr. Watson.

LADY PITTS They sound like plain clothes policemen.

VINCENT No, my lady, they're not police officers.

LADY PITTS Where are they?

VINCENT In the morning room, my lady.

LADY PITTS Tell them I shall come to them presently.

VINCENT Very good, my lady. *(Exit VINCENT)*

LADY PITTS I think our Mad Tea Party is big enough, don't you? Besides we are talking about things that strangers might not understand. I am not sure that I understand them myself. Will you forgive me? And don't dare go away, any of you!

(Exit LADY PITTS)

MAISIE That's how she walked. Right across the rotten floor.

BOB Honestly. I don't think we've any business to be here. I shouldn't think a lady like her – in *Who's Who* and well in with everybody who's anybody – I shouldn't think she'd be keen on being reminded that she was stinking tight.

HELEN Yes, I didn't want to come at all.

BILL It's Maisie's fault.

MAISIE Well, she asked us.

BILL I wonder why the hell she did that?

HELEN I think she's a bit mad.

BOB More than a bit.

BILL She does herself pretty well.

BOB I wouldn't mind being a little wet if I had an outfit like this.

BILL You're wet enough all right.

HELEN I expect she's a dipsomaniac.

BOB That's right. Outbursts every now and again.

HELEN Oooh! I think we should get out of here.

BILL No. Let's wait and see what she does.

MAISIE She's got personality. But I suppose they often have.

BILL I can't say I'd like it for breakfast every morning.

ERNEST Be silent, you abominable people.

BILL Here, here, here, a little less of that.

BOB Remember you're talking to ladies.

ERNEST I am not talking to ladies. I am talking to blue-behinded apes. It is said by your English Poet, "A blue-behinded ape I skip, Upon the trees of Paradise."

BILL Are you inferring that my lady friends . . .

ERNEST Yes. And you also. You who desecrate the moonlit temple of Artemis with your simian chatterings.

BILL I don't know who you are and I don't know what you're talking about, but we didn't fight the War to let a lot of pop-eyed foreigners chuck their weight about, as you'll damned soon find out. You get the hell out of here.

ERNEST I will not get the hell out of here. It is you who have no right to be here.

BILL From all I hear, you seem to think yourself a bit of a scrapper. Well, Bob here is a commando and I myself wouldn't mind taking a little walk with you in the shrubbery.

MAISIE No. Bill. No.

ERNEST Do you wish to fight me?

BILL Don't you understand English?

ERNEST I will fight you whenever you like with whatever weapons you choose.

BILL Okey-doke. In the meantime get out.

ERNEST *You* tell me to get out? You! You miserable, stupid salacious, suburban beast.

BILL That's enough.

BOB Yes. Quite enough. Shut up, Bill. I'll talk to him.

ERNEST You will not dare to talk to me. You ignorant pig, you are not fit to talk to anybody. ANYBODY!

(*BOB makes a dash at ERNEST, and knocks over the tea table. This checks him. The women scream.*

Enter SIR JOSEPH.)

SIR JOSEPH Did you see the *Observer* anywhere? Oh, sorry, I'm interrupting.

BILL We've had a slight accident.

SIR JOSEPH What's that? Speak up!

BILL We've had a slight accident.

SIR JOSEPH Oh? Well, there's a bell over there. You'd better ring for Vincent.

(The young people are grovelling to pick up the debris. ERNEST stands aloof.)

BILL We're most frightfully sorry.

SIR JOSEPH Ah, there's my newspaper. *(He wanders off, reading his newspaper)*

MAISIE *(to ERNEST)* I hope you're ashamed of yourself.

ERNEST I am ashamed of myself.

BILL Damned right too.

ERNEST I am so bad as you are.

BILL Thanks very much.

HELEN Should we ring the bell?

MAISIE No. Let's get some of this straight first. I don't think there's much broken. *(To ERNEST)* If you're sorry, you might lend a hand.

(ERNEST helps)

I wonder who that old guy was.

BOB Another patient, I expect.

HELEN We were idiots to come at all.

BILL Just Maisie's blasted curiosity.

(MAISIE suddenly splutters with laughter)

MAISIE Blue-behinded! It's an absolute lie.

(All laugh except ERNEST. The girls are still crawling about after debris. Enter LADY PITTS, GOOCH and the FAT MAN.)

LADY PITTS I think there are some friends of yours . . . Oh!

MAISIE I'm terribly sorry, Lady Pitts. We were fooling a bit and I'm afraid we've spoiled your lovely tea-cloth.

LADY PITTS It doesn't matter a bit. Don't crawl about on the ground like that. You'll spoil your clothes too. And that won't make it any better.

BILL We were just fooling about.

LADY PITTS In that case, here are Mr. Gooch and Mr. Watson. Perhaps they'd like to fool about too.

GOOCH Ah, your ladyship, I think we're past the time of life for that, eh? But I did want a word with your ladyship in private.

LADY PITTS Would the rest of you . . . Ernest, would you like to take them for a walk in the shrubbery?

ERNEST No. . . . Yes, if you wish that I should.

LADY PITTS Do you like shrubberies, Mr. Watson?

FAT MAN Not had much experience, ma'am.

LADY PITTS There's nothing like a lovely new experience. Go, all of you, and come back in five minutes. There's a tiny little hill. If you climb it you can see over the wall, right down to London, if the day is clear. You've seen London, though, Mr. Watson.

FAT MAN Yes.

LADY PITTS Still, you can't have too much of a good thing. I'll have something for you to eat and drink when you come back. . . . Now, Mr. Gooch, we shall have our tête-à-tête.

(Exeunt OMNES but LADY PITTS and GOOCH)

What was it you wanted to say to me?

GOOCH Lady Pitts, I spoke to you in an ungentlemanly fashion the other night. You see, I didn't know who you were. I accepted your most kind and generous invitation so that I could have an opportunity of apologising most sincerely for my uncultivated behaviour. You see, I had had a drop or two.

LADY PITTS Perhaps I had had a drop or two myself, Mr. Gooch.

GOOCH I wouldn't say that, your ladyship; and whether or not, you were always the lady. No. There was no excuse for me.

LADY PITTS Was that all you wanted to tell me?

GOOCH That's all, your ladyship.

LADY PITTS Then I accept your apology. Go and fetch the others.

GOOCH I'm more than grateful that you have taken the unfortunate incident in this spirit. I assure you it will not occur again.

LADY PITTS No, I don't suppose it will. Fetch the others, will you?

GOOCH Only to happy to oblige.

(Exit GOOCH. Enter VINCENT with whisky and soda on a tray. The sun is beginning to set and the stage is lit by a warm light.)

LADY PITTS Put the tray down here. We are having a very nice party, Vincent.

VINCENT So I see, my lady.

LADY PITTS Oh, yes. You can clear away the rubble. . . . Why didn't you tell me about all these people?

VINCENT I knew nothing about them. I saw them for a minute in the restaurant, but they were only an ordinary sort of crowd, so far as I was concerned.

LADY PITTS Except the young man who hit you on the head with *The Wealth of Nations.*

VINCENT Except him. I never knew you were going to write to them.

LADY PITTS There must have been something about them that interested me.

VINCENT I don't see it. I should think it was all part of the evening's general gaiety.

LADY PITTS You think it's quite safe to leave the whisky with me?

VINCENT Oh, yes. You've had your fling for the next six weeks. Your sort doesn't like whisky – for itself, I mean.

LADY PITTS My sort?

VINCENT Cyclothymic type. Oh, and by the way, Sir Joseph bumped into this bunch.

LADY PITTS Did he? What did he think?

VINCENT How do I know what he thought, or what he ever thinks? Will that be all, my lady?

LADY PITTS Yes, thank you, Vincent.

(Exit VINCENT. The LADY is left alone. The stage grows darker. She appears to be thinking deeply. Presently, re-enter ERNEST, alone.)

Is that you, Ernest? Where are the others?

ERNEST I found a little gate. I said to them that it would be wise for them to go.

LADY PITTS That was very impudent of you.

ERNEST I'm sorry. I did not like to see hempen homespuns swaggering here, so near the cradle of the fairy queen.

LADY PITTS I asked Vincent why I had invited them. He said it was because I was tipsy. But that is no explanation. Vincent is a very stupid man. He is a faithful watchdog, but a very stupid man. It is sad and strange that only stupid people are faithful. Have you noticed that, Ernest?

ERNEST It is not a universal law, but there is truth in what you say.

LADY PITTS I think I asked them because I was lonely. Oh God, I am lonely.

ERNEST It cannot be that the unique and exquisite can be anything but lonely.

LADY PITTS My loneliness finds expression only in drunkenness or in delirium. At other times I say: "Keep off; Keep far away from me". . . . Don't take my hand, please. Do you like my little summerhouse?

ERNEST It is a holy place.

LADY PITTS I want to plant a laurel bush, just there. We have rhododendrons and bays in the shrubbery, but no laurels. When it grows to full height, I shall be dead.

ERNEST No.

LADY PITTS I am nearly fifty.

ERNEST Fifty what? Fifty years? What are years?

LADY PITTS Years are nothing to you. You are only a boy.

ERNEST They were something to me till Tuesday night. They were made of long hours and long minutes to be filled with work and experience. Now they are nothing.

LADY PITTS There is not much meaning in what you say, Ernest. I cannot fall in love any more.

ERNEST It is not necessary that you should fall in love. There is nothing that you could give me that you have not given me already. You say that there is not much meaning in what I say. That may be. I do not well speak English. But there is a meaning for me now in the words happiness and grief, joy and sorrow.

LADY PITTS My God, if only there were! . . . Don't be a fool. You don't know me. You know nothing about me.

ERNEST I know all that need be known.

LADY PITTS Don't sit there talking like a heavenly messenger in a Notting Hill verse drama. You think you're in love with me, don't you?

ERNEST I think so.

LADY PITTS It's calf love. You think I'm your poor damned Presbyterian mother, or something. You come bleating to me because you've lost your way. I'm not a Presbyterian and I'm not your mother. And I've lost my way too. You've made a mistake. . . . You were right about only one thing – I'm a bad woman – as bad as I knew how to be. As bad as be-damned. I've been bad all over Europe and most of America – North *and* South. Now when I'm burned out and more than half mad, I'm playing at respectability with all the fervour I put into the other thing. I'm even the Chairwoman of a Marriage Guidance Clinic. I could tell them something! And now I'm a kept woman. Kept in more senses than one. Vincent, there, is my keeper, among other things. His job is to keep me out of mischief when I have the impulse to dash out and say to the first beggar in the street: "For God's sake, speak to me. Tell me I'm not the only creature in this damnable dead universe . . ." *(quietly)* I can only say that when I'm tight, you see. I think I told you that already.

ERNEST Yes. You told me.

LADY PITTS So you see, you had better go away and find some young lady in Pont Street. By the way, the service at the conventicle round the corner must be nearly finished. If you go now you will see dozens of them coming out, blushing with the beauty of holiness.

ERNEST There is the new moon.

LADY PITTS I shouldn't pay any attention to that, if I were you – unless you turn a half crown in your pocket. It's been a lovely day for the time of the year. Quite an Indian summer. But it's getting cold now. I must go in.

ERNEST You have given me something else.

LADY PITTS How?

ERNEST By speaking as you have done.

LADY PITTS What have I given you? A little common sense?

ERNEST No. You have given me hope.

(He suddenly kisses her. At the second attempt they fall into a rather

protracted embrace. SIR JOSEPH emerges out of the shadows. ERNEST sees him first, tears himself away and runs out.)

SIR JOSEPH What on earth do you think you're doing? It's cold. The barometer's falling. You should have been in long ago. Besides, the Doctor said you weren't to excite yourself. I'm damned if I know what that fellow Vincent is thinking about. In you go at once.
LADY PITTS All right, Joe darling. I'm coming.

(Exeunt)

CURTAIN

END OF ACT TWO

ACT THREE

The Scene is the same as Act Two.

A week has passed. It is now November and the light is chilly. It is early afternoon.

The only notable change in the scene is that a small laurel bush has been planted near the summerhouse.

Enter SIR JOSEPH and VINCENT. SIR JOSEPH wears a heavy coat, a cap and a muffler. VINCENT carries a couple of rugs and an armful of Sunday newspapers. He begins to prepare a nest for SIR JOSEPH who walks over and looks at the laurel tree.

SIR JOSEPH It's getting damned cold but we may as well make the most of the weather while it lasts. Switch on the electric fire, Vincent. There was a touch of frost this morning. . . . What the devil's this?
VINCENT Her ladyship had it planted last week.
SIR JOSEPH What did you say?
VINCENT Her ladyship had it planted last week. It's a laurel bush.
SIR JOSEPH I can see it's a laurel bush. But what's the sense in planting a laurel bush at the beginning of November? It'll die. What the devil's going on in her head? She seemed all right last week, too. Better than she's been for years. You've had no trouble, have you, Vincent?
VINCENT No, sir. None at all. She seems more cheerful and easy in her mind.
SIR JOSEPH What's that?
VINCENT She's all right.
SIR JOSEPH Then I don't see the sense in planting a laurel bush at the beginning of November.
VINCENT I expect she thought better late than never.
SIR JOSEPH What are you mumbling about, man? Did she tell you why she planted it?
VINCENT No, sir.
SIR JOSEPH Then wrap me up. I'll ring for you if I want a hot water bottle.

(He sits down and VINCENT wraps him up, finds his spectacles and hands him newspapers)

VINCENT Will that be all, sir?
SIR JOSEPH What? Yes, yes.

(VINCENT is about to go when something attracts his attention)

VINCENT Come out of there, will you! Come along. Look sharp about it.

(Enter ERNEST. SIR JOSEPH remains absorbed in his paper.)

(Below his breath) What are you doing here, sir, may I ask?
ERNEST I came in by the little gate.
VINCENT That's not an answer to my question.
ERNEST I thought I might see Lady Pitts.
VINCENT Than I'm afraid you can't. Her Ladyship is not at home.
ERNEST But I must see her.
VINCENT There's no must about it, sir. You'd better go back the way you came.
SIR JOSEPH Hello, what's this?
VINCENT *(loudly)* Young gentleman made a slight mistake, sir. I'll show him the way out.
SIR JOSEPH I've seen you somewhere before.
VINCENT I don't think so, sir.
SIR JOSEPH Come here and let me look at you. *(ERNEST advances)* Were you here last Sunday?
ERNEST Yes, I was.
SIR JOSEPH Then come and sit down and don't stand there looking as if you'd burst your braces. Get out, Vincent. This young man's a friend of Lady Pitts.

(Exit VINCENT)

(Pointing to his Acousticon) You can talk into that gadget. Only don't bellow. What's your name?
ERNEST Ernest Piaste.
SIR JOSEPH Italian?
ERNEST No, Polish.
SIR JOSEPH My God. Well, Mr. Whatever your name is, it seems to me that you're labouring under a misunderstanding – that's to say if you're the young gentleman I saw practising catch-as-catch-can with my wife last Sunday evening. I suppose I'm right about that, am I?
ERNEST It is not how I should describe the incident. But let us say you are right.
SIR JOSEPH I am eighty-seven years of age, Mr. Piaste. Incidents like that don't upset me as much as they might have done if I had been younger. As it is, I am able to look at the matter pretty much from my wife's point of view.
ERNEST You have spoken to her?
SIR JOSEPH Good God, no. I don't go about looking for trouble at my time of life. No. You are a foreigner but you look a decent enough young fellow. I've got some sort of vague recollection of what young men are, especially foreigners, and I don't blame you. But it's my duty to give you a word of warning. You've bitten off a damned sight more than you can chew.

ERNEST Sir Joseph, I very much love your wife.

SIR JOSEPH So do I, my boy, so do I. But that's got nothing to do with the case.

ERNEST You do not understand. It was most unfortunate that you should come upon us at the only moment when I have forgotten myself. You must believe me when I say that I worship your wife as I worship God. She is all-pervading, infinitely near at all times of the day and yet infinitely far off. To think of her in any other manner would be blasphemy.

SIR JOSEPH I see what you mean. I suppose that's why you skulk about my shrubbery on a Sunday afternoon.

ERNEST I wanted to explain.

SIR JOSEPH To Lady Pitts?

ERNEST Yes.

SIR JOSEPH Pretty much in the terms you've just used to me?

ERNEST Yes.

SIR JOSEPH I see. Seems hardly worth while, does it?

ERNEST It is tremendously what you call worth while.

SIR JOSEPH Well, it all depends on the point of view. I suppose you're quite serious about all this?

ERNEST I swear before God I am.

SIR JOSEPH Do you know anything about Lady Pitts?

ERNEST She has told me all.

SIR JOSEPH Here, take a rug. You're shivering with cold. She has told you all, has she?

(ERNEST *wraps a tartan plaid round his shoulders and sits crouching tensely forward*)

ERNEST Yes.

SIR JOSEPH What did she tell you?

ERNEST I am not at liberty to betray her confidence. But what do these things matter? They are in a different dimension from the dimension in which I live.

SIR JOSEPH Did she tell you she'd had a nervous breakdown?

ERNEST No, but I am not surprised.

SIR JOSEPH It's rather important from everybody's point of view. I don't think she can have told you very much after all.

ERNEST I tell you she told me everything and I have forgotten it. Absolutely.

SIR JOSEPH Lady Pitts' father was a parson in Sussex. He had a lot of daughters – all parsons have – but she was the clever one. She took a scholarship at Newnham and a Rockefeller Travelling Scholarship after that – just after it was founded. She had first class Honours in Economics and Modern Languages. Damned stupid, I think. A woman can't carry all that and her physiology and psychology too. Anyhow, it was no damned good to her. She had to be a governess like the rest of 'em. She had to get out of that, of course, so she married some kind of an usher at a public school. He was killed climbing Snowdon round about '25. He left her six hundred and seventy-five pounds, eighteen and fourpence, so she took her chartered accountant's examination. She couldn't bear the thought of teaching any more. From 1926 to 1937 she was secretary to a biscuit factory in Birmingham. She worked all day and ran a shelter for prostitutes at night. In 1937 I married her. In a way it's been a success and in a way it hasn't. She has outbreaks. One can't really be surprised. It's all this emancipation of women. They think they can do what they like but it's not in their nature to do what they like. They just wallop about with the tide until they're caught in some new form of slavery. I found her plenty to do to keep her mind occupied but there's more than the mind has to be kept occupied and so she has outbreaks every now and again. I don't know why the hell I'm telling you all this. I told Vincent to throw you out when you came first and that would probably have been the best plan. I wouldn't mind her amusing herself with young men, but the trouble is she doesn't know how. She has the misfortune to be a dyed-in-the-wool Puritan. Ring the bell, will you?

(ERNEST rings the bell)

By the way, how do you support yourself?

ERNEST I am a student of Arts in London University. I teach French and Polish and Russian in a Commercial College.

SIR JOSEPH Well, if I were you, I'd go on doing that and leave my wife alone. You say you worship her afar off or something. Well, the further off the better. If you keep messing around here, you'll only make her ill, and get poor enough satisfaction for yourself. And if, by any chance, it's money you're after, you won't get any here. I'm a millionaire and millionaires don't make money by giving it away.

ERNEST Sir, you are insulting. I am a gentleman.

SIR JOSEPH Gentlemen have to live like anybody else.

(Enter VINCENT with hot water bottle)

Ah, there you are. Give it to me. Have you my tablets?

VINCENT Yes, sir.

SIR JOSEPH Give me one. And a glass of water.

(He takes a tablet and washes it down)

VINCENT Are you all right, sir?

SIR JOSEPH Of course I'm all right. I've been all right for eighty-seven years. Get out, Vincent.

VINCENT Thank you, sir. *(Exit VINCENT)*

SIR JOSEPH Where were we? Oh, yes. You were saying that you were a gentleman. Well, if you are a gentleman, you'll know how to act. Lady Pitts isn't particularly happy; but then nobody is. And you can take it from an old man that she won't be any happier living on your pay. She's fifty and fifty's too late to go stravaiging.

(ERNEST rises. The plaid is still draped round him and he looks very noble and rather like a Highland chief.)

ERNEST Sir, what you have said has very much disturbed me; but it has called me back to the honesty of purpose which I have tried all my life to maintain. I am a young man; but I have experienced frustration and grief and now I am strong to bear them. I give you my sacred word of honour that I will never again attempt to see your wife. She will be to me as Beatrice was to Dante Alighieri when she had gone to Heaven. That will be to me all my happiness. It will be known to you from the works of the poet, Ovidius, that the god Apollo did once pursue Daphne, the daughter of the aged Ge. As the god was about to seize her, the aged Ge transformed her suddenly into a laurel tree. You will see the picture by Pollaiuolo in your National Gallery. As Apollo has grasped the young lady by the hips her left foot has taken root and both her arms have become enormous laurel branches. It is very sad. But it is grand also. For the laurel, Daphne, still eternally spreads her leaves, and the Sun-god, from ninety-two million, eight hundred and thirty thousand miles away, still warms and comforts her and endows her with life. It shall be so with me.

SIR JOSEPH I suppose you realise that I haven't heard a word you've said. What's the gist of it?

ERNEST *(shouting into the Acousticon)* I shall not see Lady Pitts again any more. My word of honour.

SIR JOSEPH Good. I'm glad you've taken this line. When I die, of course, she can do what she likes. Goodbye. *(He holds out his hand. After some hesitation, ERNEST takes it.)*

ERNEST Goodbye, Sir Joseph Pitts.

SIR JOSEPH I've taken rather a fancy to you. It's a pity we'll never see each other again. You know the little shrubbery gate? Go out by that. Goodbye.

ERNEST *(to the laurel bush)* Goodbye, Daphne.

(Exit ERNEST. SIR JOSEPH drowses. In a few moments enter LADY PITTS. She tucks him in softly, walks over to the laurel bush and stands touching it.)

SIR JOSEPH Eh? What? Who's that? . . . Oh, it's you, Kitty.

LADY PITTS Yes, dearest.

SIR JOSEPH Ain't you going to sit down?

LADY PITTS Yes. *(She sits beside him. SIR JOSEPH laboriously reaches for ERNEST's rug and places it round her.)*

SIR JOSEPH Mustn't catch cold. It's pretty parky out here. It's November now.

LADY PITTS Yes, dear, it's November.

SIR JOSEPH Wonderful that we can get out at all, time of the year.

LADY PITTS Yes, Joe.

SIR JOSEPH It's November all the year round, these days. But we can still get out. That's something. How's your laurel tree?

LADY PITTS I think it's going to live – if the frost stays away.

SIR JOSEPH It's a Daphne Laureola, isn't it?

LADY PITTS Yes, darling.

SIR JOSEPH Pretty name, Daphne. . . . There was a young fellow here looking for you. Young foreign fellow. . . . I had quite a little chat with him . . . decent sort of a young fellow.

LADY PITTS What did he want?

SIR JOSEPH Nothing important. I expect he'll write to you. He may not.

LADY PITTS Did you send him away?

SIR JOSEPH Me? No. Went himself. Quite a decent young fellow. A bit daft. I shouldn't worry about him, if I were you. Any more.

LADY PITTS Are you trying to tell me something?

SIR JOSEPH No. I can tell you things without trying. That's one of the things I like about you.

LADY PITTS What did he say?

SIR JOSEPH How do I know what he said? I'm as deaf as a post as you know very well.

LADY PITTS He left no message?

SIR JOSEPH No. Nothing in particular. I gathered he's taken a fancy to you. I don't blame him. You look lovely to me. I never bought anything I like more.

LADY PITTS You bought me, did you?

SIR JOSEPH Oh, I suppose so. What does it matter? It's the only way I ever had of getting what I needed. It's as honest a way as most, when all's said. I've never regretted it. Have you?

LADY PITTS I don't believe I have.

SIR JOSEPH Afar off.

LADY PITTS What did you say?

SIR JOSEPH Afar off may be just over the garden wall; but it's far enough. Or the other side of the glass on a glass case. Never mind. It's better than nothing. And, by God, it's better to be outside the glass case than in it. That's right, old Daphne, isn't it? God, don't you know it! Femina sapiens. Daphne Laureola. . . . Never mind. You're safe behind glass. No frost can reach you . . . not if I can help it. . . . Pure bloody Hepplewhite. A collector's piece. I loved you . . . how do they put it? In my fashion, Kitty. The best I could do. . . . If I had been younger, not that I wouldn't have . . .

LADY PITTS What's the matter with you, Joe?

SIR JOSEPH Death, me dear. Just death. The first natural thing that has happened to me for half a century.

LADY PITTS Where are your tablets? . . . Vincent! Vincent! Come quickly. . . . Oh, Joe, don't go. I need you!
SIR JOSEPH Do you, sweetheart? That's not so bad, then.

CURTAIN

END OF ACT THREE

ACT FOUR

Le Toit Aux Porcs, six months later.

Curiously enough, most of the people who were dining there six months ago are dining there now. The ladder and the ceiling cloth are not there, and the playful design on the wall is completed. But the bad piece of flooring is still there. This time it has a little pyramidal post at either corner with a red light on top.

The DINERS have altered their seats. The FAT MAN and GOOCH are dining at number 4. The YOUNG PEOPLE are at number 1. The SPIVS and the SLEEPY COUPLE are at numbers 3 and 2 respectively. The table on the rostrum is empty. GEORGE is in attendance.

1ST SPIV So I says to him, look, Maurice, you can't do that. Not to me you can't. And he says, look, Alfie, he says, I'd be just the same if it was my dear old grey-haired mother, he says. Fair's fair, he says. That's the sort he is.

2ND SPIV That's the sort he is, all right.

1ST SPIV You've said it.

2ND SPIV That's his blooming mark, and you can take it from yours most sincerely.

1ST SPIV I believe you.

2ND SPIV What'd you say next?

1ST SPIV I says, Look, Maurice. Business is business all right. You know me, Maurice, I says. You don't find no bluebottles on yours most sincerely, I says. I can take it with the rest of the gang, I says. I'm no Stafford Cripps on wheels, I says. But, look, Maurice, I says, have a bit of morality. Three hundred and forty-five smackers is just sheer bloody robbery with violence, I says. You're a business man and I'm a business man, I says. Picture it to yourself, I says. Have a bit of imagination, I says. Well, I ask you.

2ND SPIV Well, after all. Live and let live. We all got to stay in the same world.

1ST SPIV That's what I say. . . . George!

GEORGE Sir?

1ST SPIV Bill.

GEORGE Yes, sir.

(He produces the bill. The SPIV signs it and both SPIVS go out. GEORGE says: "Goodnight, gentlemen," but neither answers.)

GOOCH Coffee?

FAT MAN Yes.

GOOCH A likyour?

FAT MAN I don't mind.

GOOCH George, what likyours have you got?

GEORGE Van der Humm and Gin Cocktail.

GOOCH I asked for likyours. Gin cocktail isn't a likyour.

GEORGE It is these days.

GOOCH Coffee and Van der Humm, then.

GEORGE Thank you, sir.

GOOCH George! *(shouting across to Table 1)* Care for a likyour?

BILL Oh, yes, Mr. Gooch. Thank you very much.

MAISIE It's very kind of you.

GOOCH Six Van der Humms, George.

GEORGE Yes, sir.

GOOCH Not in your usual high spirits tonight.

BILL No. Matter of fact, we *are* a bit low.

GOOCH What's the matter?

HELEN Bill's lost his job. He's just been directed.

MAISIE Shut up, Helen.

GOOCH What to?

BILL Agriculture.

GOOCH My God! Still, it's healthy, they tell me.

BILL Who wants health?

GOOCH Come round and see me tomorrow. Winston Hotel. They know me there. Ask for Mr. Gooch. I don't want to see a young man like you rotting his soul out on the land. I do a bit with the dogs. I might find a place for you.

BILL Well, ta ever so much, Mr. Gooch. It's really most kind of you.

GOOCH Well, we *have* got immortal souls, haven't we? You can't play ducks and drakes with them.

(Re-enter GEORGE who serves liqueurs and coffee)

Ever see our mutual friend, Lady Pitts, George?

GEORGE No, sir. She hasn't been in recently.

GOOCH It must have been six months ago, I saw her last. Cor, that was a night!

GEORGE Was it, sir? I can't recollect.

GOOCH The lot of us went into High Society as a result of that. Didn't we, Mr. Watson?

FAT MAN That's right.

GOOCH Funny business altogether. Nice place they have, up there in Hampstead. None of you seen her since?

MAISIE No, Mr. Gooch. Here's gravel in your ear-hole.

GOOCH Thank you, Maisie. *(All drink)* Funny, us all being here tonight. It's funny world.

MAISIE Yes, it is, isn't it?

(They all meditate on the fun of the world)

BORED WOMAN Your coffee's getting cold.

BORED MAN I like it cold.

BORED WOMAN You kick up hell in the morning if it's cold.

BORED MAN This isn't the morning.

BORED WOMAN I never said it was the morning.

BORED MAN All right then. We know what time of day it is. That's something, anyway.

BORED WOMAN Well, moderate your voice. Everybody'll hear you.

BORED MAN Suppose they do? What I've got to say won't do them any harm.

BORED WOMAN Whether it does them harm or not, I don't like looking conspicuous.

BORED MAN Then what did you put on that hat for?

BORED WOMAN You leave my hat alone.

BORED MAN Wouldn't touch it with a pair of tongs.

(The BORED WOMAN snivels silently. Enter ERNEST.)

MAISIE *(in a whisper)* Look who's here.

HELEN Oh!

ERNEST *(to GEORGE)* Good evening.

GEORGE Good evening, sir. Haven't seen you here for some time. There's a table here, sir.

(ERNEST takes his old place)

Some nice hors d'oeuvres to start with, sir? We have some very nice beans and chopped turnip with a bit of salt herring and a nice bit of beetroot.

ERNEST No, please. I think I should like some Vienna steak and some pommes sautes.

GEORGE Very good, sir. Anything to drink?

ERNEST No, thank you.

(Exit GEORGE. GOOCH turns and raises his glass to MAISIE, who guides his eye to ERNEST. GOOCH gets up and goes to ERNEST's table.)

GOOCH Good evening, Mr. Piaste. How are you?

ERNEST I am very well, thank you. How are you?

GOOCH I never forget a name or a face. You are Mr. Piaste, aren't you?

ERNEST Piaste, yes.

GOOCH Remember me?

ERNEST I do not think so.

GOOCH Come along now. Weren't you here six months ago when we had an unfortunate little contertong? And haven't I met you in more genial circumstances in a certain mansion in Hampstead? Hey?

ERNEST Yes. You are right, perhaps. I am sorry.

GOOCH Any familiar faces down there?

(MAISIE and HELEN smile and wave to ERNEST)

ERNEST Ah yes . . . how do you do?

GOOCH Care to join Mr. Watson and me? We've nearly finished, but we'd be very pleased.

ERNEST No. You are very kind. But, thank you, no.

GOOCH Mr. Watson never takes no for an answer. He's a bit difficult to know, but he's worth it when you do get to know him. Come along.

ERNEST Oh, please.

GOOCH But yes, old boy, yes! We were just talking about you. And here we are all together again. It's like old times. Come along. No, dammit, I'll be offended if you don't. *(He almost drags ERNEST to Table 4)* George will set a place for you. Remember Mr. Piaste, Cecil?

FAT MAN Yes. How do? *(He shakes hands with ERNEST, who sits down)*

GOOCH Gosh, Cecil, we owe our acquaintance to this young man, in a way.

FAT MAN That's right, Tom.

GOOCH God works in a mysterious way his wonders to perform. *(Re-enter GEORGE with Vienna steak)* Bring it here, George. Set a place for Mr. Piaste. We never expected him to turn up, did we?

GEORGE. No, sir.

GOOCH Looks like Fate.

GEORGE Yes, sir, in a way.

GOOCH You know, I don't believe there's any such thing as a coincidence. There's something in the stars after all. Not that I'm superstitious. Have a little something with your dinner? Mr. Piaste? It's on me. What've you got, George?

GEORGE Rum and lemon. Gin cocktail . . .

GOOCH A large rum and lemon and six more Van der Humms.

ERNEST No, no. Please.

GOOCH You'll allow an older man to tell you what's good for you. That right, Cecil?

WATSON That's right.

GOOCH Very well, then. Run, George.

(Exit GEORGE)

Well, well, well, well, well. Mild weather for April.

ERNEST Yes.

GOOCH More like November.

ERNEST Yes.
GOOCH I suppose it's not much different in your part of the world.
ERNEST No.
GOOCH Still living in London?
ERNEST Yes.
GOOCH Go on with your chuck. Don't let my conversation interrupt you. We all need our little whack of calories, eh?
ERNEST Yes.
GOOCH Quite a party, this has turned out to be.
ERNEST Yes.
GOOCH We were all feeling a bit low till you came in.
ERNEST Yes?
GOOCH You've cheered us up quite a bit. Hasn't he, Maisie?
MAISIE Yes, he has.
GOOCH Kept pretty fit during the winter?
ERNEST Yes.
GOOCH That's a blessing. What about a cigar, Cecil? You don't mind, do you, Mr. Piaste?
ERNEST No.
GOOCH I must say I like a good cigar. I got a handful from a customer today. I don't know where we'd be if it weren't for the Merchant Navy.

(Table 1 have dropped all conversation and are listening intently to what is going on. The BORED MAN is settling his bill with GEORGE in dumb show. Then he and his wife get up and go out.)

GEORGE Goodnight, sir. Goodnight, madam. I hope you enjoyed your dinner.
BORED MAN No.

(Exit BORED MAN and BORED WOMAN. GEORGE brings over drinks.)

GOOCH Looks like we've got the whole place to ourselves, George.
GEORGE Yes, sir. The touch of sunshine today took them all out. Not doing much business anyway.
GOOCH That's a happy married couple just gone out.
GEORGE Yes, sir. They often come here.
GOOCH You married, Mr. Piaste?
ERNEST No.
GOOCH Well, I suppose it's all right for some temperaments. I'm all right, but maybe it's because my old stocking-mender and me don't see too much of each other. Even-tempered old bundle she is, too. That's the kind to look for, Mr. Piaste, if you're ever thinking of it. You married, George?
GEORGE I'm a widower, sir. *(He drifts off)*
GOOCH Aye, there's a sad side to it too. . . . We were just talking about

our genial hostess, Lady Pitts, before you came in. Seems she doesn't come here now. Just as well, perhaps. Seen her lately?

ERNEST No.

GOOCH Read about her in the papers?

ERNEST I don't read the papers.

GOOCH I saw where it said she'd resigned from most of her Boards and Committees. I'm not surprised. Funny thing was she kept going so long. Tragic case in a way, too. She must have a cool quarter of a million to her own kick; and what's she going to do with it, I'd like to know.

FAT MAN There ought to be a law against it. Women don't know how to handle money. Specially her sort.

GOOCH Sir Joseph was a sharp old citizen. She'll feel the want of advice now he's gone.

ERNEST Gone?

GOOCH Didn't you know? That's what you get for not reading the papers. He died six months ago.

(ERNEST falls forward in a dead faint and rolls on to the floor. The other diners converge on him with squeals and shouts. GOOCH takes charge of the situation.)

That's all right. He's just fainted. Stand back and give him air. Wait. I'll undo his collar. Glass of water, George.

(He dashes a glass of water in ERNEST's face)

That's better. He's coming round. Food poisoning, I shouldn't be surprised. Some of these foreigners don't get much to eat. How's that, chum? Feeling a bit better?

ERNEST Yes, thank you.

(He is helped up to his chair. His collar is loose, his hair disordered and he is dripping with water. This produces a generally wild appearance which persists till the end of the scene.)

GOOCH You gave us all a bit of a turn. Take a swig of rum. That'll steady you. George, fetch some brandy. *(Exit GEORGE)* It wasn't the cigar smoke, was it?

ERNEST No.

(The YOUNG PEOPLE are grouped round the table in varying attitudes of concern. The FAT MAN has not moved.)

You say that Sir Joseph is dead?

GOOCH Yes, chum, I thought you would know.

ERNEST I must go to her.

GOOCH Yes, of course. But there's plenty of time. Tomorrow will do. Just you trot around to see her tomorrow. *(To YOUNG PEOPLE)* He's all right, now. You'd better leave him with Cecil and me.

(The YOUNG PEOPLE return to their tables. GEORGE arrives with a glass of brandy. ERNEST absently finishes his rum and starts on the brandy.)

That's the stuff. You wouldn't like to see a doctor, or anything?
ERNEST No, thank you.
GOOCH He's all right now, George. You needn't worry. You can take away his Vienna steak and bring him a little dry toast. I don't think he's feeling much like dinner, are you, chum?
ERNEST No.

(GEORGE tidies up and goes)

MAISIE *(shouting across)* Are you feeling all right, Mr. Piaste?
ERNEST Yes, thank you.
MAISIE That's fine.
GOOCH Yes, I can see it must have been a bit of a shock to you. You were a bit struck on Lady Pitts, weren't you?
ERNEST Yes.
GOOCH There was something very attractive about her. She must have been a smasher when she was younger. And mind you, she's still got a lot of what it takes. Ladylike, too. There's even some likes the mature types best. I knew a young fellow in Leeds who married a woman old enough to be his great-grandmother, and it was a great success. She looked after him and steadied him up like. I knew the old girl too and it took twenty years off *her* age. If you'd had any ideas in your head, Mr. Piaste, don't think I'd go the length of discouraging you. To say nothing of quarter of a million not being a bad sort of thing to have about the house. Not that anyone should marry for money. Matrimony is a sacred tie, you see, Mr. Piaste, and there's got to be something else, otherwise life's a living hell for both of them. I've seen that happen too.
ERNEST Sir, you are a most impudent dog; but nothing that you have to say can either offend or distress me. I am living, sir, in a world to which even your most feverish dreams could never hope to penetrate. Your words do not affect me one way or another. You might as well spit at the sky.
GOOCH Well, I must say. . . . I don't expect gratitude these days, but I'm used to a little common civility. If you don't like my conversation you can push off. It's still a free country.
ERNEST I have told you that I do not either dislike or like your conversation. It is nothing to me. You have been very kind when I was foolish just now and for that I am grateful and I thank you very much. You may speak to me on any topic you like. Please don't misunderstand me. Whatever you wish to say is OK by me. It is quite OK by me.

GOOCH Well, I suppose there's nothing to do except accept your apology. But you're a queer character and no mistake.

FAT MAN I think that's pretty handsome of you, Tom. I wouldn't take that kind of talk from anyone.

GOOCH You got to have some give and take in this world. I'm not a hard man like you, Cecil. I've great sympathy with Mr. Piaste's point of view. I was young myself once.

FAT MAN So was I.

GOOCH Well, you see, there it is.

FAT MAN I don't see what that's got to do with it. We were all young once. I was taught manners when I was young. Nobody's taught manners in this generation.

MAISIE Oh, what a lie, Mr. Watson!

FAT MAN There you are. They're not content with eaves-dropping. They call you a liar to the back of your neck, and you old enough to be their father.

GOOCH I'm afraid you're a very hard man, Mr. Watson.

MAISIE He's nothing of the sort. He's as soft as a Swiss roll.

FAT MAN There you are. Nothing but impertinence, impertinence, impertinence, from morning till night. And all you can do is to ignore it.

HELEN (*sotto voce*) You shouldn't have said that to him, Maisie.

MAISIE I couldn't help it. Fat fool.

FAT MAN I heard that too.

MAISIE Who's eaves-dropping now?

FAT MAN Look here, I've had just about enough of that from you. Another word out of your head and I'll complain to the management.

GOOCH Now, now, now, now, now!

(*Enter LADY PITTS and VINCENT. GOOCH's voice dies away in astonishment and he says his last "now now" or two in a strangled whisper. The others gaze on the newcomers in a startled silence. LADY PITTS is in black. VINCENT is rather more gaily dressed to indicate that he has been liberated from serfdom. But he is a very much subdued VINCENT. The pair are ushered to the table on the rostrum by GEORGE, who gives no sign that he has seen either of them before.*)

GEORGE This way, madam. This way, sir. We're very quiet tonight. (*LADY PITTS and VINCENT sit*) Now can I get you a couple of glasses of sherry and some nice hors d'oeuvres?

VINCENT We ordered a special dinner by 'phone. This afternoon.

GEORGE Of course, sir. Yes. What name was it, again?

VINCENT Mr. and Mrs. Vincent.

GEORGE Yes, of course, Mr. Vincent. Thank you, sir.

(*So far LADY PITTS has given no sign that she recognises anybody in the room. Exit GEORGE.*)

LADY PITTS Yes. It's curious. It does come back to me. Bit by bit. I remember that patch on the floor. But not the lights.

VINCENT They tell me they have to wait years for permits.

LADY PITTS There was a ladder, or something. It's gone. It's rather a ramshackle place, dearest.

VINCENT Well, you would insist on coming. I didn't think it was a specially good idea myself. We might . . . good Lord . . .

LADY PITTS What's the matter? . . . Oh!

(They have both seen ERNEST)

VINCENT *(rapidly)* Want to go?

LADY PITTS No. Why should we?

(She smiles radiantly and bows to ERNEST. ERNEST stares at her.)

LADY PITTS *(to VINCENT)* Now I *know* it was sheer inspiration. *(To ERNEST)* Mr. Piaste, don't you recognise your old friends?

(GOOCH bounces out of his seat)

GOOCH You set him a bad example, your ladyship. Remember me – name of Gooch? And Mr. Watson, here? And the young folks?

LADY PITTS But of course! Now this is really extraordinary.

GOOCH Talk about the long arm of coincidence, hey? How are you, my lady?

LADY PITTS Very well, thank you.

GOOCH But perhaps I shouldn't be calling you "my lady" any more? Am I right in saying that we are to congratulate you?

LADY PITTS Yes, if you like.

GOOCH Well, I'm sure we all do. . . . Ladies and gentlemen, will you please be upstanding and drink the healths of the happy couple. . . . Mr. and Mrs. Vincent, isn't it? Mr. and Mrs. Vincent.

(All rise except ERNEST)

Long life to you and may all your troubles be little ones.

(The health is drunk. VINCENT is embarrassed and angry. LADY PITTS (as we may for convenience call her) is looking at ERNEST in a puzzled sort of way. GOOCH follows her glance.)

Hello, Mr. Piaste. You're not joining in. . . . Mr. Piaste hasn't been too well, Mrs. Vincent. . . . Come along. Pull yourself together. We're drinking the health of the bride and bridegroom. *(ERNEST makes no sign)* Well, well, please yourself.

"For they are jolly good fellows,
For they are jolly good fellows,
For they are jolly good fellows,
And so say all of us." Hip, hip, hooray!

(The YOUNG PEOPLE cheer)

> "So we'll all sit down together,
> We'll all sit down together,
> We'll all sit down together,
> And wait for his reply."

(ALL sit)

VINCENT Very kind of you, I'm sure. This is a bit unexpected, and I'm not sure that my wife and myself . . .
GOOCH Hooray!
VINCENT I'm not sure that we'd've come if we had known there was going to be this sort of thing. In fact, I know we wouldn't. But, seeing you've drunk our healths, thank you.

(Applause)

(Urgently to LADY PITTS) Come away.
LADY PITTS No.
VINCENT But, Katherine . . .
LADY PITTS I said "No".

(Re-enter GEORGE with hors d'oeuvres and sherry. LADY PITTS sips her sherry in silence and looks over the brim of her glass at ERNEST. GEORGE is going out.)

GOOCH Quite a party, George.
GEORGE Yes, sir.

(Exit GEORGE. An awkward silence falls. LADY PITTS toys with her hors d'oeuvres and then suddenly puts down her fork and addresses ERNEST.)

LADY PITTS Why do you look at me like that?
ERNEST I did not know that your husband was dead.
GOOCH Now, now. Don't bring up funerals on a happy occasion like this. The king is dead, long live the king.
ERNEST Do you believe that? That I did not know?
LADY PITTS Why should I not believe you? And what does it matter?
ERNEST *(rising)* You ask me what does it matter? You ask me that?

(VINCENT rises too, but LADY PITTS pulls him back to his seat)

GOOCH Now, Mr. Piaste. Control yourself. We're all friends here.
ERNEST I will tell you what it matters.
VINCENT *(bellowing)* Listen. We've had enough speeches. Sit down, you.

(GEORGE hurries in, but goes no further than the archway)

GEORGE Did you call, sir?

VINCENT No. . . . *(to ERNEST)* Did you hear me? Sit down.

LADY PITTS Darling, you mustn't shout.

VINCENT Let him sit down and shut up, then.

LADY PITTS He has nothing to do with you. I have told you to be quiet.

ERNEST Yes, be quiet, you poor devil.

VINCENT Look. Another word from you and . . .

LADY PITTS *(in cold fury)* I will not endure this. You were once my keeper; but I did not engage you as my bully. Sit still. Sit very still.

VINCENT Sorry, darling. He made me lose my temper.

LADY PITTS *(to ERNEST)* Do you propose to make a public speech at me?

ERNEST I must say what is in my mind. I must say it. I cannot help it. You should not have come here.

(GOOCH tries to restrain him and GEORGE advances on him)

GEORGE Come along now, sir. This isn't the House of Commons.

LADY PITTS Let him be. I am not afraid of him. Let him alone, I tell you.

ERNEST Are you married to this man?

LADY PITTS Yes. Do you mind?

ERNEST I so desperately mind that I feel as if ten thousand mad rats were tearing my heart to pieces with red hot teeth. I do not understand why you do this. You knew what you were to me. I told you. I do not understand. I must understand or I shall die.

LADY PITTS So you wish me to explain my private affairs at the top of my voice in a public restaurant?

ERNEST You were doing that when I first met you.

LADY PITTS You know English very well. Do you know what a cad is, Mr. Piaste?

ERNEST It is of no purpose to call me bad names. Besides, it is only in England that there are cads. I am not an Englishman and I am interested in the truth. Stick what label on me you like. It is nothing to me.

FAT MAN She's right, all the same. No gentleman would cast up old stories to a lady.

ERNEST It is a very old story. Has nobody told you the story of the poor peasant who worshipped a goddess? And then he found there were no gods and goddesses, only an empty sky. Has nobody told you about the god who loved a mortal girl, thinking she was as he was, and found that she was a no-good slut?

FAT MAN I'd make up my mind which it was, if I were you. You can't have it both ways.

ERNEST You *can* have it both ways, if you know what it is to love. Madame, you filled my world with wonder. If I had learned that the wonder existed only in my own imagination I could have borne it. But you exist, by

281

God, you exist. The blessed sun has changed to a huge scorpion and the great mountains to pestiferous dunghills and the green grass to bile.

GOOCH Well, my goodness gracious me!

ERNEST "Al ciel, ch'e pura luce;
        Luce intellectual piena d'amore . . ."

The pure light, the heaven, the light of the mind, the light filled with love. I asked you for nothing more; I desired nothing more. You have plunged my light in darkness to enjoy the embraces of that evil dog.

HELEN Chaps, I think we ought to go. I mean . . .

ERNEST It was nothing to me that you lied to me. I believed you when you told me that you had led the life of a woman of pleasure. It was no more to me than to be told that before the day of Creation there was chaos. On the day I first saw you, there came light, day and night came and the stars and the sun and the moon, the ocean and the land filled themselves with life and a man and a woman were born to be king and queen over all. Now it is ruin and desolation for ever and ever.

LADY PITTS Nonsense.

ERNEST If it is nonsense, you have made it nonsense. Even if I kill myself, it has no meaning.

LADY PITTS I have nothing to do with all this. It is all in your own head. I told you that. If you feel wretched it isn't my fault. I *won't* be blamed. It's not fair.

(*She gets up rapidly and goes to MAISIE, who naturally looks astonished*)

You're a woman. Tell him it isn't fair. They're in love with themselves, aren't they? They care nothing for us. Do they? They make up something out of their heads and borrow our faces and our bodies to clothe it, like washing off a line. They do, don't they? I told that fellow I had played the harlot over half Europe. He believed me. It wasn't true, but he believed me. And he didn't care, do you hear? He didn't care. There never was such a waste of a good lie. He simply wasn't interested. He wasn't interested in *me*. He wouldn't have noticed me at all, if I hadn't got tight and made a fool of myself. I burst in on his meditations and he said, "Hello, here's a woman. She'll do for Beatrice," – or whatever cloudy tart he was dreaming about. It never occurred to him that I was a human being. They're all the same – unless they're pigs. And the pigs are at least honest with themselves and with us. I've found that out now. That's why I've settled down in a nice clean pig-sty.

ERNEST Don't believe her. She is a liar. She knows she is a liar. She is a damned liar.

(*The MANAGER, a tall Cypriote in a dinner jacket, comes in hurriedly. GEORGE goes to meet him. LADY PITTS does not appear to notice him, but she detects a movement from VINCENT.*)

LADY PITTS *(to VINCENT)* Stay where you are. I can deal with this young fool.

(The MANAGER goes to VINCENT and whispers to him. VINCENT appears sulkily to assent to what he says.)

Mr. Piaste, you are an excitable, crazy, ignorant, young man. You think because you played at being a bandit in the War that everything is like that. You wanted to save the distressed lady from the ogre, didn't you? But the lady was too old to play these games, and she married the ogre and settled down. They all do, Mr. Piaste, THEY ALL DO! . . . *(to VINCENT)* Don't mumble and mutter there when I'm speaking.

VINCENT The Manager thinks we had better go home.

LADY PITTS What has he got to do with it?

VINCENT I think he's right.

LADY PITTS But we haven't had our dinner.

VINCENT We can have our dinner somewhere else. This isn't a restaurant. It's a bloody debating society.

LADY PITTS But I haven't finished what I was going to say.

VINCENT I never yet met the woman who had. Come along.

LADY PITTS I seem to have been a little silly.

VINCENT That's all right. You got over-excited.

LADY PITTS Yes. I suppose I did. Forgive me. *(She goes to ERNEST)* Will you forgive me?

ERNEST Why should I forgive you? You have done me no wrong. It is not you who have done all this.

LADY PITTS Yes, Ernest, that is true. The old people who lived three thousand years ago would not have found this strange. These things are as old as the moon. The white goddess swings the tides idly to and fro and the little coloured wriggling things in the swaying seas know her. They know that she is higher and more terrible than their simple round of eating and fighting and copulation and death. . . . But you will not be cast by the fringe of the tide on the shingle to die in the hot sun. Go back into the sea, Ernest. The moon is a silly, cold goddess. Find another god, Ernest. . . . Goodnight.

GEORGE Round the edge, please, madame. The floor isn't safe.

LADY PITTS Of course, yes, I remember. Goodnight, goodnight.

(LADY PITTS, VINCENT, GEORGE and the MANAGER go out, circling the dangerous floor)

OMNES *(except ERNEST)* Goodnight, Mrs. Vincent. . . . Goodnight, Lady Pitts.

(After a short pause, everybody gathers round ERNEST, who is sitting now, with his head in his hands)

MAISIE You're well rid of her. I think she's bats.

HELEN So do I.

GOOCH I don't know. There was a lot in what she said. I mean to say, no matter how much you like your bit of fun, you've got to settle down some time. Anyhow, you'll have another drink. Where's George? George!

ERNEST I know now what it is. I am not Dante.

GOOCH Of course you're not.

MAISIE Nothing like him.

ERNEST I am Apollo. She is Daphne. Apollo wanted Daphne so much that the old man changed her into a laurel tree. But Apollo still rode on his predestined course, day and night, day and night.

GOOCH That's right. I don't know what you're talking about, but have a drink.

ERNEST I thank you. A double brandy.

GOOCH I'm glad you take it that way. George! George!

CURTAIN

END OF THE PLAY

Note on the Performance and Text of *The Sunlight Sonata*

The Sunlight Sonata was first performed on 20th March 1928, by the Scottish National Players in the Lyric Theatre, Glasgow, and with authorship attributed to 'Mary Henderson'. It featured the following Cast:

GROUNDWATER . . . . Morland Graham
MRS. GROUNDWATER . . . . Elliot Mason
HAMISH . . . . George Yuill
PETTIGREW . . . . Halbert Tatlock
CARMICHAEL . . . . Graham Dow
MR. CARMICHAEL . . . . Meg Buchanan
ELSIE . . . . Esther Wilson
BEELZEBUB . . . . James Anderson
SUPERBIA . . . . Peggy Morton
INVIDIA . . . . Ethel Lewis
IRA . . . . Frankie Smith
ACCIDIA . . . . Jean Taylor Smith
AVARICIA . . . . T. P. Maley
GULA . . . . Caven Watson
LUXURIA . . . . Elsie Brotchie
FAITH . . . . Nan Scott
HOPE . . . . Jenny Miller
CHARITY . . . . Nell Ballantyne

The Play was produced by Tyrone Guthrie. The Costumes were designed by Ethel Lewis.

The Sunlight Sonata was first published in the collection, *The Switchback*, *The Pardoner's Tale*, *The Sunlight Sonata* (London: Constable, 1930) and was reprinted in an identical version in 1932. Emendations have been made to this single existing published text.

Explanatory Notes

p.1 Sonata is a musical form in three sections featuring two themes. The first section (exposition) states the two themes, the first in the home key, the second theme in a related key. The second section is the development where the two themes are fragmented and stirred around and the third section (the recapitulation) states the two themes again with the second, this time, in the home key. The title of Bridie's play obviously resonates with Beethoven's *Moonlight Sonata* (1801).

p.1 Seven Deadly Sins Pride, Wrath, Envy, Lust, Gluttony, Avarice, Sloth.

p.1 Farce-Morality on the face of it a 'modern' mixing of genres, but farce originally meant additional matter introduced into the liturgy; the medieval

Morality plays were pieces in verse featuring personified abstractions, usually vices and virtues. Bridie's label, then, is suggestive of how the 'real life' (the farce?) of the play might be regarded.

p.1 A Prologue an introduction to a poem or a play.

p.1 An Interlude a performance, usually light, in the interval between acts of a drama; originally during medieval miracle plays.

p.1 A Demonstration the presentation of evidence or proof, especially in the context of practical science teaching.

p.1 An Apotheosis literally the elevation to divine status; generally, the reaching of the highest or most ideal point.

p.1 An Epilogue a short concluding section of a text; sometimes a short final speech by an actor in a play.

p.1 Tyrone Guthrie (1900–71) friend

of Bridie who directed the premiere of this play for the Scottish National Players at the Lyric Theatre, Glasgow, on 20th March 1928. *See also the Introduction.*

p.1 C.B.E. Commander of (the Order of) the British Empire.

p.1 D.L. Deputy (or Second) Lieutenant.

p.1 J.P. Justice of the Peace.

p.1 2nd-LT. Second Lieutenant.

p.1 B.D. Bachelor of Divinity.

p.1 B.Litt *Latin* Baccalaureus Litterarum (Bachelor of Letters).

p.1 Beelzebub a god of the Philistines (2 Kings 1:3) known as 'the prince of Devils' and ranked by John Milton and others as second only to Satan in the infernal kingdom.

p.1 Superbia *Latin* pride.

p.1 Invidia *Latin* meaning, most precisely, 'ill will' and, here, envy.

p.1 Ira *Latin* anger.

p.1 Accidia *medieval Latin* sloth.

p.1 Avaricia alternative to the *Latin* form, 'avaritia', meaning greed.

p.1 Gula *Latin* for the throat or, here, as a metonym, for appetite.

p.1 Luxuria *Latin* luxury.

p.1 Faith Hope Charity see The Three Graces below.

p.1 Phœbus Apollo from Greek mythology: two names used, interchangeably, for the god of the sun.

p.2 Æt. *Latin* 'aetatis', at the age of.

p.2 an elder an official authority, other than the minister, party to decision-making in a parish of the presbyterian Church of Scotland.

p.2 Fettes an Edinburgh private boarding-school built in 1865–70, and which has traditionally educated many future leaders of Scottish and, indeed, British society.

p.2 Sandhurst the Royal Military Academy for the training of British military officers, Berkshire, England.

p.2 Highland Light Infantry a British army regiment that adopted this designation in 1808; by the time of World War One the battalions of the regiment had particularly strong Glaswegian associations.

p.2 Harris tweeds woollen cloth of mixed fleck colours, hand spun, woven and dyed by the inhabitants of the Outer Hebrides; traditionally associated with the middle and upper classes at leisure in the countryside.

p.2 Mæcenas a patron of letters, the name derived from Gaius Mæcenas the patron of Virgil and Horace.

p.2 a drudge someone who does menial work.

p.2 The Three Graces in classical mythology, the goddesses of beauty and charm who embodied these qualities: the sisters Aglaia, Thalia and Euphrosyne; Christianised to become Faith, Hope and Charity.

p.2 Pantomime in British music-hall tradition, often a fairy tale performed with lots of comedy, singing and cross-dressing, most usually designed to appeal to children at Christmas time.

p.2 Emil Jannings in the Faust film Jannings played the Devil in the silent film *Faust* (1926), directed by F. W. Murnau.

p.2 embonpoint *French* plumpness.

p.2 the Doric from the mid seventeenth century a term used for Scots dialects of the English language.

p.2 arum lily collar an arum lily is a flower with a pure white spathe surrounding the plant's inflorescence; hence a white, wide-spilling collar.

p.2 passion flower a climbing plant whose name is derived from the supposed resemblance of its parts to things associated with Christ's crucifixion.

p.2 Pompadour cane the Marquise de Pompadour, mistress of Louis XV, gave her name generally to ornate, stylish or strikingly coloured dress or objects; a Pompadour cane is a walking stick topped by a large silver knob.

p.3 brogues rough shoes of untanned hide, formerly associated in particular with the Highlands of Scotland and the most rural parts of Ireland.

p.3 a slut a slovenly woman.

p.3 Falstaff a fat, bragging, sensual, deceitful, witty knight who is the special friend of Henry, the Prince of Wales (the future Henry V), King of England in

Shakespeare's *Henry IV Parts I & II* (1597), *Henry V* (1598) and *The Merry Wives of Windsor* (1600).

p.3 smilax a name for various spiny, climbing plants.

p.4 Glen Falloch a place near Inverarnan, north west of Loch Lomond on the road to Crianlarich.

p.4 butt o' the nicht *Scots* the end of the night.

p.4 muckle *Scots* large.

p.4 Bens *Scots-Gaelic* peaks.

p.4 Dour and cauld and deid *Scots* stern and cold and dead.

p.4 bonny *Scots* beautiful.

p.4 wee *Scots* small.

p.4 glens *Scots-Gaelic* mountain valleys.

p.4 burn *Scots* brook or stream.

p.4 linn *Scots* waterfall.

p.4 muir *Scots* moor.

p.4 clachan *Scots* hamlet.

p.4 flittering *Scots* splintering.

p.4 cleg *Scots* gadfly.

p.4 sculduddery *Scots* fornicating.

p.4 slater *Scots* woodlouse.

p.4 ruckies *Scots* stones.

p.4 caird *Scots* a tinker or a rough person, generally.

p.4 weans *Scots* children.

p.4 bothy *Scots* a rough-hut used as temporary accommodation by shepherds and travellers.

p.4 plaid *Scots* a rectangle of twilled woollen cloth, traditionally worn as the outer garment in rural areas.

p.4 lugs *Scots* ears.

p.4 horngollochs *Scots* earwig.

p.4 hirple *Scots* limp or hobble.

p.4 brain-pan the skull.

p.4 feart *Scots* afraid.

p.4 Droll queer or odd.

p.4 e'e *Scots* opening or eye(let).

p.4 Ancient of Days a name for God (Daniel 7:9).

p.4 hosannas in the Judeo-Christian tradition shouts of praise or adoration for God.

p.4 Play the game from Henry Newbolt's poem, 'Vitai Lampada' (1897); in a passage celebrating cricket a captain encourages the last man in to 'Play up! play up! and play the game!'

p.4 the worm and the flame Jesus speaks

of the torments of Hell 'where their worm dieth not, and the fire is not quenched' (Mark 9).

p.4 Benedicamus, Domine! *Latin* Blessed be the Lord God.

p.5 Prince of Darkness a common epithet for Satan.

p.5 sarcophagous bings! *Scots* a bing is a heap, often a funeral pile.

p.5 glower *Scots* to look angrily.

p.5 weel *Scots* well.

p.5 wag *Scots* shake.

p.5 pow *Scots* head.

p.5 a'body *Scots* anybody.

p.5 a Sabbath of Witches a midnight meeting of witches, sometimes also involving demons and presided over by a devil.

p.5 hobgoblin an impish ugly sprite.

p.5 poltergeist *German* a spirit that makes noises and moves objects, usually within a house or other building.

p.5 fays a generic name like 'fairy' for small beings or sprites of supernatural power.

p.5 the boiling *Scots* Hellish bile.

p.5 duddie bit braws *Scots* ragged pieces of splendid dress.

p.5 oot o' the mirklins *Scots* out of the twilight.

p.5 widdershins *Scots* denoting anti-clockwise, the direction in which witches and warlocks are traditionally supposed to circle the Devil.

p.5 Deil hain us! *Scots* Devil protect us!

p.5 vaudie bit smatchet *Scots* vain kind of pert individual.

p.5 Son of the Morning an epithet here for Satan, Beelzebub's overlord, dismissed by God from his original position as highest among the angels for the sin of pride.

p.5 the sack to be dismissed from employment (from the seventeenthth-century French: 'On luy a donné son sac', denoting the worker removing his tools in a sack on dismissal).

p.5 Inferiority Complex a feeling of inferiority wholly or partly unconscious; made particularly popular as an idea by the followers of the psychoanalyst Alfred Adler (1870–1937).

p.5 Get ower *Scots* idiomatic imperative, 'get over there' or 'get away from me'.

p.5 **oot** *Scots* out.

p.5 **maggie-rab partan** *Scots* a 'maggie-rab' is a 'bad half-penny' and a 'partan' is a 'crab', so cumulatively we have what looks like a tumultuous flyting term carrying the implication of crookedness, or being off-centred.

p.5 **Losh** *Scots* Lord.

p.5 **Whatna dirdum** *Scots* What a noise.

p.5 **Awa' an coo** *Scots* Go away and 'coor' (crouch down).

p.5 **rap** a counterfeit coin.

p.5 **maik** *Scots* a halfpenny.

p.5 **routh** *Scots* an abundance.

p.5 **yin** *Scots* one.

p.5–6 **the black dog** *colloquial* another term for 'the blues' or even depression.

p.6 **the Neuroses** typical of Bridie, modern psychological terminology is here couched as though encompassing allegorical figures such as the Three Graces or the Vices.

p.6 **Psychasthenia** *Greek* degeneration of the soul. A psychological term for a mental disease where fixed ideas, excessive rumination and hypochondria are symptoms.

p.6 **oak-headed natives of Britain** the oak is associated with English/British identity from the time of the Druids down to the nineteenth century where it stands, among other things, for British naval power (strong wooden ships); the association generally is that of a strong, independent character.

p.6 **"They shall never be Slavs"** a pun on 'Rule, Britannia, rule the waves;/ Britons never will be slaves' (from James Thomson, *Alfred: a Masque* (1740), Act II).

p.6 **craturs** *Scots* creatures.

p.6 **nippit wee spirlie** *Scots* pinched with hunger, small, spindly person.

p.6 **creeshy pockpud** *Scots* fat, greasy dumpling.

p.6 **Gutsy Gilbert. Salivating Sam** names that sound like folk-names for minor devils found in British folk-literature; no specific sources have been identified.

p.6 **gab** *Scots* mouth.

p.6 **ow're** *Scots* over.

p.6 **in the name o'** catchphrase of Tommy Lorne, Scottish pantomime comic.

p.6 **owre wi' the lave** *Scots* over with the rest.

p.6 **randy** *Scots* generally this means wild, dissipated and excitable (but it carries also the meaning of 'beggar-woman').

p.6 **skelping** *Scots* slapping or beating.

p.6 **antre** a cavern or cave.

p.6 **Pandemonium** *Greek* literally 'all the demons'.

p.6 **yon sulphur ditch** brimstone or burning sulphur is traditionally thought to be present in Hell.

p.6 **girns** *Scots* grimaces or moans.

p.7 **Lucifer** *Latin* light-bringer; applied by St Jerome to Satan in his pride and position as chief among the angels prior to his expulsion from Heaven.

p.7 **Agog** up and ready.

p.7 **Zaharoff** Sir Basil Zaharoff (1850–1936), international financier and munitions dealer who was held by some to foment war in the interests of his own commercial activities.

p.7 **Bernard Shaw** George Bernard Shaw (1856–1950), Irish dramatist (see Introduction).

p.8 **besoms** *Scots* a term of contempt for a woman.

p.8 **'The world is asleep like a peerie . . . babies of sorrow'** a pastiche of Hugh MacDiarmid's early lyric poetry (*cf.* especially, 'The Bonnie Broukit Bairn' (1925) and 'The Eemis Stane' (1925)).

p.8 **peerie** *Scots* spinning-top.

p.8 **bumming** *Scots* humming or buzzing.

p.8 **An impromptu** *French* an improvised musical piece.

p.9 **bless my buttons** a mild exclamation of surprise of uncertain origin (probably here allusive also to the language of pantomime).

p.9 **the Morris** from 1913 the company of William Morris (beginning in Oxford) specialised in the production of motorcars that were seen to be particularly appropriate to the recreational motoring of the rising middle class.

p.9 **Crianlarich** on the western fringes of Perthshire at the junction of Glen Falloch,

Glen Dochart and Strath Fillan; this village is a popular base for tourists in the area.

p.9 Ardlui a village, popular as a resting and dining spot, at the northernmost point of Loch Lomond.

p.9 Ashtaroth a demon riding a dragon and holding a viper, notable also for his foul breath and said to be grand-treasurer in Hell.

p.10 a profiteer someone who makes an excessive profit, usually by trading in circumstances of hardship; the term was coined in the early twentieth century, probably during World War One.

p.11 Indian summer an American term for fine weather in late autumn, such weather being more common in lands occupied by the American Indians of the more western regions.

p.11 Ayala a type of champagne, very fashionable from its original production in 1850.

p.11 For pleasures are like poppies . . . into the liquid mass paraphrase of Robert Burns's 'Tam o' Shanter' (1790), *cf.* ll.58–66.

p.12 bucked *colloquial* cheered up.

p.12 attache case small rectangular case for carrying documents.

p.12 The same that oft times . . . seas in fairyland paraphrase of John Keats's 'Ode to a Nightingale' (1820), *cf.* ll.68–70.

p.12 blushful Hippopotamus Keats's 'Ode to a Nightingale': 'O for a beaker full of the warm South,/Full of the true, the blushful Hippocrene,/With beaded bubbles winking at the brim' (ll.15–17).

p.12 Shelley Percy Bysshe Shelley (1792–1822), English Romantic poet, contemporary of Byron and Keats.

p.13 opera creams a kind of biscuit made with vanilla and broken nuts.

p.13 Balloch small town in West Dunbartonshire on the southern shore of Loch Lomond.

p.13 duckums *colloquial* term of endearment.

p.13 seraph a type of angel of the highest order, usually depicted with six wings.

p.13 ruling elder see note to p.2 above.

p.13 the War World War One (1914–18).

p.13 comprendre tout, c'est tout

pardonner *French* to understand all is to forgive all.

p.14 full of oats to 'feel one's oats' is a colloquial term for being lively; of uncertain origin, but probably related to 'sowing one's wild oats'.

p.14 palliness friendliness.

p.14 poodlefaking describing a man who cultivates the friendship of women for professional advantage; more generally, a 'ladies man'.

p.14 jazz about as used here meaning to have a generally good time (but in the early twentieth century 'jazz' was also slang for sexual intercourse).

p.14 Peace, perfect peace is the title of a hugely popular hymn (1875) by E. H. Bickersteth.

p.14 vanity bag a small handbag usually containing mirror, powder-puff and other makeup.

p.14 shipshape things arranged in orderly fashion.

p.14 a daunder *Scots* a stroll.

p.15 The Corporation the Corporation of Glasgow, the city municipal authority.

p.15 oxter *Scots* armpit (here figurative): 'accompany you down to the burn'.

p.15 baking soda bicarbonate of soda used in cake-baking, and as a simple remedy for calming an upset stomach.

p.15 second oldest profession in the world the first, reputedly, being prostitution.

p.15 Kirk Session meeting of the minister and his elders in the Church of Scotland, to oversee the financial and other affairs of the parish.

p.16 cant to speak in pietistic fashion.

p.16 Gifts to the Lord! probably a humorous (by Bridie) play on the common expression 'gifts from the Lord'.

p.16 University Court the governing body of the University (of Glasgow).

p.16 highfaluting *colloquial* 'highfalutin' (from the mid nineteenth century possibly a combination of 'high' and 'fluting') meaning pompous or over-showy.

p.16 Bailie *Scots* a municipal councillor serving as a magistrate.

p.16 whole jing bang a colloquial expression of uncertain origin from the mid nineteenth century meaning the whole company or affair.

p.17 "One fine day a ship . . ." an aria from *Madame Butterfly: A Japanese Tragedy* (1904) by Giacomo Puccini.

p.17 daffing *Scots* acting playfully.

p.17 Rotary Club the world's first service club, the Rotary Club of Chicago, Illinois, USA, was formed in 1905 by Paul P. Harris, an attorney who wished to recapture in a professional club the same friendly spirit he had felt in the small towns of his youth. The name 'Rotary' derived from the early practice of rotating meetings among members' offices. By the 1920s the idea had spread to the United Kingdom, becoming a fashionable middle-class social gathering undertaking also miscellaneous works of charity.

p.17 jam day a play on the phrase 'jam tomorrow', meaning a pleasant thing continually promised.

p.17 tapsalteerie *Scots* upside down, topsy-turvy or in chaos.

p.17 Cincinnati Dip probably a recipe for a bread dip called Cincinnati Beer-Cheese dip.

p.17 sodger *Scots* soldier.

p.17 topping *colloquial* from the eighteenth century meaning excellent.

p.18 Buckingham Palace official residence of the British Royal Family in London.

p.18 stiver *Scots* a small coin, originally associated with the Low Countries.

p.18 manging *Scots* leading astray or wandering confusedly.

p.18 pococurantic indifferent or nonchalant.

p.18 kelpie *Scots* a water-demon, usually in the form of a horse that lures people to their deaths.

p.18 mutt colloquial expression current in the 1920s for a stupid or incompetent person; probably derived from the cartoon films of *Mutt and Jeff*.

p.19 Nap a card game where each player receives five cards and attempts to predict the number of tricks they will win.

p.19 bucolic rustic.

p.19 Lotos eaters in Homeric legend those who ate of the lotus tree descended into luxurious laziness, forgetting all thoughts of friends and returning to their homes.

p.19 Ach, to blazes *colloquial* meaning 'Ach, to Hell'.

p.19 Mr. Copperfield *David Copperfield* (1849–50) is a novel by Charles Dickens. The line perhaps implies that Pettigrew is taking the role of the amiable lunatic Mr. Dick with whom Copperfield lodges for a time.

p.19 "Melodious birds sing madrigals" Christopher Marlowe, 'The Passionate Shepherd to His Love' (published 1600), l.8.

p.19 Eblis a jinn, or ruler of the evil genii or fallen angels in Arabian mythology.

p.20 covey a group or party, usually of birds.

p.20 louse *Scots* to let loose.

p.20 Rhadamanthus in Greek mythology, along with Minos and Æacus, one of the three judges of Hell.

p.20 gash *Scots* ghastly.

p.20 athwart across.

p.20 pernickety *Scots* fussy.

p.20 golden trumpets in a number of places in the Judeo-Christian tradition, the coming of the Lord is heralded by the sound of ornate trumpets sometimes blown by angels.

p.20 cherubim a winged creature whose wings in some depictions help form the throne of God, and which is one rank below the seraphim.

p.20 Fourth Seat in the Christian creed, Christ is depicted 'seated at the right hand of the father', with the Trinitarian implication that the Holy Spirit is notionally on the left-hand side; Mr. Carmichael's talk of a 'Fourth Seat' then betokens his egotism.

p.20 showfoor chauffeur.

p.20 blithering *colloquial* from mid nineteenth century, senselessly chattering (perhaps related to the *Scots* 'blethering').

p.20 cocksure absolutely (presumptuously) certain.

p.20 sky-pilot *colloquial* a member of the clergy.

p.20 twenty quid *colloquial* twenty pounds.

p.20 **spoke in my wheel** interfere in my projects (from the pin or spoke once put into wheels to skid a cart when it was going downhill).

p.20 **diddle** *colloquial* from the early nineteenth century (probably from the earlier 'condiddle') meaning to swindle.

p.20 **Doll about** *colloquial* appear dressed up finely.

p.20 **stow your gab** *Scots* fill or feed (in other words, stop) your chatter.

p.20 **stingy** mean.

p.21 **shilpit** *Scots* thin or starved-looking.

p.21 **viper . . . in my bosom** coined in 1713 at Cambridge in a sermon by Waterland where, referring to pride, he talks of 'this lurking viper in our Bosoms'.

p.21 **cattishness** *colloquial* spitefulness.

p.21 **Tableau** a group of people forming a picturesque scene.

p.22 **for the love of Mike** *colloquial* 'for the love of idling'.

p.22 **Mount Etna** the highest active volcano in Europe, standing over the Straits of Messina.

p.22 **skinny** *Scots* thin.

p.22 **jaunt** an excursion, especially a pleasure trip.

p.22 **sair** *Scots* sore.

p.22 **Moloch** the god of the Ammonites to whom human sacrifices were burnt.

p.22 **awa** *Scots* away.

p.22 **Rolls-Royce** expensive and powerful car made by the company of this name.

p.22 **Upsy daisy** *colloquial* encouragement to a child on being lifted.

p.22 **Alarums and excursions** sounds of war or warlike activity; the phrase is used as a stage direction for the moving of soldiers across stage, most notably in Shakespeare's plays.

p.22 **the Limit** a situation in which behaviour has been taken to the edge of acceptability.

p.22 **an Institution** here, in its contemporary usage, a shelter or a house run by society or a private organisation taking the vulnerable or the impoverished into some form of charitable care.

p.23 **The Aunties** here Faith, Hope and Charity are described as though they were cosy (perhaps bourgeois) family characters.

p.23 **pull up your stockings** *colloquial* 'get yourself organised'.

p.23 **Diner Dansant** *French* Dîner Dansant: dinner dance.

p.24 **thix, thix, thix** six, six, six, the number of the beast or the Antichrist (Revelation 13:18).

p.24 **buthing** buzzing.

p.24 **piffle** *colloquial* talk or action in a trifling manner.

p.24 **Come wind . . . horse to back** *cf. Macbeth* V, v, ll.51–2.

p.25 **Kelvinshields** a conflation of two 'respectable' middle-class areas of Glasgow, Kelvinside and Pollokshields.

p.25 **the Peace . . . that Passeth All Understanding** 'And the peace of God, which surpasses all understanding, will guard your hearts and your thoughts in Christ Jesus' (Philippians 4:7).

p.25 **thermogene** a kind of medicated cotton wool.

p.25 **I've took** *ungrammatical* it should be 'I've taken'.

p.25 **How blue the Heavens** is possibly a frivolous reference to Walter Donaldson's highly popular song, 'My Blue Heaven' (1927).

p.25 **elevenses** light refreshment, such as tea or coffee, taken around eleven in the morning.

p.25 **Ah! catch the flitting moments . . . a jot of it** lines based on the opening lines of the poem 'To the Virgins, to Make Much of Time' (*c*.1647) by Robert Herrick:

Gather ye rosebuds while ye may,
Old Time is still a-flying;
And this same flower that smiles today
Tomorrow will be dying.

The third of the lines Lady Groundwater recites, however, paraphrases Edward Fitzgerald's 'Nor all your Tears wash out a Word of it' (l.284 of the *Rubaiyat of Omar Khayam* (1859)).

p.26 **Glittering scales below the apple-tree** not identified, probably a poetic turn of phrase by Bridie himself.

p.26 bismuth a medicinal metallic compound drunk for tonic purposes.

p.26 Barcarole a song sung by Venetian gondoliers suggestive of the rocking of a boat.

p.26 "Tales of Hoffman" opera (1881) by Jacques Offenbach.

p.26 Schumann's "Unfinished Symphony" . . . **fate knocking at the door** two movements of a symphony composed in 1829 by Robert Schumann (1810–56), a moment of the first movement does allude to a knocking at the door, but less famously than in the case of the first movement of Beethoven's Fifth Symphony (1808).

p.26 dwawm *Scots* giddiness, or, here, meaning to take one into a daydream state.

p.27 the "Tatler" originally a satirical current affairs magazine founded in 1709, and which has gone through various incarnations in several different countries since then, incorporating culture, fashion and society gossip.

p.27 "Pilgrim's Progress" a prose dream allegory (1678 & 1684) by John Bunyan in which the Christian pilgrim attains a strong awareness of the evil around him.

p.27 gigot from *French* a leg of mutton.

p.27 Do-you-believe-in-Fairies Guild Bridie here satirises the renewed belief in spiritualism and the supernatural from towards the end of Word War One into the 1920s; the most famous example of this tendency being the credulous endorsement by Arthur Conan Doyle of alleged photographs of fairies in 1917.

p.28 bye the bit idiomatic *Scots* through the hard times.

p.28 more nor I can chew idiomatically *Scots*: 'more than I can chew'.

p.28 puir *Scots* poor.

p.28 midges a small blood-sucking gnat-like insect particularly prevalent in the Highlands of Scotland in the summer.

p.28 faither *Scots* father.

p.28 bigg *Scots* build.

p.28 Gehannum 'Gehennum' has a diffuse coinage in supernatural lore, referring, among other things, to an afterlife where all is dreams.

p.28 bittie *Scots* a bit.

p.28 Lambikin term of endearment for a child.

p.29 Scottish Episcopal Church after the Reformation the Episcopal Church, Protestant with Bishops, was the established church in Scotland, but it was disestablished in 1689, being replaced by the Presbyterian Church.

p.29 distinguy a version of 'distingué', meaning to appear fine or eminent.

p.29 United Free Church in 1929 (i.e. the year after this play was written) the majority of the Presbyterian United Free Church joined with the established Church of Scotland, ending the major schism among Scottish Presbyterians which had come about in the 'Disruption' of 1843.

p.29 Trial of the Thirty-nine Bishops . . . **Bloody Mary of Argyle** a garbling of different aspects of British religious history including the thirty-nine Articles of the Church of England and the persecution of Protestants, most of them Londoners (hence the reference to Smithfield Market), by Queen Mary of England from 1555 to 1558. 'Bonny Mary of Argyle' is a Scottish ballad.

p.29 Vacuum in Venice presumably a garbling of the Vatican in Rome.

p.29 Wordsworth's "Evangelic" presumably John Wesley's eighteenth-century 'Through the Pure Evangelic Word'.

p.29 chappie in the Bible . . . **hence-forward** this is perhaps a deliberately vague, perhaps even non-existent, reference to scripture that perhaps points to Hamish's wooliness of character.

p.29 "You're for it . . . for a mucker" here are various *colloquial* phrases portending something bad to happen.

p.29 the Salvation Army an organisation founded by William Booth in 1865 in the East End of London to bring both food and shelter and the word of God to the urban poor.

p.30 "Proud rank is but a penny stamp,/For a' that and so forth" 'The rank is but the guinea's stamp,/The Man's the gowd for a' that.' (Robert

Burns, 'For a' that and a' that' (1795), ll.7–8).

p.30 douce *Scots* respectable.

p.31 a Scottish Public School in other words, a private school.

p.31 The Hebrew . . . commercial career an all too common anti-Semitic view of the money-grasping Jew current in the interwar years.

p.32 Parnathuth Parnassus, mountain in Greece sacred to the Muses.

p.33 In Nomine Angelorum! *Latin* 'In the name of the Angels'.

p.33 Skittles! a game where the player knocks over pins to demonstrate his skill.

p.33 as batty as a hatter the usual phrase is 'as mad as a hatter' supposedly because the glue used by some hat-makers could affect their senses.

p.33 the Royal Scot from 1862 a sleeper train from Euston, London, to Aberdeen, Edinburgh and Glasgow that was built for speed and comfort and which set off punctually every night from the same platform.

p.34 the baby leopard gets his Alenbury an alenbury is an early twentieth century brand of baby bottle.

p.35 cantharides 'Spanish fly', taken as an aphrodisiac.

p.35 "Sabbath Pictorial" there was a newspaper in Britain called the 'Sunday Pictorial'.

p.35 the "Queen" . . . "Homes and Gardens" . . . "Spectator" . . . "News of the World" all current periodicals of the day.

p.35 Wells Herbert George Wells (1866–1946), frequently a writer of fiction from an outside perspective, for instance, and with particular pertinence here, *The Wonderful Visit* (1895), where human life is viewed by an angel.

p.35 Barrie James Matthew Barrie (1860–1937), writer, among other works, of the immensely popular *Peter Pan* (1904), which is probably the point of reference here in the context of Bridie's play.

p.35 Beverley Nichols (1898–1983), a prolific writer on subjects ranging from religion to politics and travel.

p.35 near the knuckle *colloquial* verging on the indecent.

p.35 nincompoop *colloquial* a simpleton.

p.36 Bide a wee *Scots* wait a moment.

p.36 cockiemajinkies *Scots* variant on 'Cockmaleerie' or cock, meaning, metaphorically 'proud' ('jinkies' in Scots also can connote a wanton woman).

p.36 Hand of Glory a severed human hand used for black magic.

p.36 Deid *Scots* dead.

p.36 Nippit *Scots* pinched.

p.36 medlar there are various types of medlar tree which grow fruit to be plucked and eaten when these are half-rotten.

p.36 Bale *Scots* here a word with the connotation of 'festering' (as in a boil).

p.36 licht *Scots* light.

p.36 bricht *Scots* bright.

p.36 Oleoc ni es iuq retson r-r-r-retap a version of words from the 'Black Mass', where Satan is conjured up in parody of the Christian doctrine of the Eucharist: 'Retap Retson Iuq Tse Ni Sileac Etcnas Rutaloc Nemon Muut. Tainev Munger Muut. Taif Satnulov Aut Tu Ni Oleac Te Ni Arret.'

p.37 Sathanas Satan.

p.37 Haud you your wheesht *Scots* 'Hold you your whisper', in other words 'Don't make a sound'.

p.37 Awa' *Scots* away.

p.37 yetts *Scots* gates.

p.37 waur *Scots* were.

p.37 Pas de Quatre a ballet dance for four people.

p.37 Pests and Pandemics! here words used as oaths of annoyance.

p.38 by Eblis see note above p.19.

p.38 "The League of Pussy's Protectors" a sardonic reference to the likes of the British Union for the Abolition of Vivisection (BUAV) founded in 1898, part of the early Animal Rights movement, increasingly popular in the decades following World War One.

p.38 high-faluted see note above p.16.

p.38 the Silly House *colloquial* lunatic asylum.

p.38 Official Receiver an official appointed by the court to handle the property of a bankrupt or an insane person.

p.38 vampires a fabulous creature, often

originally the spirit of a criminal or heretic, returned from the dead in the form of a bat to suck the blood of the living.

p.38 wages of sin 'the wages of sin is death' (Romans 6:23).

p.39 the Malmaison popular name for restaurants etc, implying indulgent living (here in the context of the play, of course, the literal translation of 'bad house' is to be borne in mind).

p.39 sotto voce *Italian* in an undertone.

p.39 Goat Fell the highest mountain on the Isle of Arran off the west coast of Scotland.

p.39 Saul on the road to Damascus Saul the Pharisee, persecutor of the early Christians, was converted to Christianity after experiencing a blinding light on the road to Damascus (Acts 9:3–9 & 22:6–11).

p.39 Burgundy wine from eastern France of a very rich red colour.

p.39 swithering *Scots* dithering.

p.40 blued *colloquial* squandered.

p.40 siller *Scots* silver.

p.40 tick *colloquial* a despicable person.

p.40 mutt see note above p.18.

p.40 in such a funk *colloquial* in a state of panic.

p.41 Hymen's torch Hymen in Greek mythology is the name given to the god of marriage, depicted as a youth carrying a torch.

p.41 Ira whack them, as the Bible bids 'He that spareth the rod hateth his son' (Proverbs 8:24).

p.42 Accidia will advance characteristic of Bridie's attitude to his art (see the Introduction).

p.42 Fireman in the pit presumably the man in charge of the theatre fire-curtain and here located in the orchestra pit (though Bridie is clearly maintaining his punning on the demonic).

p.42 Propaganda Play a term in existence since at least 1905 referring to a drama written or performed to promote a particular ideology or view of life.

Note on the Performance and Text of *The Anatomist*

The Anatomist was first performed on 6th July 1930, by Robert Fenemore's Masque Theatre Company at the Lyceum Theatre, Edinburgh. It featured the following Cast:

MARY BELLE DISHART .... Evelyn Neilson
AMELIA DISHART .... Maud Risdon
WALTER ANDERSON .... Ireland Wood
JESSIE ANN .... Doreen Cayley
DR. KNOX .... Alfred Wild
RABY .... David Wilton
LANDLORD .... Halliday Mason
MARY PATERSON .... Mattie McLennan
JANET .... Doreen Cayley
DAVIE PATERSON .... William Hendry
BURKE .... Douglas Allen
HARE .... Eric Messiter

The Play was produced by Claud Gurney.

The Anatomist was first published in the collection *The Anatomist and Other Plays* [including *Tobias and the Angel* and *The Amazed Evangelist*] (Constable: London, 1930) and was reprinted with minor corrections in a revised separate edition (Constable: London, 1932). Emendations have been made to the 1932 edition, the last previously corrected edition.

Explanatory Notes

The following publications have been useful sources of historical information:

Bailey, Brian, *Burke and Hare: The Year of the Ghouls* (Mainstream Publishing: Edinburgh & London, 2002).

Edwards, Owen Dudley, *Burke and Hare* (Polygon: Edinburgh, 1980).

Lonsdale, Henry, *A Sketch of the Life and Writings of Robert Knox the Anatomist* (Macmillan: London, 1870).

Taylor, Clare L., 'Robert Knox' in *Oxford Dictionary of National Biography* Vol. 32 (Oxford University Press: Oxford, 2004).

p.43 A lamentable comedy the genre allusion here recalls 'tragi-comedy' and perhaps also 'farce', two possible readings in the mode of the play. This is the first in a surfeit of explicit genre tags in the play.
p.43 West Port Murders Burke and Hare carried out their murders in the West Port (the west gate area of the ancient city) of Edinburgh between December 1827 and October 1828.
p.43 Dedication: To Rona Mavor Rona Locke Bremner (1897–1985), wife of Dr. Osborne Henry Mavor ('James Bridie').
p.43 L.R.C.S. Licentiate of the Royal College of Surgeons.
p.43 M.D. *Latin* Medicinae Doctor (Doctor of Medicine).
p.43 modern type of chronicle play the chronicle play, charting the historic significance of a king or hero whose tale provides a lesson for the present, came to prominence from the late sixteenth century in England. Progenitors of the genre are Shakespeare and Marlowe. Bridie clearly has in mind George Bernard Shaw's *Saint Joan: A Chronicle Play* (1923) about Joan of Arc and her visionary defiance of received authority.
p.43 fable generally, a story that is circumscribed by a clear moral lesson.

p.43 Robert Knox (1791–1862), anatomist and ethnologist born in Edinburgh.

p.43 who was so theatrical in his life and habit Knox's lectures are described as being well 'rehearsed' and for these he took great care in his dress and wore fine jewellery (see, especially, the very useful account of Taylor above).

p.44 Lonsdale see bibliographical note above.

p.44 Knoxophile a lover or admirer of Knox.

p.44 versatile Frenchman more than the 'canny Scot' stereotypes of the excitable Frenchman and the cautious Scot.

p.44 confluent small-pox as a child Knox contracted confluent small-pox which left him blind in one eye as well as disfigured in part of his face.

p.44 obiter dicta *Latin* passing or incidental remarks.

p.44 dandy a fop, or a male who pays too much attention to their dress and appearance.

p.44 watch-seals small engraved figures or illustrations worn about the person decoratively.

p.44 patch on his blind eye Bridie presents Knox as a dandy, for which there is some justification, but the reason for him covering up his left eye might simply be its unsightliness (he had an 'ugly raised cicatrix in the cornea') [*Dictionary of Scientific Biography* (New York, 1970), p.414].

p.44 Waterloo battle on 18th June 1815 at which British forces under the command of the Duke of Wellington defeated the French under their emperor Napoleon Bonaparte. This battle soon precipitated the second and final abdication of Napoleon. Knox treated the wounded from the battle at Brussels.

p.44 bulldog a large-headed smooth-haired breed of dog often taken as a symbol of the British character (Bridie here, as elsewhere in the preface, plays around with racial characteristics in mimicry of Knox's own interest).

p.44 pluck referring to the heart as the metaphorical seat of courage.

p.44 South Africa in April 1817 Knox

was sent to the Cape of Good Hope as a surgeon with the 72nd Highlanders and he served also in the Cape Frontier War of 1819.

p.44 Mr. Shaw George Bernard Shaw (1856–1950), Irish dramatist.

p.44 anti-vivisectionist someone opposed to surgical operations on living animals for the purposes of research.

p.45 resetting receiving stolen goods with intent to turn them to profit.

p.45 Higher Criticism through textual and literary analysis, principally, the study of everything pertaining to the meaning and interpretation of the Bible.

p.45 fled to Glasgow and thence to London Knox went to London in 1842, but worked briefly in Glasgow in November 1844 at the Portland Street School of Medicine (by the end of that month he returned fees received from his students so as to demit their tuition). During the late 1850s and early 1860s he was again employed in London as an anatomist at the Cancer Hospital at Brompton. This brought some final acceptance to Knox who had been struck off the roll of members of the Royal Society of Edinburgh in 1848.

p.45 Leith traditionally the main sea-port for Edinburgh.

p.45 bootleggers *colloquial* a smuggler or trafficker of illicit goods.

p.45 Liston Robert Liston (1794–1847), anatomist and surgeon at the University of Edinburgh and the city's Infirmary. Highly popular with students, but renowned also for supposedly coarse manners and rudeness to his inferiors; general elements of Liston's character are incorporated into the character of Knox by Bridie.

p.45 Burke and Hare William Burke (1792–1829), born in Urney, County Tyrone, Ireland. William Hare (1790–c.1860), born in Newry, County Down, Ireland.

p.45 incaution of their race one of a surfeit of ethnic stereotypes in the play, where, in a sense, the voice of Knox the ethnologist is 'heard'.

p.45 Mary Paterson (1799/1800–1828), an Edinburgh prostitute.

p.45 **William Fergusson** (1808–77), pupil to and, from the age of twenty, demonstrator for Knox.

p.45 **Davie Paterson . . . became a hero** probably because he was allegedly author of a sixpenny pamphlet produced when the scandal broke, *Letter to the Lord Advocate, disclosing the accomplices, secrets and other facts relative to the Late Murders*. It is improbable that Paterson was, in fact, author of the pamphlet.

p.45 **Raby . . . dog-like loyalty** Raby's name is clearly a pun on 'rabid'.

p.45 **The play does not pretend to be anything but a story with an historical background** this statement clearly contradicts the earlier definition of the play as a 'fable' and should alert us to Bridie's or the preface's narrator's slippery playfulness that is of a piece with the protean self-presentation of Robert Knox himself in the play.

p.45 **mob** from the rapid increase of urbanisation in the mid-eighteenth century to the period of revolutionary unrest in the 1790s down to the present, fear of the mob as a potential interference with the rightful leader is a strong cultural phenomenon in Britain.

p.45 **stoning the prophets** Jesus cites the rejection and stoning of prophets in Matthew 23:37 (see also Luke 13:34).

p.45 **de Quincey** Thomas de Quincey (1785–1859) produced an essay, 'On Murder as one of the Fine Arts' (1827), for *Blackwood's Magazine*.

p.46 **withdrawing-room** or 'drawing' room into which bourgeois households would 'withdraw' to entertain guests.

p.46 **autumn in 1828** the play opens with Knox at the height of his reputation as a teacher. At this time his anatomy class of four hundred and five students was the biggest in Britain. He was also coming towards the end of an eleven-month period (29th November 1827–2nd November 1828) in which he received from Burke and Hare twelve cadavers who had been murdered.

p.46 **'I attempt . . . fever and pain'** A song from Act III of Henry Purcell's *The Indian Queen* (1695).

p.46 **Calais . . . Madeira** the former a port in northern France and a regular point of disembarkation for British tourists to Europe, the latter a group of Portuguese islands occupied twice by Britain during the wars with France in the early nineteenth century. In other words, both are highly predictable destinations for Britons.

p.46 **Christopher Columbus** (1451–1506), Genoese discoverer of the 'New World'. Columbus's voyaging into uncharted territory sardonically contrasts with Walter's highly predictable journeys.

p.46 **waggish** joking.

p.46 **pulled each other's hair and torn each other's clothes** the first of many references in the play, although here supposedly innocent, to the abuse of the human body.

p.47 **married . . . unhappily** the details of Knox's private life are somewhat obscure; he married Mary Russell in 1824 and she bore him six children before dying of complications from the birth of the last of these children in 1841. One version of Knox's time in Edinburgh has him keeping an 'official' residence overseen by his sister Mary and maintaining a private residence for his wife and children. Another contrary strand in the legend has him a devoted family man. The actual facts of his domestic life remain elusive, however, given much contradiction across a number of biographical accounts.

p.47 **Irish tinker in the street** itinerant mender of pots and other metal kitchen utensils.

p.47 **protégé** someone under the guidance of a superior influence.

p.47 **fey** having a premonition of doom (Mary's 'feyness' might be read as merely romantic affectation since no harm ultimately comes to anyone actually connected to her in the play).

p.47 **ogreish** an ogre is a monster, often gigantic and man-eating.

p.47 **Purcell** Henry Purcell (1659–95) English composer.

p.47 **'To make us seek ruin and love those that hate'** see note above (p.46).

p.48 skein of wool a loose coil or tangle of wool sometimes wound on a yarn.

p.48 Fife region on the opposite side of the Firth of Forth from Edinburgh. Here, in Walter's eyes, implicitly, it stands for a parochial place distant from cosmopolitan Edinburgh where he sees his real work with Dr. Knox.

p.48 Walter, please don't gesticulate here, as with Knox and Mary, we find the notion of artifice and acting in Walter's behaviour.

p.48–9 tragedy . . . French farce these further genre references, at opposite extremes to one another, counterpoint the gruesome reality at the centre of the play and incorporate Knox's behaviour in the posing, artificial realm that is prognosticated as that of the bourgeois class.

p.49 sack-'em-up men those who exhume and steal corpses; a term in current use from the 1780s.

p.49 resurrectionists those who exhume and steal corpses; a term in current use since 1776.

p.49 moulting carrion crow a bird that feeds off decaying animals, here shedding feathers, and so we have here the theme, prominent in the play, of divesting appearances to reveal reality underneath.

p.49 Buonaparte and Wellington Napoleon Bonaparte (1769–1821), emperor of France, and Arthur Wellesley (1769–1852), British general who was given much of the credit for defeating Napoleon. At the time when the play is set, both men are seen as possessors of 'great lives', and are of huge interest to biographers (a phenomenon that has never abated).

p.49 comparative anatomy of the eye during the 1820s Knox gave a series of papers to the Wemerian Society and the Royal Society of Edinburgh, confirming his brilliant reputation. The most noted and lasting of these was 'Observations on the Comparative Anatomy of the Eye'.

p.50 Amaryllis a Greek term for a country-girl, often a shepherdess, familiar in the work of Theocritus, Ovid and Virgil.

p.50 idyll a picturesque pastoral scene or a name for a genre of poetry itself featuring such subject-matter.

p.50 Mr. Daphnis Anderson Daphnis is the Sicilian shepherd who invented pastoral poetry according to Greek mythology.

p.50 Your only jig-maker this is the first of several roles that Knox facetiously offers for himself in the drawing room. Again, then, we note the theme of acting.

p.51 Une affaire des tendresses *French* an affair of love or of the heart.

p.51 Eureka 'I have found it', the cry of enlightenment associated with Archimedes, the Greek mathematician.

p.51 Ach, Gott! *German* Oh, God!

p.51 rara avis *Latin* rare bird, a phrase connoting an unusual person.

p.51 Prometheus the Greek titan who stole fire and was punished for this by the god Zeus by being chained to Mount Caucasus where an eagle ate his liver every day, since his liver was renewed during the night. In Knox's utterance the eagle has become vultures, carrion-birds, as he sardonically alludes to his own elemental quest, like that of Prometheus, and its portrayal in hideous terms.

p.51 C'est vrai. C'est juste *French* It is true. It is just.

p.51 Bartholomew pigs connotes a very fat person; famously pigs were roasted whole at Bartholomew Fair, Smithfield, London.

p.51 the Militia, with a cocked hat and a blunderbuss from 1795 down to the early decades of the nineteenth century volunteer loyalist militia were formed on a local basis to safeguard Britain against invasion from France and revolutionary insurrection at home.

p.51 prig someone of precise, but unrealistically inflexible, morals.

p.52 Dr. Bell John Bell (1763–1820), surgeon and anatomist, whose house had been the scene of a fashionable social set in Edinburgh, where musical entertainment and art were enjoyed.

p.52 piquant racey.

p.52 Sidney Smith (1771–1845) English clergyman who was part of Francis

Jeffrey's circle that established the *Edinburgh Review*.

p.52 boors coarse or rude persons.

p.52 Maga *Blackwood's Magazine*, the Tory periodical formed in 1817 in opposition to what was seen as the Whig organ, the *Edinburgh Review*.

p.52 Macaulay . . . Machiavelli Thomas Babington MacCaulay (1800–1859), English writer who wrote on Niccolò Machiavelli (1469–1527), the Italian statesman said to be a proponent of the political doctrine that evil should be done if good can come of it.

p.52 chatterbox *colloquial* someone who cannot stop talking.

p.53 canaille *French* a term current from the late sixteenth century meaning, literally, a pack of dogs and used to refer to the rabble or the populace at large.

p.53 'Crucify him!' here, as elsewhere, Knox talks of his situation in messianic and religious terms, something that might seem paradoxical from a man of science.

p.53 vampire flittermice the vampire bat, as it is more commonly termed today. We might note the paradox that Knox, who is responsible in his work for drawing blood, is someone whose own blood is sought.

p.53 your harp . . . willow if a quotation, I am unable to identify it.

p.53 'I attempt from love's sickness . . .' see note to p.46 above.

p.53 Regius Professor, Alexander Monro the Third (1773–1859) third in a patriarchal line to be professor of anatomy at Edinburgh University. Monro the third took occupancy of his chair in 1817 and was to be seen as capable rather than talented at a time of huge expansion in his subject and when contemporaries such as Knox were seen as much more exciting teachers and researchers.

p.53 You are in the right to be a fool, and a fool to be in the right Knox here talks in a paradoxical riddle, a puzzling propensity sometimes associated with the Devil in folk-culture.

p.54 Judge in Chambers in typical

Protean fashion, Knox has now assumed another role.

p.54 comes from Warwickshire Raby's journey north for his education reflects the superiority of Edinburgh University at this time over any institution in England as a medical academy.

p.54 Surgeon's Square the address of Knox's dissecting rooms near the University of Edinburgh.

p.55 Canongate a district of the Old Town of Edinburgh formed around a rough track running eastwards down the rocky 'tail' of Edinburgh Castle.

p.55 Sutton Bottom many places in England are prefixed by Sutton, but none of these are followed by 'Bottom'.

p.55 Midlothian ancient county south of the Firth of Forth containing Edinburgh.

p.55 negus a mixture of wine and hot water sweetened by sugar and other flavourings, a beverage that was very fashionable from the eighteenth century.

p.55 'O wad some poo'er . . . ithers see us' Robert Burns (1759–96), 'To a Louse': 'O wad some Pow'r the giftie gie us/To see oursels as others see us!' (James Kinsley ed. *Burns: Complete Poems & Songs* (Oxford University Press, 1969), ll.43–44). Amelia exaggerates the Scots language in these lines in keeping with the long reception of Burns in Scotland as the natural voice of his country rather than as a literary artist (working more than has been acknowledged from a basis in English print orthography). The lines also reflect on the theme of perception and of the eye and seeing in the play.

p.56 spinal cord in the chick embryo Walter moves quickly to prevent Raby talking as the latter, in his choice of such raw subject-matter, is offending the propriety of the drawing room.

p.56 Mount Vesuvius an active volcano south east of Naples.

p.57 imbroglio an entanglement, an enwrapping, or even a confused heap.

p.57 Mount Olympus a mountain in northern Thessaly, Greece, considered in ancient times to be the home of the gods.

p.57 pig in an Irishman's cabin a traditional insult against the poverty and culture of the agrarian Irish, allegedly often having their pigs live with them in their homes.

p.57 impostume an abscess, a collection of pus in a cavity on the body.

p.57 imbrue moisten.

p.58 Signorina *Italian* Miss.

p.58 lunatic intermittently insane person thought to become so due to the changing cycle of the moon.

p.58 Dieu vous remercie, mon Prince *French* May God thank you, my Prince.

p.58 affianced the pledging of the intention to marry.

p.58 Sir Matthew Goudie not identified as any historical person.

p.58 aux grands sérieux *French* of the highest seriousness.

p.59 crewel-work generally, ornamental embroidery.

p.59 musical glasses a musical instrument where hemispherical glasses are fitted on an axis turned by a treadle and dipped into water; it is played by the application of the finger.

p.59 assemblies gatherings of people for social purposes, including polite conversation, that were very popular during the eighteenth and early nineteenth centuries.

p.59 quadrilles from the early eighteenth century a fashionable card-game played by four persons; later a fashionable square dance, French in origin, involving four couples.

p.59 foolish jingles or spoiling canvas here Knox speaks contemptuously of the Romantic age of expression in poetry and painting, still very fashionable in 1828. There is irony, however, in Knox's declamation about the higher quest involved in his work, a form of thinking very much in keeping with the age of Romanticism.

p.59 typhoid fever a severe infectious fever caused by a bacterium with one of the common symptoms being delirium.

p.59 Nam fuit ante Helenam, femina teterrima causa belli *Latin* from Horace, 'For there was before Helen a most loathsome woman who was the cause of war'.

p.60 carnivora a zoological term for flesh-eating animals, usually hunters,

primarily mammals; the earliest recorded usage dates from 1830, two years after the play begins.

p.60 Caffres Kaffirs or Kafirs, members of the Bantu family of South and Central Africa; used pejoratively by Arabs as a term for non-Muslims, implying, then, primitive cultural status.

p.60 quack in use from the seventeenth century, meaning someone wielding spurious medical knowledge.

p.60 Mumbo Jumbo meaningless talk, derived from the term in use from the eighteenth century for a grotesque idol said to be worshipped by certain tribes of Africans.

p.60 pagan atheist to say so Knox here reflects one orthodox Christian position that the body is outgrown as the human soul moves beyond life. There is a tension in Christian thinking, however, as eventual resurrection, with the body once more conjoined with the soul, is also a traditional Christian belief.

p.61 Mr. Liston . . . beats the guardians Liston (see note above) was one of a number of anatomists known to have organised body snatching in the pursuit of his work (though the involvement of violence against those guarding graveyards is unlikely; probably we have an example here of Knox's exaggeration).

p.61 pot-house a name for a low-dive, or insalubrious public-house.

p.61 God's benison God's blessing.

p.61 'To arms! . . . weapons in their hands' Alexander Pope (1688–1744) wrote the mock epic poem *The Rape of the Lock* (1712) from which these lines are taken (Canto V, ll.37–43).

p.62 conjunctival sac pouch behind the lower eye-lid.

p.62 Schubert . . . Rossini Franz Peter Schubert (1797–1828); Gioacchino Antonio Rossini (1792–1868).

p.62 'I attempt from love's sickness to fly in vain' see note to p.46 above.

p.63 Tuns a tun is another name for a cask or large barrel in which alcohol is kept.

p.63 Nebby *Scots* sharp or ill-natured and 'neb' also means nose.

p.63 the nicht *Scots* tonight.

p.63 figged *colloquial* insulted.

p.63 tapped your claret a tapper is one who 'taps' or draws casks of liquor (in other words a bar-keeper) and claret here is a metaphor for blood; there is, then, a clever pun being practised by Walter in his threatening of violence against Nebby.

p.63 Nae *Scots* no.

p.63 maulies *Scots* fists.

p.63 Surgeon's Hall from 1697 to 1832 the home on the south side of Surgeon's Square of the Royal College of Surgeons in Edinburgh.

p.63 aboot *Scots* about.

p.63 owre mony *Scots* over (too) many.

p.63 Bow Street runners the first regular police force set up in London, formed in the mid-eighteenth century under the authority of the Chief Magistrate at Bow Street near Covent Garden. Here the term is used ubiquitously for the police.

p.63 speirin' *Scots* asking.

p.63 Merryandrew, the Sack-'em-up man Merryandrew was the old name given to a buffoon attendant on a quack doctor at fairs.

p.63 Spune and Moudie-warp and Praying Howard spoon, (*Scots* mole) and an unidentified name (implying, perhaps, someone who raises the dead?); these three names, clearly, belong to resurrectionists.

p.63 Mid-Calder a small village in West Lothian.

p.63 awa' *Scots* away.

p.63 wi' *Scots* with.

p.63 Aye, weel *Scots* Yes, well.

p.63 kenned *Scots* knew.

p.64 Calton area below Calton Hill in Edinburgh which was densely inhabited in the 1820s.

p.64 joe *Scots* sweetheart.

p.64 bonnie *Scots* beautiful.

p.64 neb *Scots* nose.

p.64 red, red rose . . . June from Robert Burns's song of 1794, 'A red, red Rose': 'O My Luve's like a red, red rose,/That's newly sprung in June' (ll.1–2).

p.64 frae *Scots* from.

p.64 misguggle *Scots* to handle roughly.

p.64 thrapple *Scots* throat or windpipe.

p.64 mashackerel *Scots* mash.

p.64 wheesht *Scots* silence.

p.64 hame *Scots* home.

p.64 freen *Scots* friend.

p.64 Dalkeith town eight miles south-east of the centre of Edinburgh.

p.64 cordial here meaning simply sociable, but with an ironic undertow in that a cordial drink might usually have some medicinal application.

p.65 tipsy partly intoxicated (with the implication of being unsteady or about to 'tip' over).

p.65 Puir (*Scots* poor) **wee** (*Scots* little) **thing . . . your tail a' parritch** (*Scots* porridge) **and your heid** (*Scots* head) **a' wumps** 'wumps' is baby talk for 'lumps'.

p.65 greetin' *Scots* crying/weeping.

p.65 ken *Scots* know.

p.65 mair *Scots* more.

p.65 dab *obscure* perhaps meaning 'throw away'.

p.65 Nownie *Scots* an expression of soothing or of sympathy.

p.65 partan-face *Scots* 'crab-face'.

p.65 mooshwar version of the *French*, *mouchoir* handkerchief.

p.65 Seneschal official who was top servant in a medieval household.

p.65 b' Jove (by Jove) by Jupiter (Jovis pater = 'father Jove'), supreme Roman God who determined the course of human affairs.

p.66 hap *Scots* wrap.

p.66 clash o' the toon *Scots* gossip of the town.

p.66 deil *Scots* devil.

p.66 wauken *Scots* waken.

p.66 backsettin' *Scots* relapsing.

p.66 crult a nonce word, possibly, meaning hunchback.

p.66 mangy scabby, shabby or contemptible.

p.66 Can ye sew cushions . . . bairnie (*Scots* baby) **. . . Oh, what'll I dae wi' ye?** an old lullaby collected by Robert Burns.

p.67 high-backed settle a type of seat.

p.67 lime-kiln a type of furnace in which limestone is calcined to produce lime.

p.67 gill a measure if liquid containing a quarter of a pint.

p.67 siller *Scots* silver (or coin).

p.67 Holy St. Joseph there is grim irony

in Burke's casual invocation of the saint who is patron of a good death in the Catholic tradition.

p.67 mort-cloth *Scots* a pall covering a coffin on its way to the grave. These were often hired out in the nineteenth century and so Nebby's remark implies the mercenary nature of Burke and Hare.

p.67 prate to blab or talk superfluously.

p.67 make a cat laugh presumably, because cats are usually so inattentive to what humans are doing.

p.67 shebeen a house selling liquor which is unlicensed.

p.67 puck in the gob *colloquial* a blow in the mouth.

p.67 shot a corpse used for anatomical dissection. According to the *Scots National Dictionary*, this usage was, in fact, popularised by the events surrounding the West Port Murders.

p.67 blatherin' *Scots* talking loquaciously.

p.67 Musha from the *Irish* 'maiseadh', literally, 'if it is so'. An exclamation of surprise.

p.67 laves *Irish English* leaves.

p.67 Slainthe *Gaelic* [Good] Health!

p.68 aye *Scots* always.

p.68 at a pinch in an urgent case.

p.68 the session the university term.

p.68 Lizars John Lizars (1791/2–1860), surgeon and extramural lecturer in anatomy, like Knox, to whom he was the biggest rival as an attractor of students.

p.68 sowl *Irish English* soul.

p.68 auld *Scots* old.

p.68 tea-kist *Scots* tea-chest.

p.68 gi'e *Scots* (including Ulster Scots) give.

p.68 Nellie Helen (or 'Nelly') Dougal (or McDougal), Burke's common-law wife.

p.68 Portobello in Knox's time a small seaside town several miles to the east of Edinburgh, today incorporated into the city.

p.68 stravagin' *Scots* wandering.

p.68 Grogan's ass-cart presumably a cart belonging to an Irish associate of Burke and Hare (not identified).

p.69 rickle *Scots* carelessly thrown together.

p.69 St. Patrick patron saint of Ireland;

Hare's untroubled supposition that the saint in his supernatural capability knows what they're doing is not only comical, but reinforces the theme of the play that respectable platitudes (such as saintly invocation, or the mores of the drawing room) are upheld in society even while, in their hypocrisy, people allow evil to happen.

p.69 sentries at the cemeteries during several outbreaks of bodysnatching in Britain in the late eighteenth and early nineteenth centuries, some parishes paid to have their cemeteries guarded at night (small watch-huts can still be found in some church graveyards to this day; for instance, a very fine example exists at Baldernock parish church in the hills above Torrance near Glasgow).

p.69 rampagin' *Scots* raging.

p.69 owre by *Scots* over the way.

p.69 forbye *Scots* besides.

p.69 a dram a small drink of spirits.

p.69 tripes *colloquial* bodily insides.

p.69 A wheen o' Jezebels a number of dubious women.

p.69 we'll play the pump on him pour water (from a pump) on him to help induce sobriety.

p.69 au revoir *French* goodbye.

p.70 Deevil sain us! Devil bless us.

p.70 messan *Scots* dog.

p.70 breeks *Scots* trousers.

p.70 sneck up *Scots* shut up (a sneck is a door-latch, with the metaphorical implication that this is to be closed).

p.70 phiz *slang* the face (from physiognomy).

p.71 hantle ower muckle *Scots* a great deal over much.

p.71 weeshy *Scots* silent.

p.71 warlock generally, an evil spirit.

p.71 frichtit *Scots* frightened.

p.71 shilpit *Scots* thin or emaciated. Hare's appearance.

p.71 cratur *Scots* creature.

p.71 chiel *Scots* fellow.

p.71 fushionless wee besom *Scots* fushionless means lacking in strength or mental power; besom is a term for a low woman.

p.71 slut generally, a lazy woman.

p.71 harle *Scots* hurl.

p.71 **blithe** *Scots* happy.

p.71 **give ow're skirling like a pea-hen** *Scots* stop screeching like a female peacock.

p.71 **ae** *Scots* one.

p.72 **omadhaun** *Irish* fool (*amadan*).

p.72 **alannah** *Irish* my child (*o* or *a* followed by *leanbh* = child).

p.72 **Venus herself go back into the say** the Roman goddess of beauty and love, said to have sprung out of the sea.

p.72 **gey** *Scots* very.

p.72 **demijohn** a glass bottle with a full body and a narrow neck, being often enclosed in wickerwork.

p.73 **'And if you despise my statutes . . . And I will set my face against you'** see Leviticus 26.

p.73 **twa callants** *Scots* two (fine) young men.

p.73 **feart** *Scots* afraid.

p.73 **Dr. Wharton Jones** Thomas Wharton Jones (1808–91), physiologist and ophthalmic surgeon who was Knox's demonstrator. In the wake of the Burke and Hare scandal, Wharton Jones left for Glasgow in 1829, after which he had a spell working in Ireland before returning to London.

p.73 **canting** talking with hypocritical piety.

p.73 **humbug** fraud.

p.74 **corpse-reviver** various alcohol cocktail ('hair of the dog') hangover cures are so known.

p.74 **Queensferry** small town on the south shore of the Forth river, three miles from Edinburgh.

p.74 **joco** *Scots* facetious.

p.74 **on the randan** *colloquial* riotous (usually with the involvement of alcohol).

p.74 **gey** *Scots* very.

p.74 **yon** *Scots* that.

p.74 **Book of Books. The very Word of the fairest amang** (*Scots* among) **the ten thousand of the altogether lovely** this sounds biblical but is not a direct quotation from any book of the Bible in particular.

p.74 **Dr. Barclay** John Barclay (1758–1826), anatomist, to whom Knox was first assistant and then (from 1825) partner in the provision of anatomy lessons.

p.74 **eerie** *Scots* uneasiness that something supernatural is about to happen.

p.74 **deid** *Scots* dead.

p.74 **ben** *Scots* in or towards.

p.75 **ould** (*Irish–English* old) **soldier** Burke had served for seven years in the Donegal militia.

p.75 **the colic** paroxysms in the stomach due to bowel problems.

p.75 **guinea** a sum of money equivalent to 21 shillings (or £1.05 in modern UK currency).

p.75 **Holy St. Patrick** the patron saint of Ireland.

p.76 **keek** *Scots* to peep.

p.77 **Hoots, toots** *Scots* an interjection expressing incredulity.

p.77 **a man's heart stopped when he looked at her** ironically, of course, it was here a woman's heart that stopped not long after a man looked at her.

p.78 **Rigor mortis** *Latin* stiffening of the body after death.

p.78 **trull** a prostitute.

p.78 **Et ego in Arcadia** *Latin* Et in Arcadia ego ('And I too in Arcadia'), a mysterious tomb inscription, the voice of Death, often found in classical paintings. On the face of it, Knox here is being emollient to Anderson implying that Mary Paterson has gone to the happy, pastoral place that is Arcadia; but he is also in a sense continuing his diagnosis that Walter to some extent inhabits a realm of unreality.

p.78 **divine science** an oxymoron typical of the play.

p.78 **buck** *colloquial* young male.

p.78 **blood-money** here, money paid to a hired murderer or betrayer, of which Judas Iscariot is the archetype.

p.79 **prosector** someone who dissects dead bodies or animals in the context of teaching instruction.

p.79 **gaby** the state of being talkative (from 'gab', variation of 'gob').

p.79 **poroncephalic** porous-headed.

p.79 **Lethe-like** in Greek mythology Lethe is a river in the underworld, Hades, to be tasted by all the dead so that they forget all they have done in their former lives.

p.79 Robert the Devil they call him this epithet was actually applied to Robert, 6th Duke of Normandy, father of William the Conqueror, due to his reputation for cruelty.

p.80 yon *Scots* those (yonder).

p.81 28th January 1829 as many as 25,000 people gathered in the Lawnmarket, Edinburgh to witness the execution of William Burke on this day.

p.81 Guid save us! *Scots* God save us!

p.81 louse *Scots* loose.

p.81 Michty *Scots* an exclamation meaning 'strange' or 'surprising'.

p.81 the chaise a light open carriage.

p.81 tassie o' tae *Scots* a small drinking cup of tea.

p.81 jiffy *slang* an instant.

p.81 griddle scones small sweet or savoury cakes made on a hot metal plate.

p.81 crood *Scots* crowd.

p.81 gangrel buddies *Scots* vagrant or tramp individuals.

p.82 demonstrator one who exhibits or describes specimens and who is otherwise involved in practical work with students as assistant to a university teacher or professor.

p.82 Dover port on the Kent coast of England.

p.82 Ower the heid o' *Scots* over the initiation of.

p.82 Fornenst *Scots* opposite.

p.82 causies *Scots* a street with cobblestones.

p.82 windies *Scots* windows.

p.82 naipkin *Scots* a pocket handkerchief.

p.82 surtout overcoat.

p.82 staunin' *Scots* standing.

p.83 paw paw usually this carries the meaning of handling in a lewd or licentious manner; here, in being applied to the desperate movement of Burke's feet, a rather nice image is brought about.

p.83 syne birled *Scots* then spun.

p.83 shouthers *Scots* shoulders.

p.83 begood *Scots* begun.

p.83 'Hang Knox' at Burke's execution cries went up of 'Bring out Hare!' and 'Hang Knox'.

p.83 smelling-salts ammonium carbonate mixed with lavender used as a stimulant in the result of a person feeling faint.

p.83 Up the close . . . who buys the beef a children's street-rhyme that began to circulate in Edinburgh from around December 1828.

p.83 Dieppe a channel port in northern France.

p.83 They'll catch a Tartar a name applied to Asiatic tribes (probably derived from 'Tartarus' or 'Hell'), some of whom had served under the notorious Genghis Khan who menaced thirteenth-century Europe.

p.84 Grand Tour from the seventeenth century it was common for young men from families of rank to undertake a tour of Western Europe as to complete their education with experience and language skills.

p.84 an old vagrant Irishwoman was found murdered . . . Gray gave the alarm on October 31st 1828 James Gray, his wife and their child were lodging with Burke when Mrs. Gray discovered in a bed the naked body of a bloody-faced woman they had been introduced to as Mrs. Mary Docherty (also known as Campbell). Gray reported this to the police and this led to the arrest and prosecution of Burke and Hare.

p.84 turned King's evidence Hare was offered immunity from prosecution on 1st December 1828 if he would reveal the truth about the murder of Mrs. Docherty and any other murders to which he had been a party. As a result he saved his own life, and the account of his and Burke's activities used at Burke's trial rested largely on his testimony.

p.84 November a year ago in November or December 1827, Burke and Hare sold to Knox's representatives their first body, that of a man named Donald who had apparently died owing rent to Hare in the cheap lodging house that he ran. Knox himself appearing on the scene agreed to pay the pair £7 10 shillings for the body.

p.84 cock-and-bull story an unbelievable story.

p.84 Paterson . . . and Wharton Jones bought the body before Knox had appeared and proposed the price for the cadaver, Burke and Hare had been met by three of Knox's students, William Fergusson, Alexander Miller and Thomas Wharton Jones.

p.84 Their next lodger was a woman . . . they put a pillow over her face the next body sold by Burke and Hare, the first that they murdered, was, in fact, an old man named Joseph who became ill while lodging with Hare. The use of the pillow to suffocate him was apparently the first and last time this method was used.

p.84 They killed about sixteen people most accounts from those by Burke himself to modern criminology writers agree that there were sixteen victims.

p.84 Christopher North is lashing him with lies 'Christopher North' (Professor John Wilson, 1785–1854) wrote in *Blackwood's Magazine*, March 1829, that Knox was 'accessory to murder'. Anderson here voices the views of Knox's biographer, Lonsdale, who protested indignantly against this charge.

p.85 They broke his windows . . . faced them with two pistols in his hands in fact Knox was cornered by a mob on 11th February 1829 at his home at 4 Newington Place and escaped by the backdoor.

p.85 life preserver a club or bludgeon.

p.87 offal waste from a carcase especially entrails and inner organs.

p.87 mealy-mouthed prissy.

p.88 riff-raff sweepings, from an Old French term; here the rabble.

p.88 Auld Reekie *Scots* Old Smokey, a name for Edinburgh and its traditionally crowded buildings which often produced a pall of lingering smoke over the city.

p.88 public dissection of Burke Burke was publicly dissected in Professor Monro's lecture room in the medical school of Edinburgh University on the morning of 29th January 1829, the day after his execution. This was in keeping with the enactment of the 1752 'Act for Preventing the Horrid Crime of Murder' which visited upon all executed murderers either this penalty or having their body hung in chains.

p.88 kenspeckle *Scots* conspicuous.

p.89 these provincial towns Knox alludes to London's status, not only in the eyes of the Scots, during the period 1770–1830, as supposedly the cultural and intellectual inferior of Edinburgh.

p.89 snell *Scots* sharp.

p.89 east wind the wind that frequently blows over Edinburgh from the North Sea to its east.

p.89 Modern Athens *The Modern Athens: A Dissection and Demonstration of men and Things in the Scotch Capital* by a Modern Greek (Robert Mudie) [London, 1825] popularised the notion of Edinburgh as a neo-classical city.

p.89 snob someone who sets too much store by the supposed divisions in social ranks.

p.89 pimp someone who solicits for and/ or lives off the earnings of a prostitute.

p.89 placeman a member of the House of Commons who held an office under the crown bringing significant personal profit.

p.89 cheap-jack a vendor of small goods whose strategy is to accept less for his wares than he first names so as to have his customers believe that they are obtaining a bargain.

p.89 parakeets a small parrot.

p.89 jackals a wild African animal which was wrongly supposed to act as a lion's hunting scout. The image has resonance with the public reputation of Burke, Hare and Knox.

p.89 she entraps great men and sucks their blood. Her streets are littered with their bones here the city is primitive, organic and vampiric. Knox's apprehension of the city as a sinister place has a pedigree at least as long as the conception of the city as a place of order and civilisation. Politically, Knox's image is a Tory conceit of the city's massing of irrational and difficult-to-control selfish human impetuses. A strong Scottish literary precedent here can be found in Tobias Smollett's *The Expedition of Humphry Clinker* (1771), where for the seemingly misanthropic Matthew Bramble, Bath and London are places of horrific, tumultuous human gathering.

p.89 phantasmagoria a series of fantastic images; here it pertains to the usage, from 1802, for a show of optical illusions.

p.90 400 students in a letter of 17th March 1829 to the *Caledonian Mercury* following on from the report of the committee appointed to investigate Knox's role in the West Port murders, the anatomist claimed to 'have a class of above 400 pupils'.

p.90 Jericho a city in Jordan, but used to indicate an indefinite place (carrying a connotation of Anderson's immaturity when we consider that it is probably taken from 2 Samuel 10:5 and 1 Chronicles 19:5: 'Tarry at Jericho until your beards be grown').

p.91 come with me to Italy there is perhaps an undertone of association with the Romantic poets, Byron, Keats and Shelley, who all for a time sought residence in Italy as they attempted to escape the conventions of British life.

p.91 barn-storming tenor barnstormer refers to a strolling player, often supposedly a second-rate actor possessed of an exaggerated style fit for the undiscriminating audiences who gathered for itinerant performances in village barns.

p.92 lint scraped linen for dressing wounds.

p.93 the cause is between Robert Knox and Almighty God here Knox stands on the principle emphasised in Presbyterianism of God alone being allowed to judge the individual.

p.93 monstrous fine fellow an oxymoronic, or protean identity such as is associated with the demonic (as in James Hogg's similarly oxymoronic character, Robert Wringhim, in the novel *The Private Memoirs and Confessions of a Justified Sinner* (1824)).

p.93 souteneur a protector of prostitutes.

p.93 pig-headed obstinate, as pigs are.

p.93 apostolic successor Apostle means one sent to preach the gospel; Knox here especially taunts Presbyterian Edinburgh in using the term to connote holy orders passed down through an unbroken chain, a doctrine especially associated with the authority of the Pope.

p.93 Cuvier, the great naturalist Georges Cuvier (1769–1832), anatomist and zoologist who was a pioneer of palaeontology and the classification of animal species.

p.93 blustering at poor Mary of Scots Mary plays upon Knox's name, relating it to John Knox, the leader of the Scottish Reformation who had attempted to lecture the Catholic Mary, Queen of Scots on her duties in government. Robert Knox, in fact, was wont to claim descent from John Knox.

p.95 buck basket a basket in which clothes are carried to the wash.

p.95 hunting horn there is deliberate ambiguity over whether this is in the hands of the anti-Knox mob, or the group revealed as being led by Raby.

p.96 Knoxites ironically, Knox now has a mob named after him.

p.96 small-clothes knee-breeches.

p.96 settled his hash to subdue or silence him ('hash' literally means a jumble).

p.96 Grassmarket an area in the Old Town of Edinburgh that was, in turn, a market area and a site associated with public executions.

p.96 Calton Hill one of the main hills near the centre of Edinburgh, site of the unfinished 'National Monument', begun in 1816 as a replica of the Parthenon in Athens as a memorial to those who had died in the Napoleonic Wars.

p.96 St. Giles Edinburgh's ancient cathedral.

p.97 distrait *French* absent-minded.

p.97 spinet a small harpsichord.

p.97 overture the instrumental prelude to a large-scale musical performance; Knox, then, is facetiously alluding to his own imminent lecture.

p.97 Cyprian Cyprus was famous as the centre of worship for Venus; Cyprian came to connote persons involved in lewdness, most especially prostitutes.

p.97 this intellectual Gomorrah Sodom and Gomorrah are the two towns destroyed by God in Genesis (18–19) for being especial centres of wickedness.

p.97 mountebanks most generally, a

buffoon or a charlatan; the term also
denotes a haranguing, showboating
quack.

p.98 Cuvier in the Academies of Paris
Knox studied briefly under Cuvier in
Paris during 1821.

Note on the performance and text of *A Sleeping Clergyman*

The play was first produced by H. K. Ayliff at the Malvern Festival on 29th July 1933, with the following cast:

The Clergyman	Godfrey Baxter
Dr. Cooper	Wilson Coleman
Dr. Coutts	Alexander Sarner
Wilkinson	Frank Moore
Cameron	Robert Donat
Mrs. Hannah	Beatrice Fielden-Kaye
Dr. Marshall	Ernest Thesiger
Harriet Cameron	Dorice Fordred
Wilhelmina Cameron	Dorice Fordred
Hope Cameron	Dorice Fordred
Mrs. Walker	Isobel Thornton
Cousin Minnie	Sophie Stewart
John Hannah	Bruce Belfrage
Sergeant	Arthur Hambling
Constable	John Rae
Donovan	Walter Roy
Sir Douglas Todd Walker	Evelyn Roberts
Lady Todd Walker	Eileen Beldon
Little Thing	Phyllis Shand
Lady Katherine	Pamela Carme
Dr. Purley	Whitmore Humphreys
A Medical Student	Kenneth Fraser

The text of *A Sleeping Clergyman* (Constable: London) was first published in a separate edition in 1933, the same edition being reprinted in the collection *A Sleeping Clergyman and Other Plays* (Constable: London, 1934). A slightly more expansive (not explicitly acknowledged) "second edition" (specifically with regard to the beginning of Act II Scene IV) is published also in *A Sleeping Clergyman and Other Plays* (Constable: London, 1934), ostensibly the same volume as that just mentioned but clearly different with regard to the text of *A Sleeping Clergyman*. The updated text in this instance is one that is frequently reprinted down to 1961. My revisions of the text in the present volume are made taking the 1933–1961 "second edition" as my base-text.

Explanatory Notes

p.99 Henry Kiell Ayliff (1872–1949) actor and director.

p.101 smoking-room a room in a house, hotel or club set aside for smoking tobacco.

p.101 neurologist a specialist in the human nervous system.

p.101 A wee drop of the auld Kirk "auld kirk" a jocular name for whisky from the late nineteenth century (presumably because in its literal reference to the established Scottish Presbyterian church as opposed to newer, post-Disruption (1843) Presbyterian communions in Scotland it implies that in choosing this anything more modern or new-fangled is eschewed).

p.101 Day of Judgment God's calling to account of individual human behaviour at the end of time.

p.101 Red King in *Through the Looking Glass* (1871) by Lewis Carroll, Alice is told that she, along with everything else, is a product of the dreams of the sleeping

Red King: "If that there King was to wake," added Tweedledum, "you'd go out – bang! – just like a candle!"

p.101 Harold Begbie (1871–1929) reactionary journalist and author of science-fiction and poetry (including of a jingoistic kind during World War I); he was also the persistent champion of the supernatural happening, the "Angel of Mons" (1914), taken as an article of patriotic faith by many in Britain.

p.101 the Royal Royal Infirmary, Glasgow.

p.102 Duthie Bay fictional place.

p.102 Caesarean Caesarean section, a method of delivering a child by cutting the walls of the mother's abdomen.

p.102 first-chop *colloquial* first-rate, from a Hindi word denoting the seal of approval.

p.102 by-blow an illegitimate person.

p.103 lame-dog *colloquial* indicating a person at some disadvantage to begin with.

p.104 phthisis pulmonary tuberculosis.

p.104 beatification the action of making or being blessed.

p.104 seeing eye supernatural vision.

p.104 guttapercha skin coagulated latex (usually taken from Malaysian trees).

p.105 got by a Presbyterian here Scottish Prebyterianism is associated with a puritanical outlook.

p.105 Hic jacet *Latin* "Here lies".

p.105 thraw *Scots* wring.

p.105 pullet a young animal, especially a chicken.

p.105 Spartan ma Sparta, the ancient capital of a Greek city-state, whose warriors were known for their courage and austerity; a Spartan mother famously handed her son a shield on going into battle with the instruction either to come back with it or on it.

p.105 hoast *Scots* coughing as an ailment.

p.105 beldame a grandmother, an old woman or a hag.

p.106 bairn *Scots* child.

p.106 lang syne *Scots* long ago.

p.106 steering wee smatchet *Scots* pestering little (rogue-like) child.

p.106 auscultating examining by listening, usually with a stethoscope.

p.107 archiepiscopal archbishop-like.

p.107 warstle *Scots* drive or force someone or something out (associated usually with the power of prayer).

p.107 quayside pub a public house in a stereotypically rough area.

p.107 Inspissated putrescence thick rotting matter.

p.107 Himmel *German* Heaven ("Ach Himmel" is said by way of an oath).

p.107 puir *Scots* poor.

p.107 the Faculty the Faculty of Medicine (at the University of Glasgow).

p.107 Joe Lister Joseph Lister (1827–1912), from 1861 Regius Professor of Surgery at Glasgow University; in 1867 he announced his discovery that carbolic acid was an antiseptic preventing wounds from going septic.

p.108 Pollokshields a middle-class suburb on the southside of Glasgow.

p.108 Pasteur Louis Pasteur (1822–1895) opposed the idea of spontaneous generation, taken to be a necessary plank of Darwinian evolution, through proving that life can only be begotten from its own kind. He worked with ferments, including those of beer and wine, and discovered that living organisms are the cause of fermentation.

p.109 Spallanzani Lazzaro Spallanzani (1729–1799), Italian priest and natural scientist, who, in the 1760s, conducted numerous important experiments in microbiology.

p.109 Voltaire pen-name of François-Marie Arouet (1694–1778), French philosopher and satirist; he became very interested in biology in the latter part of his life, supporting the idea of pre-formation, the idea that all organisms had pre-existed from the Creation. He was an admirer of Spallanzani, who similarly worked to refute epigenetic theories of life.

p.109 Blake seeing the air full of angels William Blake (1757–1827), English artist and poet, claimed that as a child he had seen angels in a tree in Peckham Rye in London.

p.109 Hippocrates (*c*.460–*c*.375 BC)

Greek physician known as the father of medicine for his work as a physician and surgeon.

p.109 circumambient ether with infusorial animalcula the world with breathing little animals.

p.109 tuberosities usually rounded swellings on the bones of the human body.

p.110 wee beasts . . . Leeuwenhoek Antonie van Leeuwenhoek (1632–1723), whose experiments with ever more refined lenses have him credited as the father of microbiology. In 1681 he observed parasites in the small intestine.

p.111 high tea a late afternoon or early evening meal similar to a light supper.

p.111 barge pole *proverbial*: "I wouldn't touch it with a barge pole."

p.111 dun a debt collector.

p.112 clay pipe a form of smoking at the cheaper end of the market in the nineteenth century, usually associated with the lower classes.

p.112 Of all the girls . . . her frigid manner loosely derivative of "The Ballad of Sally in our Alley" by Henry Carey (*c*.1687–1743).

p.113 hop over the tongs probably a variant on the idea of marrying over the broomstick, meaning to go through a quasi-marriage ceremony, in which the parties jump over a broomstick.

p.113 married in the Scots form the attitude to the marriage ceremony in Scotland was traditionally more minimalist than in England, not necessarily requiring a church, but merely a pledge in front of only two witnesses.

p.113 mumbo-jumbo see note to *The Anatomist* p.300.

p.113 blackguardly of obscure form a blackguard originally meant the lowest menial in a household.

p.113 fishwife stereotypically a female hawker of fish is full of invective, and so stands for a vulgar, scolding woman.

p.114 "recreation of the warrior" if a quotation, not identified; the meaning is clear enough as Cameron suggests that Harriet is a camp-following prostitute.

p.114 slut see note to *The Anatomist* p.303.

p.114 sot a stupid or drunken person.

p.114 potboys a bar attendant.

p.115 begrutten *Scots* tear-stained or sorrowful.

p.115 bilked cheated.

p.115 certes I assure you.

p.115 Jesus, Mary and Joseph invocation of the Holy Family in response to a shock.

p.116 déshabille *French* for a silky or fine nightdress (or négligé).

p.116 whooping cough a highly infectious disease mostly affecting children and caused by a bacterium.

p.117 Putney district in the south-west of London.

p.117 swell fashionably smart in appearance.

p.119 "The fathers have eaten sour grapes . . . set on edge" see Jeremiah 31:29.

p.119 the Row since 1785 Savile Row in London has had a reputation for bespoke tailors and fine clothing.

p.119 Mr. and Mrs. Browning Robert and Elizabeth Barrett Browning, poets.

p.120 "Oh, the days of the Kerry dancing . . . too soon" nineteenth century Irish song, "The Kerry Dance", whose chorus is:
Oh, the days of the Kerry dancing
Oh, the ring of the piper's tune
Oh, for one of those hours of gladness
Gone, alas, like our youth, too soon.

p.120 tapsalteerie see note to *The Sunlight Sonata* p.290.

p.120 fusees a large-headed match, especially useful for use in an outdoor location.

p.120 Barsac a wine from the place of this name in the southern part of the Bordeaux region.

p.121 tipsy see note to *The Anatomist* p.301.

p.121 In the sight of Heaven hackneyed phrase of uncertain origin meaning in God's eyes; in literature of the British Isles it seems first to appear in John Day's play, *Humour out of Breath* (1608).

p.121 damned radical from the early nineteenth century the term "radical" in Britain is used to denote those with inclinations to challenge the political and social status quo.

p.121 three-toed sloth from the arboreal edentate family of mammals, which hangs upside down from trees and is proverbially lazy.

p.121 besom see note to *The Sunlight Sonata* above p.288.

p.121 Ach Himmel see note to p.107 above.

p.121 Nihilist from the nineteenth century, a member of a revolutionary political party in Russia dedicated to overthrowing the established order.

p.121 bonnie see note to *The Anatomist* p.301.

p.122 a poor fish a weak character.

p.122 milkcan back to the lighthouse fresh milk has presumably been bought from a nearby lighthouse for the picnic.

p.122 breakin' the Sawbath mocking the accents of a Scots-speaker, Wilhelmina refers to the Presbyterian injunction on keeping the Sabbath clear from all human activity except worship.

p.122 heid *Scots* head.

p.123 arch waggish or teasing.

p.124 the phaeton a light four-wheeled carriage usually drawn by a pair of horses.

p.124 chuck *colloquial* throw.

p.126 Woodside Place, Glasgow a street in the west end of Glasgow, which in the final part of the nineteenth century was the abode of many medical consultants.

p.126 Balgrayhill an area near Springburn in the north of Glasgow.

p.126 nervous dyspepsia functional or psychological indigestion.

p.126 Blauds Pill named after a French physician, one of the first preparations to contain iron.

p.126 Valerian a plant-based sedative.

p.126 dovering dozing.

p.126 chaperone an older woman accompanying a younger one so as to ensure social and moral propriety.

p.127 Sodii carbonate *Latin* sodium carbonate.

p.127 granas *Latin* grains.

p.127 Acidi Hydrocyanici *Latin* hydrocyanic acid.

p.127 Diluti *Latin* diluted.

p.127 minimes *Latin* a unit of volume: 1 minim = approximately 0.06 ml.

p.127 compound infusion of gentian plant alkaloid from the gentian plant used to treat indigestion.

p.127 quantum sufficit ad *Latin* in sufficient quantity to.

p.127 misce ut fit haustus *Latin* mix as a drink is made.

p.127 signitur *Latin* label.

p.127 ter in die *Latin* three times a day.

p.128 seagreen incorruptibles Thomas Carlyle in his *The French Revolution* (1837) gave this epithet to Robespierre (a man of unhealthy complexion).

p.128 "The substance of things hoped for" perhaps a reference to Catharine Maria Sedgwick's novel *Married or Single?* (1857), where a character talks of his love as "the substance of things hoped for" (see Chapter 22).

p.128 havering *Scots* rambling or talking nonsense.

p.129 Dil. *Latin* (imperative) dilute.

p.129 the Volunteers probably the (Glasgow 1st or 2nd) Lanarkshire Rifle Volunteers, a reservist regiment.

p.130 shauchly *Scots* weak or unsteady.

p.130 weaver-kneed *Scots* knock-kneed, with the knees bent inwards.

p.130 brock *Scots* badger (though from the later nineteenth century a general term for a contemptuous person).

p.130 wabbit *Scots* feeble.

p.130 gomeril *Scots* stupid person.

p.131 weel-brocht-up *Scots* well brought up.

p.131 yon *Scots* yonder.

p.131 Dod *Scots* (euphemism) God.

p.131 gey *Scots* very.

p.132 cantrips *Scots* tricks or antics.

p.135 sent her to Switzerland through the nineteenth and into the twentieth century the mountain air of Switzerland and specialised sanatoriums were utilised by tubercular sufferers from Britain.

p.135 Great Epidemic although the epidemic referred to is the fictional one of the play, it clearly relates to the 1918 influenza epidemic which caused over 20 million deaths worldwide.

p.136 block *colloquial* man or fellow.

p.136 **gastric stomach** *tautological* fever involving the stomach.

p.137 **haud** *Scots* hold.

p.137 **"Cross Keys"** a commonly used name in Britain for many public houses during the nineteenth and twentieth centuries.

p.137 **"The King Over the Water"** . . . **Prince Charlie** the toast "the King over the water" was, in fact, originally raised to James Francis Stuart, the "Old Pretender", rather than his son Charles Edward Stuart (Bonnie Prince Charlie), the "Young Pretender" in the period of the Jacobite rebellions.

p.137 **syne** *Scots* see note to p.106 above.

p.138 **cleckan** *Scots* a brood or litter.

p.138 *sotto voce Italian* in an undertone.

p.138 **parole** word of honour.

p.139 **medals in every class** in the Faculty of Medicine at the University of Glasgow a medal was awarded for the top student in each course down to the early part of the twentieth century.

p.139 **dog with two tails** *proverbial* denoting especial happiness.

p.139 **dree my weird** *Scots* meet my fate.

p.140 **house surgeon** junior doctor assistant to a consultant.

p.140 **eugenic** eugenics is the science of dealing with, and proposing the improvement of, hereditary factors.

p.141 **worked like a nigger** *proverbial* to work as hard as a black man.

p.141 **bairn** *Scots* child.

p.141 **percuss their backs** striking the back with the fingers to detect air and irregularities.

p.141 **sicken them with digitalis** digitalis, an alkaloid treatment for treating heart disease in the nineteenth century, was made from the poisonous foxglove plant with potentially nauseous consequences.

p.141 **paraldehyde** a sedative used down to the mid-point of the twentieth century to treat violent or noisy patients.

p.142 **curate's egg** *Punch* for 9 November 1895, featured a cartoon drawn by George du Maurier. A timid curate has breakfast in his bishop's home, and the bishop says, "I'm afraid you've got a bad egg, Mr. Jones," to which the curate replies: "Oh, no, my Lord, I assure you that parts of it are excellent!"

p.143 **mitral stenosis** a form of valvular rheumatic heart disease.

p.143 **King's Commission** commissioned military officers in the United Kingdom all technically have their authority from the Crown.

p.143 **at the Palace** Buckingham Palace, Royal residence in London of the United Kingdom monarch.

p.144 **Hindenburg** Paul Ludwig Hans Anton von Beneckendorff und von Hindenburg (1847–1934), German Field Marshal, who served as president of Germany from 1925–1934.

p.144 **Joffre,** Joseph (1852–1931), French World War I commander.

p.144 **Balfour,** Arthur (1848–1930), one-time leader of the British Conservative Party who was active in politics until 1929.

p.144 **DSO** Distinguished Service Order, a military honour of the United Kingdom for officers, especially those who have excelled in active combat.

p.147 **The Boches** "Boche" (*French* slang) for rascal; a term applied from World War I to the Germans.

p.147 **KBE** Knight Commander of the British Empire.

p.147 **bamboozle** *colloquial* (obscure) mystify or cheat.

p.148 **phthisical diathesis** an inherited tendency towards tuberculosis (as once, erroneously, was supposed to be the possibility).

p.148 **Keats and Shelley** English poets: John Keats (1795–1821) died of consumption in Italy; Percy Bysshe Shelley (1792–1822) drowned in a sailing accident in Italy.

p.148 **year of grace** old-fashioned usage where the year is defined, by implication from the point of Jesus Christ's birth.

p.148 **brachycephalic** where a human is short-headed (thought at one time to indicate a potential criminal character).

p.149 **dyspepsia** indigestion or other abdominal pain associated with consuming food.

p.149 **eupeptic** having good digestion.

p.149 **Apocalypse** originally, the supposed revelation of the end of the world made to St. John in the Island of Patmos.

p.150 **RAMC** Royal Army Medical Corps.

p.150 **the Military Cross** before 1993 a military honour reserved for officers of the British Army.

p.150 **Croix de Guerre** *French* "War Cross", an honour awarded by both the French and Belgian military, and including award to foreign allies.

p.150 **Médaille Militaire** *French* "Military Medal" awarded for bravery, but not to Commissioned Officers (though awarded also, very rarely, to foreigners).

p.150 **Sam Brown belt** a combination of a pistol belt or garrison belt and a shoulder strap (and D-rings); named after General Sir Sam Browne (1849–1898) of the British Army in India.

p.150 **Bradburys** *colloquial* a one pound note (named after John Bradbury, Secretary to the British Treasury (1913–1919)).

p.150 **British Warm coat** also known as the British Great Coat, a heavy coat issued to British Army officers.

p.151 **Scottie** *colloquial* a "nickname" for someone of Scottish nationality.

p.152 **Northumberland Avenue** a lively area in the City of Westminster near the centre of government.

p.152 **Ides of March** in the ancient Roman calendar the 15th March, an unlucky day because of the warning supposedly given to Julius Caesar prior to his assassination: "Beware the Ides of March."

p.152 **Thermopylae** at the battle of this name in 480 BC three hundred Spartans and several hundred Greeks heroically held a strategic pass against overwhelmingly superior Persian forces until betrayed.

p.152 **595 antivirus** a fiction.

p.152 **milk of human** *proverbial* "the milk of human kindness".

p.153 **Pooh-bloody-bah** Pooh-Bah is a character in Gilbert and Sullivan's opera

The Mikado (1885), who holds many offices at the same time.

p.153 **pandemic** a disease prevalent through a country, continent or the world.

p.153 **Guy's, Bart's** Guy's Hospital near London Bridge; St. Bartholomew's in the City of London.

p.153 **Middlesex** Hospital, in the City of London.

p.153 **cerebellar** the cerebellum is the larger part of the hind brain.

p.153 **cordon sanitaire** *French* sanitary or safe cordon or buffer.

p.154 **Napoleon brandy** brandy of great age or somehow special (associated with Napoleon because it was said to be his favourite drink).

p.155 **Day of Judgment** in Christian belief, the end of the world.

p.155 **polio-encephalitis** inflammation of the grey matter of the brain due to viral infection.

p.155 **Angel of Death** sometimes associated with Satan, there are perhaps six angels of death who actually at various points in Judaeo-Christian scripture do God's bidding in taking human life.

p.155 **bumping us off** *colloquial* killing.

p.155 **"The Journal of the Plague"** *A Journal of the Plague Year* (1722) by Daniel Defoe is an account of the Great Plague of London (1664–1665).

p.155 **"The Lord have mercy upon us"** Samuel Pepys in his diary for 7th June 1665 says, "This day I did in Drury Lane see two or three houses marked with a red cross upon their doors and 'Lord have mercy upon us' writ there, which was a sad sight to me."

p.156 **PM** Prime Minister (of the United Kingdom).

p.156 **The Medical Research Council** established in 1913 to tackle, in the first instance, tuberculosis.

p.157 **medinal** proprietary name for barbitone sodium.

p.157 **infra-red camera** a camera sensitive to radiation as emitted by heated bodies.

p.158 **Bloomsbury brothel** from the nineteenth century Bloomsbury is associated with literary, bohemian and decadent living.

p.158 polio-encephalo-myelitisis pandemic variety polio cannot be pandemic.

p.158 funk *colloquial* cowering fear.

p.158 anti-vivisection see note to *The Anatomist* p.296.

p.159 *nudest* **proposal** a play on the phrase "modest proposal".

p.160 D. H. Lawrence (1885–1930) English writer of poetry and fiction who died of tuberculosis (as with Cameron in Act I Scene I, Lawrence is both a sufferer of this disease and has a reputation for bucking the moral code).

p.162 the Black Death during 1347 one third of the population of Europe was wiped out by the disease that came to be known by this name; it was carried by the oriental rat flea.

p.162 Koch, Robert (1843–1910), sought to arrest tuberculosis by means of a preparation, which he called tuberculin, made from cultures of tubercle bacilli. This was initially disappointing but it led, nevertheless, to the discovery of substances of diagnostic value.

p.162 Law of Immunity in medicine there is really no such thing.

p.163 ninety-five . . . like William Blake's Jehovah a flippant remark referencing Blake's particularly grizzled and venerable pictorial depiction of God.

p.163 "Te semper anteit, saeva Necessitas" *Latin* Wretched Necessity always preceded you.

p.166 prophylactic a medicine or vaccine that protects against the onset of a disease or illness.

p.166 Reykjavik capital city of Iceland.

p.166 Cape Horn the southern tip of South America.

p.166 Order of Merit awarded under the British honours system for a wide range of achievement including that in the armed forces, science, art, literature and culture.

p.167 order of chivalry an umbrella term for many awards in the British honours system (one of which is the Order of Merit).

p.168 Whipsnade a reference to Whipsnade Animal Park in Bedfordshire.

p.169 Now lettest thou thy servant depart in peace Luke 2:29.

Note on the Performance and Text of *Mr. Bolfry*

Mr. Bolfry was first produced in August 1943 at the Westminster Theatre, London, with the following cast:

Cully . . . . Ellis Irving
Cohen . . . . Harry Ross
Jean . . . . Sheila Brownrigg
Morag . . . . Dorothy Smith
Mr. McCrimmon . . . . Alastair Sim
Mrs. McCrimmon . . . . Sophie Stewart
Mr. Bolfry . . . . Raymond Lovell

The text was first published in Bridie's collection of five plays, *Plays for Plain People* (Constable: London, 1944). For this text, a number of minor emendations have been made to J. T. Low's separately published *Mr. Bolfry* (Constable: London, 1944), which made several changes to the first edition.

Explanatory Notes

p.172 Free Kirk (*Scots* church) dating from 1843 this Presbyterian church was formed in opposition to the established Church of Scotland after the latter had agreed to government interference in the placement of church ministers in return for state funding; the Free Church clung to the ideal of ministers appointed by local parish assent and refused the arrangement.

p.172 Manse the house of the parish minister.

p.172 Larach Larach na Gaibhre, Argyllshire.

p.172 lanky *coll.* a tall, thin person.

p.172 "Roll out the barrel" or "Beer Barrel Polka" (as published from 1939), is a song which became widely popular during World War II. The music was composed by Czech musician Jaromír Vejoda in 1927. As popular a musical piece among German as British troops during the War, the English lyrics were written by Lew Brown and Wladimir Timm.

p.172 Hoots mon! *Scots* (literally something like, "nonsense, man") where someone else's statement or opinion is doubted by the utterer.

p.172 ken *Scots* know.

p.172 Sabbath Day the seventh day of the week enjoined by God as a day of rest on the ancient Hebrews.

p.172 Gordon Montefiore Cohen Cohen is probably named after Sir Moses Montefiore (1784–1885), sometime sheriff of London, made a baronet by Queen Victoria and something of an international Jewish celebrity for his humanitarian work on behalf of his religious community.

p.172 balmy *coll.* variant on "barmy" indicating the froth on top of fermenting liquor (figuratively meaning empty-headed).

p.172 cocky (a little cock or fowl) here sardonically as a term of endearment.

p.172 Cor, stone the crows an old English expression, perhaps dating back to Anglo-Saxon times; of uncertain meaning but maybe indicating an assault on a bird associated with bad luck. Used commonly as an expletive in response to harmful or unexpected news.

p.172 billet place where troops are quartered with civilians.

p.172 darn my socks an expletive saying, perhaps of Bridie's own devising in a heightened register that we would today call "Mockney".

p.172 sour-puss a peevish, irritable person (literally "sour-face" from late-nineteenth-century slang).

p.173 bombardier a soldier in charge of

315

a bombard, and so an artilleryman; in the British army a non-commissioned officer in the artillery.

p.173 BSM Battery Sergeant Major.

p.173 Tin-eyed toy dolls of the 1930s were often "tin-eyed" in their manufacture, and so here the expression means excessively or artificially watchful.

p.173 *Meditations among the Tombs* James Hervey (1714–1758) published the extremely popular Methodist treatise *Meditations among the Tombs* in 1746.

p.173 browned off *colloquial* a phrase signifying boredom or discontent, that became particularly current during World War II.

p.174 Meenister's niece Jean here mimics the Highland accent.

p.175 Borough Road in Southwark in the south-east of London.

p.175 Ministry of Interference Jean here parodies the notion of her government ministry.

p.175 blitzed from "blitzkrieg", the "lightning war" strategy of the Nazis, later used in Britain to signify the heavy bombing of London and other British cities in the earlier part of World War II.

p.175 Conk *colloquial* from the early nineteenth century for the nose; here used in racial terms because of the supposed prominence of the Jewish nose.

p.175 After you, Claude a phrase of comical, but practical, politeness used between World War II British bomber pilots as they circled their airfields waiting to land.

p.176 Heilans here Cully mimics one Scots pronunciation of "Highlands".

p.176 Wordsworth . . . solitary Highland Lass William Wordsworth's poem "The Solitary Reaper" (1807) features a narrator who admires from afar but never engages with a Highland girl singing in Gaelic.

p.176 mizzle *colloquial* early twentieth century meaning "to do a vanishing act".

p.176 dodging the column British army slang meaning to avoid taking part in a main movement (literally a column) or activity under military operation.

p.176 A fatalist a phrase dating from the mid-seventeenth century and denoting someone who believes that all events are predetermined by fate.

p.177 longsyne *Scots* (literally "long since") long ago.

p.177 greeting *Scots* crying, wailing.

p.177 cup of gruel oatmeal boiled in water or milk, an appropriately spartan repast for the Calvinist Sabbath.

p.177 burnt offering a religious sacrifice offered by burning.

p.177 Presbyterian referring to the established Church of Scotland and some other Protestant denominations, where certain local people – "elders" at parish level and sometimes also presbyters at area level – govern the affairs of the church, as opposed to the Episcopal system employing bishops. Historically Presbyterians are associated with eschewing liturgical complexity, and hence Cully's jibe about "altars" a central part of this.

p.178 pease brose a dish of pease-meal (split peas) which is made with boiling water.

p.178 on the mat *colloquial* from the early twentieth century meaning to take down, similar to being "carpeted", or to reprimand.

p.178 Mum Cockney variant on "Ma'am".

p.178 C. of E. Church of England.

p.178 out bye *Scots* literally "beyond"; outside.

p.178 ast *Cockney* "ask".

p.178 trouble and strife *Cockney* rhyming slang: "wife".

p.178 Southend Southend-on-sea, Essex, a once popular holiday resort in the south-east of England.

p.179 Cor blimey! *colloquial* "God blind me!", a Cockney ejaculation of amazement.

p.179 North Africa between November 1942 and May 1943, North Africa was a major strategic theatre in the war between Britain and Germany and its ally, Italy.

p.179 whiles *Scots* sometimes.

p.179 chanst *Cockney* chance.

p.180 Twicet *Scots* Cohen here seems to be picking up on a twentieth-century Scots usage meaning for a second time.

p.180 **get the willies** *colloquial*, of obscure USA origin, meaning to have the jitters.

p.180 **Hitler . . . Goering . . . Rommel** Hitler, Adolf, 1889–1945, German dictator 1934–1945; Goering, Hermann, 1893–1946, "Marshal of the Empire", and the man responsible for Germany's air warfare strategy; Rommel, Erwin, 1891–1944, for much of World War II, Germany's most successful general, made Field Marshal for his particular success, initially, in North Africa.

p.180 **bogles** *Scots* an ugly or fearsome ghost.

p.180 **kelpies** *Scots*, probably of Gaelic origin, a water demon.

p.180 **mixty maxty** *Scots* all mixed up.

p.180 **My sorrow and my shame!** "sorrow" and "shame" is a fairly common collocation in the Judaeo-Christian mindset (see for instance, Jeremiah, 20:18).

p.181 **ben** *Scots* into.

p.181 **record for church attendance . . . highest illegitimacy rate in the Kingdom** the Free Church Western Highlands did, indeed, have a very high record for church attendance down to the 1960s, though there is nothing to suggest that the illegitimacy rate was higher than elsewhere in the United Kingdom in the 1940s.

p.182 **aspirin** common analgesic painkiller.

p.182 **mortal sin** in Christian theology, spiritual transgression of an extreme nature where lack of restitution condemns one to damnation.

p.183 **boils and leprosy** in the Bible, Job is tested by God through terrible disease, where one symptom is boils, long interpreted as leprosy (see Job 2:7–10).

p.183 **Milton**, John (1608–1674) author of the epic poem *Paradise Lost* (1667), in which Satan emerges as perhaps the most interesting character.

p.183 **Goethe**, Johann Wolfgand Von (1749–1832) whose drama *Faust* (1808–1831) sees Mephistopheles battling for the soul of the eponymous character.

p.183 **William Blake** (1757–1827) whose poetry and prose from the *Marriage of Heaven and Hell* (1790) meditates deeply, and often grimly, on the divine economy and the figures of God and the Devil.

p.183 **Bobbie Burns** Robert Burns (1759–1796) contemplates the Devil in several poems, including "Address to the Deil" (1785).

p.183 **Conk's ancestors . . . against Christ** the longstanding Christian, anti-Semitic myth, especially prominent in the Middle Ages, that the Jews were collectively responsible for the death of the Messiah.

p.183 **Painted blue** some ancient British tribes encountered by the invading Romans painted their bodies blue with woad.

p.183 **Institutes of Calvinism** *Institutes of the Christian Religion* written between 1534 and 1536 by French reformation theologian John Calvin (1509–1564).

p.183 **raining cats and dogs** the cat is associated with the wind in Northern mythology, and the dog (an attendant to Odin) is seen as a signal of the wind; both then are associated with stormy weather.

p.184 **gallus** *Scots* to be acting in a "gallus" fashion means to be swaggeringly self-confident.

p.184 **Players** a popular brand of cigarettes.

p.184 **a gallon of Rosie Lee** Cockney rhyming slang for tea.

p.185 **cla'es** *Scots* clothes.

p.185 **Garn!** *Cockney* "go on".

p.186 **Cissy** *colloquial* from the nineteenth century meaning effeminate (a variant on "sissy", short for "sister").

p.186 **great Goramity** *Cockney* "great God Almighty".

p.186 **Gerry** *colloquial* "German".

p.186 **forced hallelujahs** see *Paradise Lost* Book II, from line 243.

p.187 **niggers** *colloquial* black people.

p.187 **heids** *Scots* heads.

p.187 **birsey** *Scots* bristley.

p.187 **seraph** a member of the highest order of angels, usually with six wings.

p.187 **geraffe** meaning here, in the stream of nonsense, giraffe.

p.187 **camomile** creeping aromatic plant; as with "geraffe" above there is a free associationism going on (where "geraffe" has led to the unspoken "camel" to "camomile").

p.187 oinseach an "eejit" from old Irish meaning a scabby old woman.

p.187 Ochonorie cod Gaelic from "ochone", a noise of lament.

p.187 *The Discoverie of Witchcraft* book published (London, 1584) by Reginald Scot (*c*.1538–1599), debunking the idea of sorcery.

p.188 cabalistic signs from the Middle Ages; Cabbalists made up charms and spells in their search for the philosopher's stone and communion with the dead and other supernatural beings.

p.188 old boze in the opera "boze" is a variant on the American colloquialism "bozo" (meaning a stupid or despised person); the opera referred to is *Faust* (1859) by Charles Gounod.

p.188 monkey kit proverbially, monkeys are full of cleverness and tricks.

p.188 Wee Frees (*Scots* "wee" means "small") mildly pejorative name for the Free Presbyterian Church in Scotland.

p.188 red tights devils are depicted in opera and music-hall from the nineteenth century in garish red costume.

p.188 Mestify-toffles Mephistopheles, perhaps meaning "not loving the light" (from Greek), a devil or familiar, who from Goethe's *Faust* is seen as a sardonic tempter.

p.188 fore and aft hanging to his near side horn Cohen seems to be picturing his sergeant with his shirt and tie uniform (known colloquially in the navy, at least, as a "fore and aft" uniform) hanging from one of his devilish horns, though the words also convey the impression of a crude joke, not entirely intelligible.

p.188 "Battery, tails up" soldiers are presented on parade presenting devilish tails rather than military arms.

p.188 Jock *Scots* form of "John".

p.189 do as the Romans do *proverbial*: "when in Rome do as the Romans do", or live by the standards of those amongst whom you find yourself.

p.189 laughter that is like the crackling of thorns under a pot see Ecclesiastes 7, "For as the crackling of thorns under a

pot, so is the laughter of a fool: this is also vanity."

p.189 Why call ye me, Lord Luke 6:46, "And why call ye me, Lord, and do not the things which I say?"

p.189 Fourth Commandment Exodus 20:12, "Honour your father and your mother, that your days may be long in the land which the Lord your God gives you."

p.190 Sunday School Trip outing connected to children's Christian instruction taking place separately from adult worship which has been practised by a number of Protestant denominations.

p.190 set of rules for a wandering desert tribe the idea increasingly current from the Enlightenment onwards that the Bible should be read anthropologically as a series of distinctive injunctions and prohibitions that served to provide a distinctive identity for the essentially stateless Jews.

p.190 keep Saturday holy, not Sunday Saturday is the seventh day of the week (Sunday the first) and so if, literally, the Bible enjoins rests and worship on the seventh day, then this should fall on Saturday.

p.190 If you were Legion this may be a reference to the "legion of the lost ones" (including infirm elderly people), but may also be a sardonic way of saying "if you were hydra-headed" (a propos of Mark 5:9, "My name is legion for we are many").

p.190 the mouths of babes . . . perfected praise Psalms 8:2. Out of the mouth of babes and sucklings hast thou ordained strength because of thine enemies, that thou mightest still the enemy and the avenger. Matthew 21:16. And said unto him, Hearest thou what these say? And Jesus saith unto them, Yea; have ye never read, Out of the mouth of babes and sucklings thou hast perfected praise?

p.191 Father Mackintosh . . . Strathdearg here we have reinforced the idea that "moderate" Protestantism such as Episcopalianism or Anglicanism is theologically not diligent enough and that what is needed is either the trenchant dogmatism of free Presbyterianism or that of Roman Catholicism.

p.191 ignoramus is not a noun it is, in fact, indicates first person plural present indicative of "ignorare" in Latin and means literally, "We do not know."

p.191 making your holy day Sunday instead of Saturday anciently, Sunday was the day dedicated to the sun, and severe critics of Christianity claim that it is a continuation of Pagan rather than Jewish elements.

p.191 original sin the corruption of human nature with which we are born and arising in the Christian story from Adam's first disobedience.

p.191 election the choosing by God of some but not of others for salvation.

p.191 predestination the doctrine that God has immutably preordained all events (especially with regard to salvation), and which comes to be especially prominent with Calvinist forms of thinking.

p.191 Stop the horses a proverbial phrase meaning slow down.

p.191 Brains Trust originally applied by a journalist of the *New York Times* to the advisers to F. D. Roosevelt in his presidential election campaign; now used proverbially to any team of experts or advisers assembled to answer questions impromptu.

p.191 two hoots *colloquial* from the late nineteenth century a "hoot" as in the phrase here means a scarp or the smallest amount.

p.192 Stumpie Stowsie *Scots* "stumpie" is a short, stocky or dumpy person; "stowsie" may here be meant as a diminutive of "stow" meaning to gorge.

p.192 as if you was Jonah Jonah 1:17 sees Jonah having been sent out to preach by God being swallowed by a large fish, possibly a whale.

p.192 Good night, children, everywhere catchphrase of Derek McCulloch presenter of "Children's Hour" on BBC Radio during World War II.

p.192 havers *Scots* foolish or nonsense talk.

p.192 wee tottums *Scots* little children.

p.192 clacking *Scots* chatter.

p.193 Liver Fluke a flat leaf-like parasite of mammals.

p.193 cad *colloquial* a vulgar, ungentlemanly person.

p.193 tuppeny-ha'penny *colloquial* "two and a half pence" implying cheap or worthless.

p.193 shauchly *Scots* shuffling or unsteady.

p.193 sheep and the goats taken to refer to the Day of Judgement when "All the nations will be gathered before him, and he will separate the people one from another as a shepherd separates the sheep from the goats" (Matthew 25:32).

p.194 Ben Nevis the highest mountain in Britain.

p.194 transubstantiation Roman Catholic doctrine of the real presence where the bread and wine are transformed by the actions of the priest into the body and blood of Jesus Christ.

p.195 talk the hind leg off *proverbial*, "talk the hind leg off a donkey", possibly derived from the notion of being such a persuasive talker that one can make a stereotypically stubborn animal sit down.

p.195 Nazis Hitler's National Socialists.

p.195 Lloyd George, David (1863–1945), as Chancellor of the Exchequer in 1911 he responded to attempts by the House of Lords to vote down the government's budget by being one of the architects of the Parliament Act which severely curtailed the powers of the House of Lords thereafter.

p.195 Calvin, John (1509–1564), his theology emphasised individual and community involvement, and rights even towards a cultural vision that is sometimes credited with being an influence on the European Enlightenment and on the American constitution. His system of church government implies a kind of recognisable democracy, but at the same time, its strongly theocratic nature makes this comparison problematic.

p.195 Devil's Advocate the official appointed by the Roman Catholic Church to test an individual's beatification by challenging it.

319

p.195 perisher *colloquial* an annoying or pitiable individual.

p.195 beauty sleep sleep taken before midnight and supposedly important in helping one remain more youthful looking.

p.197 cheery-oh *colloquial* early-twentieth-century expression, the equivalent of "Good Health" and similarly used as a toast.

p.197 a puritan someone practising a severe (often abstemious) set of religious or moral practises.

p.197 pig-man the pig is often associated with unrestrained exercise of the appetites.

p.199 Agla and the mystic signs mystic Figures of the Hebrew Enchiridion, and used within pentagram ceremonies, include Jehovah Elohim, Agla and Elohim; Agla is invoked as the spell-caster faces north. Agla is a "holy name of God almighty" (see the description of "Solomon's Circle" in *Discoverie of Witchcraft* 15 Booke, Cap 12; 15 Booke Cap. 14; & 15 Booke Cap 33.

p.199 "Lead Kindly Light" prayer and hymn by John Henry Newman where the speaker asks for God's guidance through the darkness.

p.199 Bealphares . . . great talker . . . Bolfry in *Discoverie of Witchcraft* 15 Booke, Cap 2 Berith has three names: Beall, Berith and Bolfry, and "speaketh with a cleare and subtill voice".

p.199 Fugiat omne malignum/Salvetur quodque benignum *Latin* May all evil be put to flight./May all that is good save us.

p.199 Homo . . . sacarus . . . musceolameas . . . cherubozca *Latin* Man.

p.200 TETRAGRAMMATON Greek (literally "four letters") referring to YHWH or JHVH, the original word for God too sacred to be pronounced and so expanded to Yahweh or Jehovah.

p.200 just after twelve o'clock traditionally the "witching hour" when spirits, especially evil supernatural beings, are licensed to enter into the world.

p.201 robbed you of Time and Space the theories of Albert Einstein proposed that distance and time are not absolute.

So that, for instance, the ticking rate of a clock depends on the motion of the observer of that clock. From 1915, his theory of general relativity proposed that gravity, as well as motion, can affect the intervals of time and of space.

p.202 feared *Scots* scared.

p.202 Get thee behind me, Satan "Jesus said to Peter, Get thee behind me, Satan; thou savorest the things that be of men" Matthew 16:23.

p.202 Father of lies "You belong to your father, the devil, and you want to carry out your father's desire. He was a murderer from the beginning, not holding to the truth, for there is no truth in him. When he lies, he speaks his native language, for he is a liar and the father of lies" (John 8:43–45).

p.202 Keep your herrings for the Loch, and do not drag them across my path this would seem to be a proverbial saying of Bridie's own devising; it has connotations with the idea of "red herrings" and "fishiness", i.e. falsity.

p.203 Universe . . . as a pattern of reciprocating opposites from the third century a form of dualism, Manichaeism, combined Christian, Gnostic and pagan elements in a belief system that proposed a primeval universal conflict between light and dark where God and Satan were coeternal.

p.203 Blasphemy . . . I know my position better here Bolfry speaks with a Manichaean awareness that his place as part of the evil supernatural economy is necessarily interdependent with the good/God-led part of the same.

p.203 He goeth about like a roaring lion "Be self-controlled and alert. Your enemy the devil prowls around like a roaring lion looking for someone to devour" (Peter 5:8).

p.203 "Now there was a day . . . Satan came among them" Bolfry misquotes Job 1:6: "One day the angels came to present themselves before the Lord, and Satan also came with them."

p.203 The Devil can quote Scripture William Shakespeare, *The Merchant of Venice*: "The devil can cite scripture for his purpose" (Act I, Scene III).

p.204 **Tee-to-tum** *Scots* a spinning top.

p.204 **Highland courtesy** the supposed hospitality of the Gaelic-speaking Highlands is proverbial.

p.204 **sneck up** *Scots* "close the latch" (meaning "shut up").

p.205 **green cheese the moon is made of** current since the mid-sixteenth century; for instance, John Heywood's *Proverbes* (1546) provides the following: "The moon is made of a greene cheese," where *greene* means new, or unaged, and has to do, presumably, with the moon's distance and the visibility of its cheese-hole-like craters.

p.205 **the Kingdom of Heaven is within me** Luke 17:20–21: "Once, having been asked by the Pharisees when the kingdom of God would come, Jesus replied, 'The kingdom of God does not come with your careful observation, nor will people say, "Here it is," or "There it is," because the kingdom of God is within you.'"

p.205 **process of Evolution** here referred to is the amoral stance of the Theory of Evolution that sees elements of human nature labelled sinful by Christianity as being, in fact, part of the selfish, survival instincts that allowed the human species to survive and evolve.

p.205 **Bedlam** short for the Hospital of St. Mary in Bethlehem in London, which housed the mentally ill from the sixteenth century.

p.205 **hooey** *colloquialism* (US) nonsense.

p.205 **teleological fallacy** the expression of the error in believing that there is meaning or order moving from a beginning to a logical end in the universe or life.

p.206 **higher faculties** mental, reasoning or moral capacities.

p.206 **tinky-tonk** *colloquial* tinny or empty sound.

p.207 **Instrument of Providence who smote Job's body with boils** in Job 7, the eponymous character is plagued with scabs (and Bolfry here claims to be the instrument of evil carrying out God's testing of Job).

p.207 **Geneva in 1570** by the 1550s Geneva was a world centre of

Protestantism with, at times, both Calvin and John Knox (the father of Scottish Calvinism) living and involved in theology there.

p.207 **High Kirk at North Berwick** *Newes from Scotland* (1591), about the North Berwick witch-hunts of 1590–1591, and probably written by James Carmichael, minister of Haddington (adviser to King James on the writing of his book *Daemonologie*), contains a woodcut where a group of female witches listen to the Devil preaching a sermon in North Berwick church at Hallowe'en 1590.

p.209 **Pay Corps** traditionally seen as a safe posting within the army.

p.210 **Devil from the machine** referring to *Latin* Deus ex machina ("god from the machine" referring to the way in which gods were suspended above the stage in Classical theatre, later adopted to describe any literary manoeuvre by which a sudden unexpected intrusion of character or event resolves the action).

p.210 **Love birds** term used for a range of types of small parrot which show remarkable fondness for their mates.

p.211 **Burning Bush** In Exodus 3:2–4 God speaks to Moses as a burning bush.

p.211 **the Resurrection** the rising from the dead of Jesus Christ.

p.212 **thingummy** *Scots* thing.

p.212 **Blake who walked to Hampstead Heath** William Blake believed Hampstead Heath to be an unwholesome place associated with the devil.

p.212 **Now is the dominion of Edom . . . Adam to Paradise** from William Blake, "The Marriage of Heaven and Hell" (*c*.1790–1793), Plate 3.

p.213 **thieves' kitchen** in the 1930s the Russian communists referred to the League of Nations by this term.

p.213 **My Führer** *German* leader, a term assumed by Adolf Hitler at the head of the Third Reich.

p.213 **New Disorder** a play on Hitler's "New Order" described in his autobiography, *Mein Kampf*, which ramblingly portrays a future Europe where Aryans are the master-race.

p.213 **Mount Sinai** God commanded

Moses to the top of Mount Sinai to receive the Ten Commandments (see Exodus 20:1–2 & 34:27–29).

p.213 Tom, Dick and Harry a term from Victorian times for the man in the street.

p.213 through Fire and Water a number of biblical passages describe ritual through the use of fire and water (see, for instance, Exodus 30:20 and Leviticus 8:21).

p.213 Crucifixion . . . Victory numerous Christian lore and utterance sees Christ's execution as a victory over death.

p.213 stamp the stony laws to dust the Ten Commandments carved on tablets of stone (see Deuteronomy 5:22).

p.213 "loosing the eternal horses from the dens of night" William Blake, "A Song of Liberty" (*c.*1792), Section 20.

p.214 Gates of Hell may prevail against the armies of the Cherubim Matthew 16:18: "And I tell you that you are Peter, and on this rock I will build my church, and the gates of Hell shall not prevail against you." The cherubim is one of the order of angels and in Genesis 3:24 one is armed with a sword while guarding the tree of life.

p.214 Man's genius will burst its bonds a parody of the Christian resurrection.

p.214 Adam to eat an apple Genesis 2: 16–17.

p.214 Onward, Christian soldiers the title of a popular hymn written by Sabine Baring-Gould (1834–1924).

p.214 It's a rocky road to Zion . . . no hope in my country "The roads to Zion mourn, for no one comes to her appointed feasts. All her gateways are desolate, her priests groan, her maidens grieve, and she is in bitter anguish" (Lamentations 1:4).

p.214 Lucifer, Son of the Morning Lucifer, *Latin*, "lightbringer", the name for God's supreme angel who becomes the Devil; a name associated also with Venus in her guise as the morning star.

p.214 the Soul and the Body are one *cf.* William Blake, "The Marriage of Heaven and Hell", Plate 4, where the devil says, "Man has no Body distinct from his Soul."

p.215 In nomine Patris . . . Sancti *Latin*

In the Name of the Father and of the Son and of the Holy Ghost.

p.215 conjuro te, Sathanas *Latin* I swear you are (Satan).

p.215 gone Papist traditionally ritual and prayer in Latin, especially the Mass, are associated with an idolatrous Roman Catholicism by Calvinists and other Protestants who abjure Episcopacy.

p.215 thrapple *Scots* throat.

p.216 mixty-maxty *Scots* confusion or jumble.

p.216 gey *Scots* very.

p.217 fash *Scots* trouble (oneself or someone).

p.219 Silly House mental asylum.

p.219 up topsides *colloquial* on the upper deck.

p.219 okey-doke *colloquial* (US) okay.

p.221 Offerance there is a settlement of this name in Stirlingshire; otherwise not identified.

p.223 Beelzebub see note to *The Sunlight Sonata*, p.286.

p.223 Firth *Scots* estuary.

p.223 yon *Scots* that (over there).

p.223 nettle turns to the sun if a quotation not identified.

p.224 stooge *colloquial* a person who acts as a butt or a foil (to another).

p.224 dog's leg perhaps Cockney rhyming slang for a peg (meaning being taken up a peg a propos Cully's promotion).

p.224 Indian Rope Trick a trick, reportedly witnessed by thousands of people, involving an Indian fakir who throws a rope into the sky, which then at the top disappears into darkness or obscurity and is climbed by a small boy.

p.225 tuilzie *Scots* a dispute or brawl.

p.225 peely-wally *Scots* pallid and sickly looking.

p.225 I have nowhere seen such great Faith . . . not in Israel in the Old Testament the Jews are long-suffering but ever faithful to their covenant with the one true god.

p.225–6 big beasts . . . horns "And I stood upon the sand of the sea, and saw a beast rise out of the sea, having seven heads and ten horns, and upon his horns ten crowns" (Revelation 13:1).

Note on the Performance and Text of *Daphne Laureola*

Daphne Laureola was first presented Wyndham's Theatre, London, on 23rd March 1949, by Sir Laurence Olivier and directed by Murray Macdonald. The cast was:

Maisie . . . . Anna Turner
Bill . . . . Robin Lloyd
Helen . . . . Eileen O'Hara
Bob . . . . Alexander Harris
George . . . . Martin Miller
1st Spiv . . . . Billy Thatcher
2nd Spiv . . . . Ireland Wood
Lady Pitts . . . . Dame Edith Evans
Ernest . . . . Peter Finch
Bored Woman . . . . Diana Graves
Bored Man . . . . Kenneth Hyde
Gooch . . . . Frank Pettingell
Watson . . . . Mark Stone
Vincent . . . . Peter Williams
Sir Joseph . . . . Felix Aylmer
Manager . . . . Bernard Gillman

The play was published in one separate first edition in 1949; corrections have been made to this text for the present edition.

Explanatory Notes

p.227 Edith Evans (1888–1976) English actress who starred with Peter Finch in the 1949 West End staging of *Daphne Laureola*.

p.228 "Le Toit Aux Porcs" *French* The Roof with Pork.

p.228 Tokay a sweet, aromatic wine from the area of Tokaj, Hungary.

p.228 Spivs *colloquial* of uncertain origin in the 1930s denoting a man of flashy appearance who makes a living by dishonest means.

p.228 older than the rocks . . . their ruined day from Oscar Wilde, *The Critic as Artist* (1888), where the mysterious painting, the Mona Lisa by Da Vinci, is discussed.

p.229 something in the woodshed meaning usually that someone has a dark or unpleasant secret in their past; used at least as early as Mary Webb in her novel *The House in Dormer Forest* (1920).

p.229 black market goods and services bought and sold in unlicensed quantities or illegally obtained through underground means; this kind of "market" thrived in Britain during World War II.

p.229 tight *colloquial* drunk.

p.230 Garcon, l'addition s'il vous plait *French* "Waiter, the bill, please."

p.230 A l'instant, monsieur *French* "Right away, sir."

p.230 pud pudding.

p.230 Sir Stafford a reference, presumably, to Sir Stafford Cripps (1889–1952) Labour Chancellor of the Exchequer (1947–1950), in which office he oversaw a programme of rigorous consumer curtailment so as to counter Britain's huge war-time debt.

p.231 hors d'oeuvres *French* (literally "outside the work") a separate dish served as an appetiser to the main dinner course.

p.231 Russian salad a salad the staple ingredients of which are usually potato and carrot, but sometimes including other items such as egg.

p.231 Vienna steak one of several names once also used for a beef-burger.

p.231 **pommes sautés** fried potatoes.

p.231 **permits** a synonym here for ration-coupons (food was rationed during World War II in Britain and for some years afterwards).

p.232 **Dundee cake** a rich fruit-cake usually decorated with split almonds.

p.232 **By gum** *colloquial* an expression of surprise which can be defined as a minced-oath, since it is euphemistic for "By God".

p.232 **dog's breakfast** *colloquial* a mess.

p.233 **mild and bitter** beer.

p.233 **long-eared chickens** signalling that the dish is in fact rabbit.

p.233 **Marmite** proprietary name for a savoury sandwich spread made from fresh brewer's yeast.

p.233 **cheroot** a small cigar, originally from Southern India, which is open at both ends.

p.233 **Dutch uncle** a term for a person who issues frank and severe comments so as to educate or enlighten someone (the phrase originates in the early nineteenth century from the stereotypical view of the Dutch as an unusually censorious type of people).

p.234 **Chopin** Frédéric François Chopin (1810–1849), French-Polish composer, who wrote very technically accomplished, but emotionally accessible pieces for the piano.

p.234 *Massenet's* **ELEGIE** a piece very popular for its passionate intensity by French composer Jules Massenet (1842–1912), who sets his music to a poem by Louis Gallet.

p.234 **Mezzo-Soprano** *Italian* a female voice intermediate in compass between soprano and contralto.

p.234 **Ah, doux printemps d'autre fois! Comme tu es** *French* from the words of Gallet's "Elegie" as used by Massenet: "O sweet spring of another time"; "Comme tu" (how or thus you) does not appear in the lyric. The piece speaks of the heartbreak following lost love.

p.235 **Kummel** a sweet liqueur flavoured with caraway and cumin seeds.

p.235 **laburnum tree** a tree with bright yellow flowers followed by poisonous pods.

p.235 **Perhaps God was wrong about Adam and Eve** implying that it is the male that tempts the female.

p.236 **Pull to the shore . . . Stand to the oar** the chorus to "Pull for the shore", an evangelical hymn of hope from the nineteenth century by Philip Paul Bliss:

Pull for the shore, sailor, pull for the shore!

Heed not the rolling waves, but bend to the oar;

Safe in the lifeboat, sailor, cling to self no more!

Leave the poor old stranded wreck and pull for the shore!

p.238 **Inter-varsity rugby match** rugby match between Cambridge and Oxford universities.

p.238 **Dean Street** fashionable dining and drinking street during World War II near Soho.

p.238 **Vine Street** the location of a police station, now closed, in the City of Westminster.

p.238 **The Dark Ages** in traditional historiography the period from *c.*470 to 1000.

p.238 **menagerie** *French* a collection of wild animals in cages or enclosures.

p.238 *The Tempest* romantic drama by William Shakespeare, probably written in 1611, dealing with the life and island exile of a magician, Prospero, and his daughter, Miranda.

p.238 **Caliban . . . spangled spooks** a monstrous son of a witch that Prospero keeps in service and controlled with the help of spirits (most notably Ariel) he has set free who had previously been imprisoned by Caliban's mother.

p.239 **"An hundred generations . . . into the grave."** "an hundred generations, the leaves of autumn have dropped into the grave: and after the fall of the Pharoahs and Ptolemies, the Cæsers and Caliphs, the same pyramids stand erect and unshaken above the floods of the Nile." From Edward Gibbon's *Decline and Fall of the Roman Empire* (1776–1788).

p.239 **as Christendom and the Roman Empire did** the Christian "Dark Ages" (see note above) from the period of the break-up of the Roman Empire until the very early medieval period are seen, stereotypically, as a period of cultural barbarism.

p.239 sport among the ruins "Love Among the Ruins" (1855) is a poem by Robert Browning.

p.239 Encore! originally *French*; used in English by an audience to demand a performance "once more".

p.240 hypnotised rabbit a common metaphor from the idea that the extreme timidity of a rabbit sometimes causes it to "freeze" when pursued by a predator.

p.240 "i know i am bound . . . toujours gai toujours gai" "the song of mehitabel" by Don Marquis, in *archy and mehitabel* (1927), a series of fictions that begin life in the newspaper column of Marquis in the *New York Tribune* from 1916.

p.241 prima ballerina *Italian* principal female ballet dancer.

p.241 Young Men's Christian Association established in London in 1844 in response to the widespread depravity of the capital to provide cheap accommodation and food for poorer, especially migrant, workers and travellers.

p.241 Laplace on Probabilities Pierre Simon (Marquis de) Laplace (1749–1827), French mathematician, developer of an equation which bears his name and of the differential operator, which are important tools in the study of random and probable events.

p.241 slubberdegullion *colloquial* (from early seventeenth century) a slobbering or dirty individual.

p.241 lick-spittle a human being, a sycophant or even acting as a parasite in some sense.

p.241 codface fraud or false face.

p.242 cur name for a low-bred dog.

p.243 The Rolls Rolls-Royce make of car, which is expensive and suitably luxurious in its mechanics and passenger comfort as a vehicle associated with the rich.

p.244 clip *colloquial* hit smartly.

p.244 Might as well be in Germany Germany had just lost World War II, and

material and consumer conditions there were very much worse than in Britain in the years afterwards, though in Britain food rationing and scanty consumer goods pertained into the 1950s.

p.244 Gas oven's the only thing a traditional method of suicide by poisonous fumes, placing one's head in a gas oven with the gas on but unlit.

p.244 Where are the snows of yesteryear? from "The Ballade (of the Ladies of Ancient Times)", *c.*1461, by François Villon, French poet (b.1431).

p.245 like a ghost possibly an echo of J. T. Trowbridge's *Lucy Arlyn* (1866), in Chapter XVI of which we find the line, "Lucy vanished from the room like a ghost."

p.246 Nonconformist Chapel communicants Methodists, the denomination that broke away under John Wesley in the eighteenth century from the Church of England in the desire for a more "low-church" style of liturgy.

p.247 sotto voce *Italian* in an undertone.

p.247 cissie see note to *Mr. Bolfry* p.317.

p.248 The Bracknell Committee possibly a play on the character Lady Bracknell, doyenne of Victorian drawing-room propriety, from Oscar Wilde's *The Importance of Being Ernest* (1895); otherwise the point, generally, is a satirical one on the plethora of committees appointed in Britain in the aftermath of World War II to oversee "reconstruction" and the normalisation of life.

p.248 broken English English as spoken by a foreigner with non-idiomatic expressions, perhaps especially involving non-standard conjunctional items.

p.249 *The Wealth of Nations* by Adam Smith classic foundational text of western economics published in 1776.

p.250 naturalisation the process where someone is formally made a national subject or citizen.

p.250 maquis originally referring to membership of the French Resistance during World War II against the Germans;

and quickly in use as a generic word to refer to any resistance movement.

p.250 Presbyterian see note to *Mr. Bolfry* p.316.

p.250 a baron most generally a noble deriving his title from military or other honourable service to the monarch.

p.250 Scottish church in Cracow presumably fictional.

p.250 into Parliament on the Nonconformist vote. In 1906 in this parliament the Liberal Party gained an overall majority, and included among its traditional membership and many of its voting supporters Protestants (non-conformists) not aligned with the Church of England.

p.251 the partisans term used for resistance-members against the Germans during World War II in Yugoslavia, Italy and parts of Eastern Europe.

p.254 La Gloriosa donna della mia mente *Italian* "the glorious lady of my mind" as the writer Dante Aligheri (1265–1321) called his great love and muse Beatirice Portinari (1266–1290).

p.255 the Deaf and Dumb a reference to a charity event under the aegis of any one of many local and national deaf associations that sprang up in the opening decades of the twentieth century.

p.255 Abbott and Costello William (Bud) Abbott and Louis Cristillo, an American comedy duo, stars of radio and, during the 1940s, many films.

p.256 the commandos a unit of British amphibious shock troops formed during World War II to undertake often hazardous, sometimes behind enemy-lines operations.

p.256 compound fracture where the skin has been pierced by the bone, with the resulting high risk of infection.

p.256 Freudian Sigmund Freud is credited as the inventor of modern psycho-analysis, particularly because of his pioneering work on the unconscious.

p.256 Twa *Scots* two.

p.257 Who's Who annually updated directory of important people in the United Kingdom.

p.257 stinking tight *colloquial* drunk.

p.258 dipsomaniac a morbid paroxysmal craving for alcohol.

p.258 fling *colloquial* a period of self-indulgence.

p.258 "A blue-behinded ape . . . trees of Paradise" from Robert Louis Stevenson's "XXX. A Portrait".

p.258 Artemis Greek goddess (the Roman version of the same becoming Diana), associated with the moon.

p.258 simian ape-like.

p.258 Okey-doke see note to *Mr. Bolfry* p.322.

p.258 the Observer British "quality" newspaper.

p.260 tête-à-tête *French* "head to head" (or one-to-one conversation).

p.260 OMNES *Latin* all.

p.261 Cyclothymic behaviour characterised by swings between moods of elation and depression.

p.261 hempen homespuns hemp is a herbaceous plant, often of dull flowers, used in the making of a type of rope.

p.261 fairy queen fairies are creatures of magical power and so the contrast between Daphne in this guise and the prosaic, practical "hempen homespuns".

p.261 tipsy see note to *The Anatomist* p.301.

p.262 a Notting Hill verse drama in the 1930s there was a new fashion for verse drama (by writers such as W. H. Auden, T. S. Eliot and Christopher Isherwood). Many such works were also composed for performance furth of the mainstream commercial theatre, including the Mercury Theatre in Notting Hill Gate, which held only a maximum of 150 of an audience. It was opened by Ashley Dukes in 1933 and was home to E. Martin Browne's Pilgrim Players.

p.262 calf love young, or immature love.

p.262 Pont Street in south-west London, near Chelsea and Kensington.

p.262 conventicle an assembly or meeting of non-conformists.

p.262 half a crown in pre-decimal sterling, 12.5 pence in modern British currency.

p.262 Indian summer see note to *The Sunlight Sonata* p.289.

p.265 Acousticon a hand-held device for amplifying sound as an aid to the deaf.

p.265 catch-as-catch-can a wrestling style in which all holds are permissible.

p.266 a parson a beneficed clergyman, a vicar or rector.

p.266 Newnham a college for woman at Cambridge.

p.266 Rockefeller Travelling Fellowship one of many educational opportunities endowed by the American philanthropist John Davison Rockefeller.

p.267 Snowdon in North Wales, the highest mountain in England and Wales.

p.268 stravaiging *Scots* see note to *The Anatomist* p.302.

p.268 Beatrice was to Dante Alghieri when she had gone to Heaven after the death of Beatrice Dante went into a period of deep contemplation and writing poetry in her memory.

p.268 Ovidius . . . laurel branches Ovid (43 BC–AD 18), Roman poet, describes how the gods, to protect Daphne's virginity from Apollo's advances, turn her into a laurel or bay-tree.

p.268 picture by Pollaiuolo Italian painter, Antonio del Pollaiuolo's late fifteenth century "Apollo and Daphne" displayed at the National Gallery, London.

p.268 gist the essence.

p.268 parky *colloquial* cold.

p.269 Daphne Laureola an eastern Mediterranean species of plant which prefers sunny positions but will grow quite happily in the heavy shade of trees.

p.269 Femina sapiens *Latin* feminine wisdom.

p.271 find no bluebottles on yours a variant on the phrase "no flies on me" meaning "I'm clean".

p.271 Stafford Cripps see note to p.230 above.

p.271 smackers *colloquial* pounds sterling.

p.271 A likyour liqueur.

p.272 Van der Humm a citrus-flavoured South African liqueur made from a five-year blend of old pot-still brandy, wine distillate, the peel of Cape tangerines, herbs, spices, seeds and barks. It is

sweetened with glucose and other ingredients.

p.272 Winston Hotel not identified (though there is a hotel of this name in Paris).

p.272 High Society the echelon of society, frequented by the British upper class.

p.272 Hampstead fashionable part of north-west London.

p.272 Here's gravel in your ear-hole variant of the toast "here's mud in your eye", denoting the wishing of good luck.

p.274 contertong "contretemps" *French* meaning here a disagreement.

p.275 chuck *colloquial* food.

p.279 "For they are jolly good fellows . . . And so say all of us" traditional British song of congratulation to help toast happy events.

p.280 The king is dead, long live the king a traditional proclamation made following the accession of a new king in a number of European countries, including Great Britain.

p.281 cad a vulgar, especially "ungentlemanly", person.

p.281 poor peasant who worshipped a goddess not identified.

p.281 the god who loved a mortal girl if based on anything in particular, perhaps loosely related to the Roman legend, where the beauty of a king's youngest daughter, Psyche, was supplanting the worship of the goddess Venus; she set her son Eros (or Cupid) the task of destroying her, but instead he fell in love with her.

p.282 "Al ciel, ch'e pura luce;/Luce intellectual piena d'amore . . ." *Italian* Dante, *Paradiso*, Canto XXX, lines 39–40: "To the heaven, which is pure light/ Intellectual light full of love . . ."

p.282 before the day of Creation there was chaos . . . ruin and desolation for ever and ever Ernest here appropriates in a general way Christian language about God and human purpose to centre it on Lady Pitts.

p.282 Cypriote variation of Cypriot or Cyprian, someone from the Mediterranean island of Cyprus.

p.283 The white goddess . . . cold goddess associated with the Egyptian goddess Isis, seen to embody both nature and magic, and who is also associated with the Roman goddess Venus (a version of the Greek goddess Aphrodite), goddess of love who is sometimes seen as represented by the moon, a beautiful but changeable planetary body.

p.284 bats *colloquial* meaning eccentric or even mad, from the phrase "bats in the belfry" which denotes being damaged "on top".

p.284 Apollo . . . day and night Apollo is sometimes seen to be represented by the sun.

THE ASSOCIATION FOR SCOTTISH LITERARY STUDIES

ANNUAL VOLUMES

Volumes marked * are, at the time of publication, still available from booksellers or from the address given opposite the title page of this book.

1971   James Hogg, *The Three Perils of Man*, ed. Douglas Gifford
1972   *The Poems of John Davidson*, vol. I, ed. Andrew Turnbull
1973   *The Poems of John Davidson*, vol. II, ed. Andrew Turnbull
1974   Allan Ramsay and Robert Fergusson, *Poems*, ed. Alexander M. Kinghorn and Alexander Law
1975   John Galt, *The Member*, ed. Ian A. Gordon
1976   William Drummond of Hawthornden, *Poems and Prose*, ed. Robert H. MacDonald
1977   John G. Lockhart, *Peter's Letters to his Kinsfolk*, ed. William Ruddick
1978   John Galt, *Selected Short Stories*, ed. Ian A. Gordon
1979   Andrew Fletcher of Saltoun, *Selected Political Writings and Speeches*, ed. David Daiches
1980   *Scott on Himself*, ed. David Hewitt
1981   *The Party-Coloured Mind*, ed. David Reid
1982   James Hogg, *Selected Stories and Sketches*, ed. Douglas S. Mack
1983   Sir Thomas Urquhart of Cromarty, *The Jewel*, ed. R. D. S. Jack and R. J. Lyall
1984   John Galt, *Ringan Gilhaize*, ed. Patricia J. Wilson
1985   Margaret Oliphant, *Selected Short Stories of the Supernatural*, ed. Margaret K. Gray
1986   James Hogg, *Selected Poems and Songs*, ed. David Groves
1987   Hugh MacDiarmid, *A Drunk Man Looks at the Thistle*, ed. Kenneth Buthlay
1988   *The Book of Sandy Stewart*, ed. Roger Leitch
1989*   *The Comic Poems of William Tennant*, ed. Maurice Lindsay and Alexander Scott
1990*   Thomas Hamilton, *The Youth and Manhood of Cyril Thornton*, ed. Maurice Lindsay
1991   *The Complete Poems of Edwin Muir*, ed. Peter Butter
1992*   *The Tavern Sages: Selections from the 'Noctes Ambrosianae'*, ed. J. H. Alexander
1993   *Gaelic Poetry in the Eighteenth Century*, ed. Derick S. Thomson
1994*   Violet Jacob, *Flemington*, ed. Carol Anderson
1995   *'Scotland's Ruine': Lockhart of Carnwath's Memoirs of the Union*, ed. Daniel Szechi, with a foreword by Paul Scott

1996*	*The Christis Kirk Tradition: Scots Poems of Folk Festivity*, ed. Allan H. MacLaine
1997–8*	*The Poems of William Dunbar* (two vols.), ed. Priscilla Bawcutt
1999*	*The Scotswoman at Home and Abroad*, ed. Dorothy McMillan
2000*	Sir David Lyndsay, *Selected Poems*, ed. Janet Hadley Williams
2001	Sorley MacLean, *Dàin do Eimhir*, ed. Christopher Whyte
2002*	Christian Isobel Johnstone, *Clan-Albin*, ed. Andrew Monnickendam
2003*	*Modernism and Nationalism: Literature and Society in Scotland 1918–1939*, ed. Margery Palmer McCulloch
2004*	*Serving Twa Maisters: five classic plays in Scots translation*, ed. John Corbett and Bill Findlay
2005*	*The Devil to Stage: five plays by James Bridie*, ed. Gerard Carruthers
2006*	*Voices From Their Ain Countrie: the poems of Marion Angus and Violet Jacob*, ed. Katherine Gordon